KRANNERT ART MUSEUM
SELECTED WORKS

Selected Works

Krannert Art Museum and
Kinkead Pavilion
University of Illinois

Contents

Authors

Etta Arntzen
Gisele Atterberry
Kavie Barnes
Charlotte Bauer
Sister Wendy Beckett
Jill E. Blondin
Dana Burchfield
Anne Burkus-Chasson
Paula M. Carns
David Cateforis
Caroline A. Connelly
Michael W. Conner
Lorraine Morales Cox
Jenifer K. Dapper
Rachael Ziady DeLue
Erin K. Donovan
Sarah Eckhardt
Megan Foster-Campbell
Judith Hoos Fox
Margaret A. Frampton
Marcel Franciscono
Barbara H. Friedell
Stacy Fuessle
Michael Gaudio
Anita J. Glaze
Maxine Hixon
Alexander Hovan
Claire Huck
Margaret A. Jackson
Dolores Kilgo
Mikael D. Kriz
Joyce M. Kuechler
Amy M. Kuhl Cox
Jennifer Langworthy
Jordana Mendelson
Brenda Mitchell
Richard D. Mohr
Kerry Morgan
David O'Brien
Robert Ousterhout
Helen Peterson
Erika Pistorius-Stamper
Natasha Ritsma
Lisa Rosenthal
Dana Rush
Jordana Saggese
Muriel Scheinman
Julia Sienkewicz
Robert B. Smith
Catharine Sprugel
Roxanne Stanulis
Heidi Strobel
Ana L. Tallone
Ronald Toby
Li-Lin Tseng
Penny Van Esterik
Gabriel Weisberg
Michael Wetzel
Phoebe Wolfskill
Warren T. Woodfin
Edward Zagorski
Christine Zitrides
Mary Peterson Zundo

Acknowledgments The publication of this book is cause for great celebration. Many years in development, *Krannert Art Museum: Selected Works* is the creation of a wonderfully diverse group: graduate students of the University of Illinois at Urbana-Champaign; Illinois faculty from multiple disciplines; curators, educators, and volunteer docents from Krannert Art Museum and Kinkead Pavilion (KAM); and specialists from other museums and universities. Their rich range of voices and backgrounds speaks to the vibrancy of the museum as a campus and community resource.

Josef Helfenstein, the previous director of KAM, initiated this collection handbook project in 2001. To determine individual works for inclusion, identify essayists, and guide the publication, a handbook committee was formed, chaired by Illinois emeritus faculty member and KAM docent James B. Sinclair. Following Helfenstein's departure from KAM in 2004, it took a few years for work on the book to resume. Throughout this long process, Jim Sinclair and Illinois emeritus faculty member, KAM docent, and handbook committee member Robert B. Smith have been passionate and committed champions of the project on the occasion of the centennial celebration of the college.

The list of dedicated and talented contributors to this major undertaking is truly illustrious, as is the roster of donors. Generous financial support was provided by Krannert Art Museum Council; The Moore Charitable Trust; Emily Nichols Trees and Merle Jay Trees Collection; James B. Sinclair; James B. Sinclair in Memory of Elmer A. Uselmann; and the Office of the Dean, College of Fine and Applied Arts on the occasion of the centennial celebration of the college.

As this publication indicates, KAM has an impressive past and present with a strong commitment to building its panoramic collection, developing an equal campus and community focus, and producing ambitious exhibitions, catalogues, and educational programming. In recent years, KAM has been very aggressive in acquiring some of the most compelling works from the exhibitions it organizes. The institution is building its leadership position nationally, originating high-quality exhibitions that travel, innovative programming that cuts across disciplines and responds to diverse interests, and large-scale collaborations that create powerful curricular connections and engage the public. We thank all who recognize our potential and encourage you to be part of our exciting future.

Kathleen Harleman
Director, Krannert Art Museum and Kinkead Pavilion

ASIA THE COLLECTION

AFRICA

ANCIENT MEDITERRANEAN

EUROPE

AMERICAS

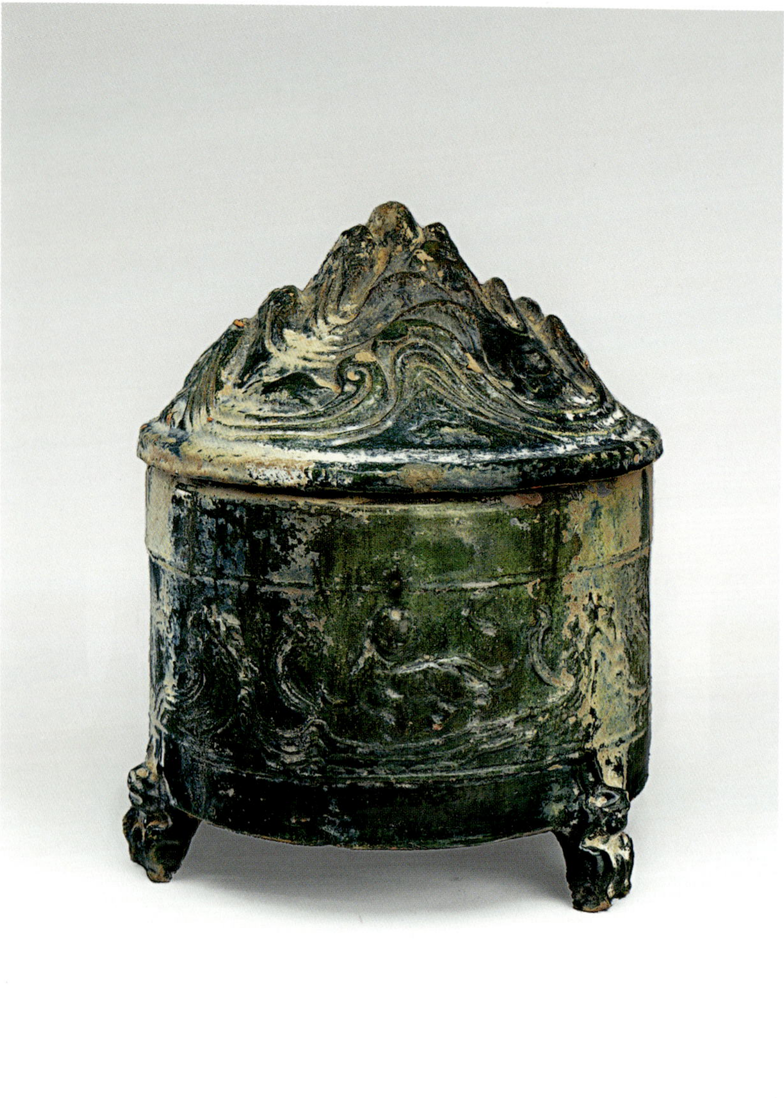

In traditional Han Chinese belief, ancestors were thought to live on in the afterlife and were thus in need of the objects they had used in everyday life. The use of *mingqi*, or "spirit goods," during the Han dynasty marked a change in Chinese funerary practices and customs. Clay models of household utensils, houses, servants, and animals were buried with the dead to aid in the afterlife. Hill jars are miniature replicas of wine-warming vessels, the surfaces of which were covered with Daoist cosmological symbols. The shape of the vessel represents the mountains where it is believed immortals exist.

The Daoist religion holds out the possibility of physical immortality to the initiate who follows prescribed rituals. Such practices traditionally included the ingestion of life-prolonging herbs and mineral drugs concocted by alchemists, which were often mixed with wine in bronze jars. The cylindrical body of this clay jar depicts hills and fantastic flying creatures in low relief. These beings represent *xian*, often referred to as "immortals," who were capable of flying on clouds and subsisting on dew.

The red clay of this hill jar is concealed by a low-fire green glaze that mimics oxidized bronze. The silver-green iridescence of the surface is an unintentional result of centuries of oxidation resulting from burial in damp soil. The conical lid was made by press-mold and finished on a pottery wheel. It depicts Mount Bo, a sacred mountain inhabited by Daoist immortals that the deceased was thought to ascend on the journey to heaven. The three bear-shaped legs supporting the vessel indicate northern Chinese artistry. Conner

China
Han dynasty
(206 BCE–220 CE)

Hill jar and cover
Earthenware with green glaze
11 × 9 1/2 inches
Sophie and Brian Leung Fund
1992 1-1

The tension that characterizes Hou Mougong's work distinguishes it from that of his Ming dynasty (1368–1644) contemporaries. Though rendered in precise and intricate detail, this crowded landscape is a realm of fantastical forms and spatial illusions that are reminiscent of earlier works of art. A net of branches created by leafless trees partially obscures the far bank of a waterway. One Western method of depicting distance includes blurring features that are farther away. In this work, the illusion of distance is contradicted by the prominent brushstrokes that define the trees throughout the work. The contours of two of the foreground trees bear clusters of dots meant to indicate bark. Beneath the trees in the lower left corner of the work, the presence of a traveler is accentuated by the pale red of his robe. Whether this figure can find a path permitting him to navigate the unfamiliar space of this landscape is unclear. The middle ground of the work is occupied by discrete and discontinuous architectural structures. The top half of the paper is dominated by hills and distant peaks set against a flat overcast sky that is tinted gray.

The text Hou inscribed at the top of the hanging scroll implies that he saw this very landscape. It reads: "In *la*, the twelfth lunar month of the year *bingzi*, I sat while it snowed and sketched at Pine Knoll Inn." Rather than depicting a specific place, however, the scroll is probably an imaginary version of this location. It shows the artist's knowledge of the work of Wen Zhengming (1470–1559) and others in his artistic circle, which was centered in Hou's native Jiangsu Province on the east coast of China. The elongated vertical format of the scroll, the composition's strong segmentation, and the distinct parts of the scene piled one on top of each other while being tied to a central axis reveal the influence of these artists. Hou also studied paintings of the Song (960–1279) and Yuan (1280–1368) dynasties. The rounded shapes of the landscape are evidence of the influence of Huang Gongwang (1269–1354), while the rock formations in the scroll's middle and upper grounds reveal Hou's familiarity with the work of Wang Meng (ca. 1308–1385). Strobel

Hou Mougong
China
active ca. 1569–1604

Untitled
1576
Hanging scroll: ink wash and color on paper
50 × 12 3/4 inches
Gift of Class of 1908
1974-5-2

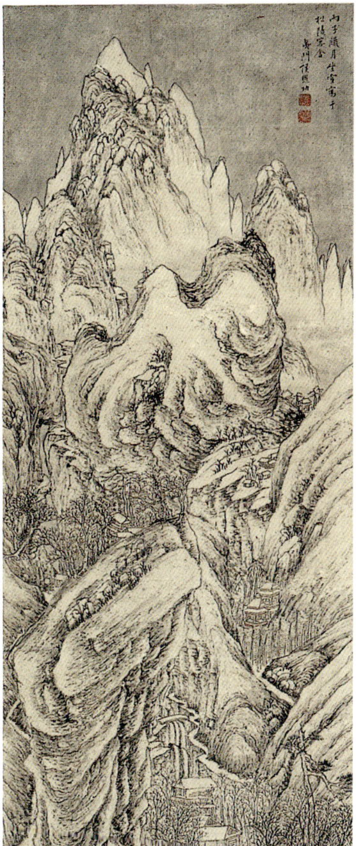
丙子臘月坐雪寫于
杜陵客舍

Chen Lian
China
active Ming dynasty
(1368–1644)

Homecoming Boat on a Wintry River
ca. 1620
Handscroll: ink and color on paper
8 1/4 × 61 3/4 inches
Gift of Class of 1908
1976-14-1

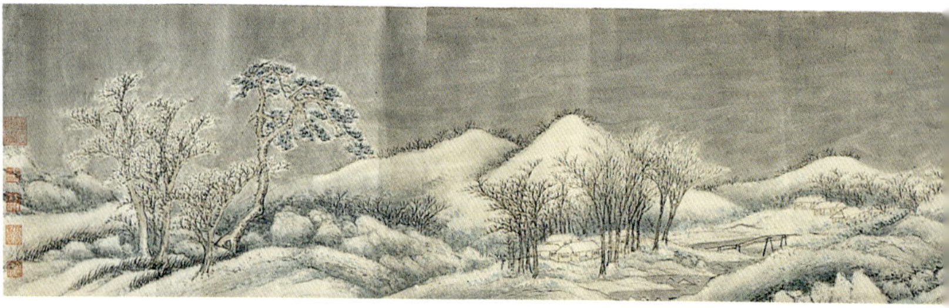

This landscape is attributed to the little-known painter Chen Lian. Following the style of the fourteenth-century landscape artist Huang Gongwang (1269–1354), Chen created abstract rounded and rectangular mountain forms and a sense of depth by depicting a clearly demarcated path at the base of the rocky promontory. However, he eliminated the austerity of Ming-period interpretations of Huang's style. Pale patches of blue, blue-green, and pink distinguish shapes and counteract their repetitiveness. Washes of ink, in some places blended with pale blue color, create an enveloping atmosphere, especially in the waterway. Chen applied ink to the dampened paper with a saturated brush, allowing the ink to bleed into the fibers. Traces of its absorption resemble cloud formations and create the illusion of motion. A fisherman in a boat in the middle of the water enhances the lyricism of the wintry landscape.

The artist created a transition from the right-hand section of the scroll to the left by transforming the waterway into a wintry sky over a shallow foreground. To the left of the waterway, a group of houses surrounded by leafless trees introduces a series of environments. The center of the scroll shows a bridge and a watercourse crossing a plain, and a grove of trees with bare branches sweeping against the sky. The end of the scroll at the left concentrates on a group of large trees that reach into the sky, balancing the first scene at the far right.

Painting texts of the late Ming and early Qing (1644–1911) dynasties indicate that Chen Lian mimicked the work of the fourteenth-century painter Zhao Mengfu (1254–1322). Much like Zhao and unlike many of his contemporaries, Chen preferred to create a landscape scene that captured the qualities of natural appearances. Burkus-Chasson

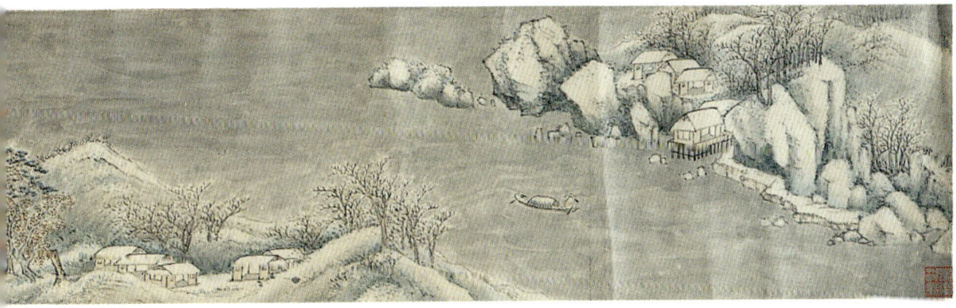

Zha Shibiao – painter, calligrapher, poet, and art collector – was a native of Huizhou in the Anhui province in east China, though he spent his later life in the city of Yangzhou on the northern bank of the Yangtze River. After the fall of the Ming dynasty (1368–1644), Zha referred to himself as the "old man from Plum Blossom Gulley" and abandoned his pursuit of a government office position to devote himself to painting and calligraphy. As a commercial painter, protesting the usurpation of the imperial throne, he often emulated the barren landscapes of the fourteenth-century artist Ni Zan (1301–1374), which reflected Zha's own attitudes toward modern society.

As a calligrapher, Zha similarly transformed familiar models of writing to fashion a new style. In the poem on this scroll, which describes a melancholy scene in early autumn, Zha imitated the "running script" (*xingshu*) of the seventeenth-century artist Dong Qichang (1555–1636). Zha sometimes used the side of a brush to gently modulate the strokes and enhance their sensuous, wavelike effect. To accentuate the sense of movement within the characters, Zha extended several vertical strokes into ragged ends, or agitated the lines by wobbling the brush as he pulled it across the surface of the satin. At the same time, he exhibited restraint in the even alignment and structural containment of the characters. The poem and its dedication read:

The wind is up. Remnants of summer's heat dissipate.
Alone with my staff: calmly, I take pleasure in this.
In the color of the countryside, I prolong quiet steps.
Against the sound of autumn, I enter the later years of life.
The sun's rays slant. The shadows of birds are confused.
The water level drops. The roots of trees are suspended.
I turn my head. An old friend is faraway.
Someone plays a frontier pipe in evening mists.

Going by the creek, I recorded this poem and presented it to Hanyuan, Mister Nian, Old Man of the Way.

Three seals of the artist appear on this work and read: *Mouhe* ("so-and-so gulley"); *Zha Shibiao yin* (Zha Shibiao's seal); and *Erzhan shi* [?] ("Scholar Who Looked Twice"). The recipient of the poem is not identified. Burkus-Chasson

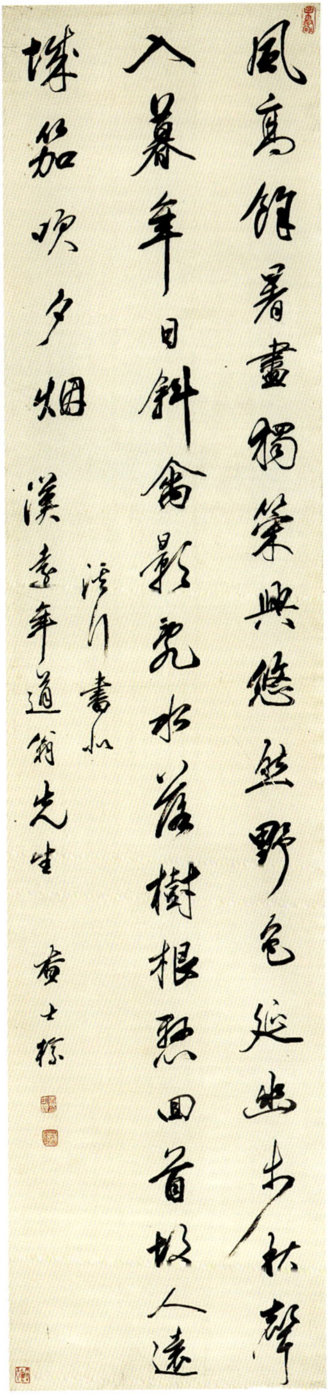

Zha Shibiao
China
1615–1698

Untitled (*Poem*)
17th century
Hanging scroll: ink on satin
81 1/4 × 19 1/2 inches
Sophie and Brian Leung Fund
2001-9-1

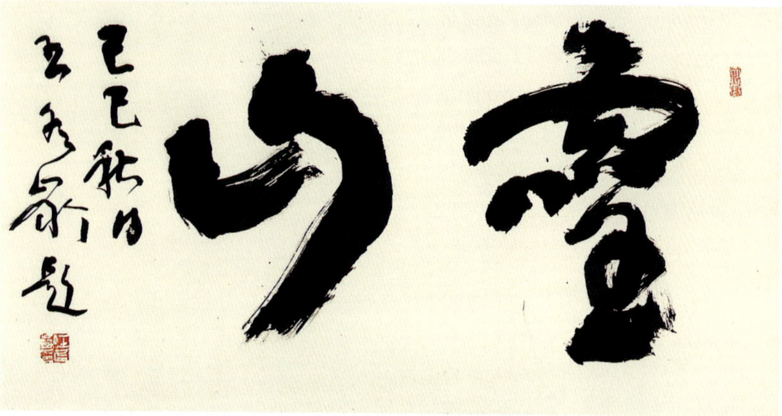

Wang Dongling
China
b. 1945

Ling Shan
(Numinous Mountain)
1989
Ink on mulberry bark paper
68 1/2 × 134 3/4 inches
Gift of the artist
1989-10-1

Wang Dongling, a teacher and historian of calligraphy, practices a variety of Chinese script forms that reflect his traditional training. His work ranges from the archaic "seal script" prevalent in the third century BCE to the "cursive script" that was established by the fourth century CE. Additionally, the influence of certain aspects of late twentieth-century European and American painting distinguish his calligraphy from that of many of his contemporaries.

"Cursive script" is an abbreviated form of writing in which the number of strokes that compose a character is radically reduced. *Ling Shan* exemplifies Wang's command of the form with two large characters – to the right, *ling* (meaning "numinous" or "magical"), and to the left, *shan* ("mountain"). At the far left of this work is a dated signature that reads: "On an autumn day in the year *jisi* [1989], Wang Dongling wrote [these words]." Two seals of the artist are also included: *Wang Dongling yin* (Wang Dongling's seal) and *Zhiguan* (meaning "calm").

Ling Shan was painted for an exhibition of Chinese landscape art held at Krannert Art Museum in 1989 that was curated by the late Illinois professor of art history, Kiyohiko Munakata. Wang created the work in front of a public audience to celebrate this event. Wang Dongling used a large, stiff, animal-hair brush to produce the characters. By using both the sides and tip of the brush, he varied the strokes to give them ragged or smooth edges. Variations also resulted from the dampness of the brush: a saturated brush spread wet ink that bled into the fibers of the mulberry bark paper, while a drier brush with spread bristles scratched against its surface. The two primary characters are formally opposed: the fluid complexity of *ling* counters the bold spiral movement of *shan*.

Wang violated norms of orthodox calligraphy in this work. The loaded brush dripping with dark ink left a conspicuous trail around the characters. A spatter of ink emanates from the knobby head of the second, right-hand stroke in the character *shan*. The splash, which emphasizes the instability of the character, occurred when Wang reversed the direction of his brush several times as he began the stroke. Such haphazard drips and splatters, partially controlled by the calligrapher, have an abstract effect, evidence of Wang's interest in modern European art. Burkus-Chasson

This stele from a Buddhist *stupa* ("reliquary mound") was made in the northwest region of Pakistan and Afghanistan in what was then known as Gandhara. Until the first century CE, Buddhist sculpture in Gandhara was aniconic. The Buddha was not represented in human form but signified symbolically by the depiction of a thematic event in his life or an object related to that event. Subsequently, Buddhist form became codified and the divine image of the Buddha was incorporated into the art.

This stele depicts two of the eight miracles associated with the life of the Buddha. The lower register depicts the Great Miracle of Preaching the Law at Sravasti, when manifestation of the Buddha's divine power led unbelievers to convert. The Buddha is seated in a pillared pavilion in *padmasana* (with legs folded and interlocked) on a raised lotus flower (signifying divinity), his hands in *vyakhyana mudra*, the preaching gesture representing the pure wisdom of a deity. Beneath him on either side of the lotus are two *nagas* ("serpent spirits") and flanking him are two Bodhisattvas (beings dedicated to attaining enlightenment) with their right hands raised in *abhaya mudra*, the gesture of protection.

On the upper level of the pavilion in the middle of the stele are female *devas* (powerful non-human beings) framed by arched *chaitya* windows. In the center window, the robed figure on the right with the *ushnisha* (cranial protuberance) is the Buddha. The figure on the left may be King Prasenajit, a follower of Buddha who had the pavilion constructed; there is precedence at the *stupa* sites of Barhut and Sanchi for inclusion of the donor's image in the reliefs.

The upper register of the stele represents the Buddha's ascendance to the *Trayastrimsa* heaven, where he converted his mother Maya, an event that occurred immediately after the Miracle at Sravasti. The Buddha is seated under an umbrella on an inverted lotus with his right hand raised in *abhaya mudra*. Standing on lotuses beside the Buddha are the gods Indra, on his left, and Brahma, to his right. Devotees stand alongside with their hands in *anjali mudra*, the gesture of devotion. Friedell

India, Gandhara
2nd century

Buddhist stele
Stone
30 3/4 × 21 inches
Gift of Ellnora D. Krannert
1965-16-1

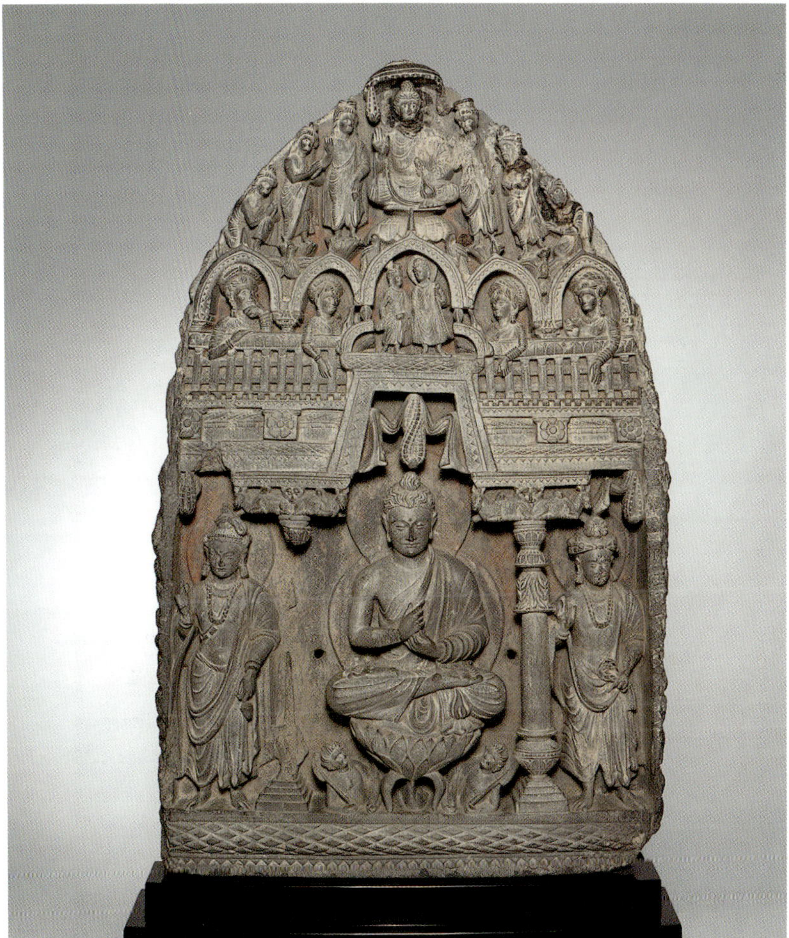

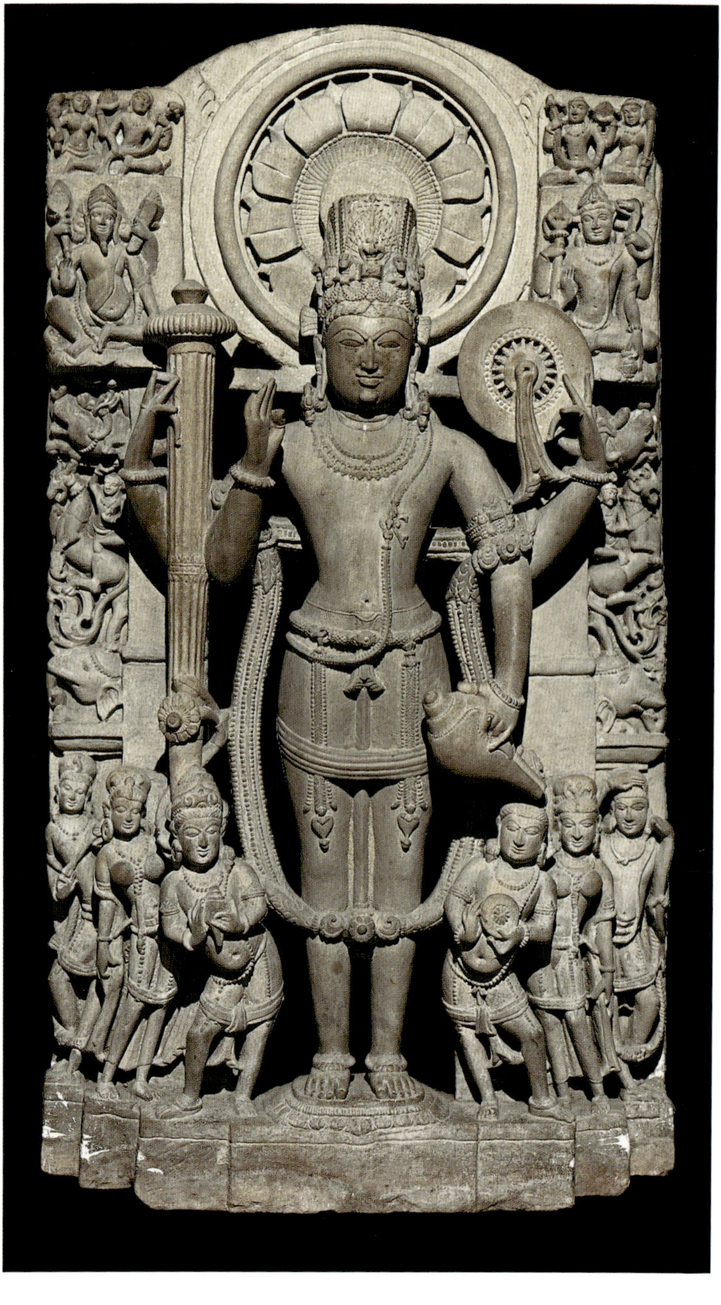

Hindus believe in a formless god whose three primary manifestations are Brahma the creator, Siva the destroyer, and Vishnu the preserver. Vishnu was first mentioned as a deity in the ancient Indian sacred collection of hymns, the *Rigveda*, in 1200 BCE.

The earliest known Hindu images are from the first century BCE from the Mathura region of northern India. By the third century CE, freestanding figurative sculpture began to appear on the outsides of Hindu temples and became an increasingly important component of temple architecture. This figure of Vishnu was probably placed in an interior sub-shrine or in the sanctum of the temple. The sanctum is the venue for *darshana*, the active visual and mental interaction between god and devotee. If the rituals surrounding this act are performed correctly, it is thought the god or divine spirit will inhabit the image.

This four-armed figure can be identified as Vishnu because of the attributes he holds in his hands. The conch in his lower-left hand represents the sacred sound *om*, which calls existence into being. The *gada*, or mace, in his lower-right hand symbolizes the power of knowledge, and the *chakra*, or discus, in his upper-left hand denotes divine power and protection. His upper-right hand is raised in *abhaya mudra*, the gesture of protection. Vishnu periodically descends to earth in various human and non-human forms, known as avatars, to preserve the *dharma* ("law") and return order to the universe.

In this stele, Vishnu stands on a lotus flower with an elaborate lotus-shaped halo behind his head. His facial expression is benign, and he wears an elaborate crown and large earrings indicating his royal status. To the immediate right and left of his feet stand the anthropomorphized figures of his attributes, the *chakra*, called Sundarshana, and the conch, Shankha. To their left and right are the diminutive figures of devotees. At the top of the stele, sitting on lotuses, are the figures of Brahma on the left and Siva on the right. Friedell

India, Rajputana
ca. 12th century

Vishnu stele
Stone
40 1/2 × 22 3/4 inches
Gift of Ellnora D. Krannert
1969-10-1

This painting is one of four illustrations of the *Bhagavata Purana* in Krannert Art Museum's collection. The works are from different areas of India and therefore differ stylistically from one another. The *Bhagavata Purana*, a popular Hindu text dating from the ninth or tenth century, narrates the life and adventures of Krishna, an avatar or incarnation of the god Vishnu. Hindus believe in a formless god whose three primary manifestations are Brahma the creator, Siva the destroyer, and Vishnu the preserver. Vishnu's Krishna avatar is known as "the dark one" and is usually shown with black or dark-blue skin.

In this work, Krishna has turned away from the goddess Radha, who looks dismayed by his actions. It seems not even the lotus in Krishna's hand pacified her. As the rejected Krishna departs, his annoyance is evident on his face. He wears a saffron yellow *dhoti* and a crown such as the god Vishnu would wear, denoting his divinity. Radha, referred to as a *gopi* ("cowherd") in the *Bhagavata Purana* text, is depicted in this painting as a princess in her palace.

Until paper became commonly used in India in the fifteenth century, illustrated texts were made on horizontal pieces of palm leaf which were pierced and threaded together with a wooden cover. The artists were usually anonymous and the works unsigned. Some patrons were *rajas* (kings) who employed a studio of artists. Other patrons hired itinerant painters, both Hindu and Muslim, to illustrate their favorite texts. By commissioning this work, donors gained religious merit as well as aesthetic pleasure. The paintings were not meant to be hung on the wall but rather held in the hand for examination and admiration. Paintings of this genre embody *bhakti*, an intense personal devotion to a god. The love between Krishna and Radha was that of a divine union. Friedell

India, Guler-Kangra
18th century

Krishna Leaves Radha
Opaque color on paper
8 1/2 × 6 1/2 inches
Gift of George P. Bickford
1970-10-5

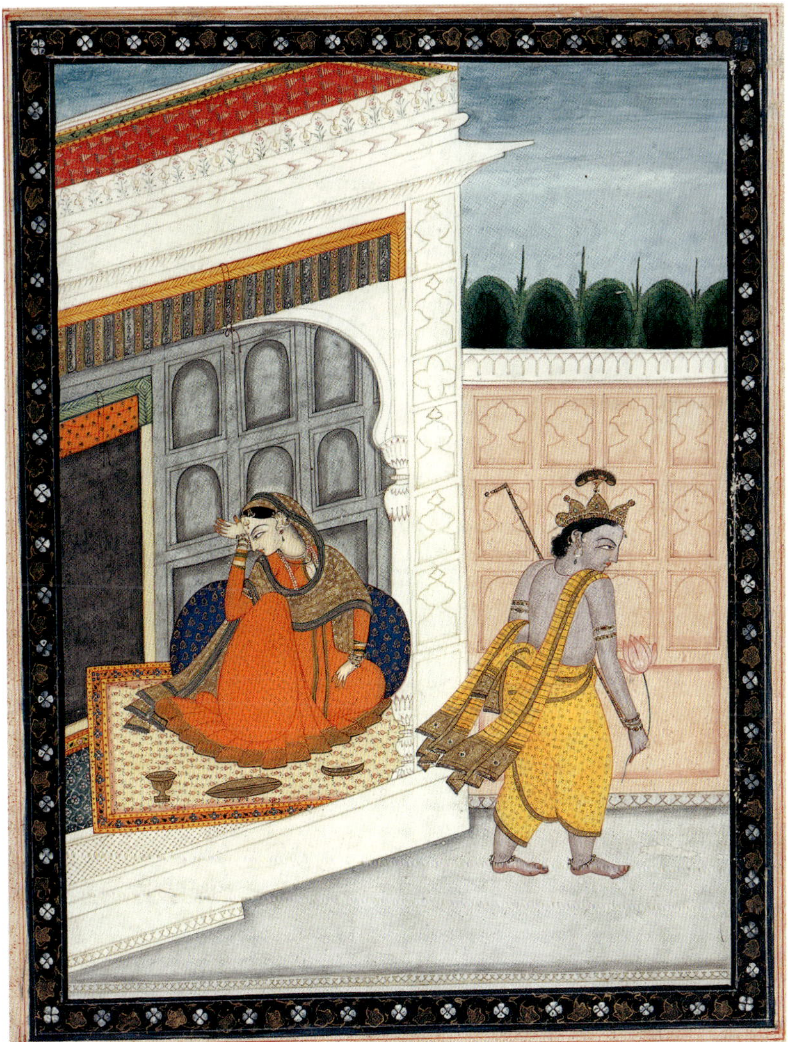

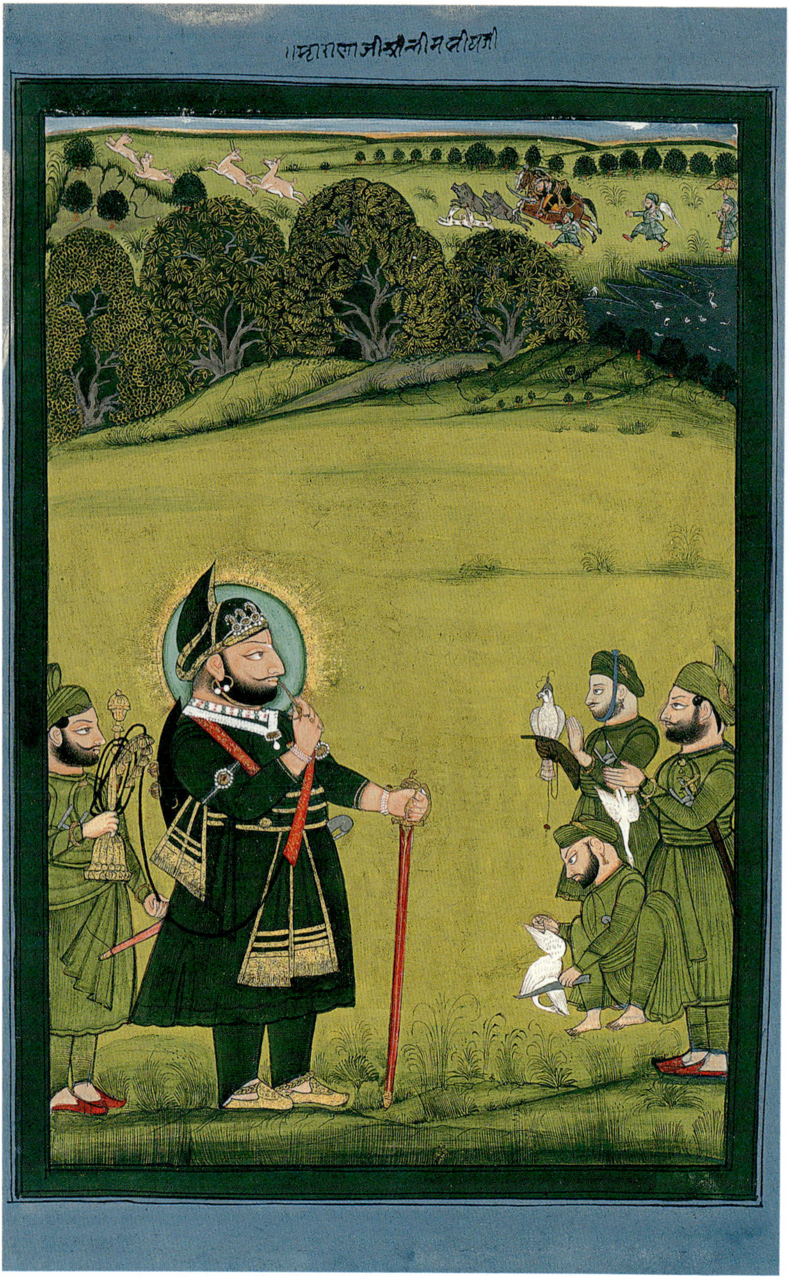
।।म्हाराणाजीश्रीभीमसींघजी

Rajput painting from the Rajputana or Rajasthan area of India was first differentiated from paintings created under the Mughal Empire (early-sixteenth to mid-nineteenth century) by the scholar Ananda Coomaraswamy in the early twentieth century. The Mughals were responsible for creating a new school of painting that was influenced by the engravings in the bibles that arrived with Jesuit missionaries in 1549.

Hindu and Muslim artists of the Mughal style adopted from these prints the concept of perspective, among other conventions, which had been lost in Indian painting since the second-century BCE Ajanta cave paintings in west-central India. Artists commissioned by *rajas* ("kings") also assimilated into their work the Mughal symbols of royalty. The pose and position of the *raja* became hieratic, as seen in this painting. Here, the *raja* at the left is prominently placed and larger than the other figures. Most *rajas* were worshipers of Vishnu and equated themselves with the god. The golden-ringed nimbus behind the *raja*'s head denoting this status was originally a symbol borrowed by the Mughals from images of western saints.

Portraiture such as this is not found in Mewar painting of Rajasthan before 1670. The *raja* in this painting stands in the foreground smoking a *huqqa* after the hunt while his servants kill two birds that the falcon has brought down. The falcon and its keeper, whose beard strap and turban identify him as a Sikh, are nearby. Time has been condensed. The *raja* is depicted twice, at two different moments in the story – in the foreground and also in the background to the upper right where, on horseback, he follows his dogs in their pursuit of two boars and four frightened deer. Behind him in the background are the keeper and falcon and a courtier holding an umbrella. The figures all wear green camouflage clothing suitable for a hunt, perhaps reflecting British influence in India. Friedell

India, Rajasthan
ca. 1800

Portrait of a Standing Rajah at Hunt
Opaque color on paper
12 1/2 × 9 inches
Gift of George P. Bickford
1975-12-6

Fudō is the Buddhist god of wisdom and fire and the central deity of the Myōō, or Five Great Kings of Light, that has its origin in Hindu influence on Vajrayana or Esoteric Buddhism. Fudō Myōō's role is to uphold Buddhist law and to attack evils such as ignorance and passion. Although he is depicted as a menacing figure, his anger is compassionate and protective. Esoteric Buddhism emphasizes the use of ritual to reach spiritual enlightenment. Symbolizing the magical element, Fudō Myōō became a primary object of worship in the Shingon (meaning "true words" or "mantra") sect of Esoteric Buddhism, which was popular among the aristocracy of the Heian period. Shingon Buddhism contributed significantly to the art and literature of this time.

Sculptures of Fudō Myōō are placed on platforms both inside (in image halls) and outside Buddhist temples to drive away evil spirits. The figure is that of a robust adolescent. He holds a *ken* ("sword") in his right hand and originally held a *kensaku* ("rope lasso") in his left. The two objects assist him in the battle against ignorance: the rope lassoes individuals and leads them to salvation, while the sword conquers doubt and illusion with intelligence and truth.

The face, however, is the visual focus of the sculpture with many of the features representing the deity's power and exemplifying the period's artistic style. The right eye bulges and the left is nearly shut, alluding to the fact that even with one eye closed, Fudō Myōō sees all. While the mouth is tightly drawn, a lower right tooth is exposed, pointing upward, and an upper left tooth projects downward. The direction the teeth point is symbolic: downward suggests unlimited compassion, while upward the desire to obtain truth. In contrast to the striated hair of earlier depictions of Fudō, the hair of this figure is composed of shell-like curls. Marks on the forehead symbolize water waves. The eye, teeth, and wave pattern of the hair refer back to the style of Kukai (774–835), the monk and artist who founded Shingon Buddhism. Smith

Attributed to the
En-School at Sanjo
Japan
Late Heian Period
(Fujiwara) (794–1185)

Standing Fudō Myōō
ca. 12th century
Cypress wood, crystal, glass, lacquer, polychrome, gold leaf
26 3/4 × 12 inches
Gift of Class of 1908
1982-5-1

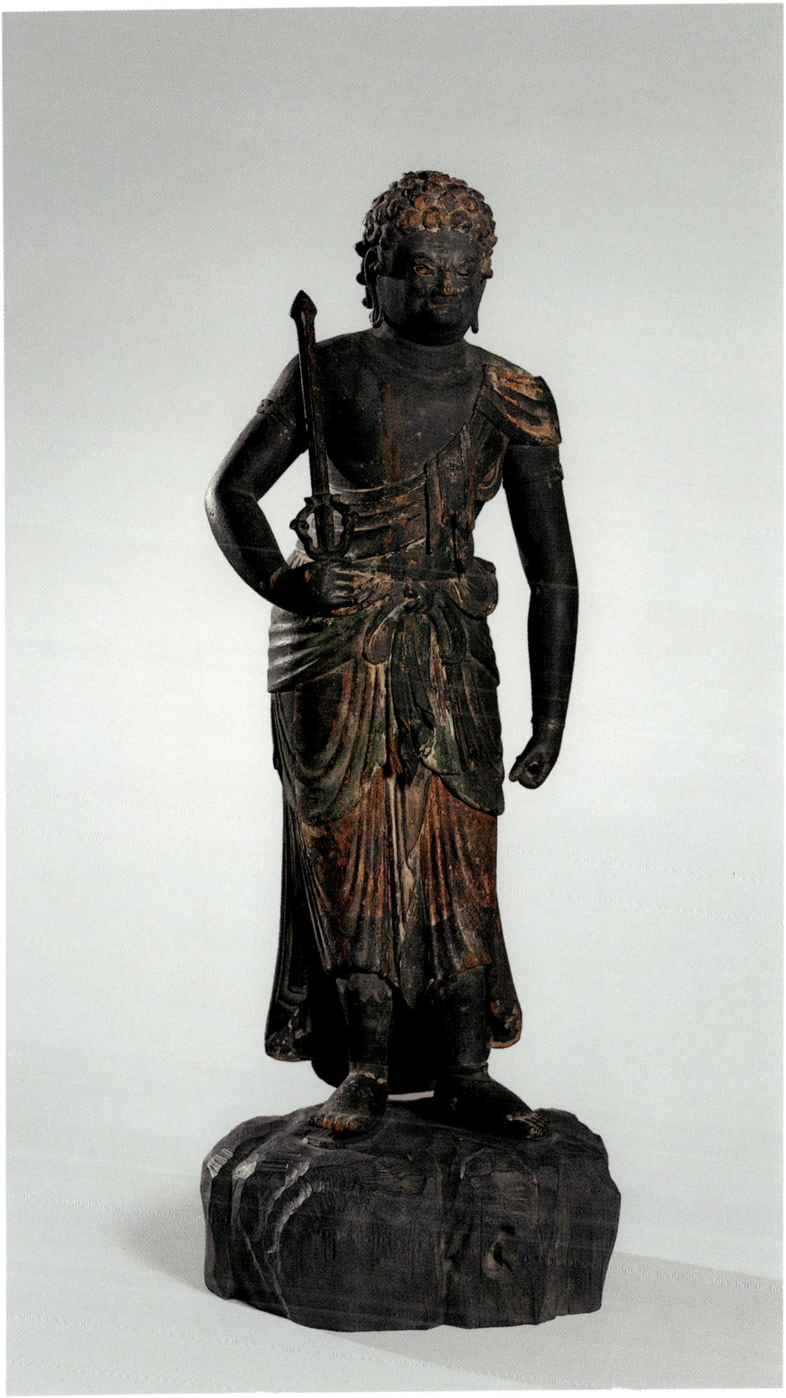

Some consider the eleventh-century Heian-period *Tale of Genji* by the noblewoman Murasaki Shikibu (ca. 970–ca. 1020) to be the world's first novel. The work certainly holds pride of place as the greatest masterpiece of classical Japanese prose literature. Its countless subplots have been reworked as themes in Nō and kabuki theatre, puppet plays, and fiction, and favorite passages have been visualized in paintings and prints.

In the image of the "Utsusemi" chapter, Prince Genji is in frustrated pursuit of a woman who denies herself to him. He is already married, but monogamous fidelity was alien to polygamous courtier culture of the time. Genji has spent the night at the lady's mansion, hoping in vain that her younger brother might help him press his suit, but she has refused to see him. In the image depicting the "Suma" chapter, Genji rides off into exile in a seaside village because of his political and amorous indiscretions.

The medium of screen painting originated in China but was adapted by the Japanese elite to suit their own purposes. Not only were screens objects of beauty, displaying the taste and culture of their owners, but they served as room dividers in spacious mansions where rooms flowed into each other without fixed walls.

Yamato-e (native "Japanese," as distinct from "Chinese," pictures), a style practiced by Iwasa Matabei and his school in the early seventeenth century, illustrated subjects from Chinese and Japanese legend and classical literature in a highly decorative manner. Matabei is a controversial figure in the history of Japanese art. Some scholars claim him for the classical tradition while others appropriate him as one of the new, energetic "town painters" of the early modern period; his body of work is expansive enough to justify both views. Matabei also painted contemporary genre scenes; his work is thought to have been highly influential on the seventeenth-century development of *ukiyo-e*, or "pictures of the floating world" that were popular in urban entertainment districts. Toby

(following pages)
"Utsusemi," *Tale of Genji*
ca. 1650–70
Color and gold on paper
mounted on wood panels
63 × 143 3/4 inches
Gift of Class of 1908
1980-16-1

"Suma," *Tale of Genji*
ca. 1650–70
Color and gold on paper
mounted on wood panels
63 × 145 inches
Gift of Class of 1908
1980-16-2

School of
Iwasa Matabei
Japan
1578–1650

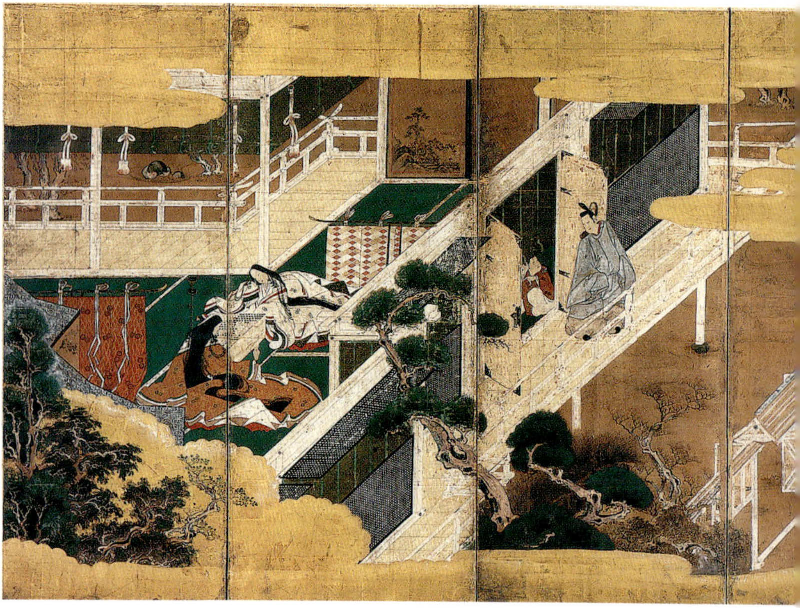

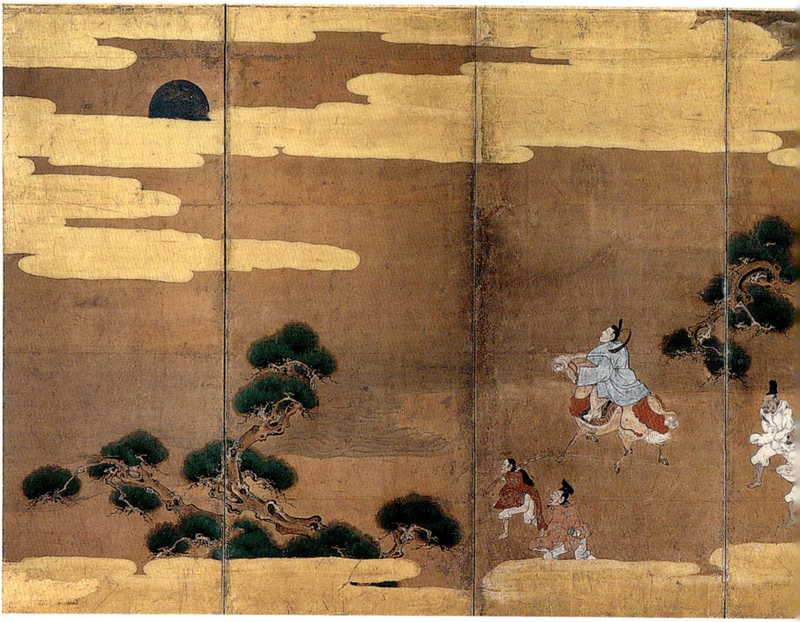

"Utsusemi," *Tale of Genji*
"Suma," *Tale of Genji*

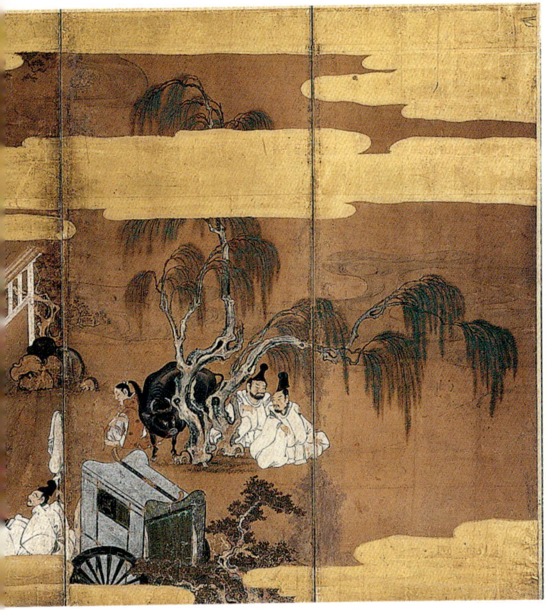

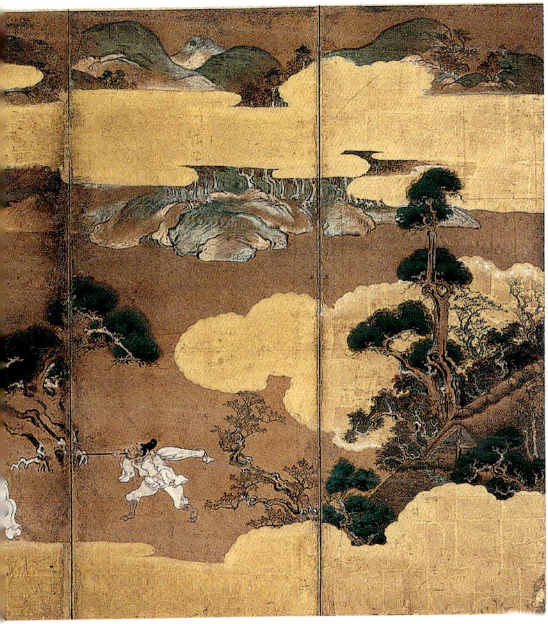

Isoda Koryūsai is best known for his work in two subjects: portrayals of "beautiful women" (*bijin-ga*) and depictions of "birds and flowers" (*kachō-ga*). Although born into the samurai or military nobility class, he abandoned his privileged status to pursue a career as an artist of *ukiyo-e* ("pictures of the floating world"), paintings and prints depicting landscapes, theatre scenes, and urban entertainment quarters. Though few details of Koryūsai's biography are known, it is thought that he studied with the *ukiyo-e* master Suzuki Harunobu (1724–1770); early in his career, Koryūsai signed himself "Haruhiro," using one character from Harunobu's name, a common sign of discipleship.

After Harunobu's death, Koryūsai emerged as a master of the erotic print, producing suggestive but relatively demure works such as this one, as well as more explicit images of the genre sometimes called *abunae*, or "dangerous prints." His *hashirae*, or "pillar prints," an exaggerated vertical format popular in the eighteenth century, are especially prized for their contrast of rich, powerful pigments with the soft, graceful curves of female figures in the *yanagi-goshi* or "willowy posture" associated with beauty and erotic allure.

This *bijin-ga* print exhibits the best of Koryūsai's talents. The voluptuous young woman steps from her bath onto the veranda of a tatami-matted room. She has yet to fasten her robe, reaching up first to adjust her *kanzashi* ("hair ornaments"). Adding to the sensuality of the subject is a gnarled budding and flowering plum tree in the background just beyond the veranda. The young woman refastens her elaborate, fashionable upswept *taka shimada* coiffeur with a stylishly carved tortoise-shell comb. The room, like the figure, is in slight disarray, with her tobacco pipe lying where it has fallen on the mat behind her. This mildly disheveled appearance was a common erotic theme in Edo-period (1603–1867) prints, a sign of the woman's accessibility or desirability. Toby

Isoda Koryūsai
Japan
1735–1790

Standing Courtesan
1775
Woodblock print
25 1/2 × 4 1/4 inches
Gift of Class of 1908
1974-15-1

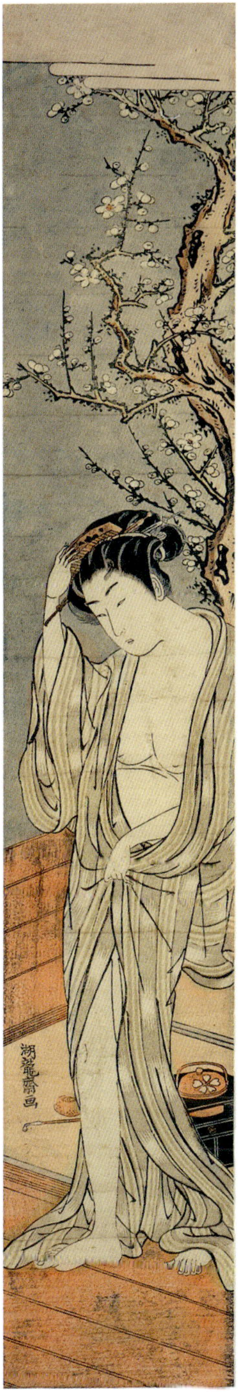
湖龍斎画

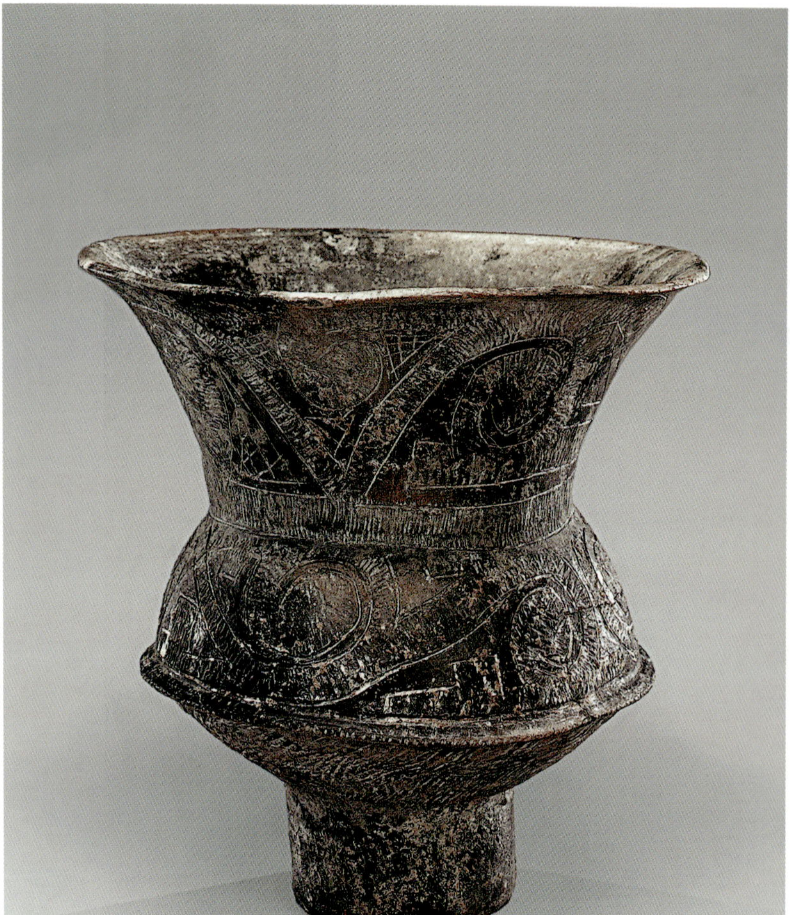

This black incised vessel is similar to pottery found at the lowest levels of excavations at Ban Chiang in northeast Thailand. There is much disagreement on dating artifacts from the site, but recent radiocarbon dating by accelerator mass spectrometry (AMS) suggests that Ban Chiang was probably first occupied around 2100 BCE. As in related sites on the Khorat Plateau, there is evidence here of cultivated rice, domesticated cattle, and mold bronze casting by around 1500 BCE. The excavations suggest that the Ban Chiang area was the center of an advanced civilization of communities with well-developed ritual systems.

Black incised pottery is commonly found in burial sites accompanied by food offerings, perhaps suggesting rituals that may have been related to ancestor worship. The black color indicates controlled firing in a kiln, or oven. The pottery was made by hand with a paddle and anvil, and decorated with incised cross-hatching. The complex geometric and curvilinear designs with double triangular shapes and spirals do not appear to be representational, although for their makers and users they undoubtedly carried symbolic and ritual associations. A foot ring stabilized the vessel, suggesting that it may have contained offerings such as rice.

By 1000 BCE, the black incised burial ware was replaced with a dramatic painted red-on-buff pottery, one of the most striking pottery traditions in Southeast Asia. However, since so many burial vessels – both black incised and red painted – were looted from the Ban Chiang site, it is difficult to confirm dates for individual pieces or to trace the relationship between the two styles. Van Esterik

Thailand, Ban Chiang
4th–3rd millennium BCE

Ban Chiang vessel
Earthenware
10 1/2 × 10 3/4 inches
Gift of Class of 1908
1979-9-1

ASIA

AFRICA THE COLLECTION

ANCIENT MEDITERRA

EUROPE

AMERICAS

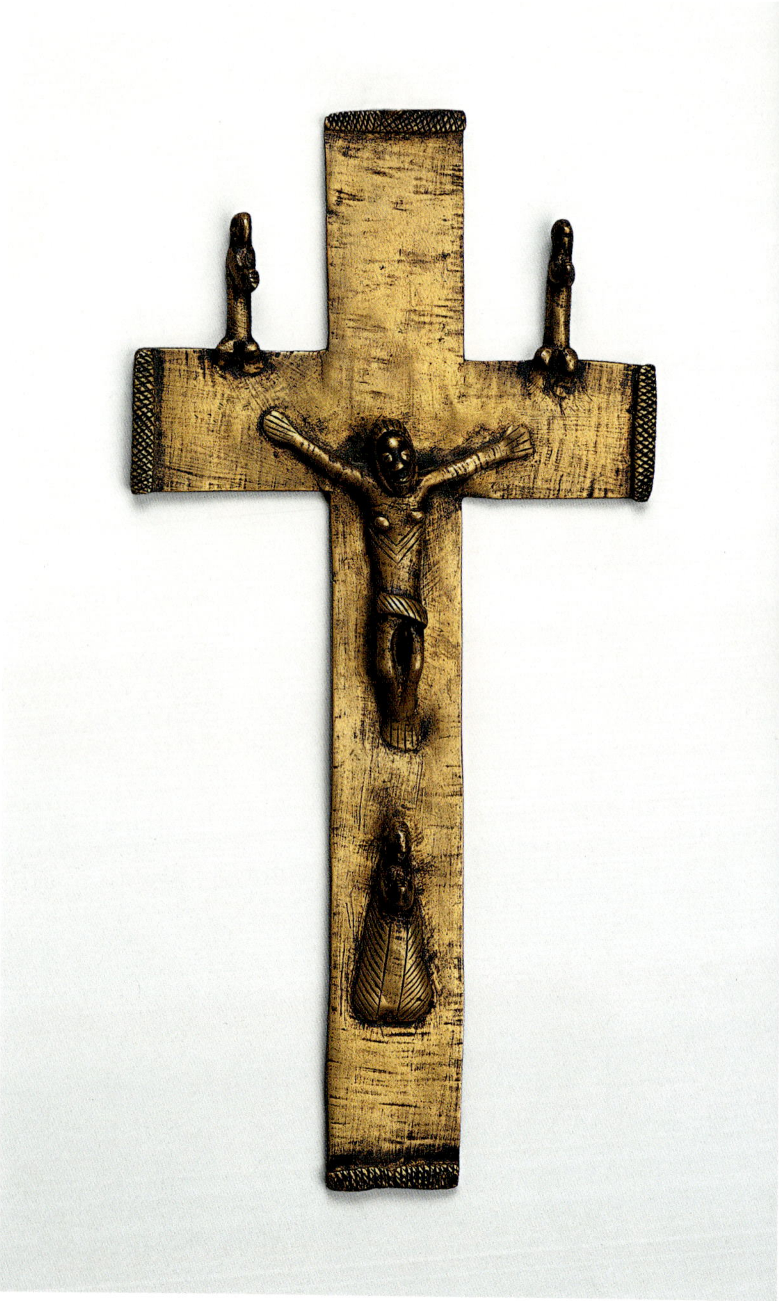

This Christian-influenced Kongo cast-brass crucifix (a cross bearing the figure of Jesus) represents two political empires, two religious systems, and two aesthetic preferences. Such crucifixes were originally venerated as religious and political icons, but with the decline of Christianity they became emblems of rank used by Kongo chiefs.

The southwest-central African Kingdom of Kongo was founded about 1400. The arrival of the Portuguese explorer Diego Cão at the mouth of the Congo River in 1483 initiated a centuries-long trade relationship between Portugal and the Kingdom of Kongo. Within two months of Cão's arrival, the Kongo king Nzinga was baptized; other dignitaries and titleholders followed his lead, understanding that adopting Christianity as the state religion was a diplomatic rather than a religious gesture.

The adaptation of Christianity within the kingdom was facilitated by the fact that the symbol of the cross already represented a major existing philosophical ideology. Iconic representations of a cross correspond to the Kongo belief that life and death are continual. Known as the "Four Moments of the Sun," the endpoints of a cross within a circle mark sunrise, noon, sunset, and midnight, which represent the trajectory of a human life as it traverses the realms of the living and the ancestors, and then begins again.

Initially, Kongo artists adhered to the European prototypes of the crucifix introduced by missionaries. As time passed, however, artists began to incorporate additional figures and details into their crucifixes, giving them a decidedly Kongo character. The small abstract figures kneeling on the arms of this cross probably represent mourners in a traditional Kongo pose of respect. The figure at the bottom of the cross may be a Kongo representation of Mary, the mother of Jesus. The facial features on the figures are clearly African, and the wide-open eyes of Jesus may suggest a possessed person in touch with the supernatural world. Rush

Democratic Republic of Congo or Angola
ca. 16th–18th century

Crucifix
Brass
12 1/2 × 6 1/4 inches
Gift of Richard J. Faletti Family Collection
2001-16-21

Epa is an ancient category of ancestral commemoration masks that are performed by members of age-grade societies (in which individuals pass through certain stages at specific ages in life) during feasts marking the annual agricultural cycle, or presented during the post-burial rites for titled men. Epa masks typically represent dignitaries, ancestral spirits, gods, and cultural heroes. The characteristic type of Epa mask is a double-faced helmet mask surmounted by one or more figures. Some are astonishingly elaborate with many figures, and can weigh up to seventy pounds. Each mask is associated with a distinctive dress and style of dance, which may range from slow and powerful to highly energetic. The most important masks are stored in shrines where they are ritually fed to increase their power and efficacy. Over time they become encrusted with sacrificial millet-gruel, feathers, and blood.

Whereas the majority of Epa-related masks are naturalistic in style and almost classic in their refinement, this example has been greatly abstracted, as if to give expression to the brutality of war, the courage and nobility of a great warrior, and the awesome power of Ogún, the Yoruba god of iron, hunting, and war. Ogún is revered for his power to create and destroy. Here he is portrayed as the very image of death. This mask is from the center for the cult of the god Ogún in the Oye Ekiti region in Nigeria.

On his left arm Ogún holds a shield with spikes, and in his right hand a long iron lance. From his chest protrudes an armor breastplate charged with protective talismans and magical substances. Medicine gourds are intertwined in his helmet, and a snake zigzags up his long, braided hair. Ogún's helmet is attached by a long strap that hangs down around his face and connects to his breastplate, giving the impression of a second beard. The steed Ogún sits on is diminutive compared to its large, important rider, but the horse's flaring nostrils and abstracted face transform it into a fearsome supernatural beast. Conner

Nigeria,
Oye Ekiti region
Yoruba
mid–late 19th century

Epa-related mask (*Jagunjagun*)
Wood, iron nails and bands, fiber, sacrificial materials
49 × 23 inches
Gift of Richard J. Faletti Family Collection
2001-16-11

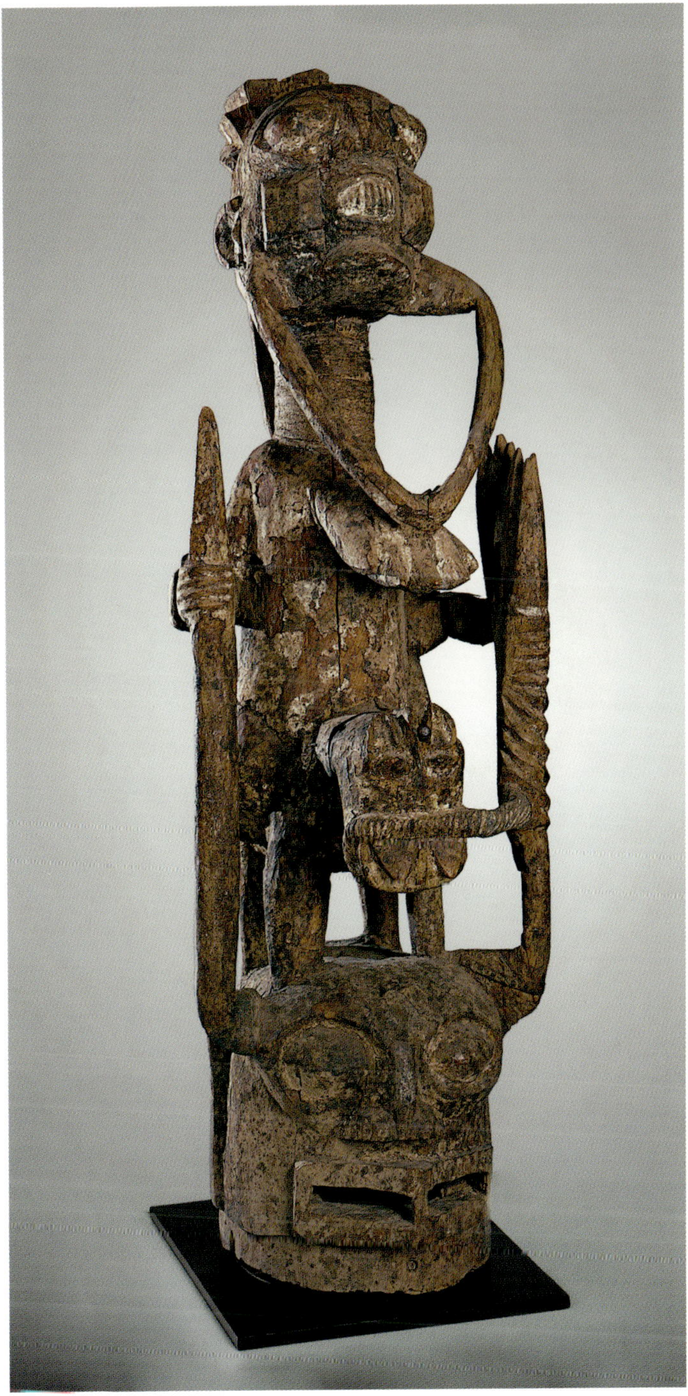

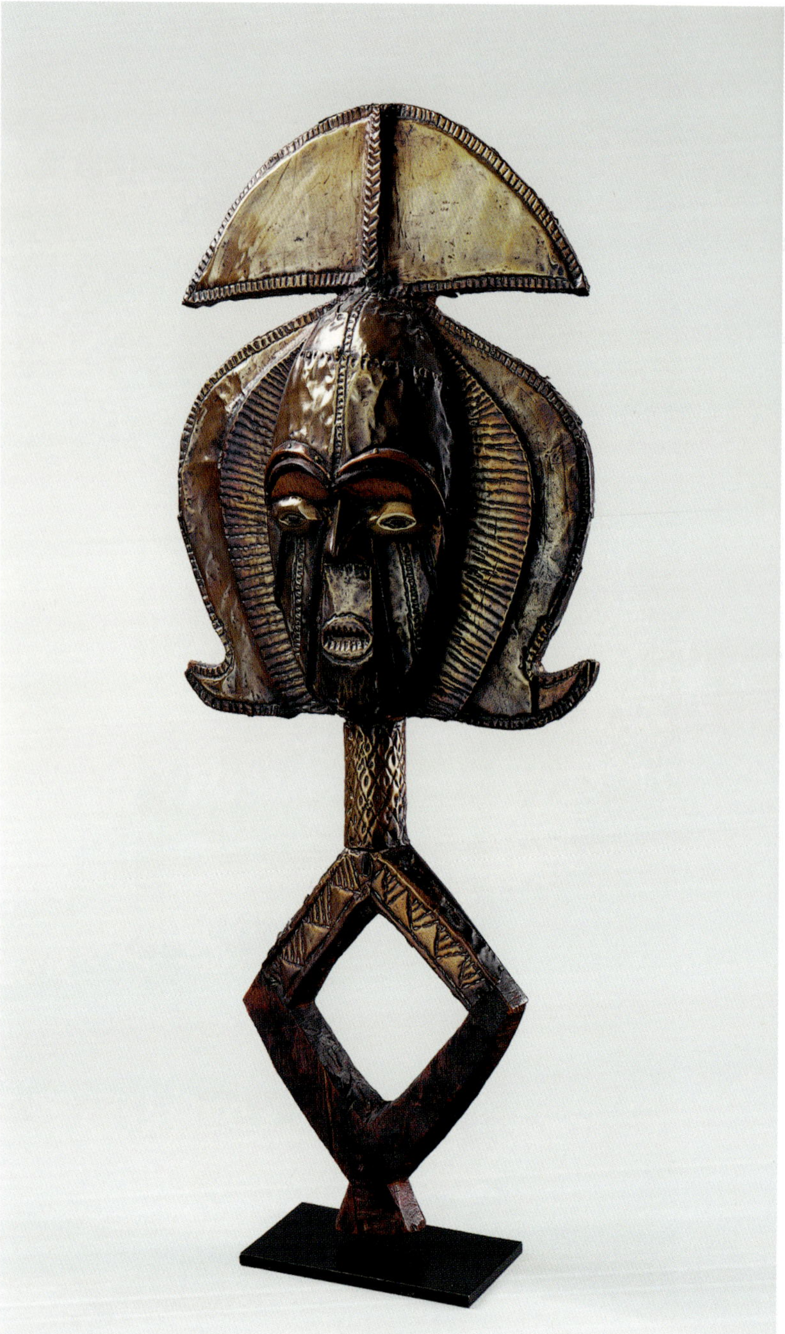

The Kota people live in Gabon in west-central Africa along the Ogowe River and in the northwestern part of the Democratic Republic of Congo. Along with several closely related groups, they are renowned for creating distinctive anthropomorphic spirit figures that watch over reliquary baskets containing the bones and skulls of important ancestors. On special occasions, reliquaries representing different lineages within a single community might be brought together.

The face of this reliquary figure is "dressed" with sheet brass, a precious material that has the power to deflect malevolent forces. It is tacked down with flat, hand-wrought copper nails, and copper lines the upper eyelids. There is no carving or metal on the back. The figure is surrounded by a semi-circular crest that may relate to an ancient style of headdress with a curved lateral form that is slightly flared at the ends to suggest ear ornaments.

Compared to the abstracted features of figures made by related peoples, the oval face of this southern Kota-Obamba sculpture is almost realistic. It has a bulging forehead, lozenge-shaped eyes, and a mouth half-open to reveal pointed teeth. Iron wire insets articulate the brow and tear-like lines radiate vertically from the eyes. These insets, which indicate facial scarification, create a penetrating gaze. Delicate *repoussé* work (metal relief that has been hammered from the back) outlines the form all around the head, and geometric triangles and diamonds ornament the neck and the "arms" of the body. The crescent forms above and on either side of the face may represent a coiffure or headdress.

In the early twentieth century, Kota religious beliefs changed and these figures, as well as reliquary baskets, were destroyed, sold, or taken to Europe, where their abstract forms became a source of inspiration for modern artists. Conner

Gabon, southern
Kota-Obamba
19th–20th century

Reliquary guardian figure (*Mbulu-Ngulu*)
Wood, brass, iron, copper
24 × 12 3/4 × 4 1/2 inches
Gift of Richard J. Faletti Family Collection
2004-5-2

A *babalawo* ("diviner") of the West African Yoruba people uses an *Opon Igede Ifa* to store the tools of his trade. These include a divination tray, beads, cowrie shells, kola or palm nuts, divination chains, and a tapper used to awaken the gods. The inside of the bowl is segmented to keep these tools respectfully isolated.

Divination serves to reveal and help shape one's destiny. The divination bowl emulates the form of a human head (*ori*). There are at least six related bowls attributed to the artist Areogun. One can infer from them that the piece missing from the top of this bowl was once a four-part braided topknot. The Yoruba believe that one's head is essentially the "self," and the cone formed by a top-knot houses the ebb and flow of the life force. The "face," or main figure on this bowl, depicts a male priest of Osanyin, whose head is shaved bilaterally, with a tuft of hair projecting to the right. Divination bags hang at his sides. In his left hand, he holds a horn containing medicines, and in his right, a wrought-iron staff with bells, surmounted by a bird.

The Yoruba define an artist as one who is a skilled designer. The word for "art" (*ona*) encompasses both craftsmanship and elaboration. Carvers apprentice with a master for years, and often more than one craftsman was involved in carving important works. Areogun himself apprenticed for 16 years to Bamgbose (d. 1920), a master carver from Osi Ilorin. The sculpture of Bamgbose and Areogun share certain stylistic aspects, but while Bamgbose skillfully incorporated open areas, Areogun is renowned for his masterly arrangement of multiple figures in a condensed space.

Areogun was intimately familiar with both the ritual and iconography of divination. This knowledge is expressed in the accoutrements of the twelve figures that circumnavigate the top of this bowl, and in the nine figures around the bottom, which include women and musicians celebrating the more important personages depicted above. There is no narrative in the organization of any of these figures, but they are all familiar Yoruba types. Together they express the fluctuating circumstances of life and the interdependence of the human and divine. Conner

Attributed to
Areogun of Osi Ilorin
Nigeria
ca. 1880–1954

Bowl for divination implements (*Opon Igede Ifa*)
early 20th century
Wood
18 1/2 × 17 1/2 inches
Gift of Richard J. Faletti Family Collection
2001-16-24

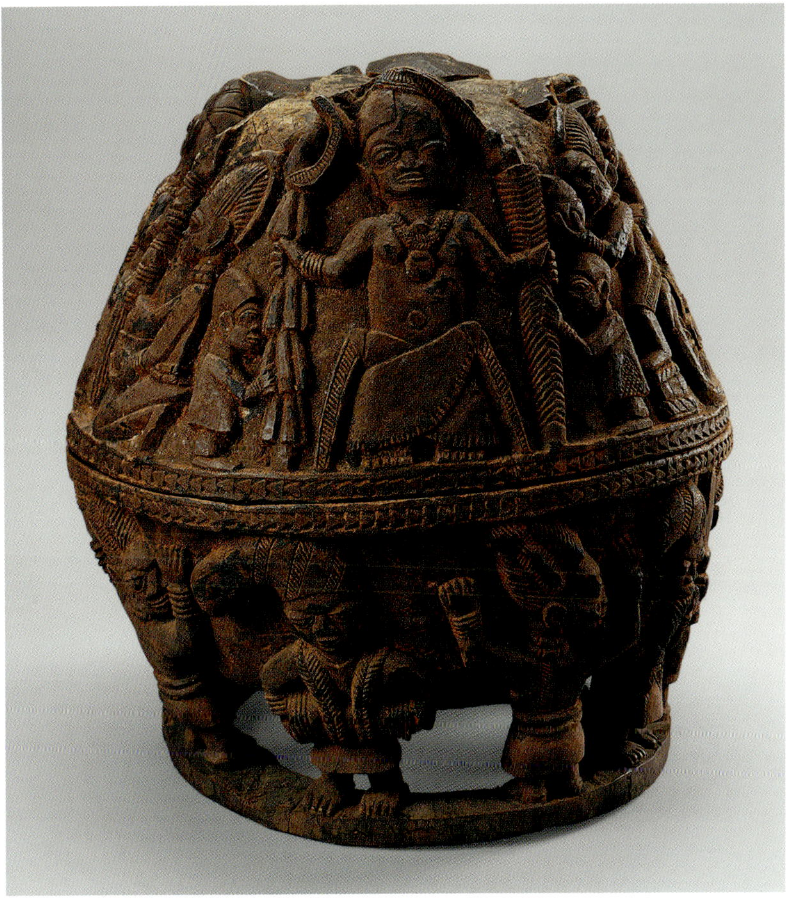

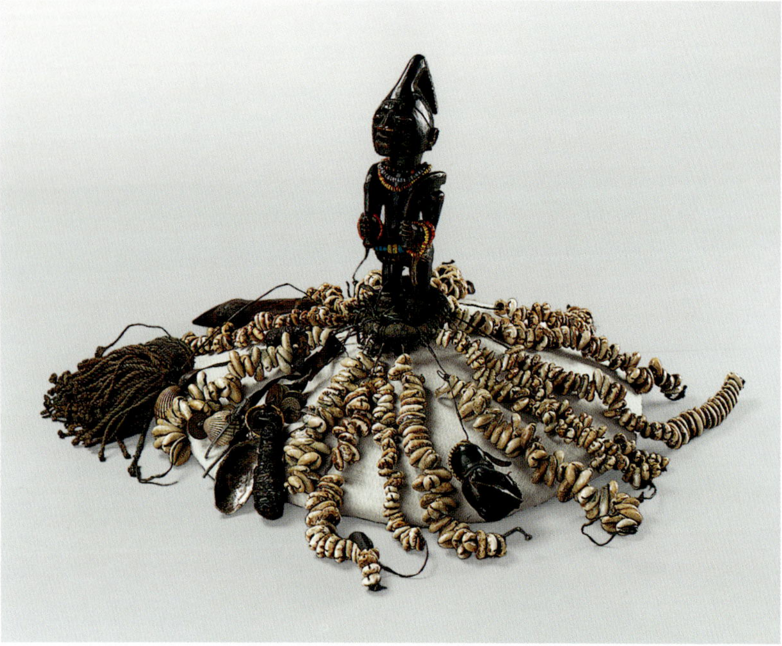

Serving as dance staff, priestly insignia, and altar sculpture, this Yoruba object honors the deity Esu, divine mediator and transformer of destinies. Esu, also known as Elegba, plays a pivotal role in the Yoruba pantheon of *orisa*, or "spirit beings." As spirit messenger and intermediary, Esu bears offerings and prayers to the god of divination, Orunmila or Ifa. The Ifa system of divination reveals the cause of and solutions to the problems that arise in one's life journey. One of the praise names of Esu is the Roadmaker, who opens the way through correct ritual. As an activator of forces that transform and reshape, Esu is unpredictable and can create confusion, deception, and conflict.

This dance staff is a superb example of African "accumulative sculpture," a composite of materials and objects designed to merge aesthetic impact with ritual efficacy. When set in motion by a priest dancing in homage to Esu, the multiple strands of cowrie shell-money and other attachments visually accent the musical beats and the dancer's movements. Even when the staff is resting on an altar, its kinetic nature is suggested in the fluid strands of cowries, coins, and shells symbolizing the flow of wealth that homage to Esu can provide. It is unusual for these staffs to have their component elements preserved intact and therefore their full iconographic dimension accessible to informed reconstruction. Each object has a particular meaning or reference, from the carved flute seen at the left back (an allusion to Esu's messenger role) to the stuffed and ornately braided medicinal packet at left-center (indicating spiritual and temporal powers). Invoking the dynamic relationship of earthly and metaphysical powers, the sculptor offers a visual pun in the formal interplay of Esu's knifelike hair braid, the rigid tube sack of medicine he holds out for display, and the thrust of the elongated phallus. In Yoruba cosmology, the head is the seat of spiritual or individual power. Glaze

Nigeria, Yoruba
early 20th century

Esu dance staff
Wood, hide, cowrie shells, coins, fiber
8 × 18 inches in diameter
Gift of Cecilia and Irwin Smiley
1985-32-5

An Efe-Gelede celebration is generally a two-day event in which masks are divided into those that make their appearances at night (Efe), and those that appear on the following day (Gelede). The nighttime Efe performance takes place in the market area, which is generally regarded as the economic and social realm of women. Efe-Gelede ceremonies recognize and honor the formidable powers of Yoruba female elders, referred to collectively as "our mothers." This celebration involves masqueraders, dancers, singers, and orators who impart social commentary, legend, and history through performance.

A wide variety of masks are worn in Efe-Gelede performances, all of which touch on aspects of Yoruba life. Snakes, birds, tortoises, and lizards, as well as historical public figures, fashion trends, and foreigners, are frequently depicted. This Efe mask is unusual in its representation of a bearded Muslim man from northern Nigeria, distinguished by seven carved amulets (three across his forehead and four flanking his beard). These amulets signify evil-averting devices containing verses from the Qur'an, which empower the mask. There has been a strong Muslim presence in Yorubaland since the seventeenth century, and aspects of Islam have been incorporated into local religious traditions. The white color of this mask tells us that it would be danced at the nighttime Efe ceremony in order to educate and entertain the community on both secular and spiritual matters, while both placating and honoring Yoruba women.

An Efe-Gelede performance exemplifies the Yoruba tradition of synthesizing the arts of mythology, poetry, sculpture, dance, and music through masquerade. Efe-Gelede is performed in times of celebration and of calamity to honor and appease the mothers. If admired and respected, the women will protect and bless the community. If neglected, they may use their supernatural powers to wreak havoc on society. Known for their beauty and athletic display, Efe-Gelede festivals honor and celebrate all women, especially mothers, a significant phenomenon in a patriarchal society. Rush

Republic of Benin,
Ketu-Ohori
Yoruba
early 20th century

Mask depicting warrior hunter (*Oro Efe*)
Wood, pigment
15 × 13 inches
Gift of Cecilia and Irwin Smiley
1998-13-12

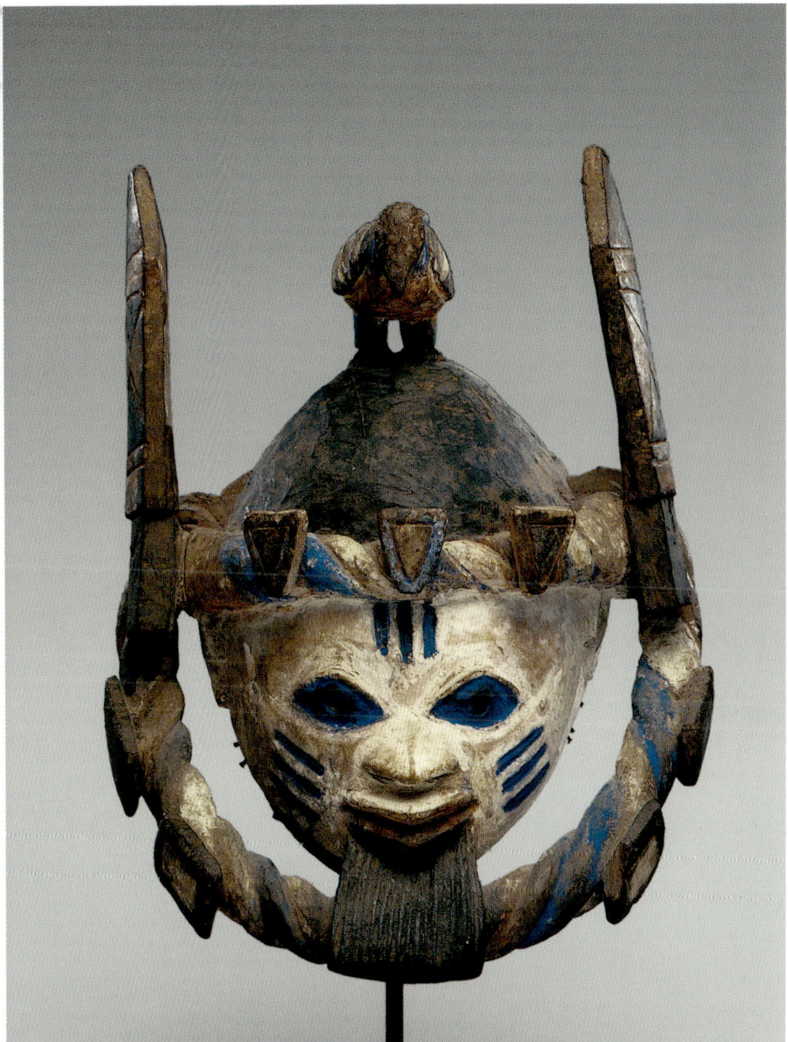

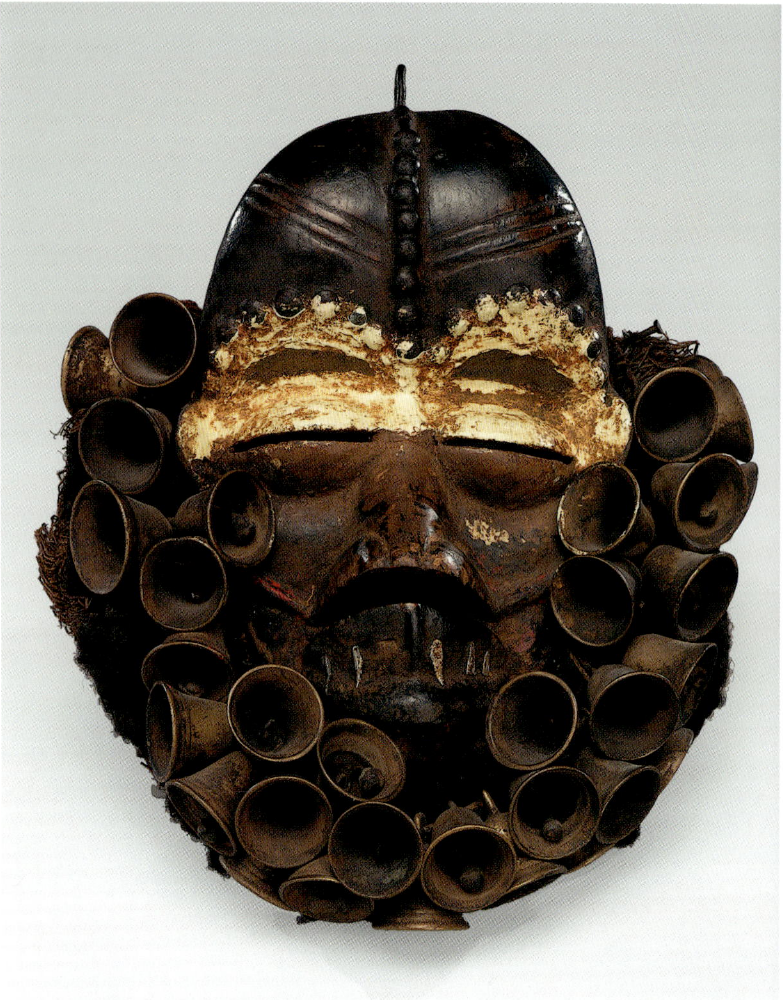

Throughout the cultural regions of Liberia and the Ivory Coast, where the We language is spoken, face masquerades have played a central role in all areas of life and government. Masks with slit, elliptical eyes painted over in white are considered "female," while those with round or projecting tubular eyes are "male." The white paint symbolizes the kaolin that is often used to decorate young girls' eyes as they go through initiation practices. Kaolin used to be part of a daily cosmetic routine in We-speaking cultures, and signifies both beauty and an absence of hostility. The vertical ridge on the forehead of this mask is an ethnic marker of northern We cultures, while the semi-circular relief that links the nostrils to the temples is a scarification pattern specific to We women.

The brass bells on this We mask, together with the generic female features, mark it as either a "singer" or a *griot* ("poet and musician") mask. The purpose and visual character of a We mask can change over time. It is the headdress and other attachments that establish a mask's particular character and its position in the masquerade hierarchy. The more important the spirit mask, the more elaborate the crowning and framing of the "face" with natural and fabricated materials. A We mask with generic female features such as this may begin life as a low-ranking "beggar" dance masquerade used strictly for entertainment, to earn money for its owner's family by its antics, and to sing the praises of notables. The same carved mask can move up in the hierarchy through successive transformations of form and repeated performance, evolving into a "singer" or, in some cases, into a "griot" masquerade. Such masks are sacred keepers of We history and cultural traditions.

Each "singer" masquerade has a "life history." Passed down from one generation to another within a family lineage, a "singer" builds its language skills and repertory of texts as it increases in age, reputation, and sanctity. Very old "singer" masks are venerated as the "mothers" of younger "singer" masks. Glaze

Ivory Coast
We
early 20th century

"Singer" dance mask
Wood, bells, fiber, chalk
11 3/4 × 9 1/2 inches
Gift of Richard J. Faletti Family Collection
2000-5-1

The Poro Society is a complex initiation system responsible for the educational and spiritual formation of the young and the upholding of law and moral order in Senufo village life. The *Kponyungo* helmet mask is primarily a funerary mask that serves both as an honorary tribute to deceased Poro elders and as an instrument of protection from malevolent sorcery and spirits. The distinctive long horns of this zoomorphic mask are emblematic of ethnic identity and its exclusive use by Senufo farmer groups.

Loaded with symbolic and magical weaponry, *Kponyungo* is also a "combat" masquerade designed for supernatural warfare. The masquerade ensemble – mask, costume attachments, performance design – is the fearsome manifestation of contesting powers and strong medicine. Charged by secret ritual and by medicine bundles and altars hidden in a sacred grove, the mask destroys the snares laid by sorcerers. The medicine cup on top of the mask alludes to its magical and healing powers.

The *Kponyungo* mask is intended to conjure up a "monster," its aggressive imagery in keeping with the reputed ability of sorcerers to transform themselves into ferocious beasts. In this example, the open, devouring jaws of a hyena, the lance-sharp horns of larger antelopes, and the dagger-like warthog tusks on top of the snout are all suggestive of effective defensive weaponry. This mask is crowned at the back of the head by a bird with a chameleon in its beak, signifying the first two creatures on earth. In Senufo literature and art, these two icons have many associations. The hornbill bird is linked in myth to agricultural productivity and the eternal duality of the male and female couple. The chameleon is an important spirit messenger, carrying the affairs of diviners and their clients to the gods. The animal's ability to change color is associated with transformational and mediating powers, making it an ideal symbol for display by diviners and healers. Glaze

Zana Soro
Ivory Coast, Senufo
20th century

(following pages)
Poro Society mask (*Kponyungo*)
1970
Wood
14 1/2 × 40 inches
Gift of Professor Anita J. Glaze
1986-31-1

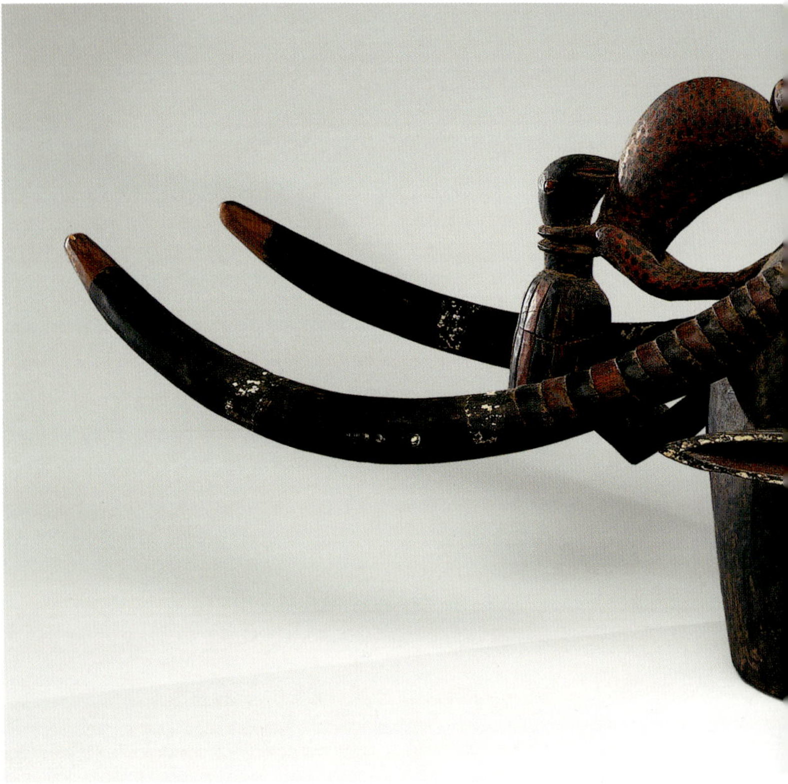

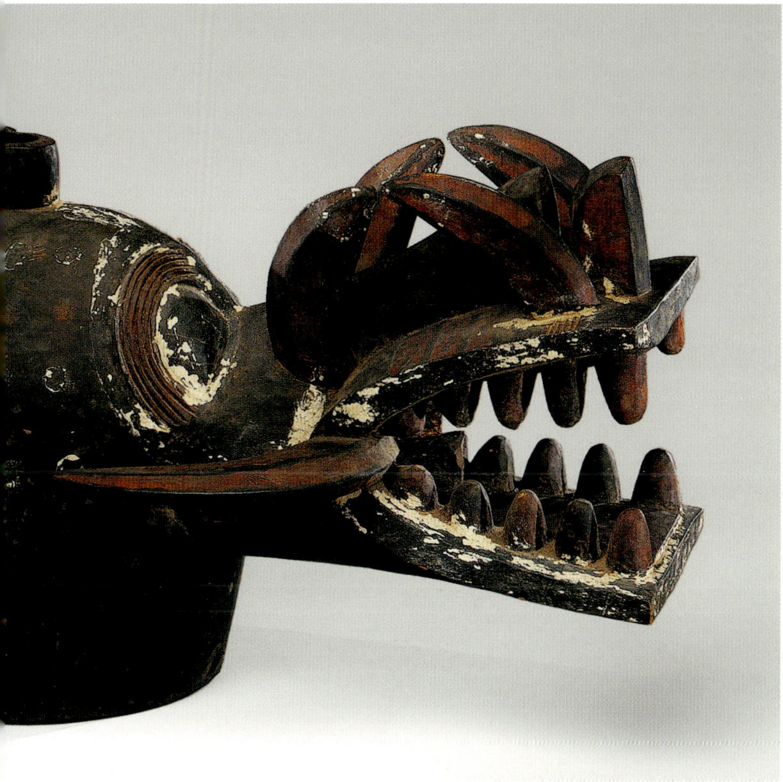

ASIA
AFRICA

ANCIENT MEDITERRANEAN

THE COLLECTION
EUROPE
AMERICAS

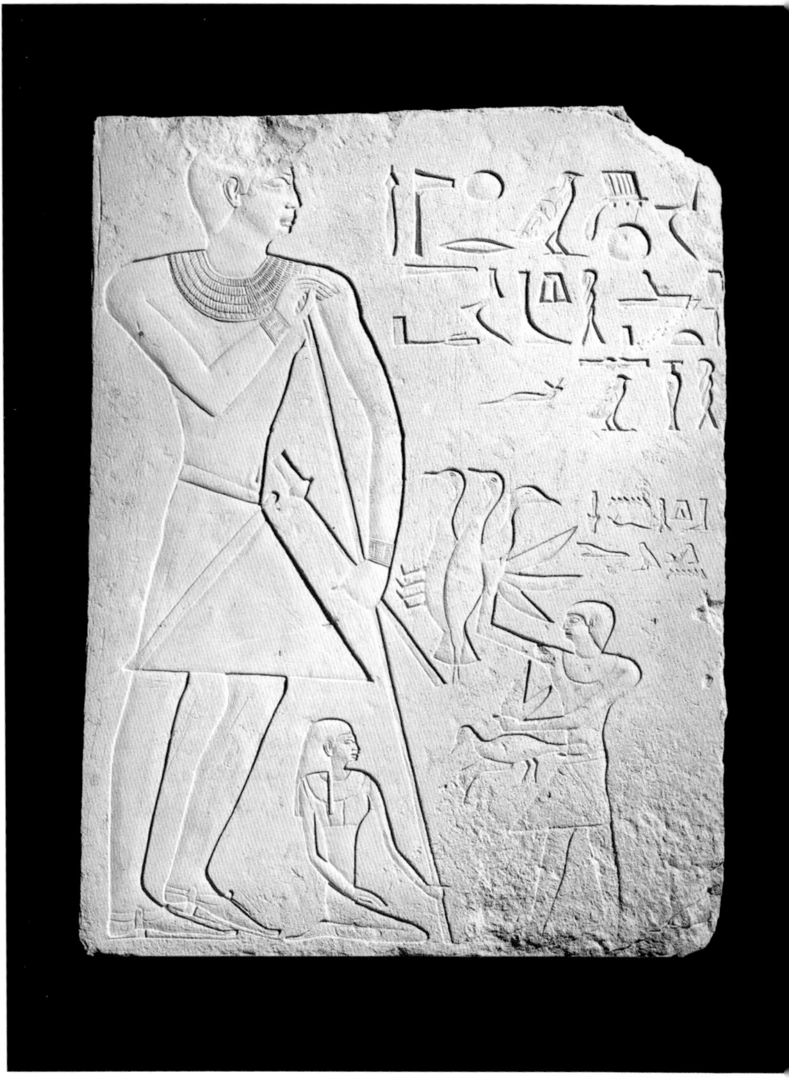

This partially preserved limestone stele, or commemorative marker, would once have been a part of a larger work. It is believed to have come from the desert plateau of Saqqara, one of the principal Old Kingdom burial grounds of Lower Egypt, just west of the ancient city of Memphis (and south of present-day Cairo).

This stele shows a tribute scene in sunken relief, a type of sculpture in which the image projects from the background. Typical of Egyptian art of this period, it has a hierarchical arrangement of figures, with the most important shown at a larger scale than the secondary ones. The large male figure on the left receives a tribute of ducks from the smaller male figure to the right. Kneeling at the feet of the largest figure is the diminutive figure of a woman who appears to assist him in acceptance of the gift.

The hierarchy is emphasized by variations in the degree of depth in the relief: details such as the figures' sandals are rendered in lower relief than the main focal points of the image. In addition, the garments and accessories worn by the figures signify their place in the hierarchy. The largest figure wears a starched triangular kilt, short wig, and elaborate necklace. He holds two staffs, indicators of his position and power. His imposing stride, a traditional stance in Egyptian art, further emphasizes his importance in the composition. Egyptian relief sculpture was often painted with vibrant colors that highlight the main elements of the image. This stele may once have had such painted decoration, though none is preserved today.

Limestone reliefs such as this one decorated tombs and palaces throughout ancient Egypt. One common iconographic theme exemplified here is the glorification of a pharaoh or other important figure in the Egyptian social structure through the presentation of tribute. The hierarchy of Egyptian society was observed both in day-to-day life and in the afterlife. Zitrides

Egypt
Old Kingdom, 6th dynasty
(ca. 2325–2160 BCE)

Stele
Limestone
26 × 19 3/4 inches
Gift of Ellnora D. Krannert Fund
1974-11-1

Beginning in the early seventh century BCE, pottery workshops in Corinth – then one of Greece's more prosperous cities – produced vessels in a distinct style later referred to as Corinthian or Orientalizing. This style is characterized by motifs that reflect contemporary trends in the visual arts of Egypt and the Near East, such as dancers, warriors, and creatures from myth, which are generally arranged in bands or registers that wrap around the vessel. The use of local, buff-colored clay and a decorative technique of incised and painted decoration, mainly in red, black, and white, also typify Corinthian ceramics. This vessel is attributed to an unknown artist called the Moore Painter in honor of the object's donor.

Registers of decoration cover almost the entire surface of this single-handled wine jug. Each one carries depictions of mythical animals, with the bodies rendered in profile and the heads shown both in profile and frontally. The spaces between the figures are filled with stylized rosettes and geometric forms, which add liveliness to the composition and diminish the horizontal emphasis of the registers. The long, thin vertical handle and black neck appear to elongate the vessel.

Corinthian potters would have had access to this visual vocabulary through the Egyptian, Persian, and Phoenician traders that came to Greek ports, and whose exports – pottery, textiles, metalwork – would have been available in the local markets. Like later Athenian pottery, Corinthian vessels have been found throughout the Mediterranean, an indication of their high quality and desirability. These vessels may have been exported by the Phoenicians and other traders who made Corinth one of their primary mercantile centers. Zitrides

Moore Painter
Greece
ca. 600 BCE

Corinthian *olpe*
Earthenware, slip
17 × 9 inches
Gift of Theresa E. and Harlan E. Moore
1970-9-2

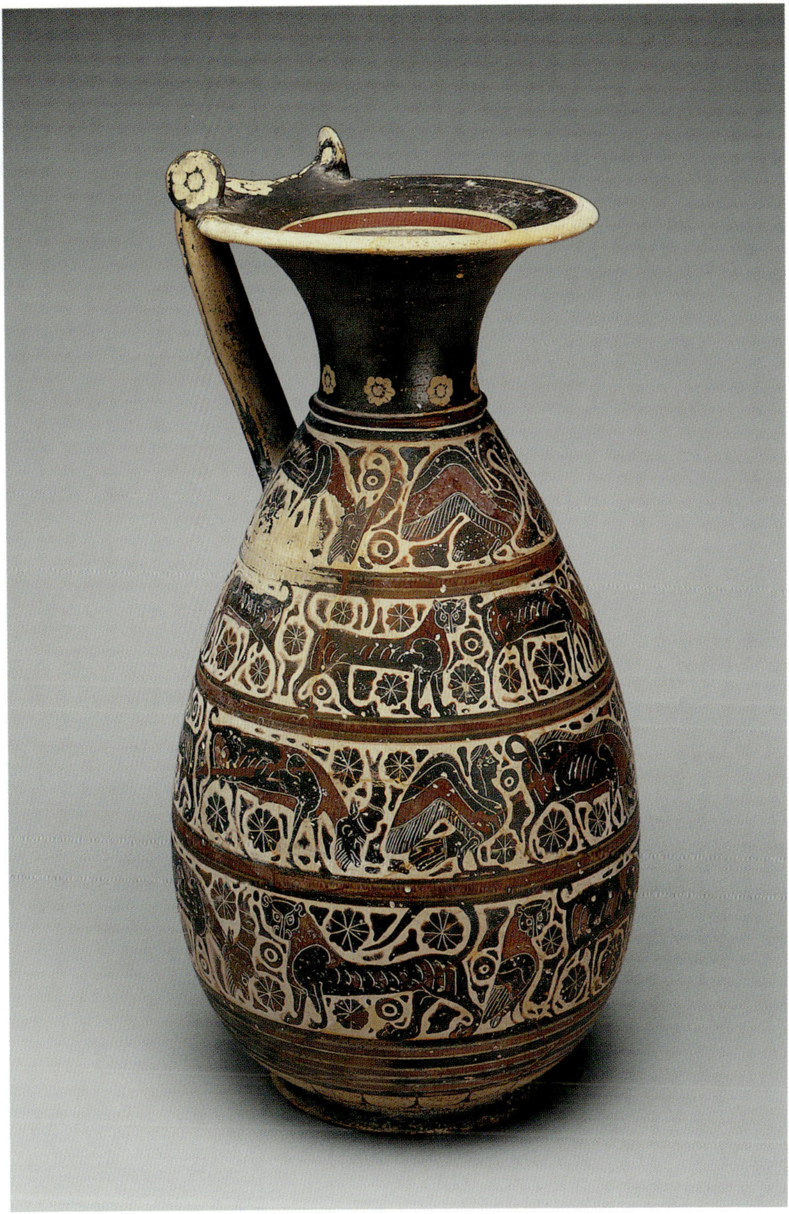

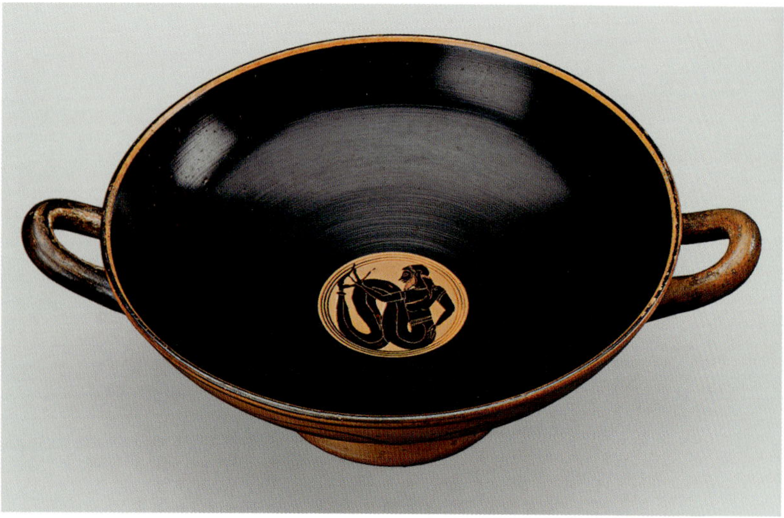

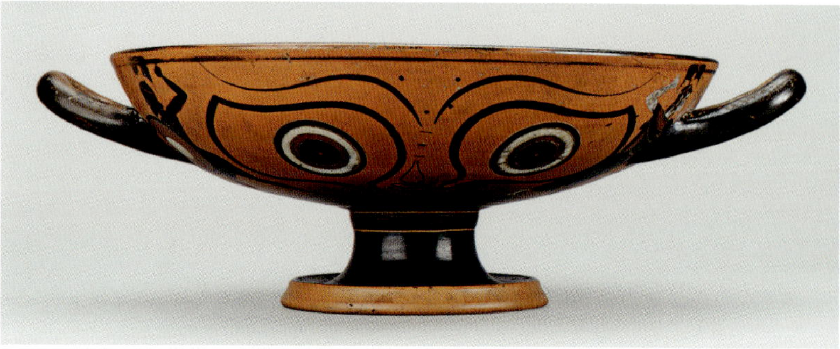

Follower of Exekias
Greece
(active ca. 550–525 BCE)

Attic black-figure kylix
ca. 530 BCE
Earthenware, slip
4 1/2 × 14 1/2 inches (including handles)
Gift of Theresa E. and Harlan E. Moore
1970-8-1

Beginning in the mid-sixth century BCE, Athens was the center of ceramic production and decoration in Greece. A wide variety of Athenian vessels have been found at sites throughout the Mediterranean, pointing to extensive exportation of these works. The signatures of the potter and sometimes the painter on these vessels indicate that several hands were involved in the production process. Even though these vessels were generally manufactured for everyday household use, the desirability of a vessel was to some degree determined by its association with an artist or group of artists.

Black-figure is the earliest of the three main Attic decoration techniques. Wheel-thrown vessels were covered with slip, a watered-down clay, which rendered a glossy reddish surface. The decoration was then painted in silhouette against the red ground with some additional incised and painted details, mainly in red and white. After the decoration had dried, the vessels were fired.

The interior of this kylix, or drinking cup, depicts a triton – a mythical beast with human torso and head and serpent body. On the outer face of the cup, four apotropaic eyes, believed to ward off evil, are shown in the spaces between two narrative scenes depicting Athena, the warrior goddess of wisdom, battling the Giants. This mythological episode is one that enjoyed widespread popularity in Athenian art during this period because it symbolized both the military prowess of Athens and the role of Athena as patroness and protectress of the city.

Although the name of the painter of this kylix is not known, it is thought that he worked near or within the workshop of Exekias, a potter and painter of the black-figure style who signed some of his works. Because of the existence of a few signed works among thousands of anonymous examples, early scholars and collectors established a hierarchy of objects. Greek vases by known artists such as Exekias became more desirable than those whose artists remained unknown. It is possible that the original owner of this piece may have associated it with Exekias in order to increase its market value. Although such an association is perhaps appealing, it may be more appropriate to appreciate this piece as a vehicle for glimpsing everyday life and aesthetics in sixth-century Athens.
Zitrides

In this Late Roman Empire grave stele, or commemorative marker, two parents mark the passing of their only child. The simple yet poignant inscription on the base reads: "Aurelios Alexandros and Flavias built this for Kyrilla and for themselves, being alive, as a memorial." The stele originated in the region of Phrygia in western Asia Minor (present-day Turkey); its Greek inscription includes the date *etous TKD*, or 239–240.

Within the arched niche of the stele, three wide-eyed figures with distinctive, large hands are depicted in various depths of relief and carved in a crisp, linear style. The father, Alexandros, seen at the left, holds a pruning knife, and the mother, Flavias, a spindle and distaff, implements of agriculture and weaving. The twisted garland draped over their heads may signify their marital bond. Their child, Kyrilla, stands between them. All three figures are dressed in simple tunics covered by cloaks. The shrine is given rudimentary architectural form, with pilasters (shallow columns) decorated with grapevines and a pediment (triangular section supported by columns) incised with foliate *acroteria* (architectural ornament on a pediment). A shaft originally anchored the stele to a plinth, or base. The dedicatory inscription on the base is off-center due to a break on the right-hand side; the date appears between the heads of the parents. The tombstone was probably a shop piece, purchased "off the rack" and inscribed to suit the buyer.

As a representative of the tumultuous third century, the stele reflects a world in transition. Exemplifying a type of object widespread in the Late Roman Empire – distinguished by common subjects, formulaic inscriptions, and a non-classical style – it marks the transformation of artistic expression from the natural and idealized forms of the art of Greco-Roman antiquity to the significant and symbolic forms that continued through and typified the art of the Middle Ages. Ousterhout

Grave stele
239–240
Marble
34 × 19 1/4 inches
Gift of Katherine Trees Livezey Estate

Phrygia 1979-7-1

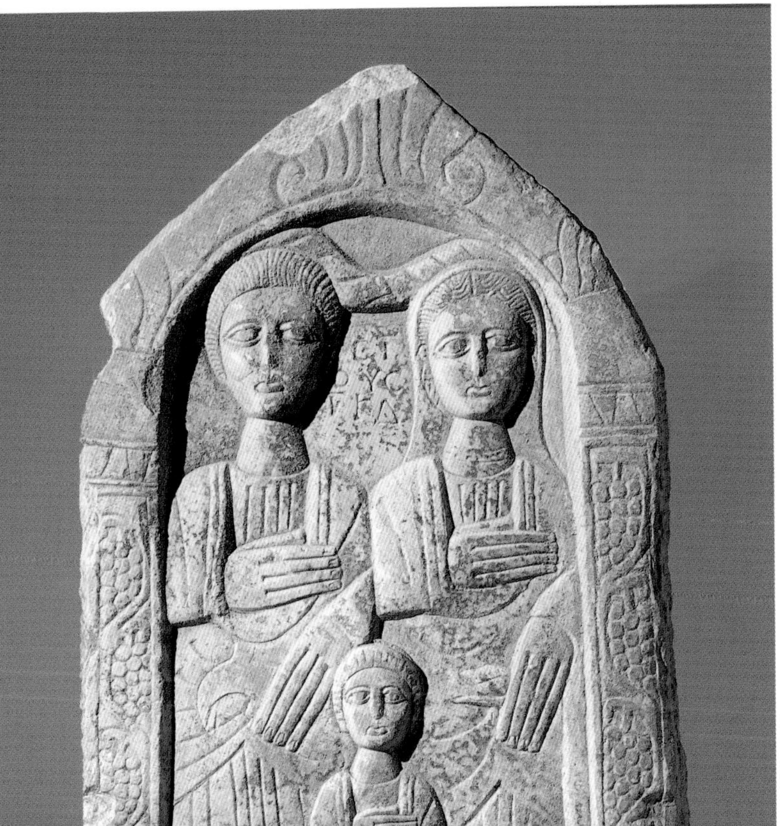

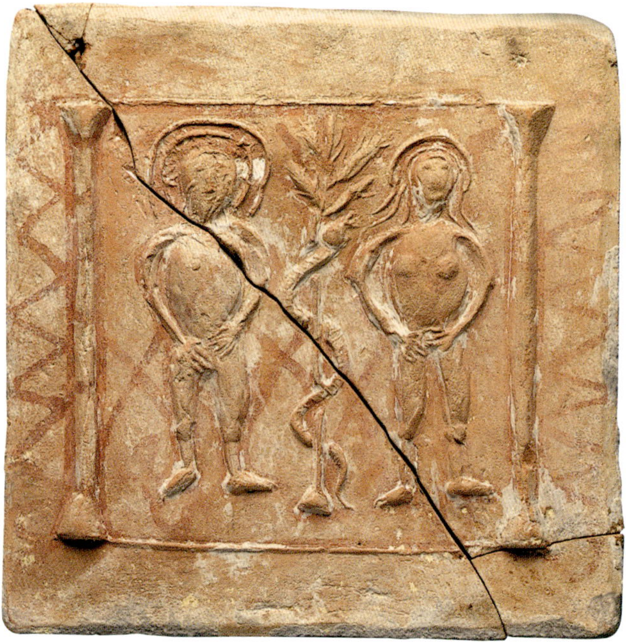

Terracotta plaques such as this one were a common element of early Christian church decoration in North Africa. Major find sites include Tunisia and Algeria, but examples have also been unearthed in southern Spain, France, and the Balkans. While production of the tiles seems to have peaked in the sixth and seventh centuries, they were produced in smaller quantities at earlier dates as well. Made from molds, they were relatively easy and inexpensive to manufacture, which may account, in part, for their popularity and the abundance of examples recovered. Despite their proliferation, they have yet to be thoroughly studied. The images depicted on the plaques most often reflect Greco-Roman mythological and allegorical themes, Christian subjects – whether popular early Christian stories or the figures of Jesus, his mother Mary, and saints – and decorative vegetal or animal motifs. Such tiles would have decorated the walls or ceiling of a church, complementing mosaic, marble, and painted decoration.

This plaque shows an abstracted representation of Adam and Eve in the Garden of Eden, a common subject in early Christian art. The figures stand on either side of a tree with a serpent wrapped around the trunk. Two columns frame the composition and decorative zigzags of red ochre pigment appear throughout the panel. Literally, the image represents the biblical Old Testament account of mankind's expulsion from Paradise and, as such, would have conveyed a moral message to the early Christian viewer. Symbolically, the image signifies the concept of mankind's salvation through the martyrdom of Christ. Embedded in this salvation imagery is the notion that the Old Testament was superseded by the New, embodied for the community of believers in the belief that access to Paradise, lost by Adam and Eve, was regained through Christ's crucifixion.
Zitrides

North Africa
ca. 6th century

Temptation of Adam and Eve
Molded earthenware
9 3/4 × 9 3/4 inches
Harlan E. Moore Charitable Trust
1986-38-1

ASIA
AFRICA
ANCIENT MEDITERRANEAN
EUROPE THE COLLECTION
AMERICAS

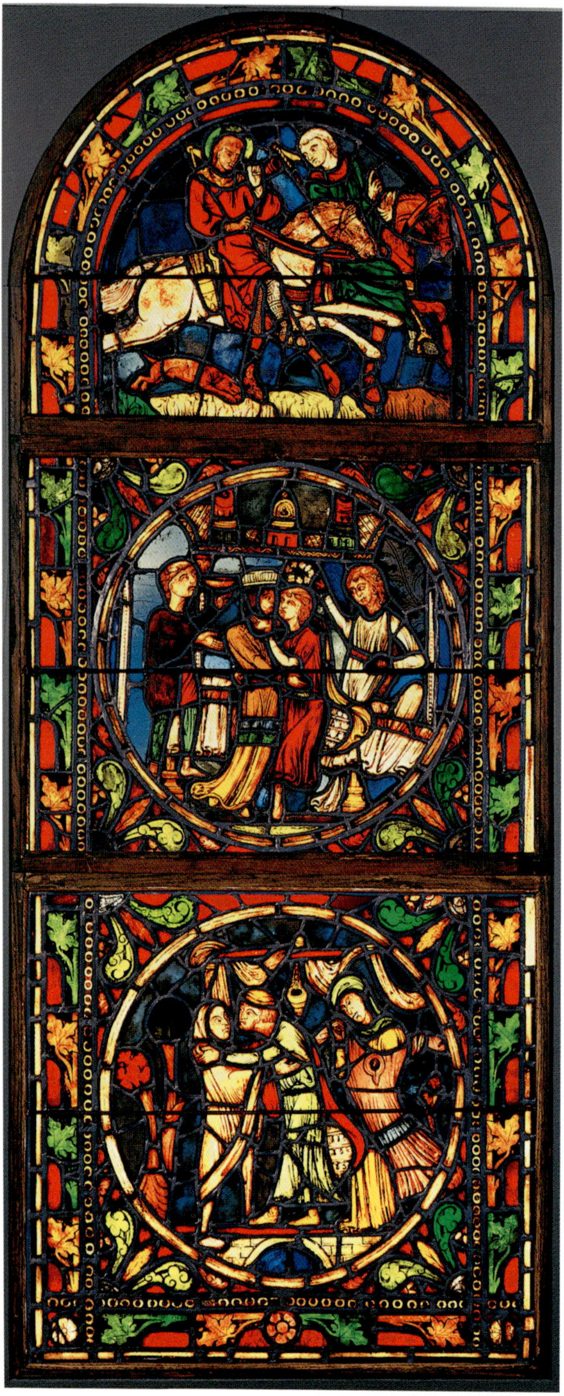

This Gothic window presents a rich visual account of the biblical parable of the prodigal son (Luke 15:11–32). The tale begins in the lunette at the top with the young man and a companion riding to the city to seek their fortunes. It continues in the rondel below with a scene showing the son and his cohorts squandering money on a prostitute. Though the Gospel mentions only that the young man lost his wealth through riotous living, medieval artists often portrayed him spending it on brothels, gambling, and drinking. The small architectural features above the figures in this scene indicate that they are in a city tavern. The story concludes in the bottom rondel with the son, poor and dejected, returning home, where he is warmly welcomed by his father as his elder brother looks on.

As is typical in Gothic stained glass, the narrative is relayed through simple forms and bright colors, and is surrounded by stylized foliate forms in the borders and spandrels. The artist not only captured the plot but also, through a skillful manipulation of form, the parable's themes of redemption and forgiveness. The images of the son meeting with the prostitute and with his father both show witnesses to his warm embraces. The visual parallel encourages a reading of the father's gesture as an expression of love and pardon. The small size of the rondels, the presence of religious imagery, and the style of figuration suggest that the window probably once decorated the lower portion of a French Gothic church. Carns

France
ca. 1215–25

Parable of the Prodigal Son
Pot metal, glass, vitreous paint
60 1/2 × 27 1/2 inches
Gift of Mr. and Mrs. Herman C. Krannert
1963-45-1

This single manuscript leaf displays the characteristics of Gothic bibles produced between the mid-thirteenth and the mid-fourteenth centuries in northern France, particularly Paris. It contains the first four chapters of the Book of Amos as well as a short prologue, and was probably once part of a single-volume Bible. In the Gothic period, bibles were made for secular readers by professional rather than monastic scribes and artists. The scribe first marked the parchment with ruling lines and then wrote out the text with a reed pen and ink, leaving spaces for illustrations and decorative initials to be added later by the artist. The ruling lines are clearly visible on this leaf, as are corrections to the text in the margins.

The historiated initial on the front of this leaf depicts the shepherd Amos, one of the minor prophets in the Old Testament, who prophesied God's judgment of the people of Israel. Enclosed within the "V" of the Latin word *verba*, Amos among his sheep receives God's word. This is the largest and most elaborate initial on the page because it begins the text proper. The intermediate and smaller initials decorated with trellislike vines are placed at the beginnings of the prologues and chapters, respectively. This hierarchy of decoration helped the medieval reader find passages in a book, much like chapter headings and subheadings today.

Other Gothic features are the use of two narrow columns of text, the vertical, spiky script, and the red, blue, and gold color scheme. One especially notable element is the long extension of the decorated initials. The letters terminate in playful depictions of foliage and animals – in this case, a dragon and a monkey – which usually have little to do with the main text but must have delighted readers nonetheless. Bauer

Page from the Book of Amos
Ink, colors, burnished gold on parchment
15 1/4 × 9 3/4 inches

France
ca. 1300

University of Illinois Foundation Fund
1958-4-1

Hic amos propheta non fuit pater
ysaie prophete: quemadmodum
et ille propheta extiterit. Nam
alius scribitur ille alius iste
apud hebreos scribitur. Diff
erentia litterarum apud la
tinos non habetur: Et ille fortis vel robustus
hic vero avulsus interpretatur: quia locutus
est contra x tribus que prevaricatam a cultu
dei vel etiam a regno domus david erant avulse: que
fuit autem cognatio eius ex oppido thecue quod
vi miliaribus distat a bethleem: ante magis gre
cus proximum in latitudine camporum, qui
qui sunt proximum oppido thecue. in quibus hu
mi arido atque harenoso nichil omnino fru
gum gignitur: sed inhabitantes pascuis ha
bundant: Et ideo cuncta sunt pastoribus plena:
et sterilitas terre compensatur pecorum
multitudine: Ex hoc numero pastorum fuit
amos: imperitus sermone sed plenus scientia;
Prophetavit autem eisdem temporibus quibus io
el, naum, ionas, osee, ysaias: sed aliquantu
lum exorsus est prophetare ante quam ysaias; q
ui tamen autem contra x tribus locutus est:
preter de duabus miseris: Hunc ablatum de
numero pastorum misit dominus ut in sa
maria prophetaret: quem amasias sacerdos fre
quenter plagis affligit; Tandem filius eius
ozias vecte per timpora transfixit; Post hec se
minivivus in terram suam evectus: post aliquo
t dies dolore vulneris expiravit. sepultusque
est cum patribus suis; Explicit prologus. Incipit liber a
mos prophete;

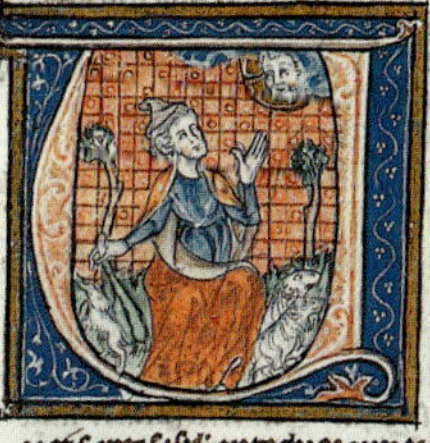

I Verba amos
qui fuit in
pastoribus
de thecue
que vidit
super israel
in diebus o
zie regis
iuda et in
diebus iero
boam fili
i ioas regis israel: ante duos annos terre motus.
Et dixit: Dominus de syon rugiet: et de ierusalem
dabit vocem suam; Et luxerunt speciosa pasto
rum: Et exsiccatus est vertex carmeli; Hec
dicit dominus: super tribus sceleribus damas
ci et super iiii non convertam eum eo quod trituraverunt

verunt in plaustris ferreis galaad; Et mittam
ignem in domum azael: et devorabit domos be
nadab; Et conteram vectem damasci: et dis
perdam habitatorem de campo idoli: et tenentem
sceptrum de domo voluptatis: et trans
feretur populus syrie cirenen dicit dominus;
Hec dicit dominus: super tribus sceleribus gaze et super
iiii non convertam eum eo quod transtulerint
captivitatem perfectam ut concluderent eam in
ydumea. Et mittam ignem in murum
gaze: et devorabit edes eius; Et disperdam
habitatorem de azoto et tenentem sceptrum de as
calone; et convertam manum meam super
accaron. et peribunt reliquie philistinorum:
dicit dominus deus; Hec dicit dominus super
tribus sceleribus tyri et super iiii non convertam e
um: eo quod concluserint captivitatem per
fectam in ydumea et non sunt recordati federis
fratrum: Et mittam ignem in murum tyri:
et devorabit edes eius; Hec dicit dominus: super tribus
sceleribus edom et super iiii non convertam eum: eo quod per
secutus sit in gladio fratrem suum: et violaverit misericordiam
eius: et tenuerit ultra furorem suum: et indignationem
suam servaverit usque in finem; Mittam igni
em in theman: et devorabit edes bosre; Hec dicit
dominus super tribus sceleribus filiorum ammon et
super iiii non convertam eum: eo quod dissecuerit
pregnantes galaad ad dilatandum termi
num suum. Et succendam ignem in muro rabbe:
et devorabit edes eius in ululatu in die belli
et in turbine in die commotionis. Et ibit melchom
in captivitatem: ipse et principes eius simul di
cit dominus;

II

Hec dicit dominus: super tribus sceleribus moab
et super iiii non convertam eum: eo quod
incenderit ossa regis ydumee usque
ad cinerem; Et mittam ignem in moab, et devo
rabit edes carioth: et morietur in sonitu mo
ab, in clangore tube; Et disperdam iudicem de me
dio eius: et omnes principes eius interficiam
cum eo dicit dominus; Hec dicit dominus super tribus sce
leribus iuda et super iiii non convertam eum eo quod
abiecerint legem domini: et mandata eius
non custodierint: Deceperunt enim eos idola
sua post que abierant patres eorum; Et mittam
ignem in iuda: et devorabit edes ierusalem; Hec
dicit dominus: super tribus sceleribus israel et super iiii non
convertam eum: pro eo quod vendiderint argen
to iustum et pauperem pro calciamentis. Qui con
terunt super pulverem terre capita pauperum: et viam

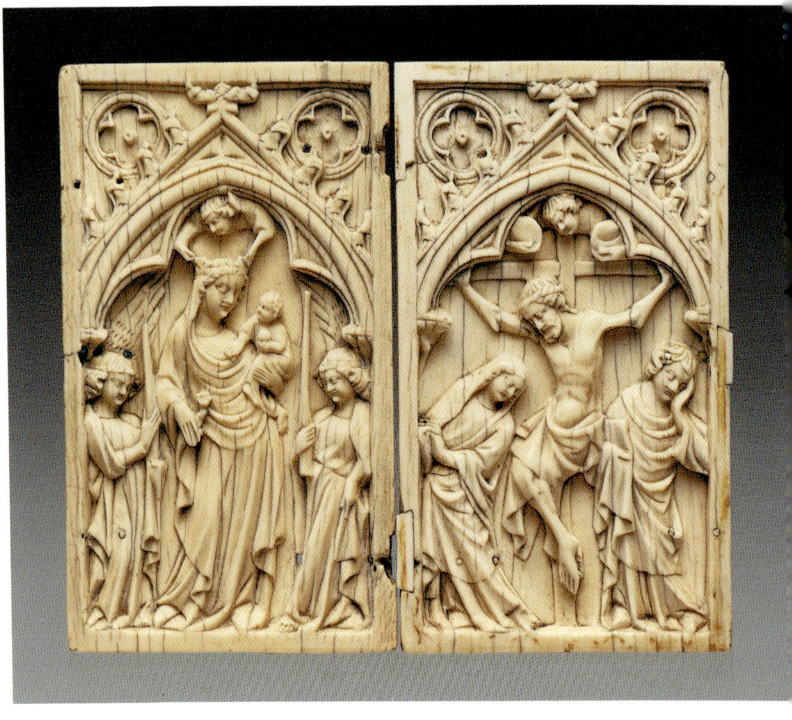

On the left-hand leaf of this diptych, flanked by two angels holding tapers, the Virgin Mary cradles the Christ Child with one arm and holds a rose in the opposite hand. The young mother looks lovingly at her son and he returns her gaze. In one hand, Jesus grasps an orb – a sign of his dominion over heaven and earth – and with the other tugs playfully at his mother's mantel. An angel hovering above the pair places an elaborate crown on the Virgin's head. On the right-hand leaf, Christ hangs on the cross as Mary and John the Evangelist lament his passing. Above, an angel carries the sun and moon – a reference to the eclipse that occurred at Christ's death.

The original owner of this small, portable object probably used it for personal devotion in the home or in church. The juxtaposition of scenes from the early and late parts of Jesus's life – with both him and Mary embodying Christian values – made it a particularly effective tool for meditation or prayer. Four interrelated themes emerge: Mary's glorification in heaven, her role as intercessor between her son and the faithful, Christ's sacrifice on the cross, and his future role as Savior.

The diptych's style and iconography along with the high quality of its carving suggest that it was probably made in Paris, the center of ivory production in Europe at the time. The artist would have worked in one of the many small shops in the city specializing in such objects. Carns

France
ca. 1340–60

Coronation of the Virgin and
Crucifixion with the Virgin and St. John
Ivory
Diptych, each panel 5 1/4 x 3 inches
Harlan E. Moore Charitable Trust
1982-6-1

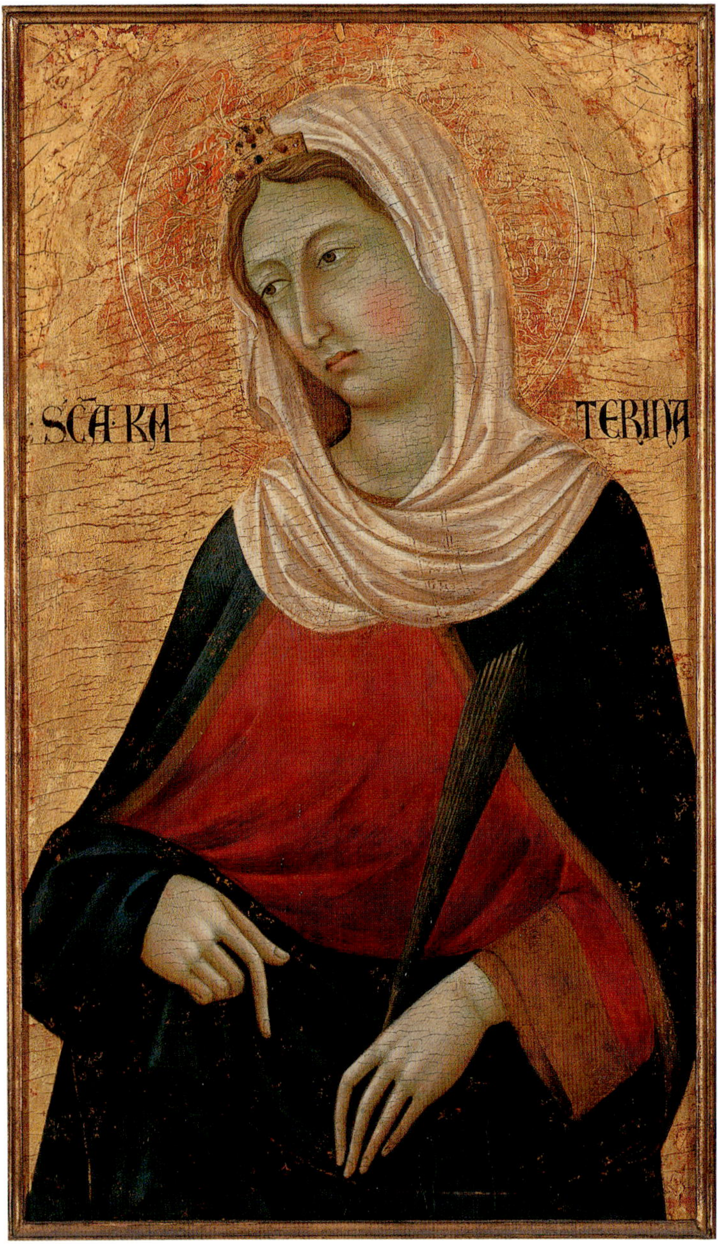
SCA·KA
TERINA

This early-fourteenth-century panel painting is attributed to Ugolino di Nerio (also known as Ugolino da Siena), a Sienese artist active in the first half of the fourteenth century. Born into a family of painters, Ugolino may have trained under Sienese painter Duccio di Buoninsegna; some scholars believe that Ugolino assisted Duccio on his renowned *Maestà* altarpiece (1308–11). Ugolino's best-known commission was the high altarpiece for the Florentine church of Santa Croce, a work now divided among several American and European collections.

The Krannert Art Museum panel was once part of an altarpiece, the central panel of which probably represented the Madonna and Child. Various specialists have attempted to reconstruct the original work from material and stylistic evidence, but to date no single version has been universally accepted. This particular panel represents one of Ugolino's early commissions as a master in his own right. Its media and support – egg tempera and gold leaf on wood – were widely used for devotional works in the later Middle Ages.

The austerity and emotional depth of Ugolino's rendition of the popular Saint Catherine are characteristic of his work. Catherine's almond-shaped eyes and rounded, elongated facial features and hands are typical of other Italian work of this period, which ultimately derived from Byzantine art. Although sometimes portrayed with a wheel of torture, here Catherine displays the martyr's palm leaf, symbolizing her victory over death. The combination of rich colors and minimal but exquisitely fine detail, as in Catherine's tooled gold halo, makes this work particularly striking. Bauer

Ugolino di Nerio
(Ugolino da Siena)
Italy
active 1317–27

Saint Catherine of Alexandria
ca. 1320
Tempera, gold leaf on panel
21 3/4 × 12 3/4 inches
Gift of Ellnora D. Krannert
1965-16-4

Painted representations of the *sacra conversazione* – the Virgin Mary, the Christ Child, and saints appearing to "converse" with one another in a unified space – were popular throughout western Europe in the fifteenth and sixteenth centuries. In this panel, the enthroned Virgin holds the Christ Child, who rests his left hand on a prayer book while blessing the viewer with his right. The four saints are identifiable by the attributes they wear or carry. From left to right they include: Augustine (wearing bishop's robes and holding a crozier, the staff used in Mass); John the Baptist (in a hermit's brown cloak, gesturing to the sacrificial Lamb); Monica (Augustine's mother, dressed in a nun's habit, reading a prayer book); and Nicholas of Tolentino (an Augustinian saint, wearing monk's robes and holding lilies and a star). Only John the Baptist is historically contemporaneous with the Virgin and Christ. The other three saints are thematically related, and their inclusion hints at the devotional interests of the (unknown) patron of this painting.

This sacred gathering occurs within a fifteenth-century interior, as evidenced by the tiled floor and the pictorial convention of a distant view of a northern European landscape through a window. The room is decorated with canopies, including one embroidered with pomegranates directly behind the Virgin and Child.

The panel has been attributed to the Master of the Saint Ursula Legend on the basis of comparison with known works by the artist. Underdrawings on the panel, recently discovered through infrared reflectography, are characteristic of the Master's artistic practice. His customary diagonal hatchings are especially evident beneath the angular folds of the Virgin's robe where the paint has become transparent with age.

The moderately large size of the panel suggests that it was originally designed as an altarpiece for a small private chapel. Foster-Campbell

Master of the Saint Ursula Legend
Flanders
active ca. 1470–90

Madonna and Child with Four Saints
ca. 1465–70
Oil on panel
29 1/2 × 37 inches
Gift of Katherine Trees Livezey and George S. Trees, and the Ellnora D. Krannert Fund
1976-20-1

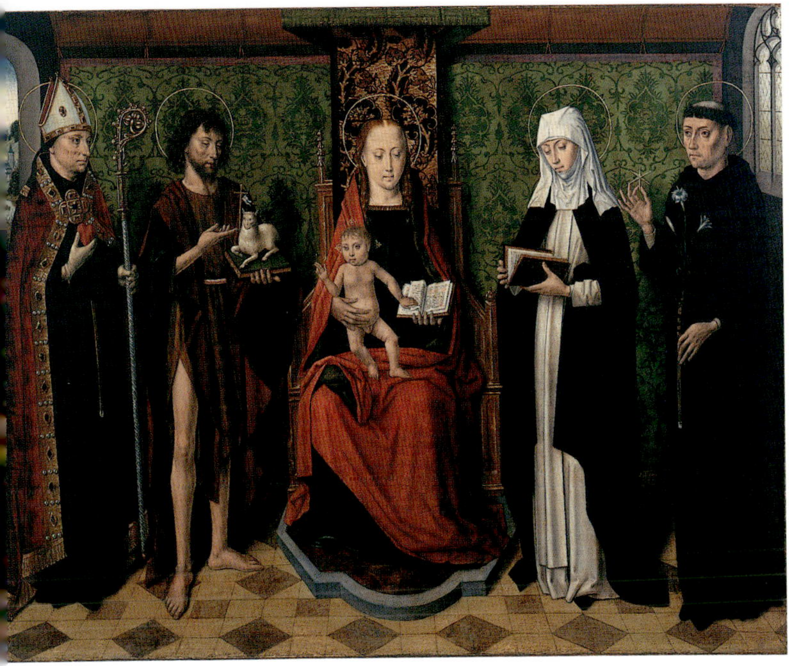

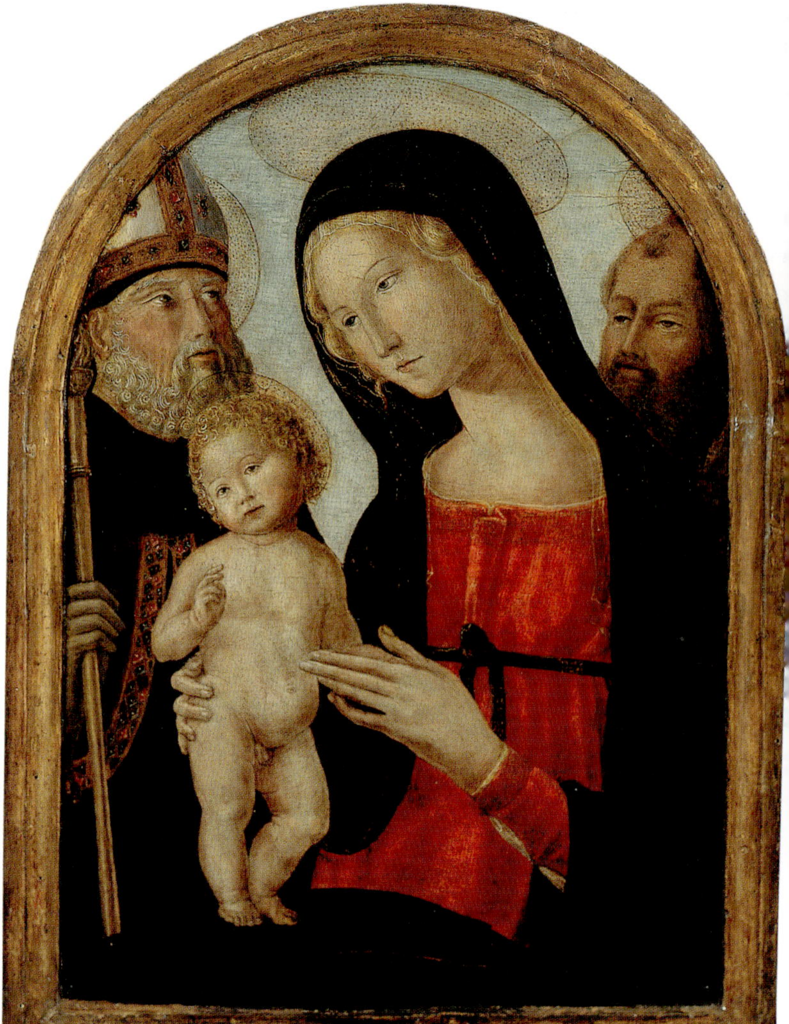

he Sienese painter and sculptor Neroccio de' Landi trained in the workshop of orenzo di Pietro, called Vecchietta (1412–1480). Neroccio specialized in intimate evotional paintings, such as this one, that were displayed in private homes and eligious institutions. These compositions were so popular in late-fifteenth-century iena that artists had workshop assistants execute small versions. The demand or Neroccio's paintings reached its peak during the 1490s, when the busy artist mployed at least seven assistants in three workshops.

he Krannert Art Museum panel exemplifies a type of devotional image popular in he 1460s, in which saints and angels flank central figures. Here, the Madonna nd Child and two saints – delicately painted with tight brushstrokes – are posed n a shallow space against a blue background. The portrayal of the Madonna ollows Renaissance conventions: young, beautiful, blonde, and dressed in a red obe and blue mantle. The gold leaf used for the halos also appears along the dge of her cloak. She leans her head, covered by the mantle and a veil, toward he Infant. Her neck and fingers are gracefully elongated. She solemnly holds the Child as he stands in contrapposto – with his weight on one leg – as he raises his ight hand to bless the viewer. The unidentified saints are shown in three-quarter view. One, partially obscured by the frame, stands behind the Madonna and the other, holding a staff, wears a bishop's hat and vestments over a monastic habit.
Blondin

Neroccio di
Bartolomeo de' Landi
Italy
1447–1500

Madonna and Child
ca. 1496
Tempera on panel
20 3/8 × 14 3/4 inches
Gift of Mr. and Mrs. Merle J. Trees
1943-1-3

The events depicted in this woodcut by Albrecht Dürer are taken from Luke's gospel (2:42–50), which recounts the travel to Jerusalem of the twelve-year-old Jesus and his family to celebrate Passover. Leaving the city afterward, Mary and Joseph realize that their son is not with them and return to search for him. After three days, they find him in the temple engaged in a scholarly debate on the scriptures with a group of rabbis.

Dürer's composition is enclosed within a vast and elaborate architectural setting framed by a large rounded arch. The mathematically accurate representation of three-dimensional space indicates the artist's familiarity with Italian theories of one-point linear perspective.

Rather than occupying the foreground, Christ sits at a lectern under an ornate canopy in the far-right background. Learned doctors are scattered throughout the scene, intently listening to him. Mary and Joseph emerge from behind the large pier at the left, not yet, apparently, having discovered that Jesus is in the temple.

This image was originally part of a series of 20 prints depicting events from the life of Mary, which Dürer made over a period of years. He did not originally conceive the group as a series, but probably did so after finishing a few images. Most, including this example, were completed before he made a second trip to Italy in 1505, though three were not made until 1510. In 1511, *Life of the Virgin* was published in book form, with explanatory texts in Latin on the verso of each image. Foster-Campbell

Christ Among the Doctors
ca. 1504
Woodcut
12 × 8 1/4 inches
Art Acquisition Fund
1992-3-1

Albrecht Dürer
Germany
1471–1528

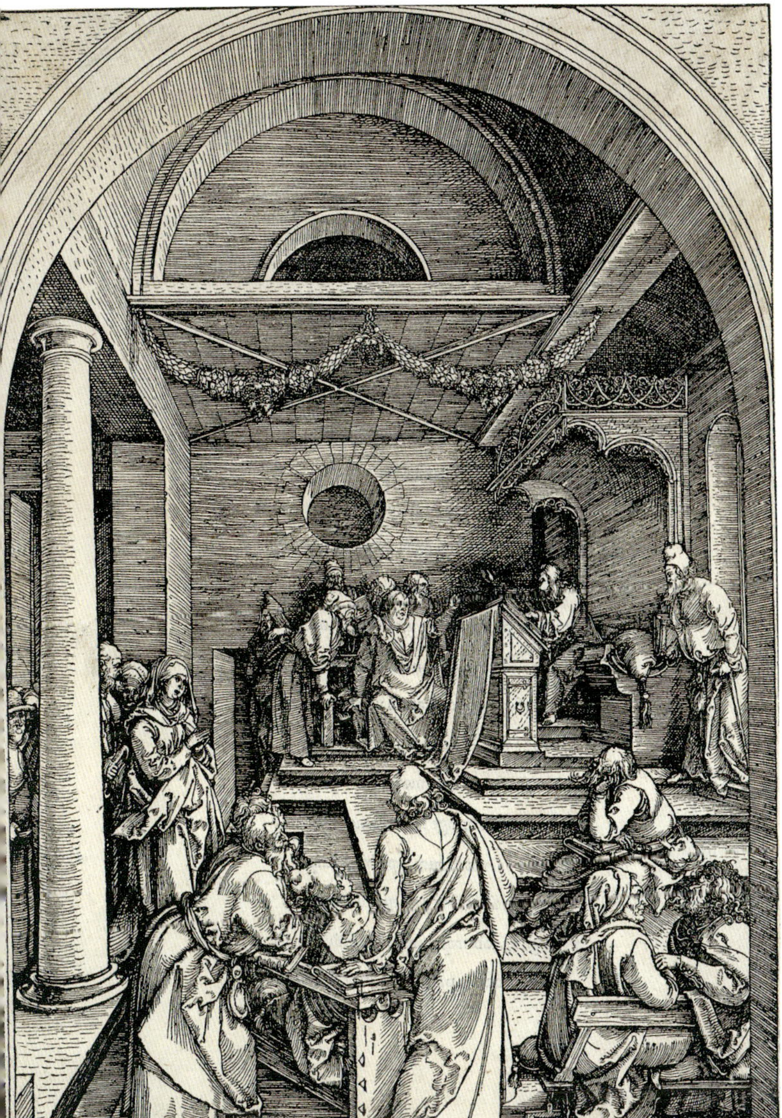

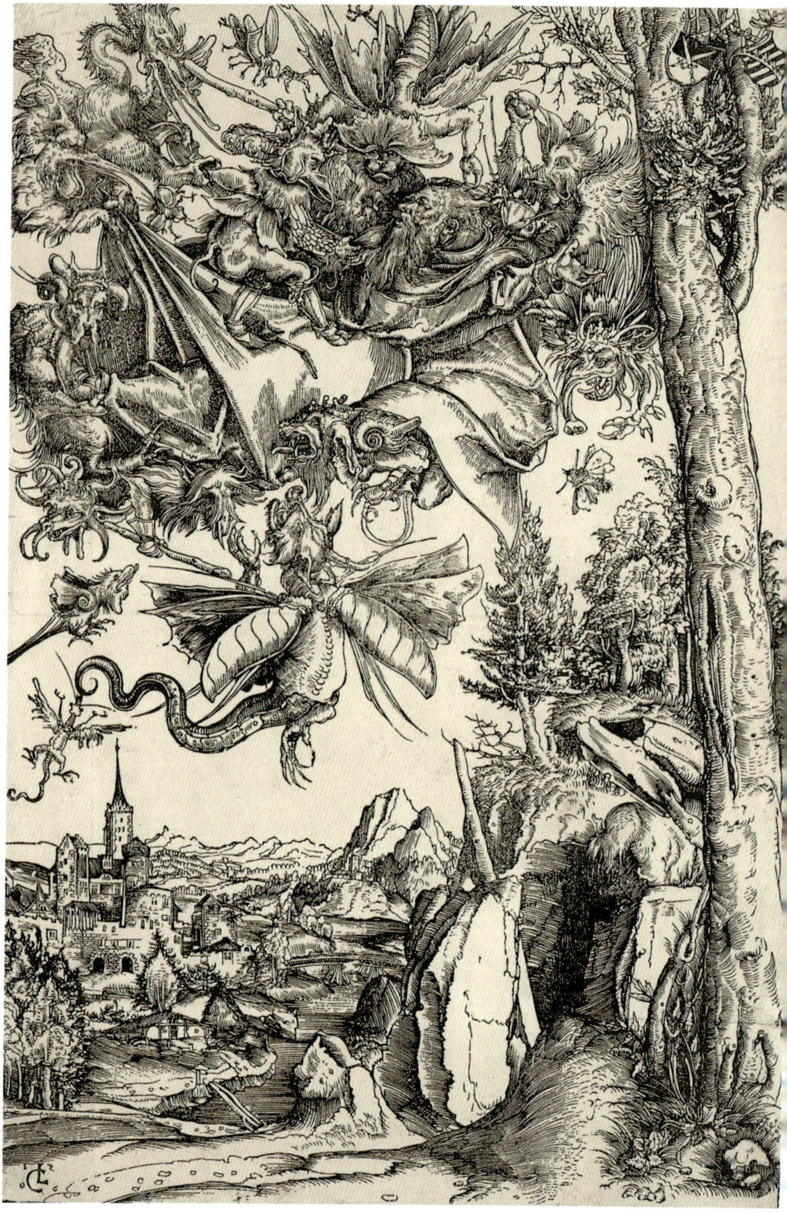

Lucas Cranach the Elder, a celebrated painter of portraits and religious subjects, was also an acclaimed printmaker. He was undoubtedly familiar with the prints of Albrecht Dürer, and may have had contact with the artist himself at Dürer's workshop in Nuremberg during the first decade of the sixteenth century.

Saint Anthony was an ascetic holy man popular in the late fifteenth and sixteenth centuries. According to his *vita* by the fourth-century writer Athanasius, as a young man Anthony gave his wealth to the poor and went into the wilderness to live in solitude. He devoted himself to prayer yet was repeatedly tempted and tormented by the devil. Cranach's print shows the saint besieged by a multitude of demons: he is enveloped by a swarm of giant insects and winged, horned, and fanged creatures that pull at his cloak and beard. The effect is that of a turbulent mass floating in mid-air, in the midst of which the saint remains calm.

The scene is set in a contemporary German landscape, with craggy hillsides and a river at the lower center. It has been proposed that the structure at the lower left is Rosenberg Castle – one of the largest medieval fortifications in Germany – in the artist's native city of Kronach (the source of his surname). While demons swirling around the hovering figure of Saint Anthony had already been interpreted in art (most famously in an engraving by Martin Schongauer of ca. 1480–90), the introduction of landscape was Cranach's innovation.

Foster-Campbell

Lucas Cranach the Elder
German
1472–1553

The Temptation of Saint Anthony
1506
Woodcut
16 × 11 inches
University of Illinois Purchase
1957-21-2

The scene on this plate is taken from the apocryphal biblical Book of Tobit. The story relates that Tobias, son of Tobit, paused during a walk with the angel Raphael to bathe in the river Tigris, where a large fish tried to swallow him. Here Tobias, the central figure, has, at the behest of the angel, pulled the fish to the riverbank. He turns to face his angelic companion, who appears to instruct him. To the left is a third figure, dressed as a shepherd and accompanied by a pair of goats. In the background are views of a city and an Italian hill-town. The scene is depicted in vivid colors, primarily bright blues and greens.

Maiolica is the Italian term for tin-glazed earthenware. The name derives from Hispano-Islamic products made on the island of Majorca and imported into Italy in the fifteenth century. In the mid-sixteenth century, the city of Urbino became famous for *"istoriato" maiolica*, which was adorned with narrative paintings. Manufacture reached a peak during the reign of Duke Guidobaldo II, who strove to improve the quality of production. The duke acquired a large print collection, including works by Raphael (a native of Urbino), Albrecht Dürer, and Georg Pencz, to serve as models for pottery reproductions.

The illustration on this example is from an etching of ca. 1543 by Pencz, the Latin title of which, *Tobias exiterat pisciem*, appears on the back of the plate.
Smith, Sprugel

Plate showing *Tobias and an Angel*
Maiolica (tin-glazed earthenware)
9 1/2 inches in diameter
Gift of Harlan E. Moore
1976-2-1

Italy, Urbino
ca. 1550

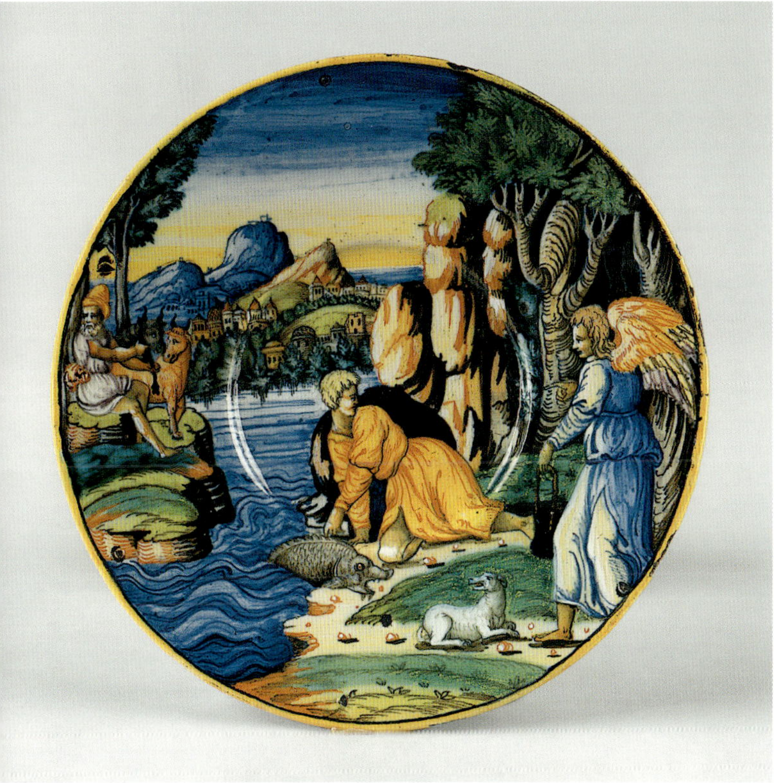

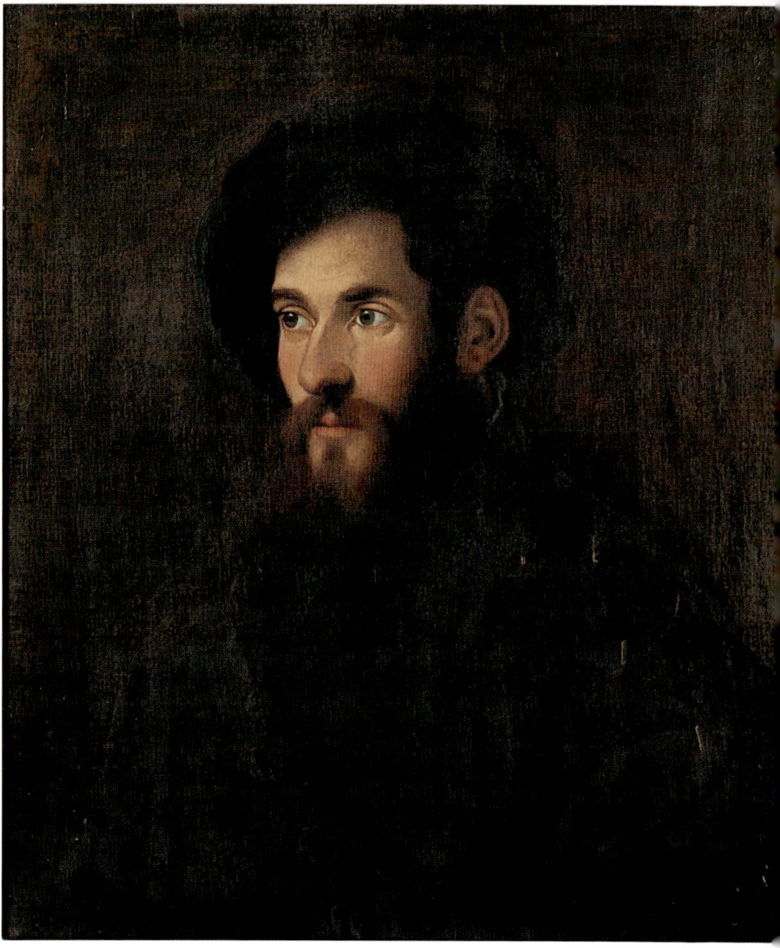

One of the leading sixteenth-century northern Italian artists, Moretto da Brescia worked primarily in his native Brescia. Born into a family of painters, Moretto was taught by his father and Floriano Ferramola, with whom he decorated the choir loft at the Old Cathedral in Brescia (1518). Moretto had a number of students, including Giovanni Battista Moroni (1523–1578), who served as his assistant as well. Although best known for his altarpieces and religious works, Moretto was also an exceptional portraitist. He is credited with painting one of the first full-length portraits in Italy (*Portrait of a Man* [1526], currently at the National Gallery, London), ten years before Titian, who influenced his modeling and brushstroke. Moretto's exposure to northern Italian (including Venetian), Roman, and Flemish art further affected his style.

This half-length portrait of a young man in three-quarter pose is characterized by an evocative use of chiaroscuro – the emphatic contrast of light and dark. The young aristocrat wears a grayish-green velvet cloak trimmed with satin ribbon and ornaments. Focusing on the face and gaze and treating the beard with great detail, Moretto strikes a balance between idealizing and individualizing the sitter. The figure has traditionally been identified as Marco Foscari, but the attribution is unsupported by inscriptions or archival information. Blondin

Moretto da Brescia
(Alessandro Bonvicino)
Italy
ca. 1498–1554

Title unknown
(*Portrait of Marco Foscari da Venezia*)
16th century
Oil on canvas
22 1/4 × 19 3/4 inches
Gift of Mr. and Mrs. Merle J. Trees
1945-1-2

Jacques Callot produced two etching series on "the miseries and misfortunes of war." The so-called "large" version, published in Paris by his friend Israel Henriet in 1633, was sold as a booklet of 18 small sheets – a title page and 17 oblong plates. The earlier set of even smaller plates, known as *The Small Miseries*, was left unfinished.

One of the most innovative printmakers of his time, Callot apprenticed to a local goldsmith in his native Nancy in 1607, and traveled at a young age to Italy. In Rome he learned printmaking from the French engraver Philippe Thomassin. By 1612 he was in Florence working with Antonio Tempesta, whose celebrated theatrical designs influenced his style. In 1621 Callot returned to Nancy, where he was active until his death in 1635.

Callot executed *The Miseries of War* during the Thirty Years' War, a conflict that involved most of Europe. The narrative recounted in the plates, each of which contains six lines of verse attributed to the French translator Abbé de Marolles, contrasts military glory with the reality of the suffering caused by war. Callot depicted the brutality of soldiers' actions as well as the punishments and abuses they endured, and in the last plate showed the distribution of rewards for outstanding performance in battle.

Callot brought to the art of etching two important technical innovations. He used a hard etching ground material, resulting in greater control and depth of line, and he developed a special tool, the *échoppe*, an oval-pointed cylinder that allowed him to vary the width of the mark. Krannert Art Museum holds 15 plates from the series. Pistorius-Stamper

The Hanging and *Distribution of Rewards*
From *Les grands misères et malheurs de la guerre*
(*The Large Miseries and Misfortunes of War*)
1633
Etchings on warm white paper
Plate mark: each 3 1/2 × 7 1/2 inches
Gift of Gordon Ray
1960-6-36.9, 1960-6-36.15

Jacques Callot
France
1592–1635

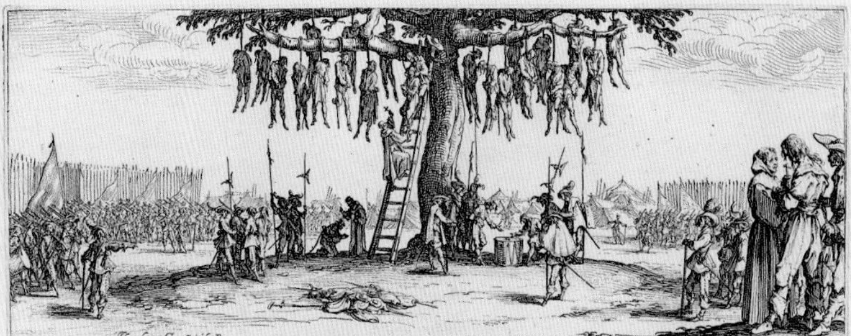

A la fin ces Voleurs infames et perdus,
Comme fruits malheureux a cet arbre pendus

Monstrent bien que le crime (horrible et noire engeance)
Est luy mesme instrument de honte et de vengeance,

Et que cest le Destin des hommes vicieux
Desprouuer tost ou tard la iustice des Cieux. 17

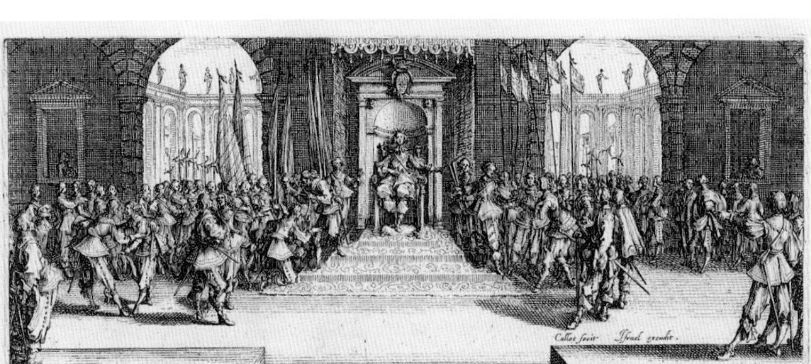

Cet exemple d'vn Chef plein de reconnoissance,
Qui punit les méchans et les bons recompance,

Doit picquer les soldats d'vn aiguillon d'honneur,
Puis que de la vertu, depend tout leur bon-heur,

Et qu'ordinairement ils reçoiuent du Vice,
La honte, le mespris, et le dernier supplice. 18

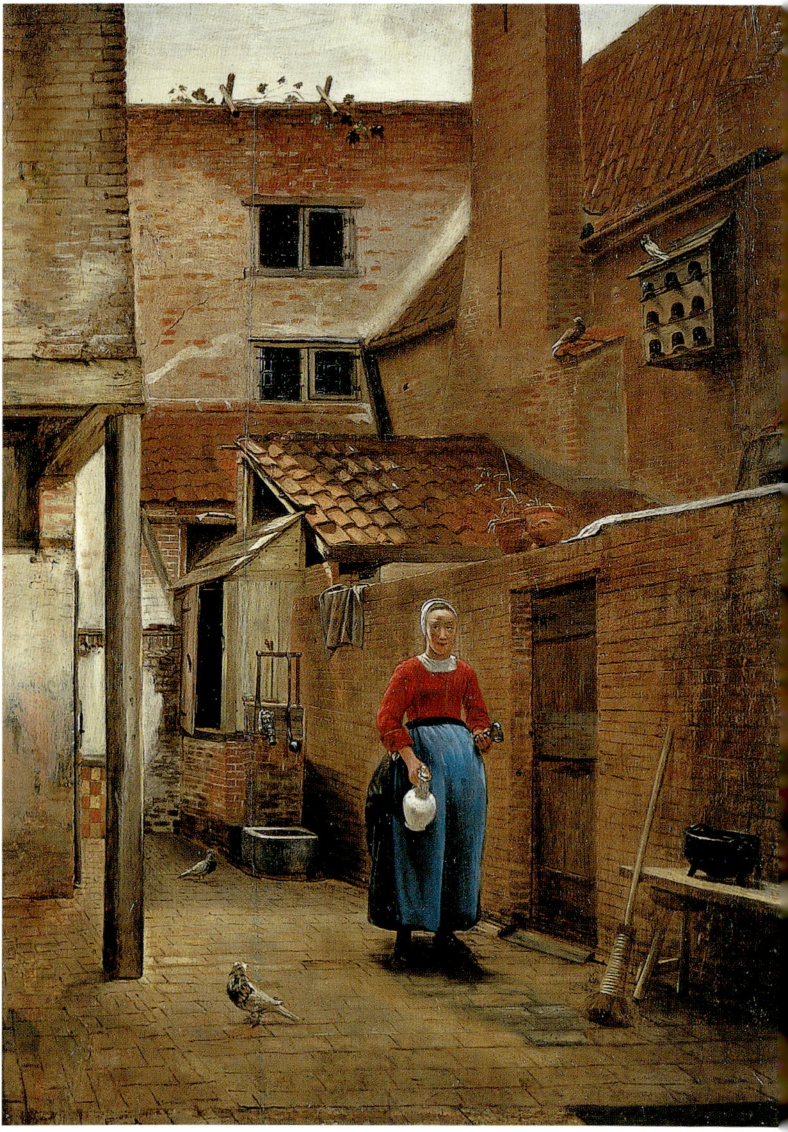

This small painting by Hendrick van der Burch was thought for many years to be the work of Pieter de Hooch. De Hooch had a close relationship with van der Burch, who may have been a relative of his wife, Jannetge, and with whom he co-signed several legal documents in Haarlem. Van der Burch's painting style was greatly indebted to de Hooch, as well as to Johannes Vermeer.

Courtyard Scene was identified as the work of van der Burch in 1921, when the art historian Hofstede de Groot discovered the monogram "HB" on the column on the left side of the image. Sometime between 1921 and 1929, the monogram was removed or painted over, likely by a dealer or restorer. The painting was erroneously attributed to de Hooch while in a Minneapolis private collection in the 1920s. The error persisted when the Art Institute of Chicago purchased it in 1940 but sold it eight years later as a van der Burch. In 1951 it was acquired by the Trees family for Krannert Art Museum.

The following description was written by Frederick A. Sweet in *Bulletin of the Art Institute of Chicago* 35 (Jan. 1941), 3:

There is a diffusion of light, a delicacy of texture, and a modulation of color which is at variance with de Hooch's more precise manner of painting. The figure of the maid is a trifle less static and a little more human. She hesitates a moment with her freshly-drawn jug of water before entering the door rather than posing stiffly for a picture. Her clear red bodice and blue apron together with the sparkling white of her guimpe and cap and of the Delft jug which she carries hold the center of attention.

Smith

Hendrick van der Burch
Netherlands
ca. 1627–1666

Courtyard Scene (*Maid in a Courtyard*)
ca. 1650–70
Oil on oak panel
19 × 14 inches
Gift of Mr. and Mrs. Merle J. Trees
1951-1-1

During Frans Hals's long career, which spanned virtually the entire golden age of Dutch art, he invigorated painting with a new naturalism, in both the portraits that account for the majority of his surviving work and a smaller output of genre paintings. Known as the "portraitist of Haarlem," he acquired a fame that peaked in the 1630s with nine large group portraits – six of military groups and three of regents. Despite his renown, he was never financially successful and died deeply in debt.

This portrayal of the mayor of Haarlem shows Hals's distinctive brushwork – swift strokes suggest a cuff, a hand, and a glove, broadly brushed areas of light and dark create strong shapes, and deep shadow contrasts with fine tonal gradation to model the subject's face. Hals refrained from making preliminary sketches or drawings in order to convey the vitality of his sitters with fresh and direct painting.

Hals was virtually forgotten for almost two centuries after his death, until his rediscovery by the French impressionists, who admired the way he caught fleeting moments animated by light. This portrait began traveling soon after Krannert Art Museum opened in 1961. The committee for the centennial celebration of the Frans Hals Museum in Haarlem selected it as one of 80 paintings from museum collections throughout the world for display in 1962. Peterson, Smith

Cornelis Guldewagen, Mayor of Haarlem
ca. 1660
Oil on oak panel
16 × 12 inches
Gift of Mr. and Mrs. Merle J. Trees
1953-1-1

Frans Hals
Netherlands
ca. 1581–1666

Given that Bartolomé Esteban Murillo was esteemed in seventeenth-century Europe, it is puzzling that his international reputation faded with relative rapidity. At the court in Madrid, he was overshadowed by Diego Velázquez, though in his own city of Seville he was much admired for paintings such as *Christ after the Flagellation*. This work dates to the beginning of an important late period in the artist's career, which came to a close when he fell from a scaffold in his mid-sixties. During this stage, Murillo used fewer and fewer colors, and the ones he chose were soft and subtle. Here, he depicts the tortured body of Christ with delicate touches of faint color and gradations of tone and light; the marks of the whips are minimized and the figure, though constrained by pain, collects his garments with dignity. The understated manner in which Murillo treats this potentially dramatic scene is sometimes taken by critics as sentimentality. Beckett

(following pages)
Christ after the Flagellation
ca. 1670
Oil on canvas
50 1/4 × 57 1/2 inches
Gift of Ellnora D. Krannert
1960-1-1

Bartolomé Esteban Murillo
Spain
1616–1682

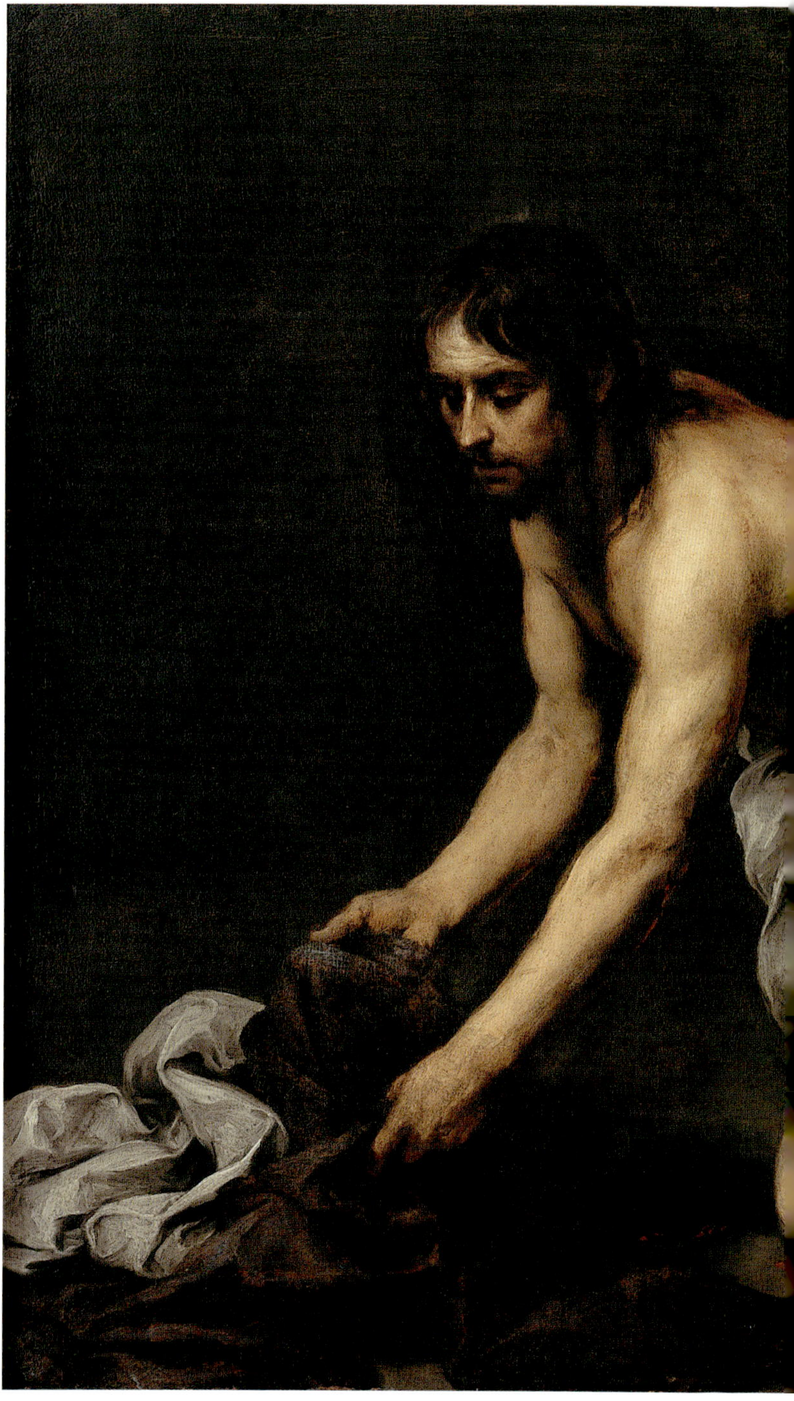

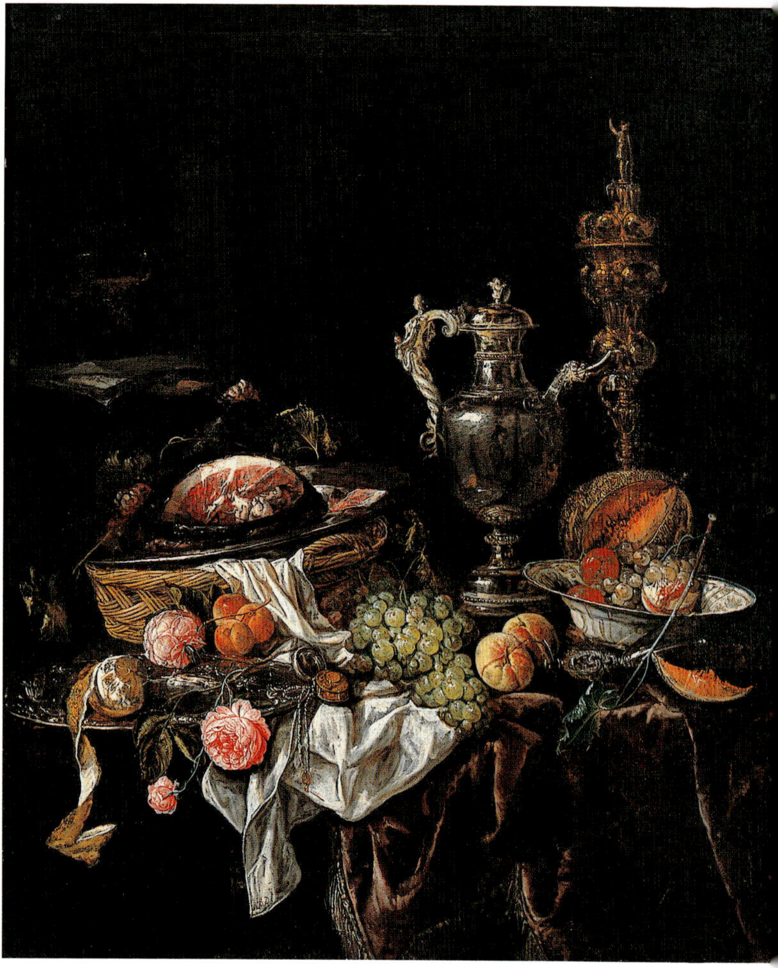

Sumptuous displays of food, flowers, and tableware proliferated in paintings from the second half of the seventeenth century in the Netherlands. The primary audience for still lifes – the merchants and bankers of the Dutch Republic – had achieved remarkable wealth by the middle of the century, due largely to the vigor and scope of Dutch trade. Such pictures would have hung in middle-class households where monied burghers imitated aristocratic manners by providing excessive banquets for important guests. But even as Abraham van Beyeren celebrates material pleasures, he includes in the foreground an opened watch, a symbol of *vanitas* in Dutch painting. Here, it invites viewers to ponder the vanity of worldly pursuits and concentrate on the need to prepare their souls for the afterlife. Thus Calvinist values of austerity and sobriety collide with materialism in an image that mixes interdiction and delight.

Van Beyeren signed this painting twice: with the initials "AB" on the gold watch, and "AVBf" ("f" is an abbreviation traditionally used by painters for the Latin *fecit* or "made this") on the corner of the white napkin spilling over the edge of the table. A final "signature" is the artist's reflection on the silver ewer, where he stands in profile facing an easel. With this device, common among still-life painters, van Beyeren proclaims the imitative power of his artistry. Rosenthal

Abraham van Beyeren
Netherlands
1620–1690

Still Life
ca. 1670
Oil on canvas
46 3/4 × 39 3/4 inches
Ellnora D. Krannert Fund
1972-2-2

In this scene, Jacob van Ruisdael, one of the best known of the seventeenth-century Dutch landscape painters, orchestrates earth, water, and sky into a unity of atmosphere and light. Temporal changes are suggested by birds in flight and clouds pushed along by the wind. Tiny walking figures blend with the landscape, and a grouping of three trees stabilizes the composition. There is no apparent narrative in this work, but the presence of a fallen log and the pairing of a dead and a living tree suggest life, death, passing time, and the endurance of land and sky. The artist signed his name on the ground at the lower right.

Little is known about van Ruisdael's life. The style and subjects of his late period – woods, stream, and waterfalls – reflect a journey he made to the border provinces of Holland and Germany in the early 1650s, documented by surviving sketches.
Arntzen, Smith

Jacob van Ruisdael
Netherlands
1628/29–1682

Ford in the Woods
ca. 1670
Oil on canvas
20 3/4 × 23 3/4 inches
Gift of Mr. and Mrs. Merle J. Trees
1953-1-2

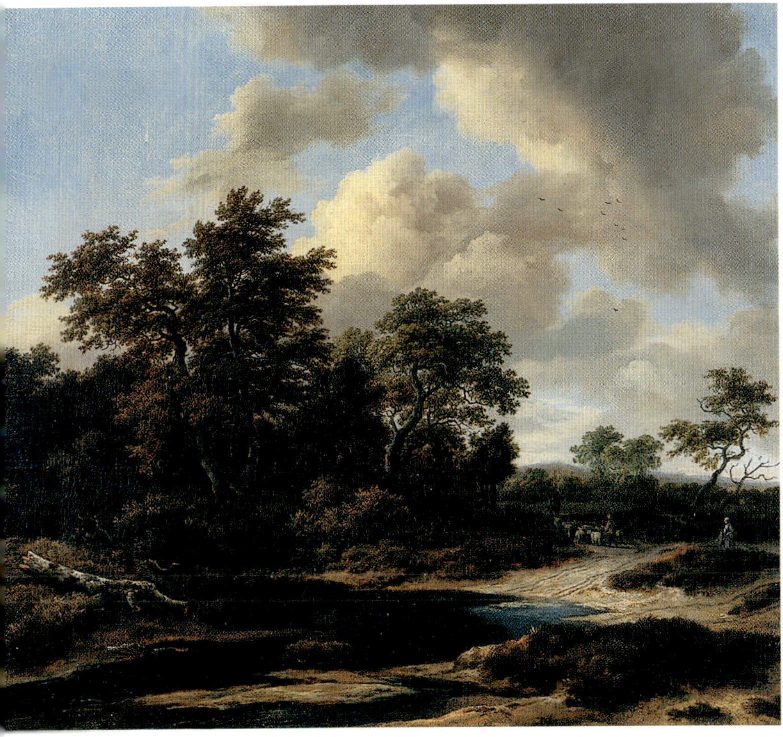

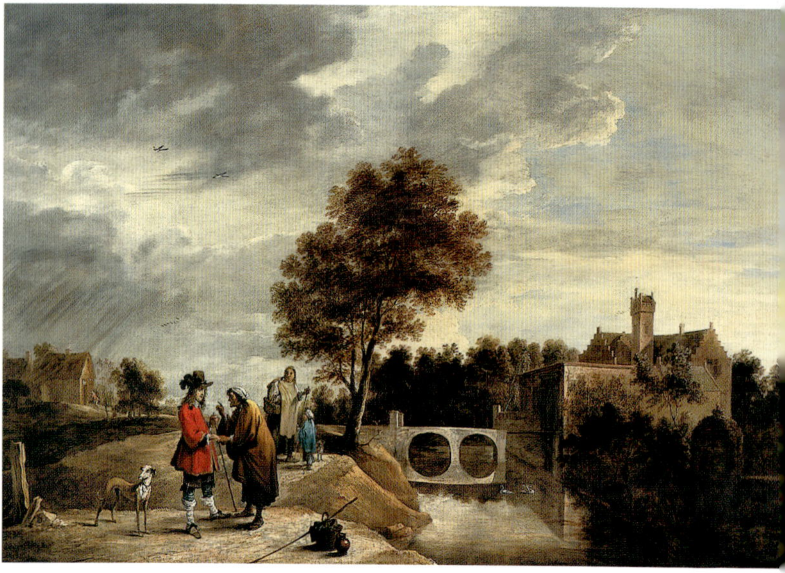

n the foreground of this painting, an old gypsy fortuneteller – a common figure n the narrative paintings of David Teniers the Younger – holds the hand of a well-dressed young man accompanied by a dog. To the right, across a bridge over a moat, is Steen Castle, Peter Paul Rubens's home on the outskirts of Antwerp. To the left is a more rustic building. The sky is clear and sunny over the castle, while a storm approaches from the left. A few birds flying in formation suggest the onset of autumn. A tree in the middle ground anchors the composition.

Teniers was a prolific artist: he and his workshop are credited with over two thousand paintings. The son of a well-known painter, David Teniers I, David the Younger married into another well-known artistic family: his wife Anne, the daughter of Jan Breugel, was a student of Rubens, who was also her guardian. In 1632, Teniers was promoted to the rank of master painter by the Painters' Guild of Saint Lukein Antwerp. At that time, he came under the influence of Adriaen Brouwer, who had studied with both Frans Hals and Rubens. The presence of peasant figures and the color scheme of this painting are reminiscent of Brouwer's work. Scholar Peter Sutton has remarked that the features of the young man resemble those in Teniers's known self-portraits, suggesting a self-insertion that the artist often practiced in genre paintings. Smith, Sprugel

David Teniers the Younger
Flanders
1610–1690

Steen Castle
17th century
Oil on canvas
47 1/4 × 64 1/4 inches
Gift of Mr. and Mrs. Merle J. Trees
1948-1-2

The Lambeth fecundity dish displays the many sources of English Delft pottery. The palette, some of the decorative patterns, and the medallions are derived from Ming porcelains, while other details are influenced by Italian *maiolica*, or tin-glazed earthenware. The yellow overglaze and the rust dots on the rim border are borrowed from earlier Dutch Delft pottery, and the shape and sculptural design are taken from a dish by the French artist/artisan Bernard Palissy. The "earth mother" subject reflects the Renaissance and baroque revival of classical motifs.

During the seventeenth and eighteenth centuries, Chinese porcelain vases were highly prized in Europe, and artisans frequently emulated their forms and styles. The first technique to inspire imitation was tin-glazing, which had been perfected in the Middle East and brought to Europe by Muslims early in the eighth century. In the French faience "Bleu de Nevers" dish (p. 112), the characteristic color scheme of the Ming dynasty is inverted, with white designs appearing against a deep blue background. The central motif is an amphora-shaped vase of tulips surrounded by flowers, vines, swooping and flying insects, and birds.

The secret of Chinese porcelain was discovered in the early eighteenth century by the young chemist Johann Friedrich Böttger, who identified its components as kaolin, quartz, and feldspar added to clay. As a result of Böttger's research, the Royal Saxon Porcelain Manufacture was established in Meissen, Germany, in 1710. The "swan" service (p. 113) is an achievement of the Meissen factory. Designed by Johann Joachim Kändler, it comprised over two thousand porcelain pieces and took four years to complete. Its motifs all relate to water: flowing water, swans, herons, and water plants are worked in relief, with painted decoration kept to a minimum. The only color on the plate appears in the coat of arms and on small scattered *kakiemon* ("Japanese-style") flowers on the border. Smith

Lambeth Delft fecundity dish
ca. 1650
Maiolica (tin-glazed earthenware)
15 × 18 inches
Gift of Harlan E. Moore
England 1975-13-1

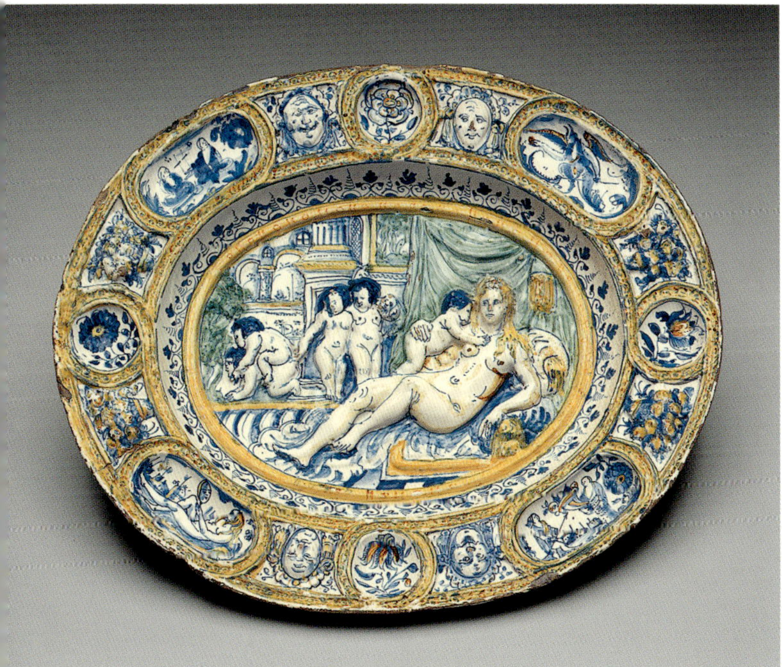

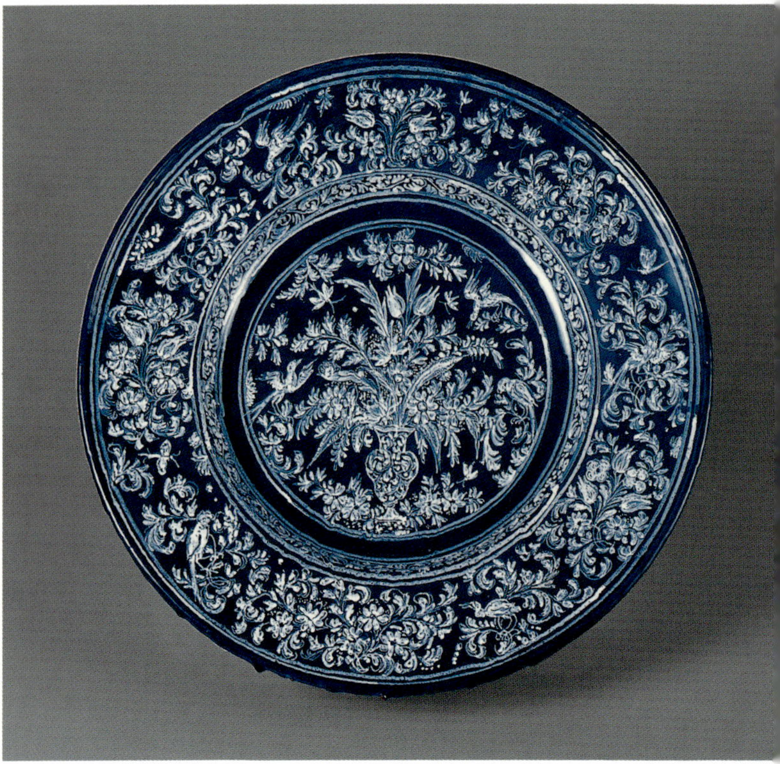

France, Nevers

"Bleu de Nevers" dish
mid-17th century
Persian blue-and-white faience
28 inches in diameter
Harlan E. Moore Charitable Trust
1996-10-1

THE HISTORY OF KRANNERT ART MUSEUM BEGINS WITH A SMALL COLLECTION

OF PLASTER CASTS
AND LOFTY GOALS
FOR THE FUTURE OF
THE VISUAL ARTS AT
THE UNIVERSITY
OF ILLINOIS AT
URBANA-CHAMPAIGN.

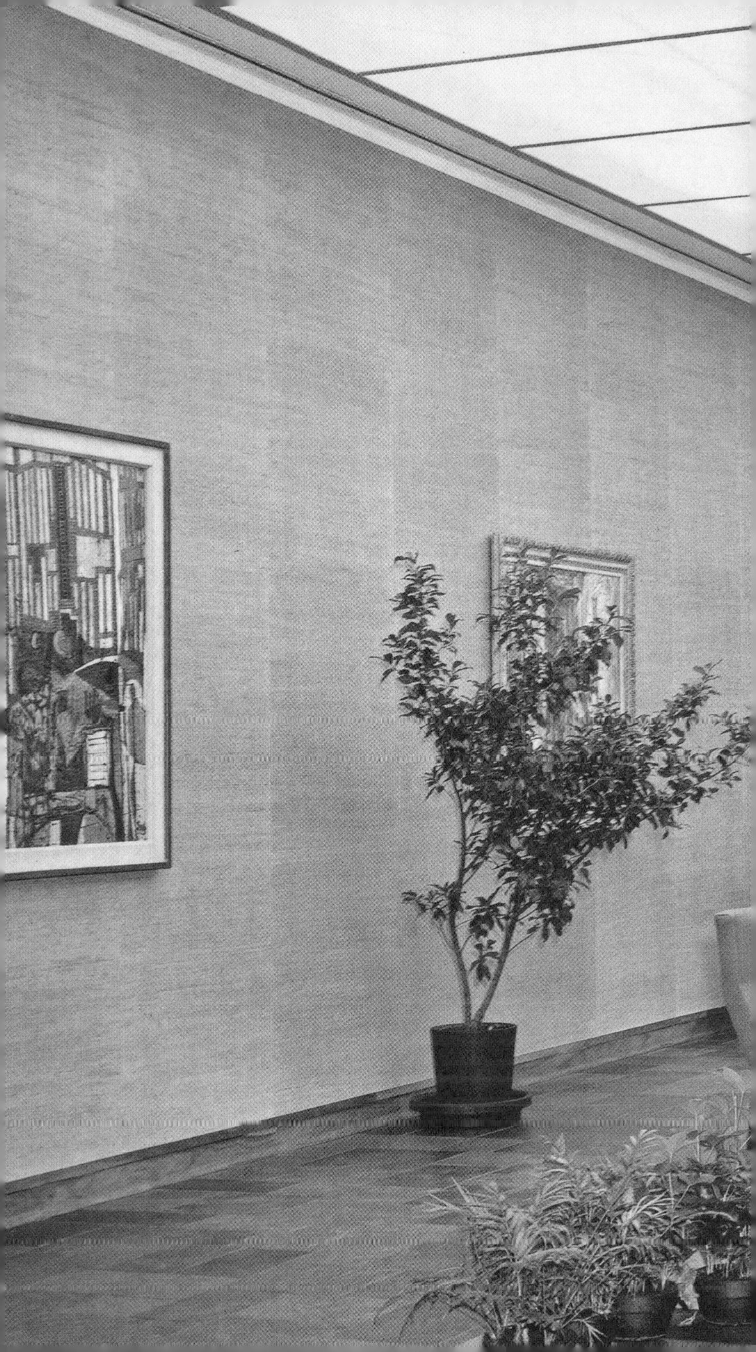

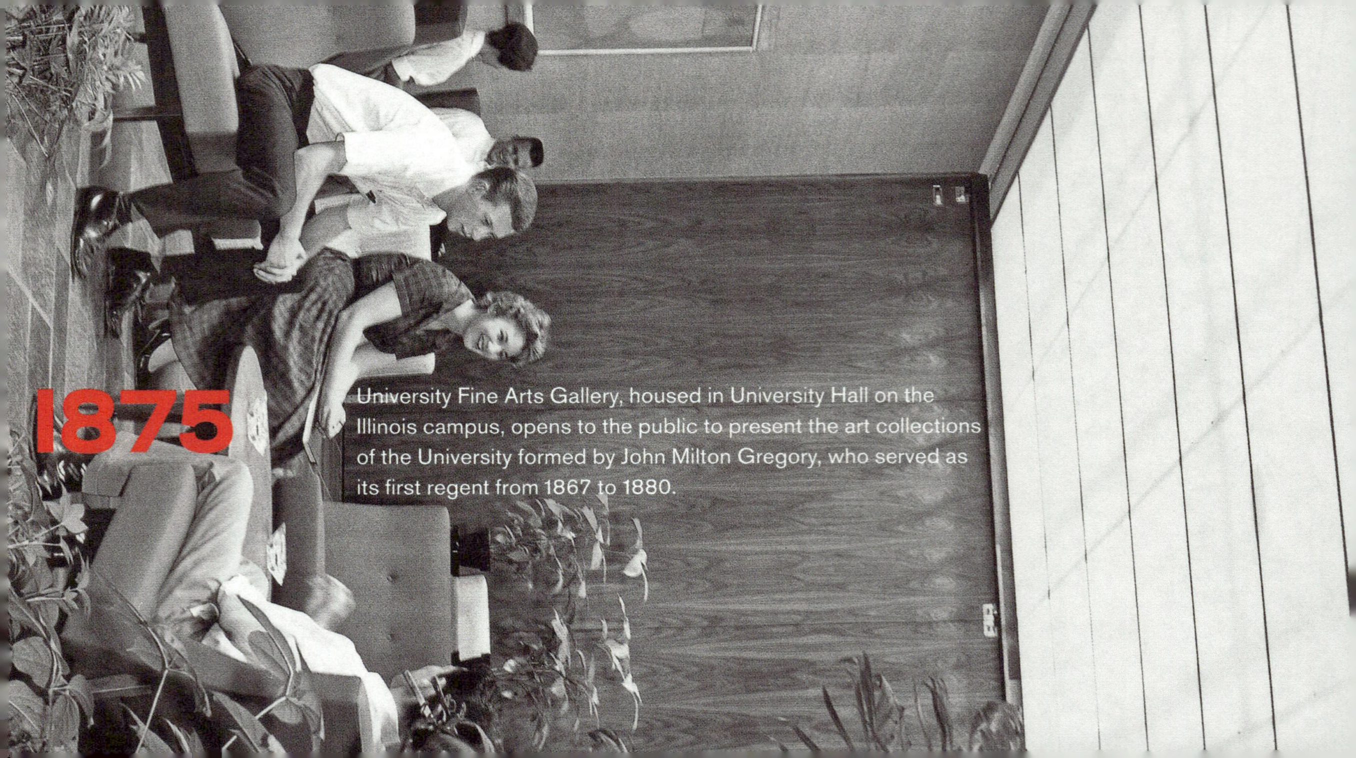

1875

University Fine Arts Gallery, housed in University Hall on the Illinois campus, opens to the public to present the art collections of the University formed by John Milton Gregory, who served as its first regent from 1867 to 1880.

1931

$12,000 to purchase contemporary paintings and sculptures for display in the new Architecture Building, which also serves as a venue for traveling exhibitions and elevation of the academic status of the arts at the University leads to the founding of the College of Fine and Applied Arts this year, and attracts major gifts and purchases for the collection.

1934–43

The University adds 35 paintings and 450 drawings from the New Deal Works Progress Administration (WPA) Federal Art Project.

1936

The University buys the contents of the Chicago studio of sculptor Lorado Taft (1860–1936).

1938

Alumni Merle Jay and Emily Nichols Trees (Class of 1907 and 1905, respectively) begin donating paintings from their collection, ultimately numbering 41 objects ranging in date from the fifteenth through the early twentieth centuries – religious scenes, landscapes, still lifes, portraits, and depictions of urban life by prominent European and North American artists, notably Frans Hals, John Singleton Copley, and Camille Pissarro.

1944

A group of 48 examples of so-called Far-Eastern art, including temple hangings, textiles, ornamental weapons, and sculptures, are donated by Spencer and Lena Ewing to form the basis of the Asian art holdings at the gallery.

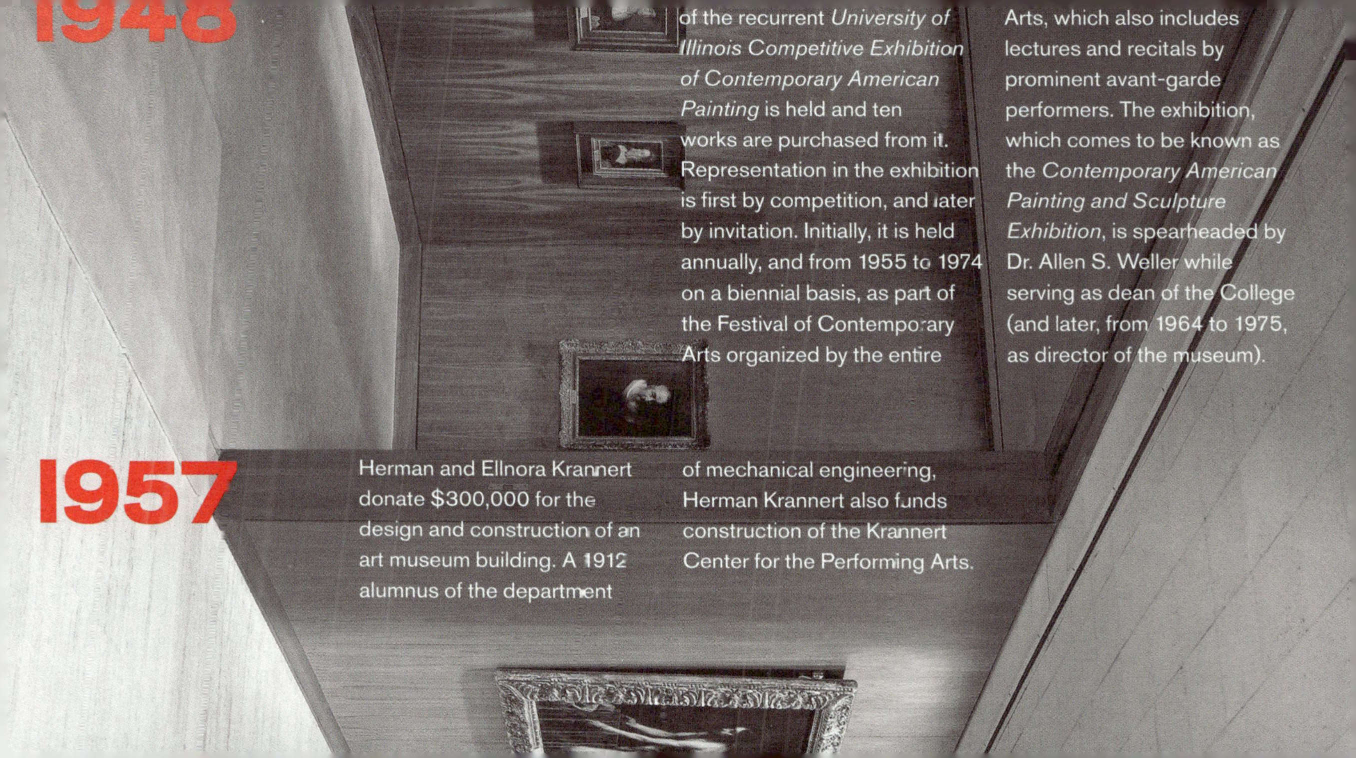

1948

of the recurrent *University of Illinois Competitive Exhibition of Contemporary American Painting* is held and ten works are purchased from it. Representation in the exhibition is first by competition, and later by invitation. Initially, it is held annually, and from 1955 to 1974 on a biennial basis, as part of the Festival of Contemporary Arts organized by the entire Arts, which also includes lectures and recitals by prominent avant-garde performers. The exhibition, which comes to be known as the *Contemporary American Painting and Sculpture Exhibition*, is spearheaded by Dr. Allen S. Weller while serving as dean of the College (and later, from 1964 to 1975, as director of the museum).

1957

Herman and Ellnora Krannert donate $300,000 for the design and construction of an art museum building. A 1912 alumnus of the department of mechanical engineering, Herman Krannert also funds construction of the Krannert Center for the Performing Arts.

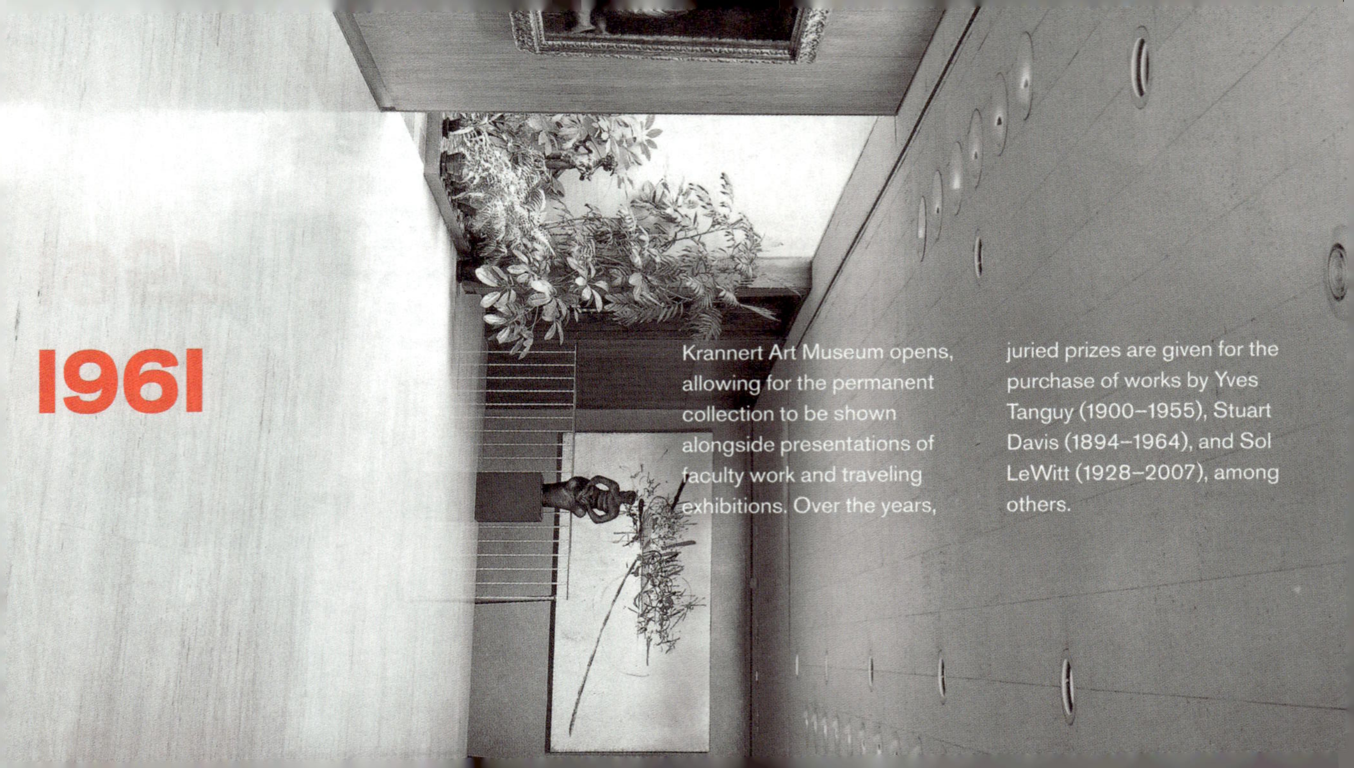

1961

Krannert Art Museum opens, allowing for the permanent collection to be shown alongside presentations of faculty work and traveling exhibitions. Over the years, juried prizes are given for the purchase of works by Yves Tanguy (1900–1955), Stuart Davis (1894–1964), and Sol LeWitt (1928–2007), among others.

1964

fundraising activities and programs.

1966

The museum's Asian art collection is enhanced through acquisition funds established by the Class of 1908, who supported construction of a dedicated gallery for its display in 1958.

1967–68

The expanding collections and exhibitions program necessitate two major architectural campaigns at Krannert Art Museum. In 1967 the Kranners fund an expansion that adds 17,800 square feet on the east side of the original building. Fred Olsen donates over 600 objects of Pre-Columbian and ancient Andean art that were shown at the museum in 1965.

1970

Local businessman Harlan E. Moore and his wife Theresa E. Moore donate a collection of eighteenth- and nineteenth-century English and American ceramics and glass to the museum.

1980s

The museum's African art collection is expanded by gifts from Mr. and Mrs. Richard Faletti and Mr. and Mrs. Irwin Smiley. The estate of William S. Kinkead, a mechanical-engineering student at Illinois from 1919 to 1920, provides monies for erection of the William S. and Anita H. Kinkead Pavilion. Under construction from 1986 to 1988, the Kinkead Pavilion nearly doubles the size of the museum, furnishing 20,000 additional square feet for exhibiting the collections and providing for administrative and curatorial activities.

1993

The museum creates the first Web site for an art museum in the United States, and pursues projects with technology groups on campus that continue to the present, some of which are realized at the museum's CANVAS: Electronic Gallery, launched in 2005.

2001

Krannert Art Museum begins a decade of acquiring aggressively from the exhibitions it organizes. Artists whose work thereby enrich the collection include Conrad Bakker, Amy Barkow, Louise Bourgeois, Charles and Ray Eames, Jackie Ferrara, Laurie Hogin, Huang Yan, Annette Lemieux, Jacques Lipchitz, Jennifer Maestre, John McCracken, Luke Batten and Jonathan Sadler (New Catalogue), Kenneth Noland, Richard Pettibone, Julia Scher, Hedda Sterne, David Svensson, Tony Tasset, and Zhao Bandi.

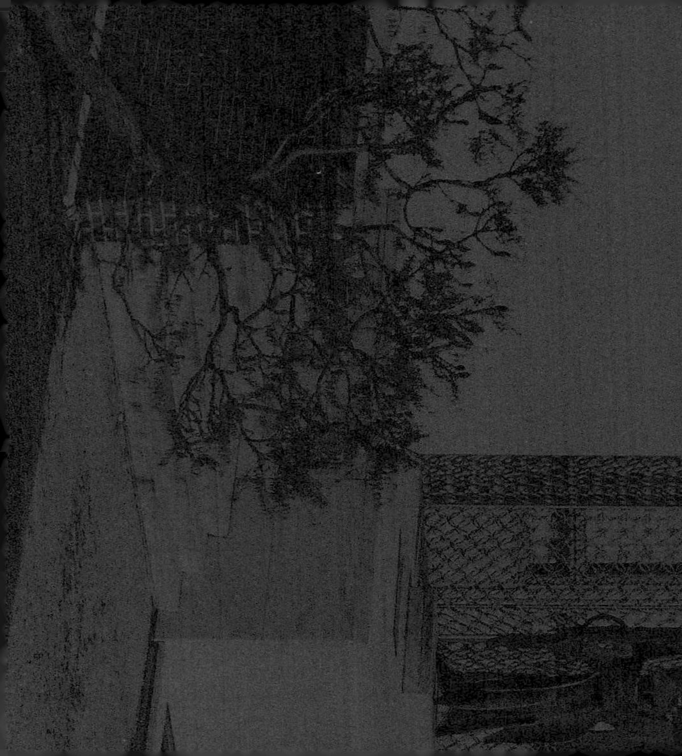

By Alexander Hovan, from sources including Muriel Scheinman, *A Guide to Art at the University of Illinois* (Urbana and Chicago: University of Illinois Press, 1995); Chris Quinn, "The History of the Krannert Art Museum and Kinkead Pavilion," in *Humanities Collections* 1, no. 2 (1999): 61–115; and an unpublished timeline by Robert B. Smith, head of the docent research committee.

Cover: View of Krannert Art Museum facade with *Initiation* by Mirko and reflecting pool, 1961

Inside pages: View of Light Court Gallery at Krannert Art Museum, 1961

View of entrance hallway at Krannert Art Museum showing the Trees Gallery, 1961

All photos courtesy of the University of Illinois

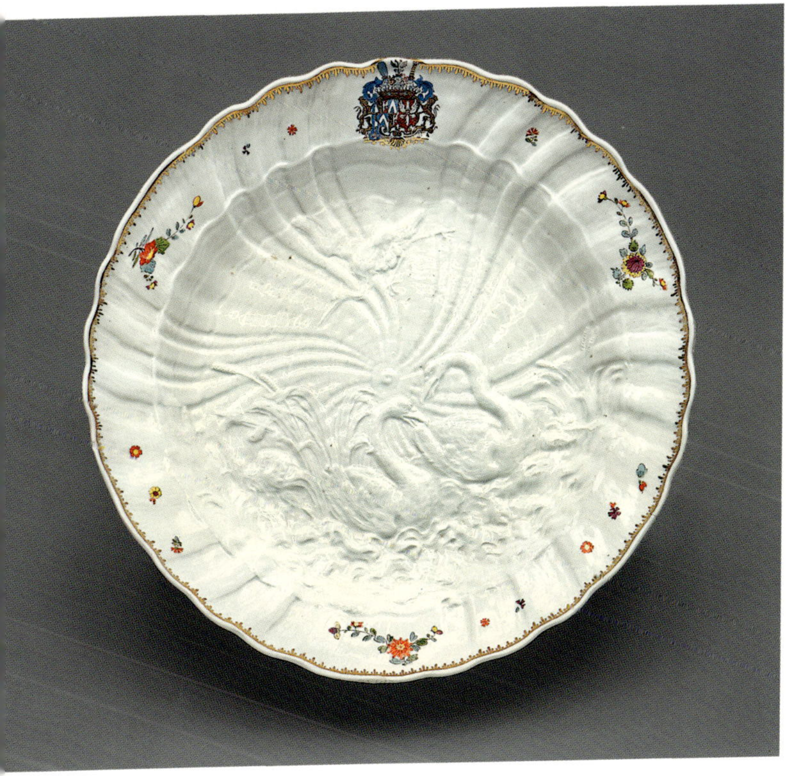

ohann Joachim Kändler
Germany
706–1775

Dish from "swan" service
1734–41
Hard-paste porcelain
13 inches in diameter
Gift of Harlan E. Moore
1976-3-1

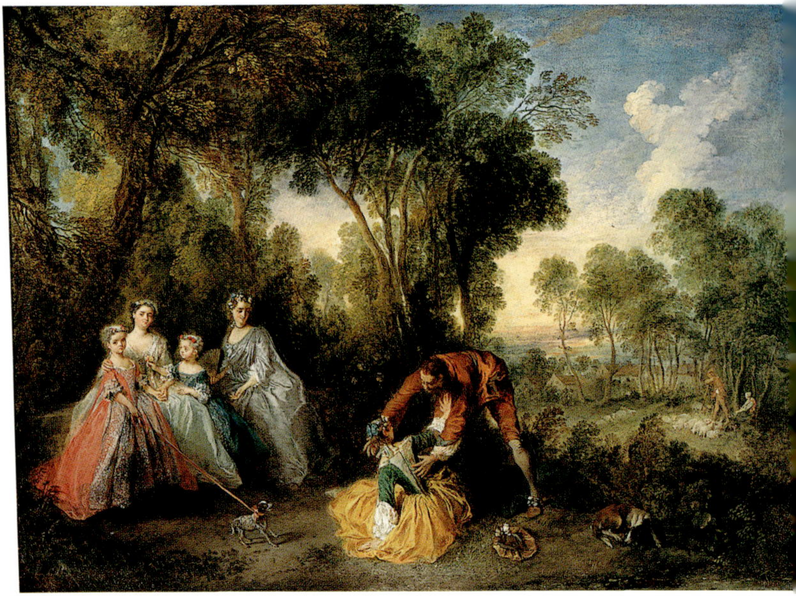

This charming small canvas exemplifies the *fête galante*, in which the upper classes engage in outdoor entertainment. A man in red awkwardly bends to embrace a young woman dressed in green and yellow, while a dog naps to their right. To the left, a girl in blue offers flowers to an older companion, who holds close a second girl pulled forward by her barking dog. Behind them, a young woman clutching a fan leans towards the girls, but her gaze lingers on the couple. In the distance, a shepherd and shepherdess tend a flock of sheep.

This lyrical, painted pastorale represents the changing roles of women. The amorous couple occupying the central position reflect the onset of puberty and sexual activity; the younger girls innocently collect flowers under their guardians' protection.

Nicolas Lancret completed this scene in 1737; it may have been exhibited in the Paris Salon of that year. Its cryptic subject matter, delicately atmospheric color, and small scale show the influence of Jean-Antoine Watteau and rococo art. Associated with, but not limited to, interior decoration, this short-lived style was in part a reaction to the monumental baroque style of the court of Louis XIV.

Arntzen, Smith

The Bourbon Conti Family
(also known as *Les plaisirs champêtres*)
1737
Oil on canvas
10 1/2 × 26 1/4 inches
Gift of Ellnora D. Krannert
1967-3-5

Nicolas Lancret
France
1690–1743

This small painting resembles six other oil sketches by Giambattista Tiepolo, the content and purpose of which are unclear. An example in the Kunsthaus Zürich, also depicting saints Maximus and Oswald, is likely the *modello*, or oil sketch, for a canvas in the main chapel of Santi Massimo e Osvaldo in Padua. The others include figures in similar poses under a vault supported by semicircular arches on piers. As in the museum's painting, the figures' attributes are insufficient to identify them with certainty, and they may be other saints. All the paintings in this group may be related to large-scale works now lost or destroyed.

Tiepolo and his workshop produced numerous painted sketches (*bozzetti*) that served a variety of purposes. *Modelli* were used to propose ideas to patrons, while *ricordi* documented completed projects. Krannert Art Museum's canvas is probably a replica of a painting at the Accademia Carrara in Bergamo, and may have been produced to meet the growing market for preliminary sketches; the painting is more detailed, particularly in the faces and garments, than *modelli* customarily were at the time. Several additions to the painting appear to have been made after it left Tiepolo's studio, perhaps to provide color incident. These include the keystone, the gold borders of the courtier's cape, the embroidery on the bishop's cope, and the red cord holding the chandelier, which is mistakenly shown rising to the top of the arch instead of the vault. Thin brown contour lines have been added around many motifs to provide greater definition. Some aspects – for example, the uncertain handling of the courtier's face – suggest that much of the original painting is the work of Tiepolo's assistants. Yet the overall composition, the dramatic poses, and the faces of the saints either come directly from or closely follow the hand of the master. O'Brien

Giovanni Battista
(Giambattista) Tiepolo
Italy
1696–1770

Saint Maximus and Saint Oswald
ca. 1740–45
Oil on canvas
23 × 14 1/2 inches
Gift of Ellnora D. Krannert
1965-16-3

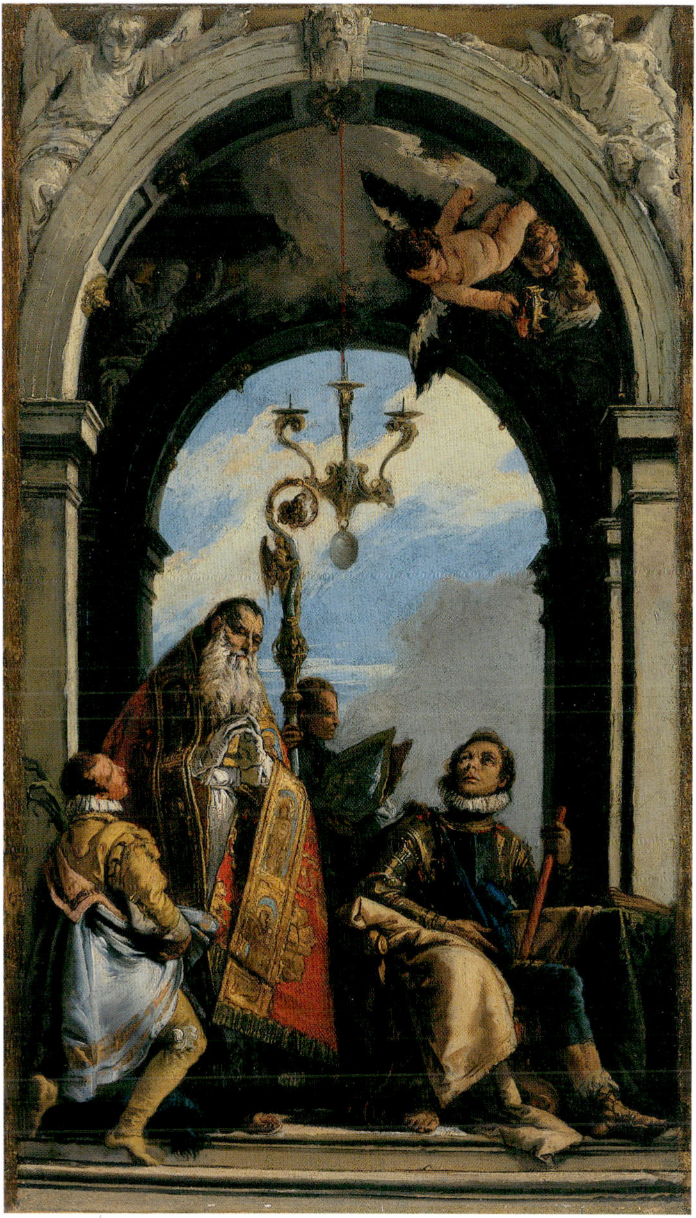

BEER STREET.

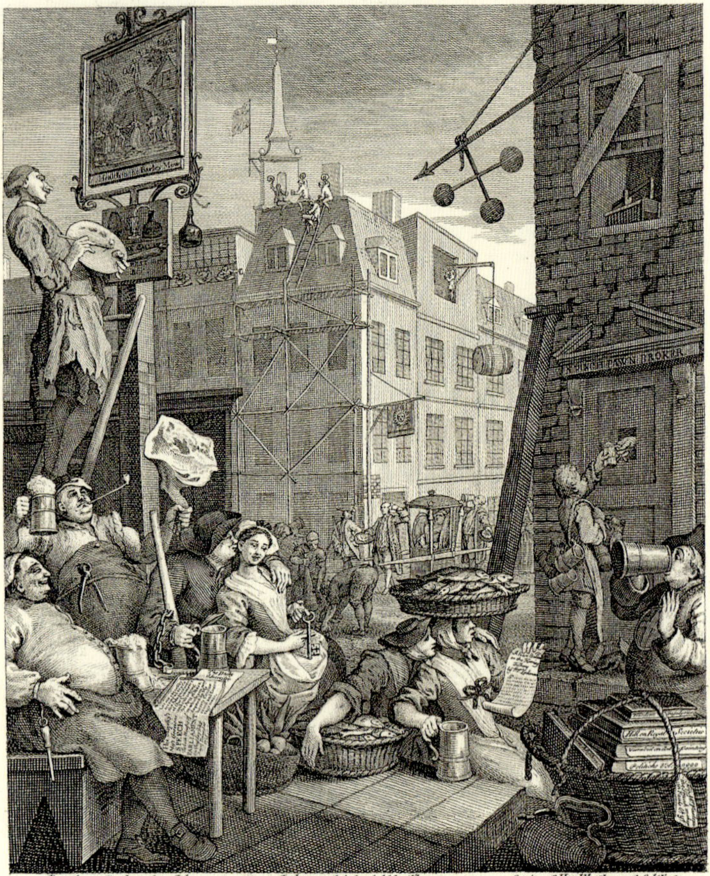

Beer, happy Produce of our Isle
Can sinewy Strength impart,
And wearied with Fatigue and Toil
Can chear each manly Heart.

Labour and Art upheld by Thee
Successfully advance,
We quaff Thy balmy Juice with Glee
And Water leave to France.

Genius of Health, thy grateful Taste
Rivals the Cup of Jove,
And warms each English generous Breast
With Liberty and Love.

Design'd by W. Hogarth. Publish'd according to Act of Parliament Feb. 1. 1751. Price 1s an age of great literary satirists such as Jonathan Swift and Alexander Pope, Villiam Hogarth had a similar reputation in the graphic realm. His "modern moral" ubjects, as he called his satirical engravings, ridicule the social types of London hile conveying ethical instruction. In his early series, such as *The Harlot's Progress* (1732) and *The Rake's Progress* (1733–35), the artist addressed the alues of London's "polite society" by presenting it with the spectacle of its own ailures. His vision of urban life was far from simplistic. He had a keen eye for he social and political complexities of Georgian London, and graphic satires like *Beer Street* are ultimately ambivalent about where virtue and vice can be found vithin the modern city.

Hogarth described *Beer Street* as a scene of virtue where "all is joyous and hriving." In contrast to its companion piece, *Gin Lane*, where "virtue and truth" re "driv'n to despair" by "foreign" gin, patriotic beer leads to contentment mong its portly advocates. A pipe-smoking artisan waves a shoulder of mutton another patriotic symbol), while a pawnbroker whose dilapidated quarters signify he irrelevance of his services receives a beer through a small opening in his ront door. *Beer Street* paints an ambiguous picture of urban prosperity, since Hogarth's vision of social contentment is easily confused with one of vulgar overindulgence. It is significant that the only thin and ragged individual in the cene is an artist, a sign-painter who leans back and gazes with admiration n his picture of festive beer-drinkers, as perhaps Hogarth did himself. Gaudio

Villiam Hogarth
ngland
697–1764

Beer Street
1751
Engraving
15 1/2 × 13 inches
Gift of Gordon Ray
1960-6-14

Étienne-Maurice Falconet's *Les mangeuses de raisins* was inspired by François Boucher's painting *Pensent-ils au raisin?* (*Are They Thinking about the Grape?*) (1747), which exists in tondo form at the Art Institute of Chicago and as a rectangular version at the Nationalmuseum in Stockholm. The themes of *Les mangeuses de raisins* – with its pretty country adolescents – are love and the pleasures of the senses. In its fluid and expressive movement, the statuette displays a characteristically rococo charm. Its modeling and detailing are technically superb.

To create such statuettes, artisans pressed clay into molds. The figures were prepared in small sections and joined with slip before firing. After firing, the seams were ground smooth, and details such as fingers or eyes were finished by hand. The result of the first firing was "biscuit" porcelain.

This little group in unglazed white porcelain imitates marble sculpture. The original model or mold was made under the supervision of Jean-Jacques Bachelier, a painter in charge of the Sèvres sculpture atelier from 1751 to 1757. This statuette is identical to one in the Musée National de Céramique in Sèvres, and bears a scripted "B," the control mark of Bachelier. Arntzen, Smith

Étienne-Maurice Falconet
(after François Boucher)
France
1716–1791

Les mangeuses de raisins
(*The Grape Eaters*)
ca. 1755
Soft-paste biscuit porcelain
8 1/2 × 10 inches
Harlan E. Moore Charitable Trust
1986-12-1

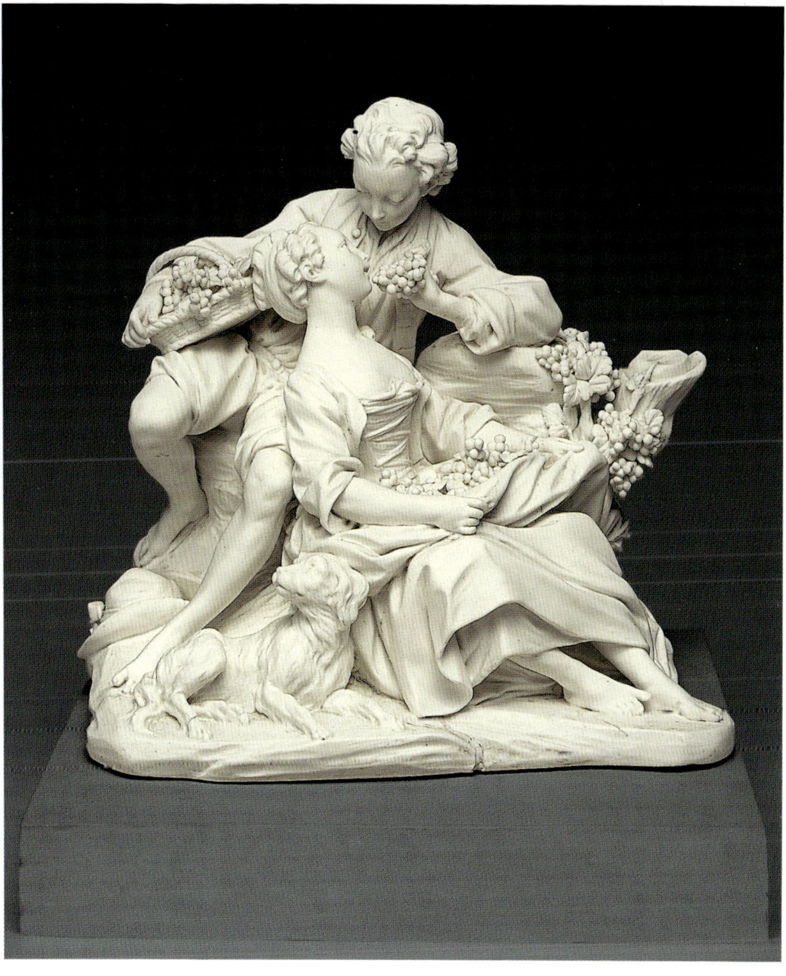

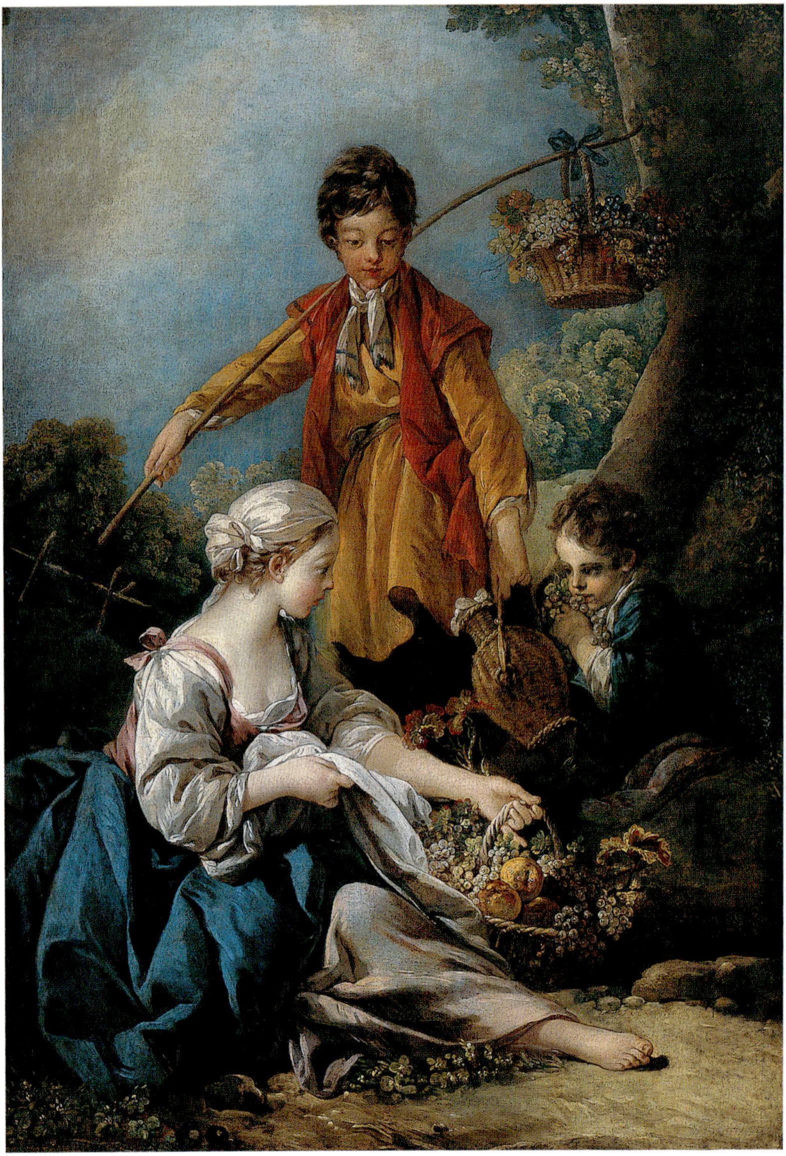

François Boucher, an acclaimed painter as well as teacher and court painter to Madame de Pompadour, began his professional career by engraving the works of Antoine Watteau for publication. He won the Prix de Rome in 1723 and later spent four years in Italy, where his major interest was the paintings of Titian, Paolo Veronese, and Giovanni Battista Tiepolo. He was most influenced by the latter, acclaimed as heir to the celebrated Venetian decorative tradition.

Boucher began designing tapestries in his thirties and became inspector for the Gobelins tapestry works in 1755. *Les vendanges* is a cartoon for part of a larger tapestry on view at the Huntington Library in San Marino, California. Two children in the foreground pose as if harvesting grapes, but their spotless clothing and gracious gestures place them in the realm of pastoral poetry, far removed from the sweat and labor of a real vineyard. The tanned skin and simpler clothing of a third child, standing in the background, are more consistent with the appearance of an actual worker. The children and decorative foliage create a scene that would have been ideal for decorating the walls of a drawing room in mid-eighteenth-century Paris. Indeed, the painting is an excellent example of the rococo style, filled with charm and gaiety.

Structural details strengthen the composition; the three children form a triangle and the lines of the stick the boy carries combine with the girl's extended leg to create a second shape. The fluidity of the clothing, the figures' gracefulness, and the softness of the colors are all characteristic of Boucher. Frampton, Smith

François Boucher
France
1703–1770

Les vendanges (*The Grape Harvest*)
1756
Oil on canvas
65 × 46 1/2 inches
Gift of Ellnora D. Krannert
1972-12-1

Giovanni Battista Piranesi's artistic career was divided between two of the grea centers on the eighteenth-century Grand Tour: Venice and Rome. He trained as an architect and printmaker in Venice, where he learned to etch in the manner of Marco Ricci and Canaletto, a style characterized by a loose, expressive handling of the needle and an emphasis on the evocative play of light across surfaces. At this time, Piranesi was also introduced to two forms of pictorial composition ther growing in popularity, largely in response to the demands of visitors: the *veduta*, or topographical view, and the *capriccio*, or architectural fantasy. In 1740 Piranes left Venice for Rome where, inspired by what he called the "speaking ruins" of the ancient city, he carried the *veduta* and *capriccio* to unprecedented levels of pictorial expression in works such as the *Vedute di Roma* (ca. 1748–78) and the *Invenzioni capricci di carceri* (ca. 1745, later reworked and republished as the *Carceri d'invenzione*, ca. 1761).

The significance of the *Carceri* (*Prisons*) has long been debated. As a demonstration of the power of ruins to inspire the artist's fantasy, they belong to the genre of *capricci*. But while the *Carceri* are indeed evocative of Roman architecture, theirs is an architecture without clear purpose. In this example, tiny figures emerge from or disappear into shadows as they wander aimlessly up and down staircases; pulleys and ropes with no obvious use hang from rafters of unfathomable height; and, at the lower right, menacing but unidentifiable spiked instruments of torture rise from a darkness that, one can only imagine, continues into unseen recesses. The viewer looks on an enclosed and prisonlike space that seems, paradoxically, to be of infinite extension. The "sublime" quality of the *Carceri* would find admirers among the romantic imaginations of the following generation. Gaudio

Giovanni Battista Piranesi
Italy
1720–1778

Carceri d'invenzione, plate XIV
ca. 1761
Etching
16 1/2 × 22 1/4 inches
Gift of Max Abramovitz
1973-1-1.3 n

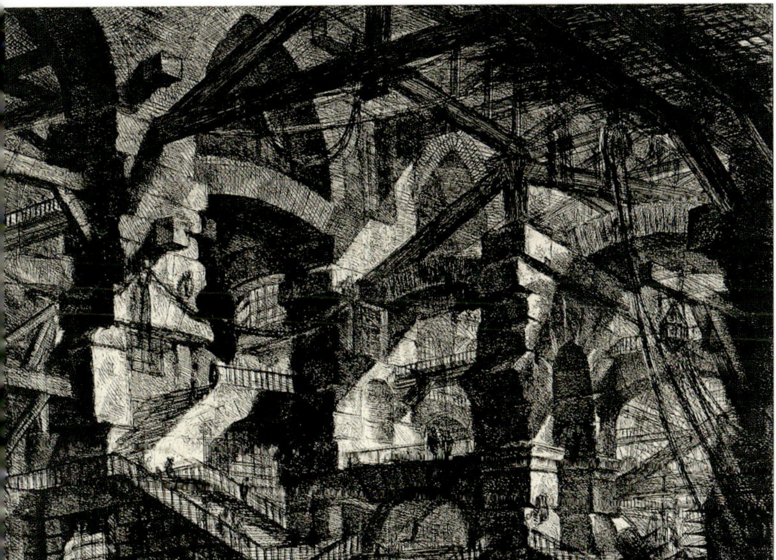

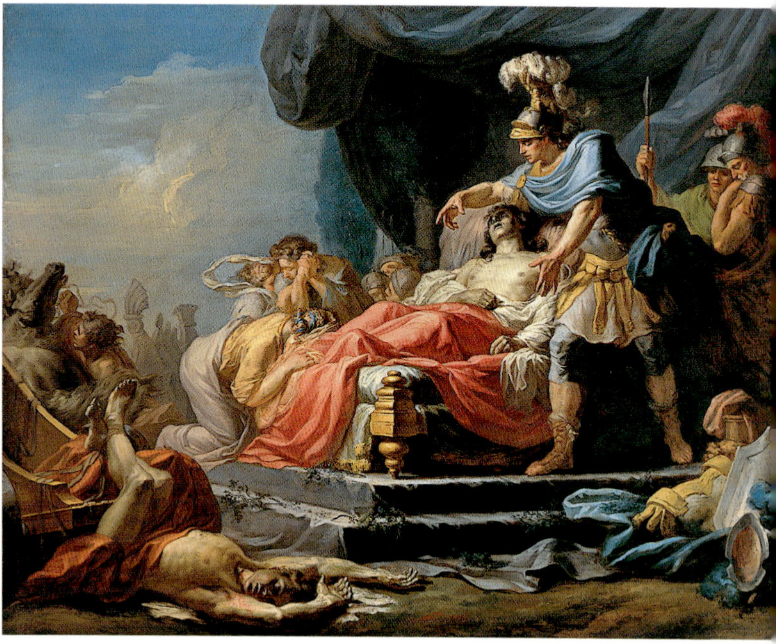

ean-Joseph Taillasson painted *Achilles Displaying the Body of Hector at the Feet f Patroclus* in 1769 for the Prix de Rome, a rigorous competition whose winner eceived a scholarship for three to four years of study at the Académie de France Rome. For the final round of the contest, painters were assigned a subject om history, mythology, or the Bible, secluded *en loge*, and given approximately vo months to complete a history painting. These paintings were exhibited to e public and judged by members of the Académie Royale de Peinture et de culpture. In 1769 the finalists were required to paint the moment in Homer's *iad* when Achilles, having dragged the body of Hector around the walls of Troy, eturns to the Greek encampment and displays it before the body of his companion atroclus, whom Hector has killed in battle. This choice of subject was highly nusual at the time: Homeric themes had never been used in the Prix de Rome, nd no representation of this episode existed in the history of art.

Remarkably, three other paintings from the final round of the competition survive. hose of the winner, Joseph-Barthelémy Le Bouteux, and the runner-up, Pierre acour, form part of the collection of the École Nationale Supérieure des Beaux-rts, Paris, and that of Joseph-Benoit Suvée is held by the Musée du Louvre. he many similarities among the paintings suggest that the artists broke the ontest rules and looked at one another's work. Indeed, a letter that Taillasson vrote to his mother during the competition suggests that he had seen the work f other contestants. Perhaps the young competitors were watching one another specially closely because they were obliged to give form to such unfamiliar ubject matter. Taillasson produced the most individualized of the surviving ntries. While Lacour and Suvée developed planar compositions and strictly linear nagery in accord with the newly fashionable classical style, Taillasson offered ısh brushwork and a de-centered, pyramidal composition that recedes diagonally nto space. O'Brien

ean-Joseph Taillasson
rance
745–1809

Achilles Displaying the Body of Hector at the Feet of Patroclus
1769
Oil on canvas
44 1/2 × 57 1/4 inches
Gift of Ellnora D. Krannert
1965-16-5

Nearly as famous as the Duchess of Devonshire, Jane, Duchess of Gordon (1749–1812) was well known for her role as confidante to Prime Minister William Pitt and the Tory party. In this portrait by George Romney, she is depicted with her eldest son, George, Marquis of Hartley, later the last Duke of Gordon. In 1794 mother and son created the army regiment of Gordon Highlanders, which was commanded by the youth.

According to Romney's ledgers, the duchess and her son sat for him in 1778, as he entered a period of intense creativity. Following a two-year period of study in Italy, the artist had established a studio in Cavendish Square, London, where he surpassed the productivity of more expensive portraitists such as Thomas Gainsborough and the president of the Royal Academy, Sir Joshua Reynolds, who also painted the Duchess of Gordon.

In addition to a rapid work pace, Romney's approach was characterized by loose brushstrokes and a thick application of paint. These elements are seen both in the duchess's white gown and in the background landscape. The pair's informal pose was influenced by the rise of so-called conversation pieces, one of the portraiture genres popular in late-eighteenth-century Britain. Romney typically painted his sitters' faces in greater detail than the rest of the composition. With a pensive look the Marquis of Hartley here studies a drawing in his mother's hand that perhaps came from the portfolio he holds in his right arm. The duchess does not look at the sketch, but into the distance.

Krannert Art Museum holds a preparatory sketch for this painting, which in turn may be a preliminary study for a larger version now at the Scottish National Portrait Gallery in Edinburgh. Strobel

George Romney
England
1734–1802

Jane, Duchess of Gordon and Her Son George, First Marquis of Huntly
1778
Oil on canvas
24 3/4 × 20 inches
Gift of Mr. and Mrs. Merle J. Trees
1940-1-6

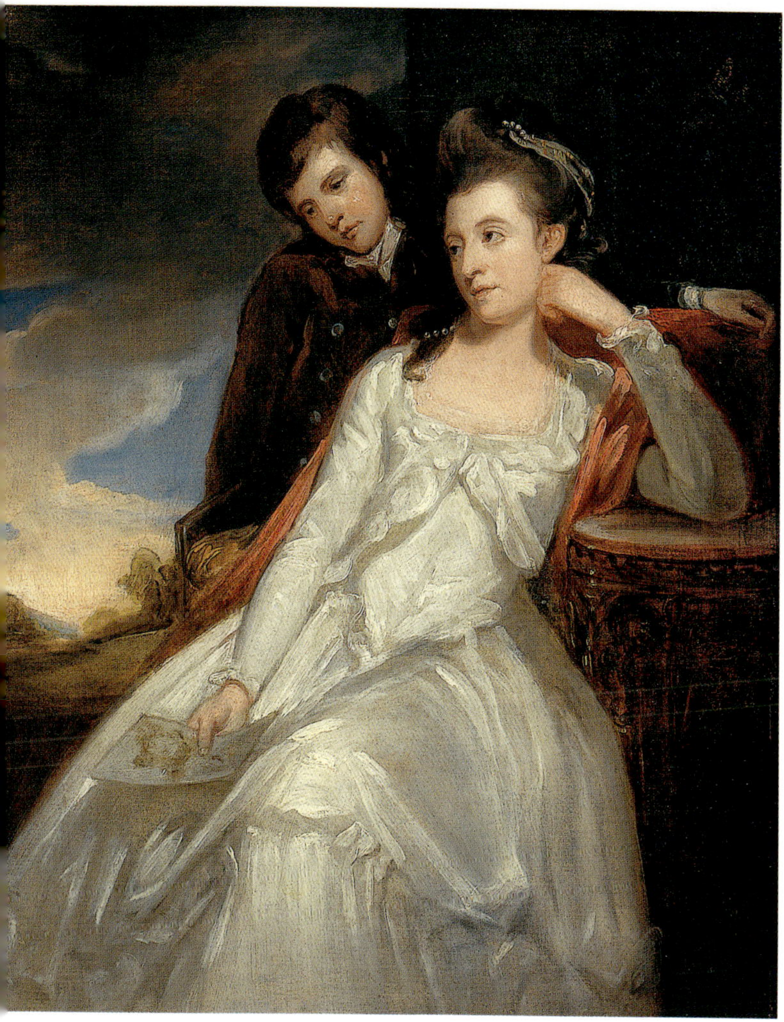

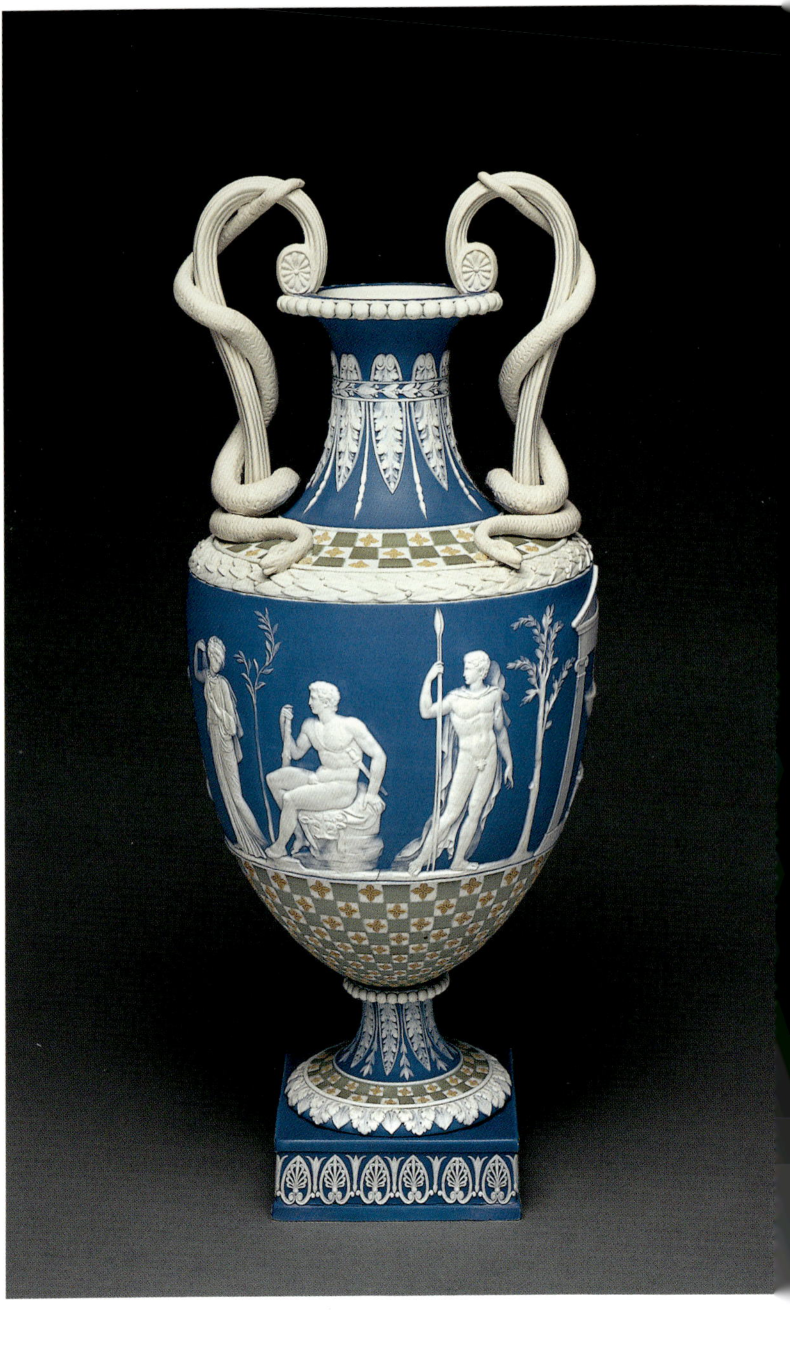

Vith the opening of his first factory in 1759, Josiah Wedgwood transformed :nglish ornamental pottery from a luxury item for the upper class into a commodity hat the increasingly prosperous middle class could afford. In 1782, after ten 'ears of experimentation, Wedgwood introduced jasperware to the public. His nost significant contribution to the history of ceramics, it remains in production o this day. Wedgwood's creation and perfection of jasperware coincided with the scendance of the neoclassical style; the new medium was ideal for the emulation f antique vases.

)n commission from Wedgwood, the leading neoclassical sculptor John Flaxman lesigned some of the most distinctive and successful jasperware. This vase is notable example because of its elaborate form and decoration. Inspired by a Greek vase he saw in an English collection, Wedgwood asked Flaxman to depict lercules's labor of gathering golden apples in the garden of the Hesperides. laxman adapted the painted design of the ancient source to a jasperware vase, he general appearance of which was based on Roman marble urns with figures n carved relief. Roman cameo glass inspired the blue-and-white color scheme, o which Wedgwood added touches of ocher and green. The intricate handles f the vase, shaped like entwined serpents, are also derived from Roman models.

)ecorated with tales from antique mythology, jasperware harmonized well with he classically inspired interiors then popular with leading architects. A shrewd usinessman, Wedgwood was sensitive to changing fashions and taste, which, ombined with his technical prowess, made a success of jasperware. It became highly sought-after collectible, elevating English ceramics manufacturing to a osition in the marketplace it had not enjoyed before. Langworthy

ohn Flaxman (designer
or Josiah Wedgwood)
ngland
755–1826

"Hercules in the Garden
of the Hesperides" vase
1785
Jasperware
20 × 6 inches in diameter
Harlan E. Moore Charitable Trust,
Ruth Miller, Rosann and Richard Noel
1990-8-1

Anne Batson was the daughter of Avon Turrell and the banker Edward Buckley Batson. In 1778 she married Henry Fane, a Member of Parliament and the second son of the eighth Earl of Westmoreland. Thomas Gainsborough twice painted her portrait, once around 1782 and again around 1786.

Both the internal evidence of costume and the style of Krannert Art Museum's canvas recall seventeenth-century portraits by Peter Paul Rubens. Mrs. Fane wears an elaborate lace collar, a gown with slashed oversleeves tied with ribbons, and a jeweled chain hanging from a central brooch. Her hat, decorated with ostrich plumage, tilts at a stylish angle, and she holds a fan made from a second feather. All these details are found in a portrait by Rubens of his second wife, Helena Fourment, painted in the 1630s. The "Rubens's wife" fashion was extremely popular at masquerades in the 1780s. Furthermore, when Gainsborough exhibited this portrait in his studio at Schomberg House, London, in 1786, he accompanied it with a notation explaining that it was "in the habit of Rubens's wife." The painting displays virtuoso brushwork, particularly in the undersleeves, where the agitated strokes suggest both the bunched, diaphanous cloth and the flesh beneath. The feathers and hair also provide passages of painterly bravura and set off the delicate treatment of the face and hands. O'Brien

Thomas Gainsborough
England
1727–1788

The Honorable Mrs. Henry Fane
ca. 1786
Oil on canvas
36 × 28 inches
Gift of Ellnora D. Krannert
1973-9-1

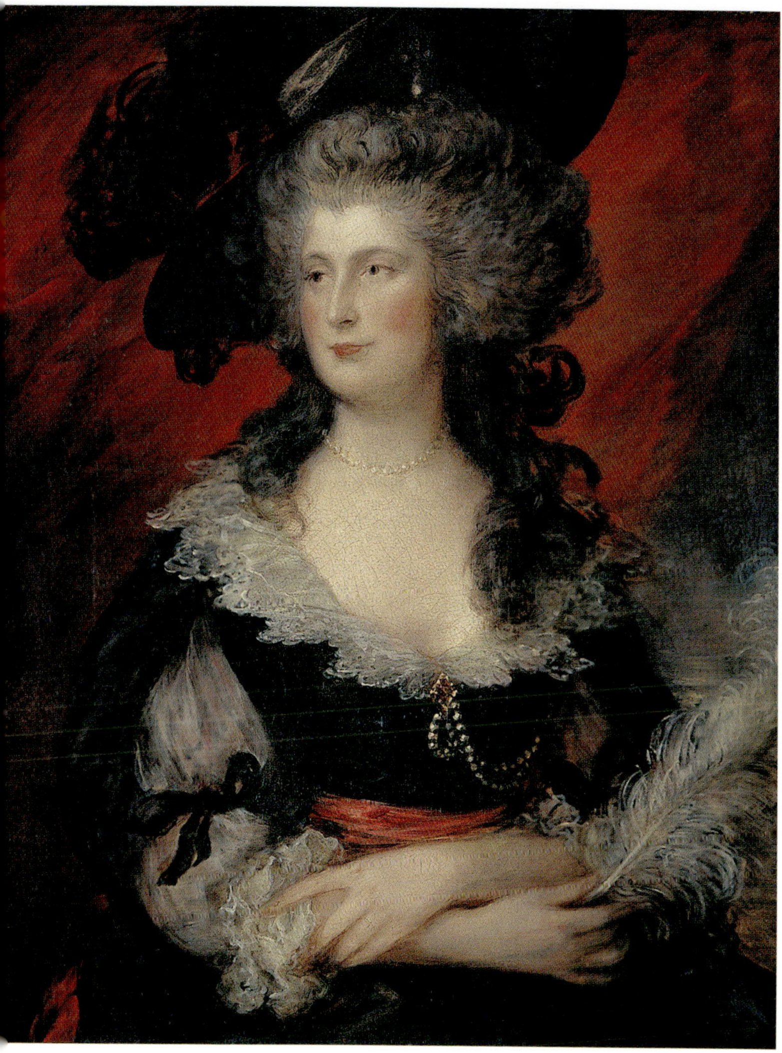

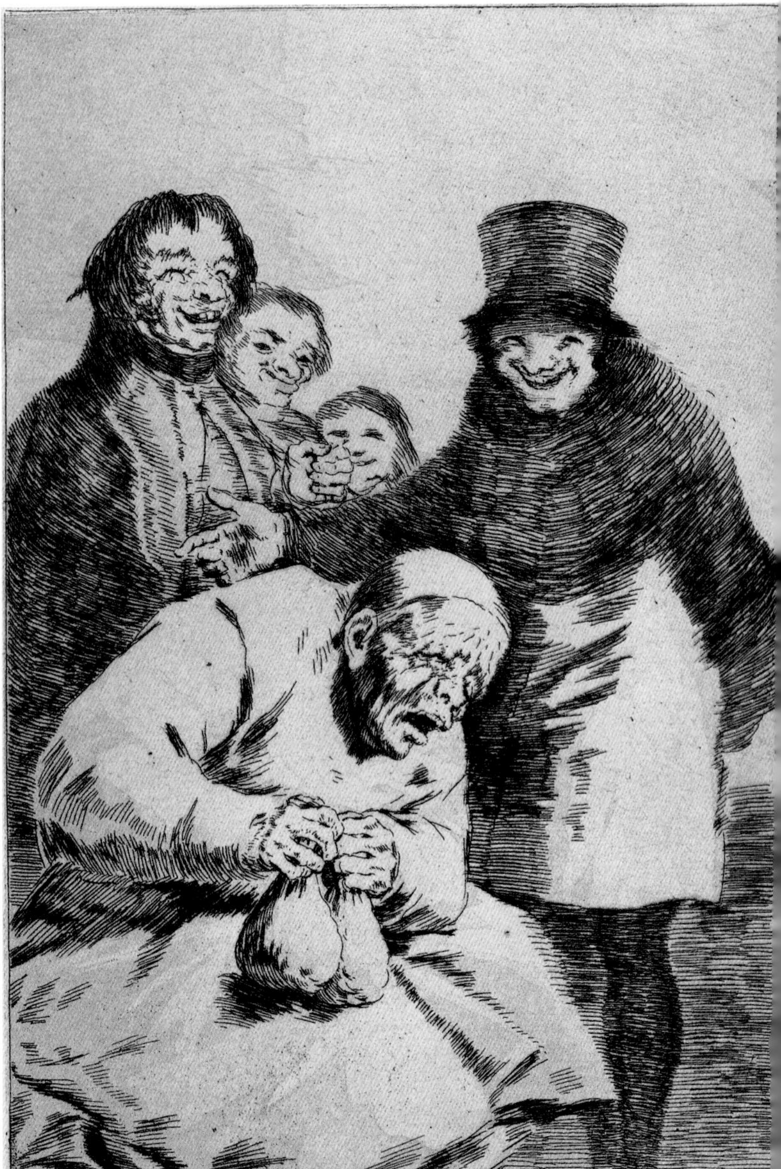

Porque esconderlos?

n the 80 plates of *Los caprichos* (*Caprices*), Francisco de Goya caricatured uthority figures and exposed the follies of Spanish society. The images reflect change in the artist's general outlook as well as his reaction against established cademic teaching. Some historians have correlated this shift with an illness n 1793 that left Goya deaf. Satire and irony pervade his illustrations of vice nd foolishness, such as alcoholism, greed, lechery, prostitution, superstition, nd abuses by the church, nobility, and government. Each image bears Goya's andwritten title and commentary. *¿Porqué esconderlos?* depicts onlookers aughing at an old bishop, and responds to the question posed in the title with he annotation "the answer is simple.... Because he doesn't want to spend them, nd doesn't spend them. Even though he's already eighty years old and won't ve a month, he's afraid that he'll survive long enough to end up short of money. So mistaken are the calculations of avarice."

The *Los caprichos* series was first rendered as ink-wash and sanguine (red-chalk) drawings, which were then translated into masterly line etchings. On he plate, Goya laid out broad tonal areas of aquatint that created contrasts of mysterious shadow against luminous open spaces. Pointed tools were used o enhance lines and deepen shadows. Surviving proofs have shown that the drypoint and some of the aquatint deteriorated quickly with successive printings, even in the first edition. Zundo

rancisco de Goya
Francisco José de
Goya y Lucientes)
Spain
746–1828

¿Porqué esconderlos? (*Why Hide Them?*)
Plate 30 of *Los caprichos*
1797–99
Etching, aquatint, drypoint
Plate mark: 8 1/2 × 6 inches
Gift of Gordon Ray
1960-6-48

This painting is an icon, an image created for use in worship in the Orthodox Church, rooted in the art of the Byzantine Empire (323–1453). For the icon to be an effective aid in devotion, its subject has to be recognizable. In this case, the saint's rounded, youthful face with a full head of curly brown locks, his horse and armor, and the Greek inscription near his right hand identify him as St. George. The winged dragon, the castle, and the princess rescued from sacrifice are elements from the popular legend of St. George and the Dragon. The diminutive figure mounted behind St. George on his horse, carrying a Turkish-style ewer, is from another legend of the saint, the Miracle of the Young Man of Mytilene. In the story, a Christian boy who had been captured by Arab raiders was made a page in the court of the Emir of Crete. Just as the young man was pouring water into the ruler's goblet at a banquet, St. George miraculously appeared and carried him – still clutching the ewer – back to his grateful parents.

Byzantine artistic traditions are evident even in this late work. Most obvious is the gold leaf background, which counteracts the illusion of depth. Also Byzantine is the stylized face and the abstract patterning of the folds of St. George's cloak, which billows into precise curves that defy the laws of gravity and wind resistance. At the same time, details such as the intricately patterned cuirass, or armor covering the torso, and blanket suggest the European baroque and Ottoman Turkish art characteristic of the eighteenth century. Woodfin

School of Epirus
Greece,
Macedonia/Epirus
18th century

Saint George and the Dragon
Gold leaf and tempera on wood
31 1/4 × 18 1/4 inches
University of Illinois Foundation Fund
1962-11-1

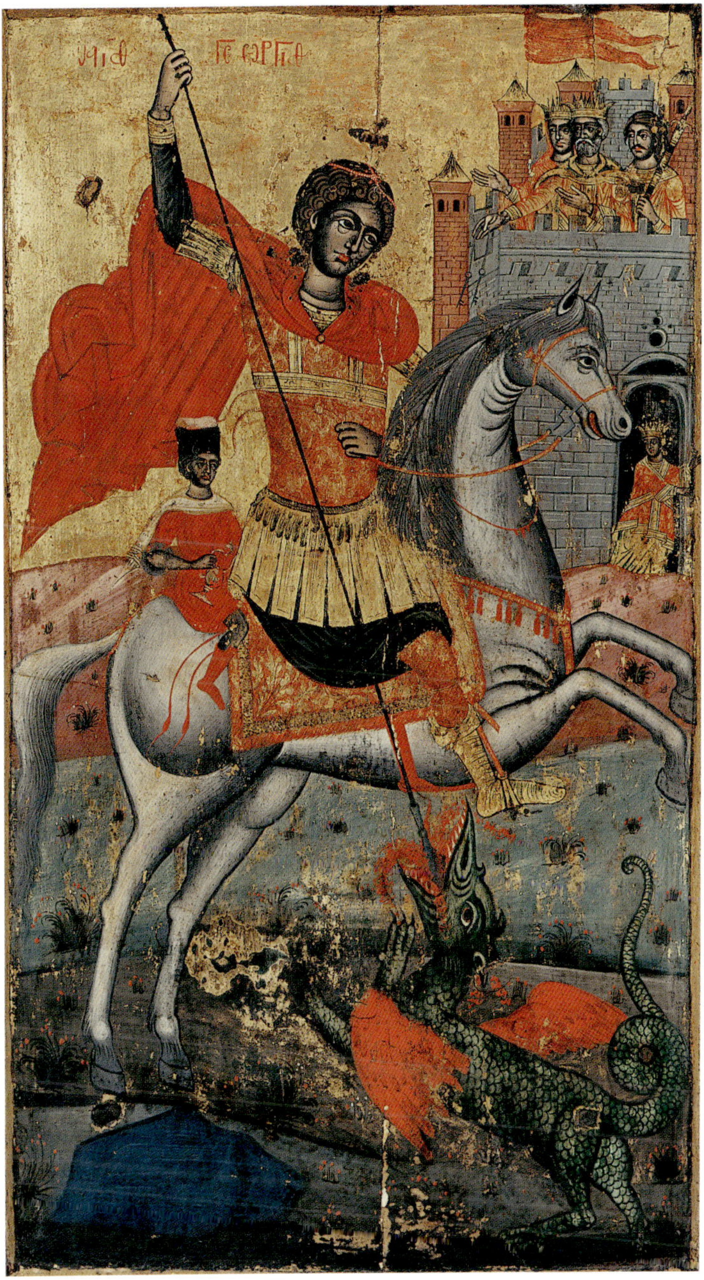

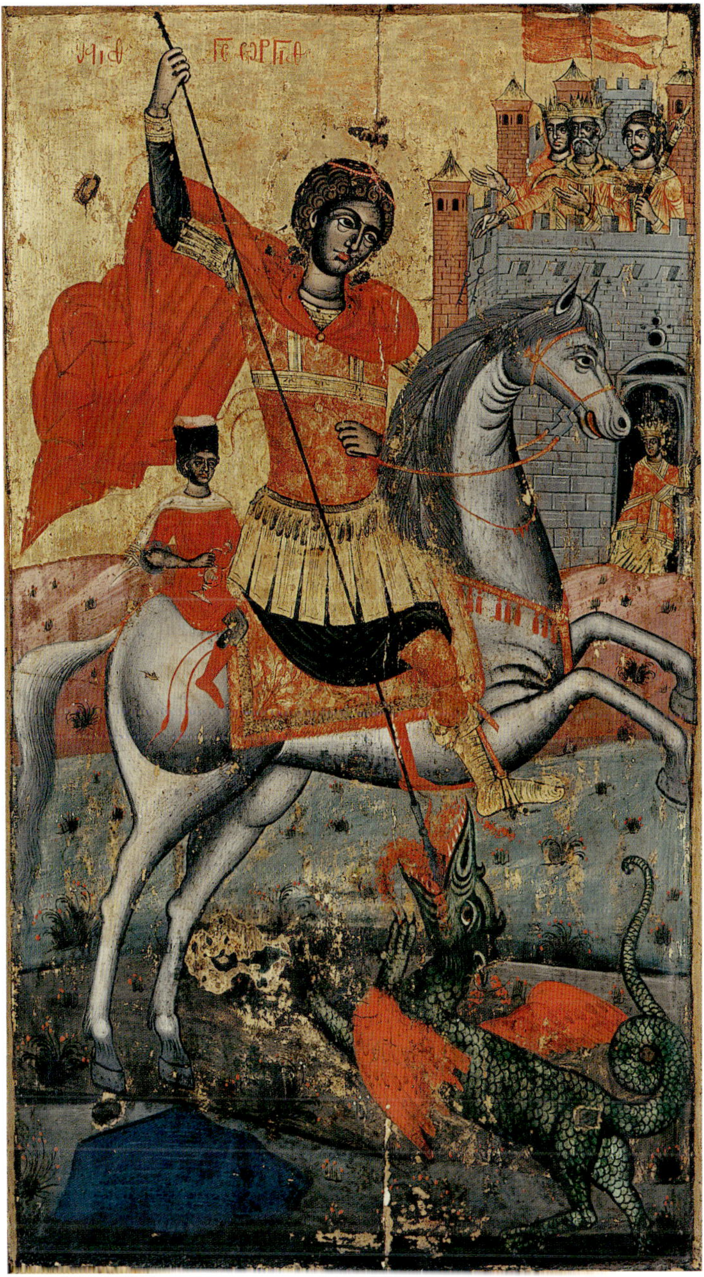

The Bateman silversmith dynasty began in 1760 with the death of Hester Bateman's husband, John, who bequeathed to her his most significant asset, the tools of the silversmith trade. In the following decade, Hester changed the Bunhill Row, London, business from that of jeweler, chain maker, and occasional silversmith to the firm of Hester Bateman, silversmith. She worked with her sons Jonathan and Peter. After Hester's retirement, Peter and Ann, Jonathan's widow, registered their own silversmith mark. Another generation was added when Ann's son William joined the firm. He became a full partner in 1800 and was co-designer with Peter and Ann until he inherited the business from them in 1815. Hester's granddaughter Sarah married Crispin Fuller, a silversmith, who also continued the Bateman tradition of fine sterling distinguished by simplicity and an elegance of shape and line.

The small beading of the sugar tongs (p. 140, top) is characteristic of Hester's designs until 1785; the bright-work (the highly polished areas of the piece) was executed by Jonathan and Peter. The form is highlighted by bright-cut designs in addition to the beading. The scallop-shell tea scoop (p. 140, bottom) was completed a short time before Hester's retirement in 1790. It is a simple in concept: a small ladle shape distinguished by a scallop-shell design and a small hand-grasp extension.

The continuity of the Bateman dynasty is exemplified by the four silver teaspoons (p. 142) produced by Peter, Ann, and William, infused with beauty of line and design. The simplicity of Bateman designs was unusual in this turbulent period of English silver-making. The discovery of Sheffield plate had led to much cheaper silver, and other silversmiths competed with the new products by producing ornate baroque designs.

The shape of the Crispin Fuller teapot (p. 143) is reminiscent of a pot William Bateman had made some five years earlier that, however, lacked decoration. Fuller rounded the shape of his work and added restrained fluting. The result is a simplified example of the fluting and half-fluting characteristic of Regency silver. The Regency (ca. 1795–1839) refers to the period when the future King George IV was appointed regent on account of the mental illness of his father George III. Smith

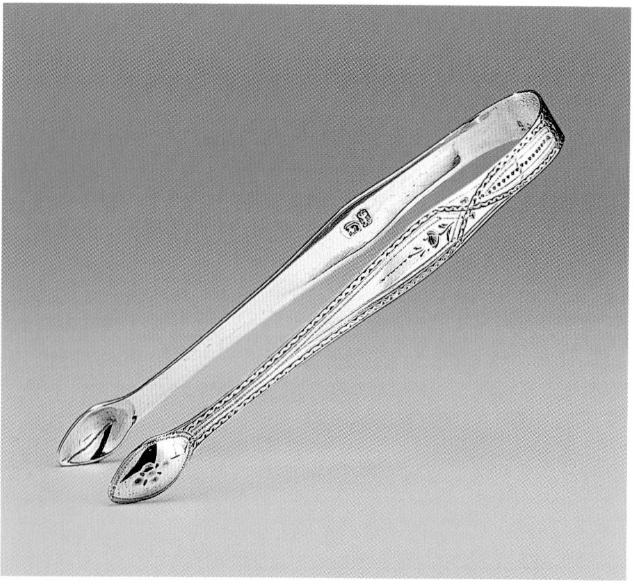

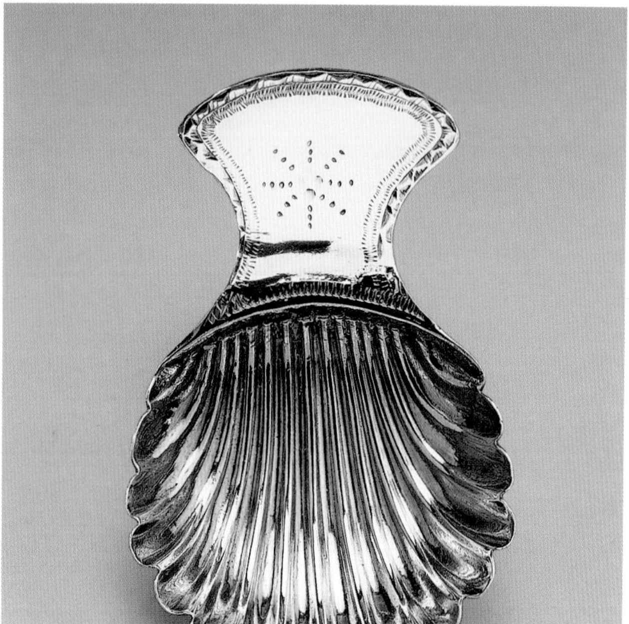

Hester Bateman
England
1709–1794

Sugar tongs
1784–85
Silver
5 1/2 × 1 1/2 inches
Gift of Theresa E. and Harlan E. Moore
1967-24-306

Tea scoop
1780–90
Silver
2 5/16 × 1 3/8 inches
Gift of Theresa E. and Harlan E. Moore
1967-24-310

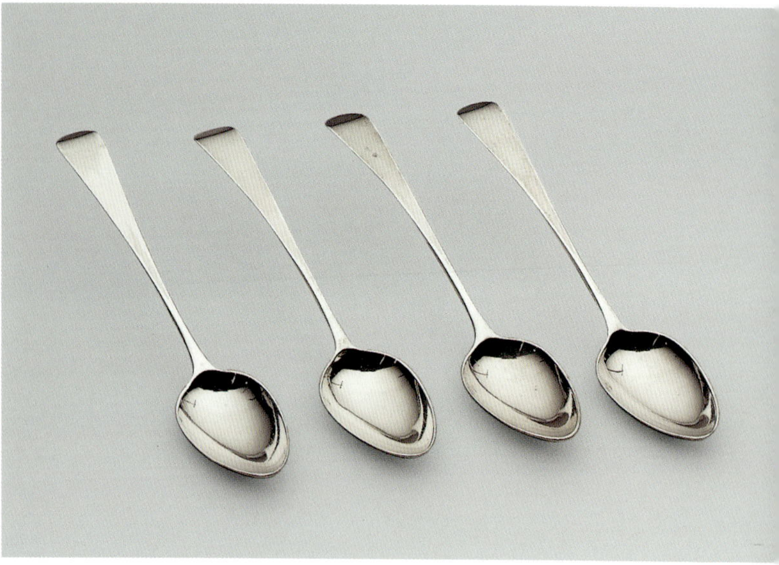

Peter, Ann, and
William Bateman
England
1740–1825,
1748–before 1813,
1774–1850

Teaspoons
1802
Silver
Each 5 1/2 × 1 1/2 inches
Gift of A. Doyle Moore
1979-6-1.1/1.4

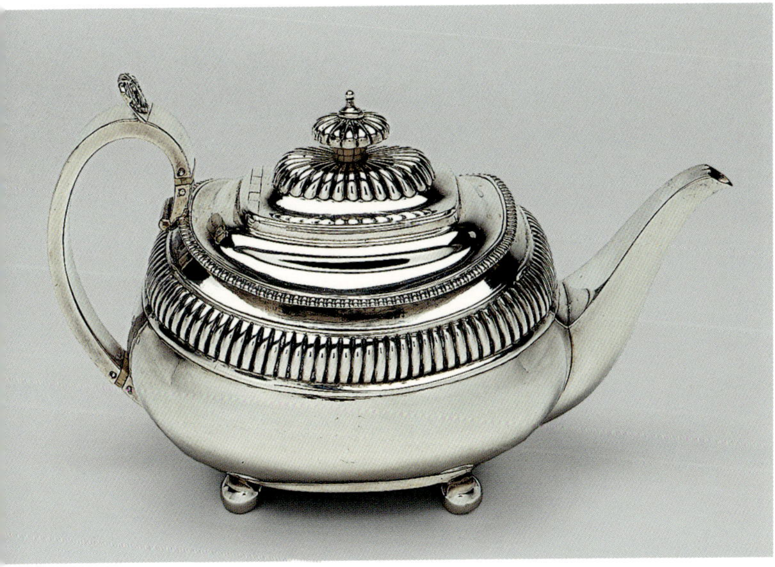

Teapot
1814
Sterling silver
5 3/4 × 10 1/2 × 5 inches
Gift of Joseph B. Harris
1996-9-1

Crispin Fuller
England
active 1792–1827

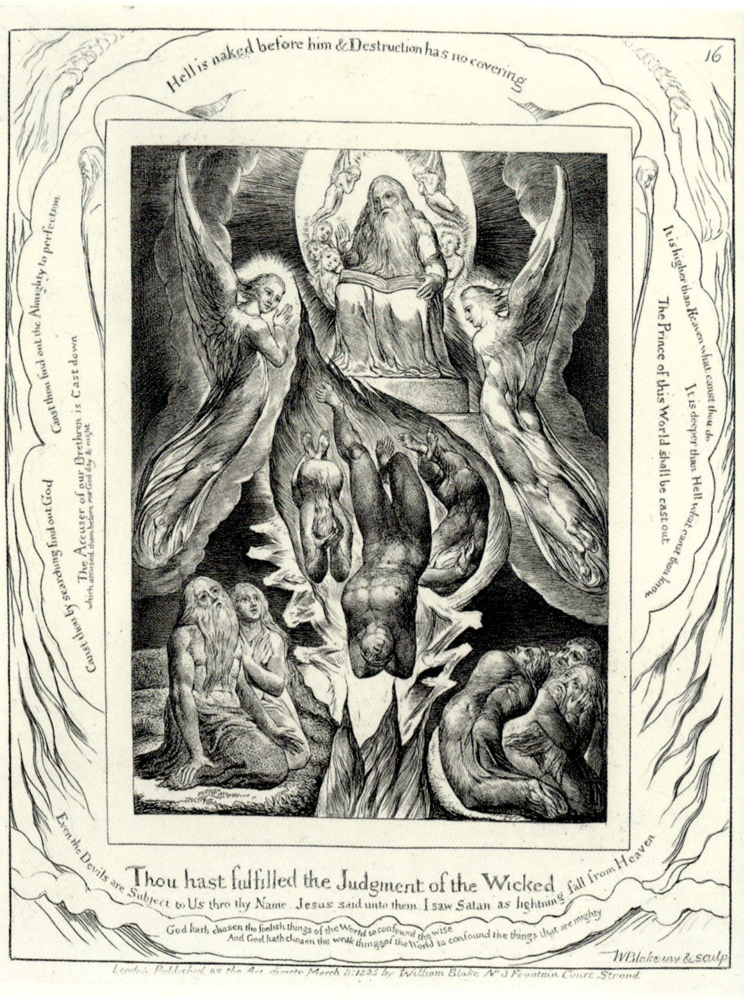
16
Hell is naked before him & Destruction has no covering
Canst thou by searching find out God
Canst thou find out the Almighty to perfection
The Accuser of our Brethren is Cast down
which accused them before our God day & night
It is higher than Heaven what canst thou do
It is deeper than Hell what canst thou know
The Prince of this World shall be cast out
Thou hast fulfilled the Judgment of the Wicked
Even the Devils are Subject to Us thro thy Name. Jesus said unto them. I saw Satan as lightning fall from Heaven
God hath chosen the foolish things of the World to confound the wise
And God hath chosen the weak things of the World to confound the things that are mighty
W Blake inv & sculp
London Published as the Act directs March 8:1825 by William Blake No 3 Fountain Court Strand

spired by the ideology of the American and French Revolutions, the poet, ainter, and printmaker William Blake rejected the traditional English institutions at governed artmaking and religious practice. He embraced printmaking as a emocratic art form, and in his numerous illustrated books used his own writings nd others, including the Bible, as vehicles for communicating his personal piritual beliefs.

lake saw in the story of Job a parallel to his own inner journey from strict belief church doctrine to the view that spirituality has nothing to do with official religion. the early 1820s, English landscape painter John Linell commissioned Blake to roduce engravings of the Book of Job, based on a series of watercolors he had ade in 1805. In plate 16, *The Fall of Satan*, Blake extended God's judgment of ob to others. The deity appears seated in heaven with the Book of Life on his lap hile Satan, with Job and his wife, falls toward the earth. To the left, the couple neels and watches in calm acceptance, while to the right, Eliphaz and the other wo friends who visited Job during his affliction cower in fear.

haracteristic of Blake's approach are the division of the scene into distinct ones, the use of well-defined contours, a shallow pictorial space, overall ymmetry, and the symbolic use of poses and hand gestures. Throughout his euvre, Blake synthesized a highly personal visual vocabulary that looked to arlier artistic styles he considered sincere and spiritually attuned. Langworthy

Villiam Blake
ngland
757–1827

The Book of Job (Thou hast fulfilled the Judgment of the Wicked)
1825
Relief etching
8 × 6 1/2 inches
University of Illinois Purchase
1950-21-5

The French realist Honoré Victorin Daumier is best known for his witty and sometimes acerbic observations of nineteenth-century French society and politics, opinions that led to his arrest more than once. Though he aspired to recognition as a painter, it was his prolific work in lithography that gained him fame.

This print, its title translatable as "supposedly the most comfortable position for a nice daguerreotype portrait," was part of a collection of 82 lithographs known as *Les bons bourgeois* (*The Good Bourgeois*). In this series, which appeared in the journal *Le Charivari* between 1846 and 1849, Daumier chronicled the work, leisure, and daily activities of the modern French middle class. In this example, he satirized the narcissistic obsession with the new medium of photography in portraiture, evidently sharing the attitude of writer Charles Baudelaire, who declared this public passion a form of lunacy.

Louis-Jacques-Mandé Daguerre pioneered the development of early photography on metal plates in the 1830s. The daguerreotype was so popular by the 1840s that itinerant photographers such as the one depicted in Daumier's print traveled widely to serve the middle class, as well as working in studios with fancy props and elegant drapery. The paunchy sitter here poses outdoors, hand in vest, while an exaggerated contraption immobilizes his head to prevent blurring during the long exposures required by early photography.

Lithography, a method of printing from stone, was used in the nineteenth century to reproduce pictures in journals and newspapers. The text was printed first in a relief press, and images were added in a lithographic press during a second run. Here, the text shows through from the reverse of the newspaper page on which the caricature was printed. Daumier also sold his popular series individually by subscription. Zundo

Honoré Victorin Daumier
France
1808–1879

Positión reputée la plus commode pour avoir un joli portrait au Daguerreotype
No. 49 from the series *Les bons bourgeois*
1847
Lithograph on newspaper
12 1/4 × 8 1/4 inches
Gift of J. Theodore Gleick
1980-2-1

LES BONS BOURGEOIS.

N° 49.

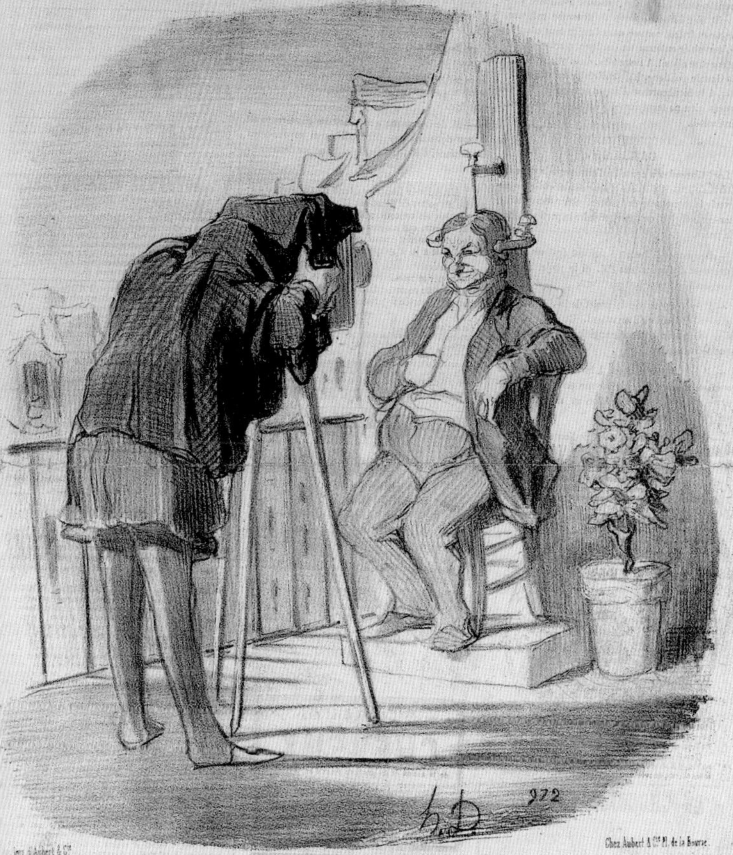

Imp. d'Aubert & Cie

Chez Aubert & Cie Pl. de la Bourse.

Position réputée la plus commode pour avoir un joli portrait au Daguerréotype.

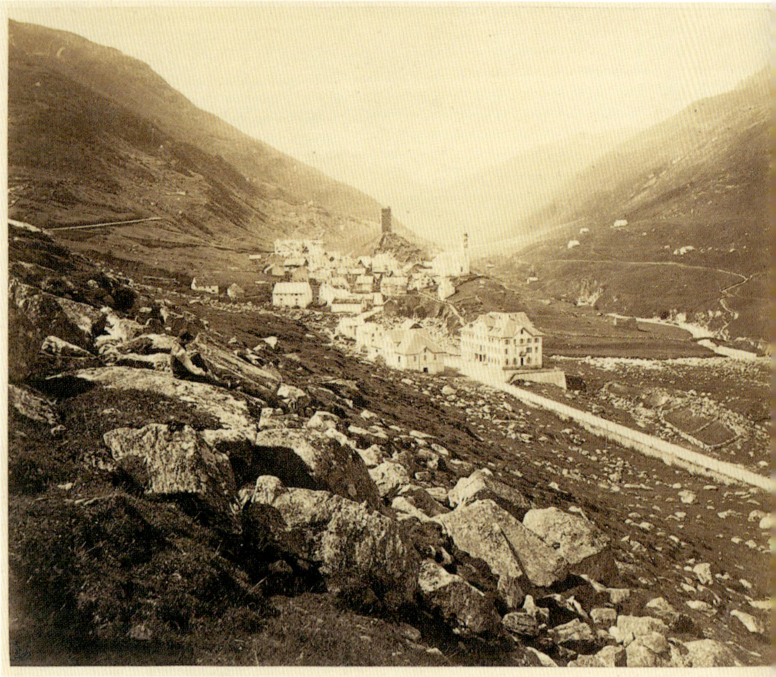

dolphe Braun was a successful textile designer when he began making hotographic flower studies for use by other fabric designers. When his pictures arned him a gold medal at the Exposition Universelle in Paris in 1855, Braun egan devoting himself exclusively to photography. He quickly mastered the ecently introduced collodion process, in which glass negatives were used to reate multiple positive prints on albumen-coated paper. By the early 1860s raun was operating one of Europe's most successful and respected photographic stablishments, headquartered in the Mulhouse suburb of Dornach in his ative Alsace.

o meet the steady demand for mass-produced views of popular tourist sites, raun and his assistants recorded thousands of scenic and historic locations in urope. Alpine scenes such as *Rue du St. Gothard* was one of the company's pecialties. This expansive vista shows Hospenthal, a small village on the ancient oad leading up the mountains to the famous St. Gothard Pass separating witzerland from Italy. For centuries, this narrow cobbled road was the principal orth-south transalpine route. The terrain pictured here lies south of the pass Switzerland's rugged south-central canton of Uri.

Braun's sweeping view, the Reuss River appears at the far right. At the center ar left, barely visible amid the mottled rocks, is a seated man wearing a white shirt nd a wide-brimmed hat. Braun routinely used figures to add visual interest and sense of scale to his landscapes.

lthough he was one of Europe's greatest producers of commercial landscape iews during the second half of the nineteenth century, Braun is now best emembered for his photographs of fine-art masterworks, a genre he pioneered the late 1860s. Kilgo

dolphe Braun
rance
811–1877

Rue du St. Gothard (Canton d'Uri)
ca. 1860
Albumen print
6 1/2 × 7 1/2 inches
Gift of William Becker
1985-40-20

While Jean Auguste Dominique Ingres is known for his intellectually ambitious history paintings and his sensual female nudes, portraiture also figures prominently in his paintings and drawings. This late example depicts the wife of his friend and occasional collaborator, French architect Jacques-Ignace Hittorf. The painting is part of a series of six decorative medallions depicting gods and goddesses designed for Hittorf's Paris home.

Mme Hittorf appears in the guise of Juno, wife of Jupiter and queen of heaven, and the goddess of light, birth, women, and marriage. Posed against a pristine azure background, she wears a gold crown and holds a scepter, both attributes of her royal status. Ingres was a master at rendering elaborate nineteenth-century women's fashions, but here he limited himself to simple, white, diaphanous drapery evocative of antique dress, delicate earrings, and a gold bead necklace. In his straightforward portraits, Ingres faithfully reproduced the sitter's features. When he incorporated the likeness of a female patron into a work that was not strictly speaking a portrait, or into a hybrid work such as this one, he characteristically invoked classically derived ideals of feminine beauty. Idealization is evident here in the figure's face, an almost perfect oval framing large, smoothly modeled eyes surmounted by arched brows. This series of curving shapes echoes the contour of the medallion frame. The sitter's light blue eyes reflect the background and complement her chestnut brown hair and rosy complexion.
Langworthy

Jean Auguste Dominique Ingres
France
1780–1867

Portrait of Madame Jacques Ignace Hittorf as Juno
1864
Oil on canvas
12 3/4 inches in diameter
Gift of Ellnora D. Krannert
1967-3-1

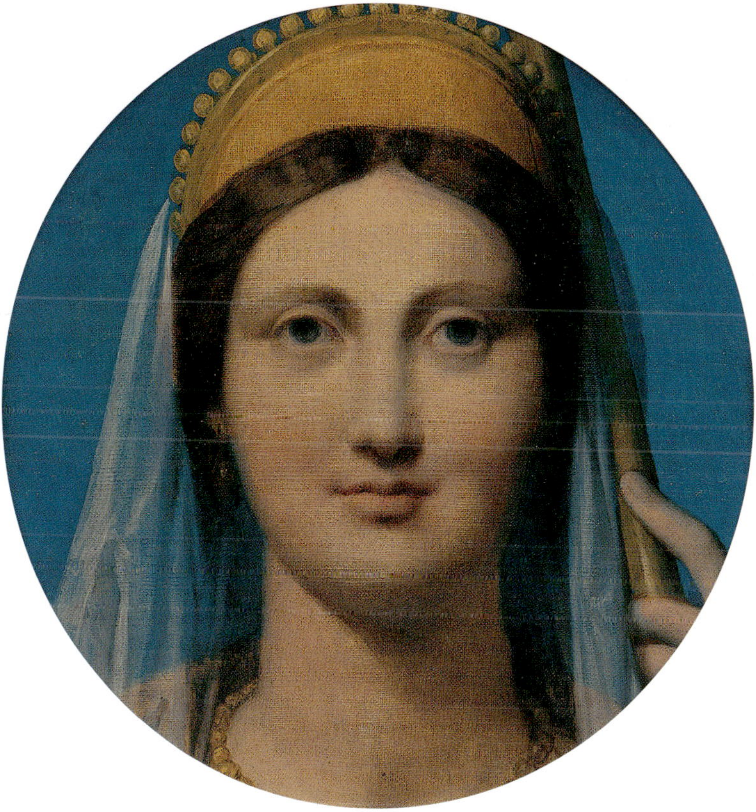

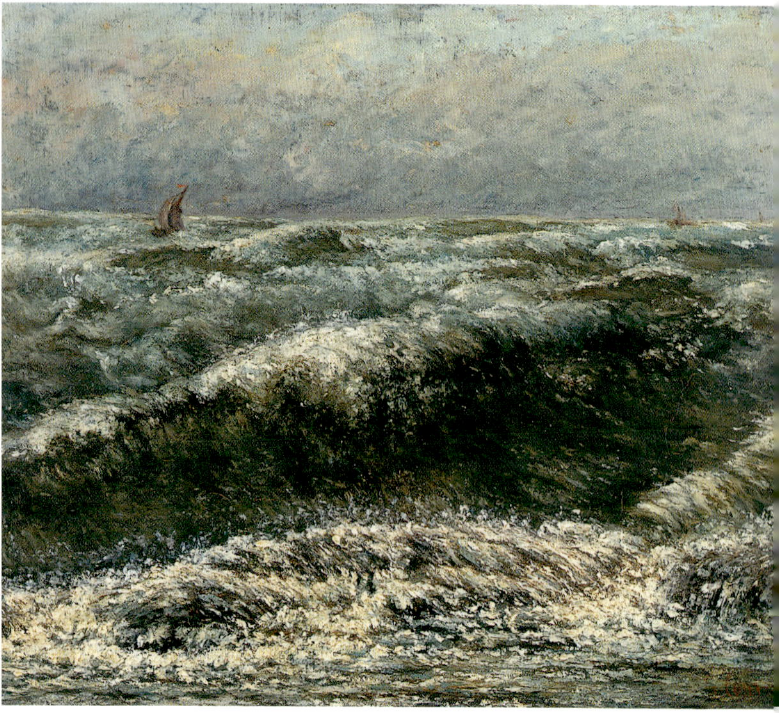

Gustave Courbet first began painting seascapes intensively in 1865 during a visit to Trouville in Lower Normandy. In 1869 he returned to the area, this time to the village of Étretat, where he completed a group of paintings of stormy seas that resemble Krannert Art Museum's picture. In this small yet powerful painting, a large wave has just broken on the sand and a second one crests behind it. The human element is reduced to three distant boats; the high horizon further dramatizes the roiling sea. Courbet applied paint energetically and thickly, often with a palette knife, creating a rough surface as aggressive as the waves that nearly conceal the rocks beneath them.

Courbet sought to render the material world realistically and to honor the materiality of his medium. The paint itself contributes as much to the appreciation of the work as the imagery it constructs. Rising up vertically, the sea seems to merge with the surface of the canvas. O'Brien

Mer d'Orage (*Stormy Sea*)
n.d.
Oil on canvas
18 1/4 × 21 3/4 inches
Gift of Mr. and Mrs. Herman Cooper
1961-7-1

Gustave Courbet
France
1819–1877

According to Claude Monet, it was Eugène Louis Boudin who opened his eyes to the value of working *en plein air*, or "in the open air." When painting beaches, tourists, and seascapes in Normandy and Brittany, Boudin began the canvases outdoors to directly capture shifting skies, water, and light, and completed them later in the studio.

Krannert Art Museum's work shows a rocky coastline under billowing clouds that sweep across an expansive horizon. The brushstrokes in the clouds swirl in various directions in contrast to the uniformly straight marks that constitute the sea below. The landmass in the foreground, covered with rocks, grasses, and wildflowers, is cleaved by a chalky path leading to the water. Earth, sea, and sky envelop and dwarf the three figures in the center. Shown from behind, the family trudges toward the sea, where small boats are indicated by touches of white paint. In the hazy background, Boudin has included a windmill, implying the towns that dot the seashore. Human activity is subsumed by the vast and wild coast.
Donovan

Eugène Louis Boudin
France
1824–1898

Untitled (also known as *The Cove*)
1871
Oil on paper mounted on canvas
10 1/4 × 14 1/2 inches
Gift of Mr. and Mrs. Herman Cooper
1958-14-1

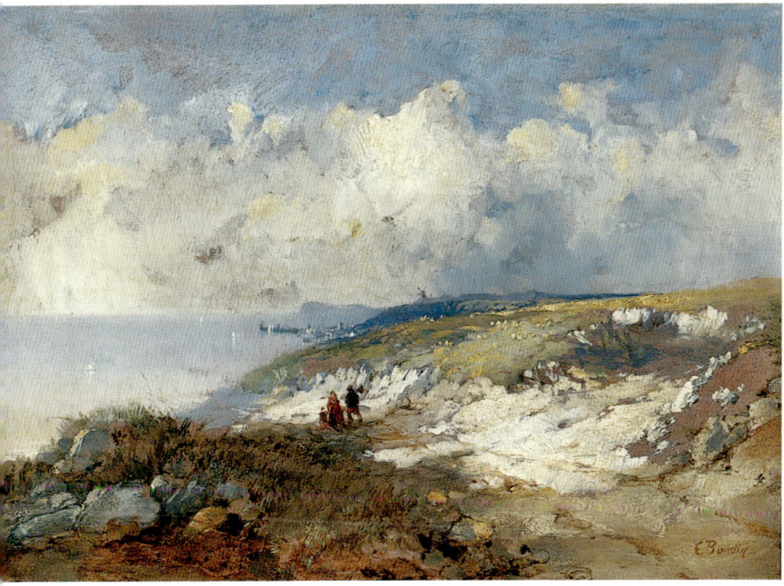
E. Boudin

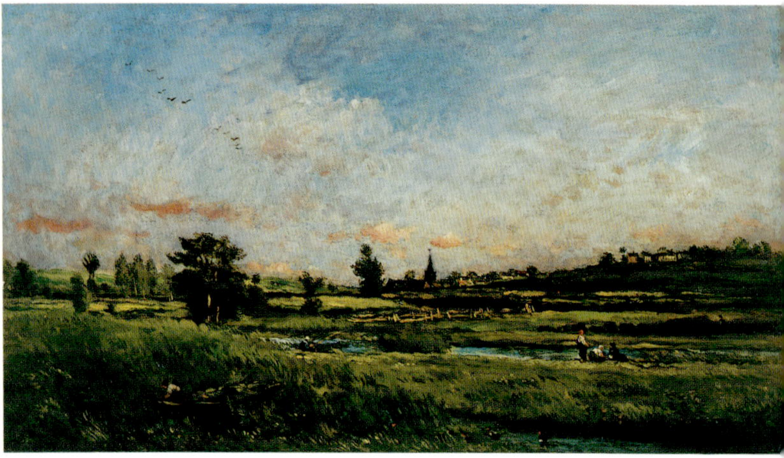

Among the Barbizon painters, a group of French artists moving toward realism in art, Charles-François Daubigny most clearly anticipated the procedures and techniques of the impressionists. Painting outdoors directly before the motif was so important to him that in 1857 he built a studio-boat from which he could view a changing landscape. Over the course of the 1860s, his handling became increasingly loose, and he developed the short, choppy brushstrokes, textured surfaces, fresh colors, and panoramic views typified by Krannert Art Museum's canvas. His lack of finish was poorly received by contemporaneous critics, with Théophile Gautier famously complaining that he gave only "an impression" of the scene.

Though the painting technique of this work appears to be spontaneous, the composition is highly calculated. The landscape is symmetrically arranged around the spire of a distant church, and horizontal bands allow the eye to gauge distances and move into the pictorial space. The scene is pastoral and serene; work is accompanied by fishing and boys playing games. The church, breaking the horizon and silhouetted against the sky, appears to preside over the community.
O'Brien

Charles-François Daubigny
France
1817–1878

Sur la Marne (*On the Marne*)
1871
Oil on cradled mahogany panel
15 1/4 × 26 3/4 inches
Gift of Mr. and Mrs. Merle J. Trees
1942-1-1

Primarily known for his paintings, Édouard Manet was at the forefront of the movement to revive printmaking as an artistic medium in France. By the middle of the century, photography had begun to replace reproductive engraving and lithography, leaving print shops free to work with innovative young artists like Manet.

Manet first met Berthe Morisot in 1868 at the Musée du Louvre, where Morisot was copying a painting by Peter Paul Rubens. They formed an intense, lifelong relationship, and Morisot became one of the elder painter's favorite models. Since Manet was already married, he suggested that she wed his younger brother, Eugène, which she did in 1874. Between 1872 and 1874, Manet based five prints on a single portrait of Morisot, including an etching in three states and a lithograph in two states – one in contour line and this one, which was not published during his lifetime.

When Morisot began posing for Manet in 1868, he was perhaps the most controversial and independent artist in Paris. He inspired her artistically and supported her goals to paint professionally. In turn, Morisot provided Manet with a link to younger artists, who regarded him as their intellectual leader. As a woman, Morisot felt deeply the gendered social restrictions that prevented her from participating in the intellectual exchanges of artists in the Paris cafés. While the male artists were free to paint the urban spectacle of modern Paris, as wife, mother, and daughter she had to pursue her work within the domestic world of family and friends to which women of her class were confined. Her favorite model was her daughter Julie, born in 1878, whom she showed making music, playing in the garden, sewing, and drawing throughout her childhood and early adolescence.

Colored pencils that Julie received as a gift in 1888 motivated her mother to take up the medium once again, resulting in a series of very personal drawings. In three sketches of Julie drawing, Morisot used the active, loose mark-making typical of her paintings. At the same time, in her paintings she lengthened and solidified her formerly light, broken brushstrokes, suggesting that her preparatory drawings and pencil sketches may have influenced her work in oils. In these sketches, Morisot drew Julie's head in profile with her back turned toward the viewer. Julie appears in the same pose, with minor variations, in an oil painting of 1892, *Jeune fille peignant*, executed in the dining room of their home. Zundo

(following pages)
Berthe Morisot
1872
Lithograph

.douard Manet	Image: 9 3/4 × 7 inches
'rance	Gift of James Russell Vaky
832–1883	2002-1-1

Untitled (also known as *Julie Manet*)
1888–92
Colored pencil or conté crayon on paper

3erthe Morisot	7 1/4 × 10 1/2 inches
'rance	Gift of Grant J. Pick
841–1895	1961-10-1

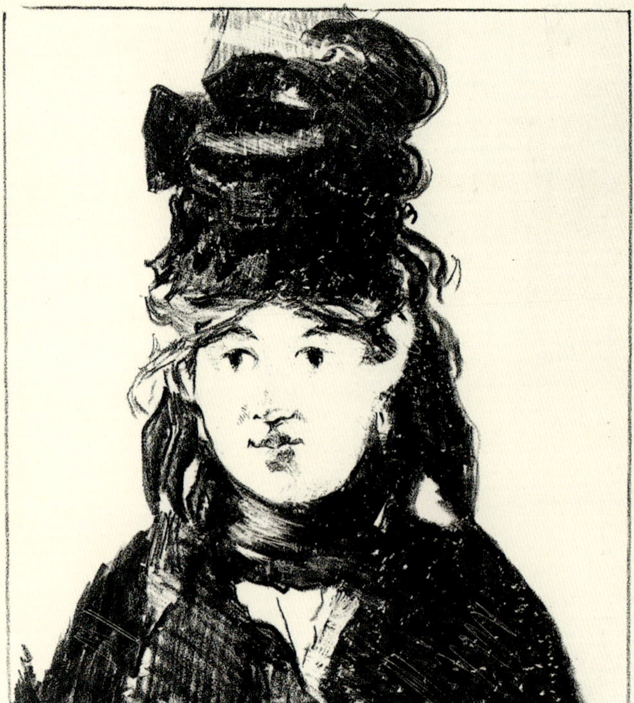

Imp. Lemercier & Cie, Paris

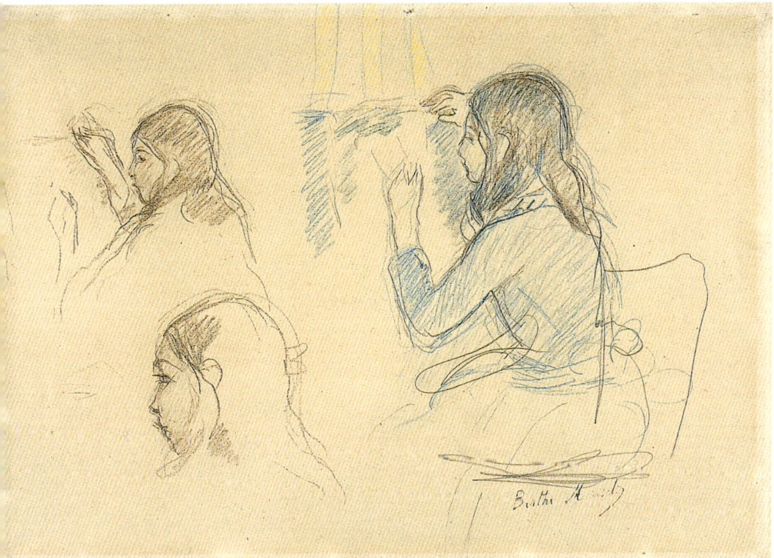

Berthe Morisot
Untitled (also known as *Julie Manet*)

This poster for champagne is the first of a small number of posters Pierre Bonnard designed early in his career, and also the first of his lithographs. In the novelty and brilliance of its conception, it rivals the well-known posters of Henri de Toulouse-Lautrec. Commissioned by an E. Debray in 1889, the date given for the work was inconsistent for many years. In 1976, however, a published excerpt from a letter Bonnard wrote to his mother established that the poster was first displayed on billboards in late March 1891, a few months before the first of Lautrec's posters, *Moulin Rouge–La Goulue*. *France-Champagne* so impressed Lautrec that he sought out the younger artist for advice on printing.

Like other poster artists of the 1890s, Bonnard adopted Jules Chéret's popular strategy of marketing products with portrayals of seductive women. But where Chéret modeled forms and created the illusion of depth, Bonnard made flat images that echo the stylized patterns of Paul Gauguin and Japanese prints, influences common among artists of his generation. These sources are felt in the continuously curving lines, and in such specifically Japanese elements as the fan and the distinctive turn of the head over the shoulder, a pose frequently found in representations of courtesans in Japanese woodblock prints. Here, the pose conveys demure inebriation, the comic effect of which is heightened by the witty economy of line. The champagne bubbles spill out of the glass to envelop the lower half of the figure, and their ruffled contour is taken up in the frills of her hair and gown. The young woman is made one with champagne. Franciscono

Pierre Bonnard
France
1867–1947

France-Champagne
1891
Lithograph
35 3/4 × 27 1/2 inches
Gift of the Estate of William S. Kinkead
1984-44-51

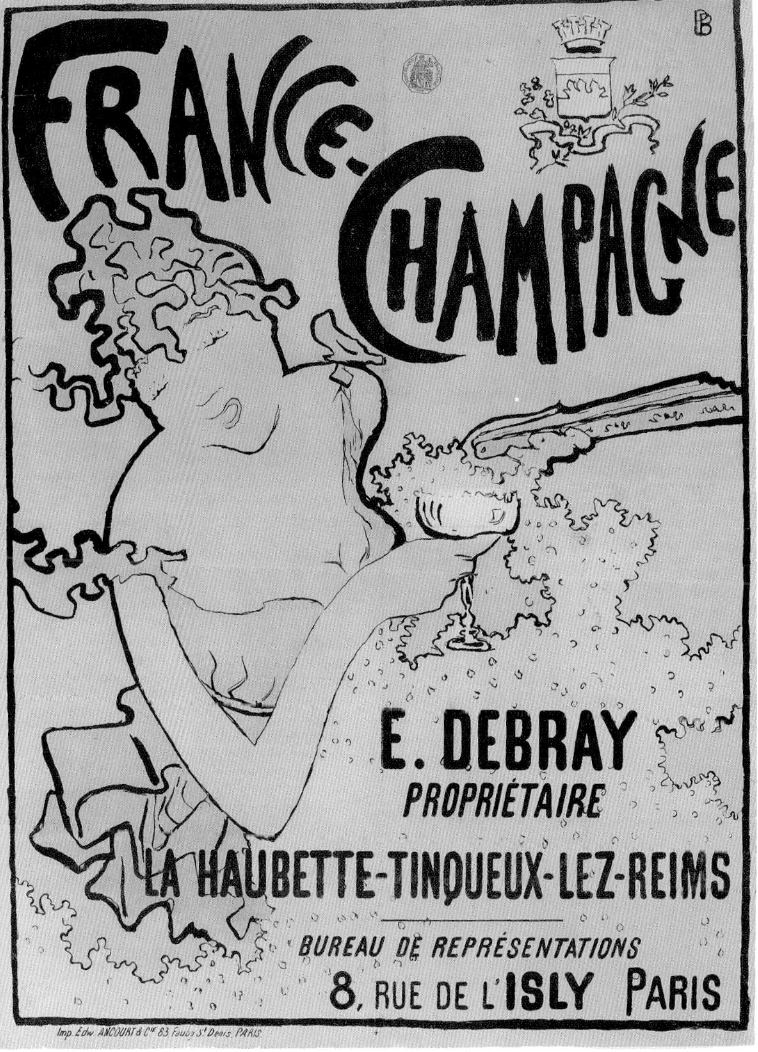
FRANCE-CHAMPAGNE
PB
E. DEBRAY
PROPRIÉTAIRE
LA HAUBETTE-TINQUEUX-LEZ-REIMS
BUREAU DE REPRÉSENTATIONS
8, RUE DE L'ISLY PARIS
Imp. Edw. ANCOURT & Cie 83 Faubg St Denis, PARIS.

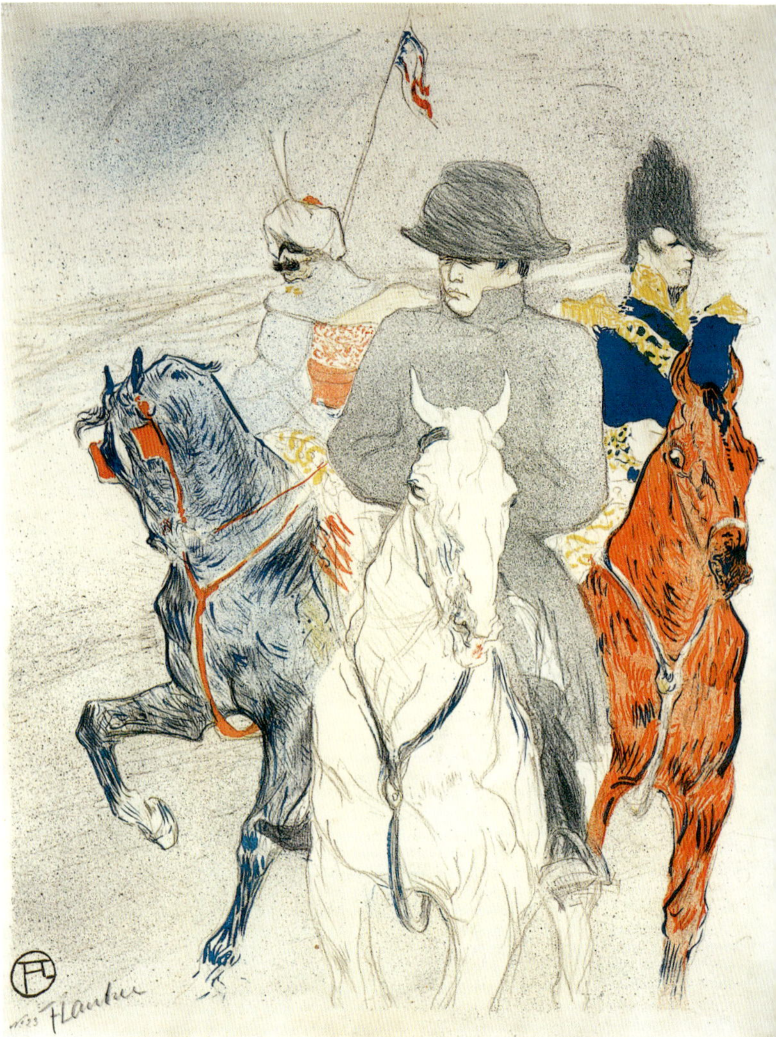

By 1895 Henri de Toulouse-Lautrec was firmly established within avant-garde circles in Paris and beyond. Since 1887 he had been represented by the Paris gallery Boussod and Valadon, where Vincent van Gogh's brother Theo was the first to promote his work. By 1891, when Lautrec conceived his famous poster for the notorious Moulin Rouge cabaret and dance-hall, his artistic career was flourishing and he had begun to explore the multicolored lithograph as a fine-art as well as commercial medium.

Napoléon was a submission to a competition sponsored by Boussod and Valadon for a poster to advertise a new biography of the emperor. Lautrec's composition is relatively conservative in its drafting and naturalistic in its detail, yet it is infused with a characteristic sense of immediacy and unconventional symbolism: the red, white, and blue horses suggest the French tri-color and the soldiers' costumes evoke Napoleon's campaigns in North Africa and Europe.

Though Lautrec had tempered his style to suit the academic tastes of the jury, the winner of the competition was Lucien Métivet – like Lautrec, a former pupil of Fernand Cormon – who submitted an emblematic and heraldic design. Despite his third-place ranking, Lautrec was satisfied enough with his image to produce it in an edition of 100, without lettering, for an ever-growing market of collectors of fine-art lithographic prints.

Napoléon is one of more than forty works on paper by Lautrec held by Krannert Art Museum. Atterberry

Henri de Toulouse-Lautrec
France
1864–1901

Napoléon
1895
Crayon, brush, spatter lithograph
33 × 28 inches
Gift of the Estate of William S. Kinkead
1984-44-6

Théodule Ribot was a largely self-taught painter who followed the model of Gustave Courbet in embracing realism in the second half of the nineteenth century. After a short period of formal training, in 1845 he moved to Paris where he worked briefly in the studio of Auguste-Barthélémy Glaize. Once independent, Ribot supported his family with commercial work, making painted signboards, colored lithographs, and decorated window shades, and copying works by Jean-Antoine Watteau for the American art market. In addition to producing portraits, genre scenes, and religious representations, Ribot became a prolific still-life painter. His interest in extremely simplified forms and down-to-earth themes recalls the Spanish and Dutch baroque masters.

Ribot painted the ordinary objects he would see in his own home. *Nature morte aux oeufs au plat (Still Life of Eggs on a Plate)* is one of at least eight works he made that show a plate of fried eggs on a table along with a jug and other elements of a meal. Lucidly organized in a restricted space, the objects create an impression of directness and honesty. Weisberg

Théodule Augustin Ribot
France
1823–1891

Nature morte aux oeufs au plat
(formerly known as *Kitchen Still Life*)
n.d.
Oil on canvas
29 × 39 3/4 inches
Gift of Mr. and Mrs. Merle J. Trees
1942-1-5

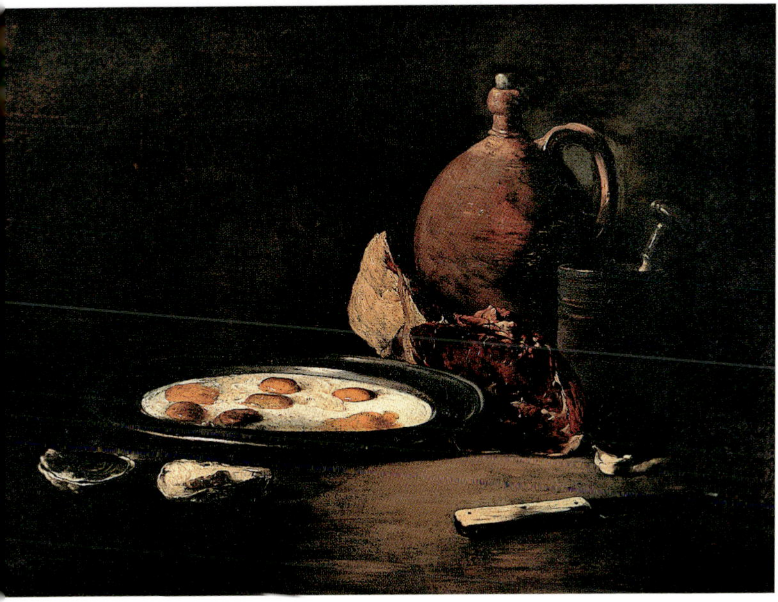

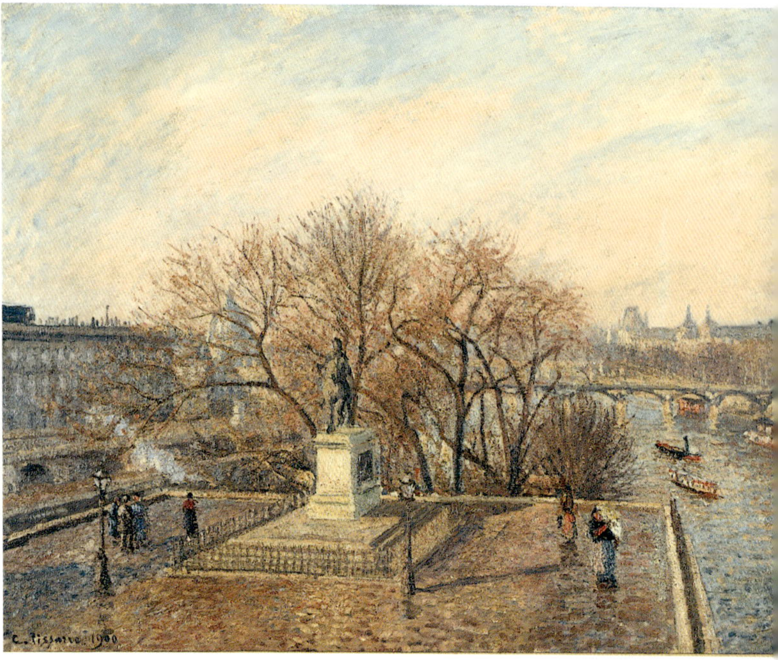
C. Pissarro. 1900

Although the impressionist Camille Pissarro is primarily remembered for depictions of rural life, during the last decade of his life he produced over three hundred paintings of French cities. In Paris he made several series of paintings from different rooms he rented in hotels or apartment buildings. Many of them were painted on the Île de la Cité, and among these most, like Krannert Art Museum's canvas, show the Vert Galant, a park at the island's westernmost tip.

Pissarro's late Parisian paintings took up the imagery that Gustave Caillebotte, Pierre-Auguste Renoir, and, especially, Claude Monet had focused on in the 1870s: tree-lined boulevards, strolling pedestrians, traffic, and the architecture of Paris. This direction was in part a consequence of Pissarro's failing eyesight, which required him to work indoors, but it may also reflect a new curiosity about urban life (and perhaps a shrewd awareness of the marketability of such images).

Statue d'Henri IV, matin, soleil d'hiver harkens back to a motif frequent in Pissarro's work of the 1870s: screens of trees in front of architectural backgrounds or the sky. Juxtaposing near and far, ethereal and solid, and dark and light, here Pissarro dabbed on paint to capture the color of a distant roof bleeding through the space between two branches. His varying handling of paint – from agitated, heavily reworked passages to areas of broad wet-into-wet strokes – provides a rich and textured surface. Pissarro's commitment to perceptual experience is evident in his efforts to capture the fleeting visual effects of the season, weather, and time of day. O'Brien

Camille Pissarro
France
(born Danish
Virgin Islands)
1830–1903

Statue d'Henri IV, matin, soleil d'hiver
(*Statue of Henri-IV, Morning, Winter Sunlight*)
1900
Oil on canvas
29 × 36 3/4 inches
Gift of Mr. and Mrs. Merle J. Trees
1951-1-2

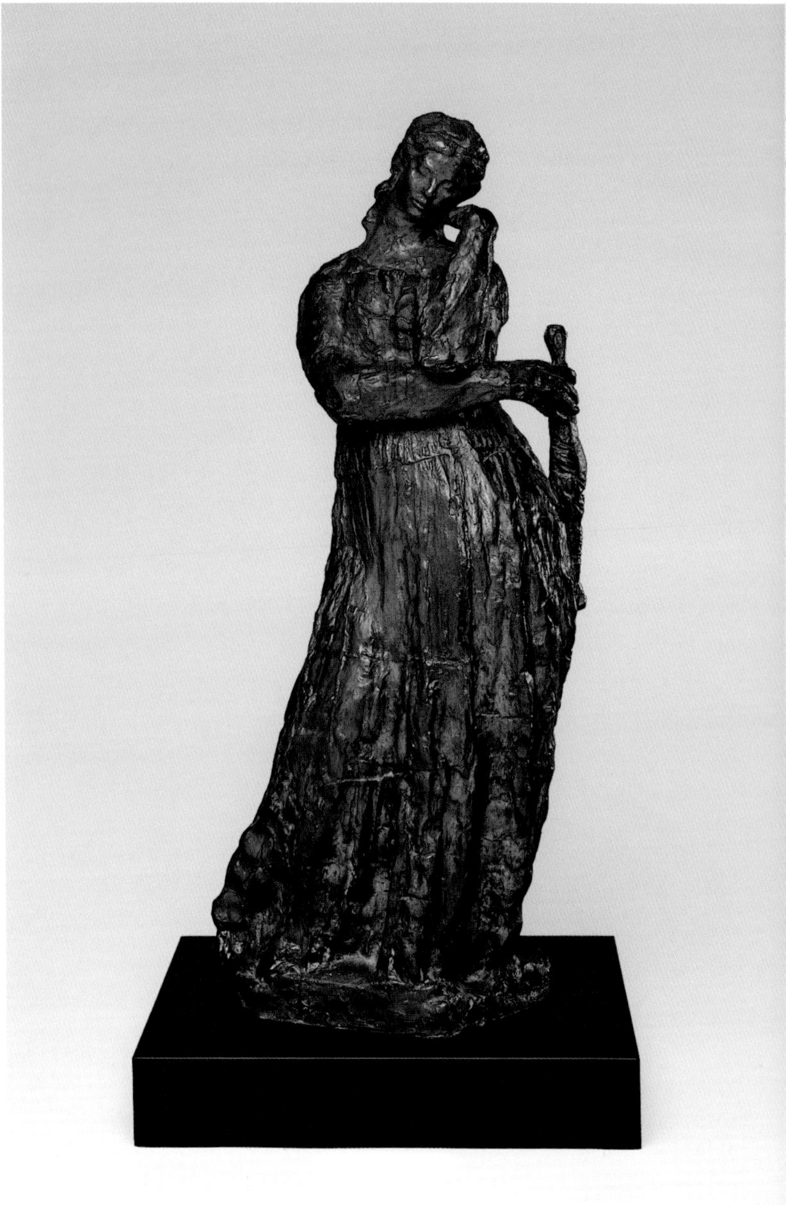

This bronze figure by Émile-Antoine Bourdelle evokes the patient suffering of the wife of the ancient Greek hero Odysseus. Penelope is shown in an attitude of resignation, carrying a spindle that represents years of a subterfuge that she used to stall the suitors who swarmed around her while she awaited her husband's return from the Trojan War. Insisting to them that she finish a burial shroud for Odysseus's father, Laertes, before responding to their entreaties, for ten years she wove by day and unraveled by night.

Bourdelle began his career by making sculptural furniture ornaments in his father's cabinet shop. Like many art students, he learned the art of modeling in clay by copying plaster casts of antique statues. After moving to Paris, he began working as Auguste Rodin's assistant, roughing out the master's plaster casts in marble. Bourdelle was a committed teacher and served as an instructor at the Académie de la Grande Chaumière, a position he occupied until his death in 1929. For three years, the modern Swiss sculptor Alberto Giacometti was one of his students in life drawing and sculpture, and Henri Matisse studied with him briefly in 1900.

This study is a bronze cast of a preparatory model for a monumental bronze *Penelope* (1912). Among the models he completed, this is the only one to include the spindle. It reflects Bourdelle's admiration for what he called "the classic harmony of ancient statues." Indeed, his work inspired Rodin to call him "a Greek from Southern France." In the realm of early-twentieth-century French sculpture, Bourdelle is still exceeded in reputation only by Rodin. Arntzen, Smith

Émile-Antoine Bourdelle
France
1861–1929

Study for *Penelope*
1905
Bronze
21 1/2 × 9 inches
Gift of Class of 1908
1961-18-1

In his early years as a struggling avant-garde artist in Paris, Pablo Picasso tended to identify with social outsiders: the circus performers, beggars, and prostitutes who lived in the neighborhoods where he could afford a studio. During this period the theme of the opposition of love and death emerged repeatedly in his work, in part due to the 1901 suicide of his close friend Carlos Casagemas.

The biblical subject of Salome and John the Baptist was fashionable in art and literature at the *fin de siècle*, or "end of the century," for its blend of the morbid and the erotic. Here, the naked Salome dances provocatively in front of her stepfather, the obese Herod Antipas. Her mother, Herodias, stands half-naked by his side, averting her eyes, while in the corner a dark-skinned female servant strokes the hair of the Baptist, whose severed head lies on a platter on her lap. These figures appear elsewhere in Picasso's work of 1905: Salome's pose mimics that of a girl on a circus horse, and the Herodias figure appears in an image as a gentle circus wife who toys with her hair.

Known for his rapid-fire stylistic innovations and experimentation in a wide variety of media, Picasso was a prolific printmaker. For this image he scratched the copper plate directly with the etching needle. His delicate lines are confident; the only change in design occurred in the dancer's right foot. Spare contour lines define the figures against the white ground while drypoint shading emphasizes their faces and hair. Zundo

Pablo Picasso
Spain
1881–1973

Salome
1905
Drypoint
Plate: 15 3/4 × 13 3/4 inches
University of Illinois Purchase
1950-12-2

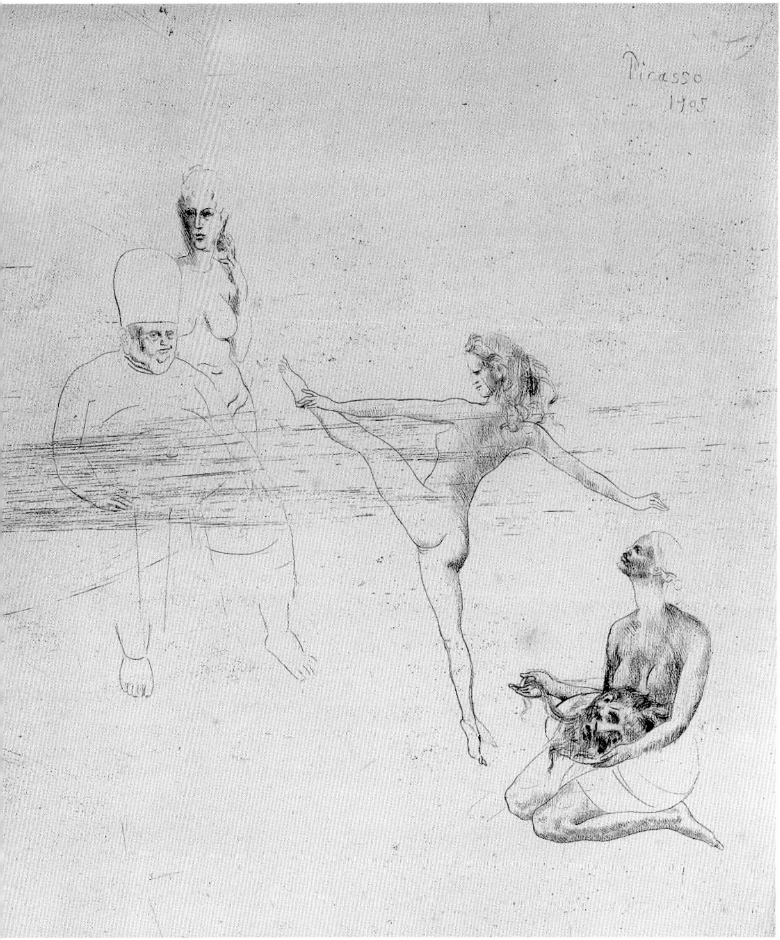
Picasso
1905

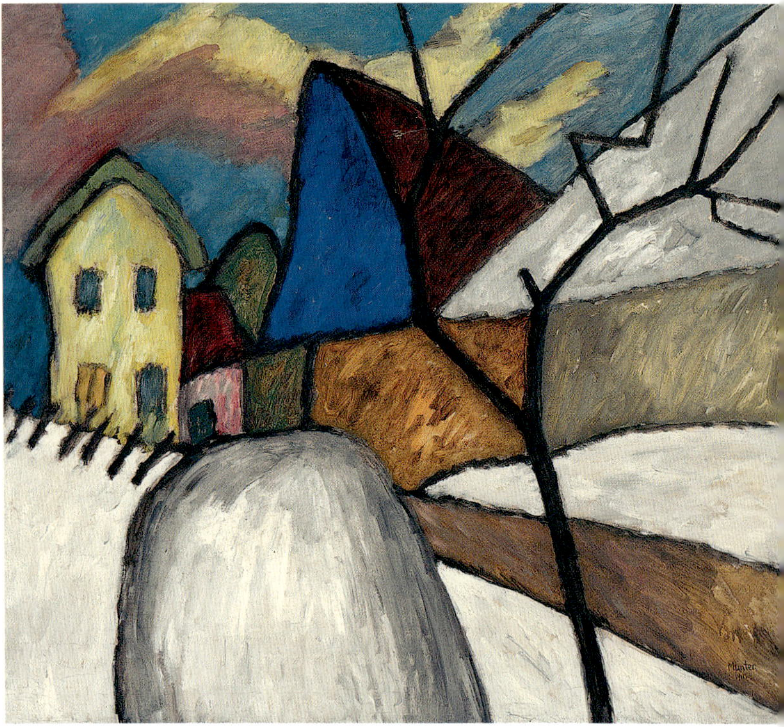

Gabriele Münter was one of the charter members of Der Blaue Reiter (The Blue Rider), a German expressionist group founded in 1911 that was united not by style but by the shared desire to convey spirituality and transcendence through art. In 1908 Münter settled in the town of Murnau, near Munich, where she envisioned a utopian community of artists living outside the context of urban life. For Münter, the rural landscape allowed for an expression of spiritual purity, a dominant theme in her art.

Münter painted the village as a refuge from modern life, a place that might restore the harmony between humankind and nature disrupted by the modern city. The broad white areas of snow on the ground contrast with the glowing pinks, blues, and yellows of the cottages, which are tightly pressed together and overlapping, distorting perspectival depth. Although the brown pathway pulls the viewer's eye in, the space is simultaneously flattened by a network of thick black outlines that draw attention to the painting's surface. Wolfskill

Gabriele Münter
Germany
1877–1962

The Blue Gable
1911
Oil on canvas
35 × 39 3/4 inches
Gift of Albert L. Arenberg
1956-13-1

With Otto Dix and Max Beckmann, George Grosz developed the subversive social realism known as the Die neue Sachlichkeit (New Objectivity) in Germany after World War I. These artists channeled into their work the disillusionment and cynicism they felt about the Social Democratic government. Grosz presented his politicaland social satire in both paintings and coarsely drawn cartoons, such as those in the Ecce Homo series of 100 lithographs published in magazines and books. Mocking the bourgeoisie, as well as social pariahs such as prostitutes and crippled war veterans, Grosz portrayed the moral collapse and social disorder of postwar Germany.

In this drawing, Grosz caricatures the entire social spectrum. Described in sharp angular lines, his characters include a middle-class man wearing a coat, tie, and bowler hat who glances nervously to his left; an older bourgeois woman, her affluence signaled by her ornamental hat, earrings, and handbag, who moves away from the crowd; and a prostitute in a transparent garment who stands in the background, gazing nonchalantly at the viewer. Other figures include an elderly man and a crippled, impoverished soldier who extends a matchbook apparently intended for sale. The lack of shading and the distorted perspective create an ambiguous space, making the composition unstable and unsettling. Grosz exposes an uncomfortable public space where social classes converge, holding them all up to sharp critical inspection. Wolfskill

George Grosz
Germany
1893–1959

Nach Ladenschluss (*Rush Hour*)
No. 45 from the *Ecce Homo* series
1919
Brush and ink on buff paper
23 1/2 × 18 1/4 inches
University of Illinois Purchase
1949-20-9

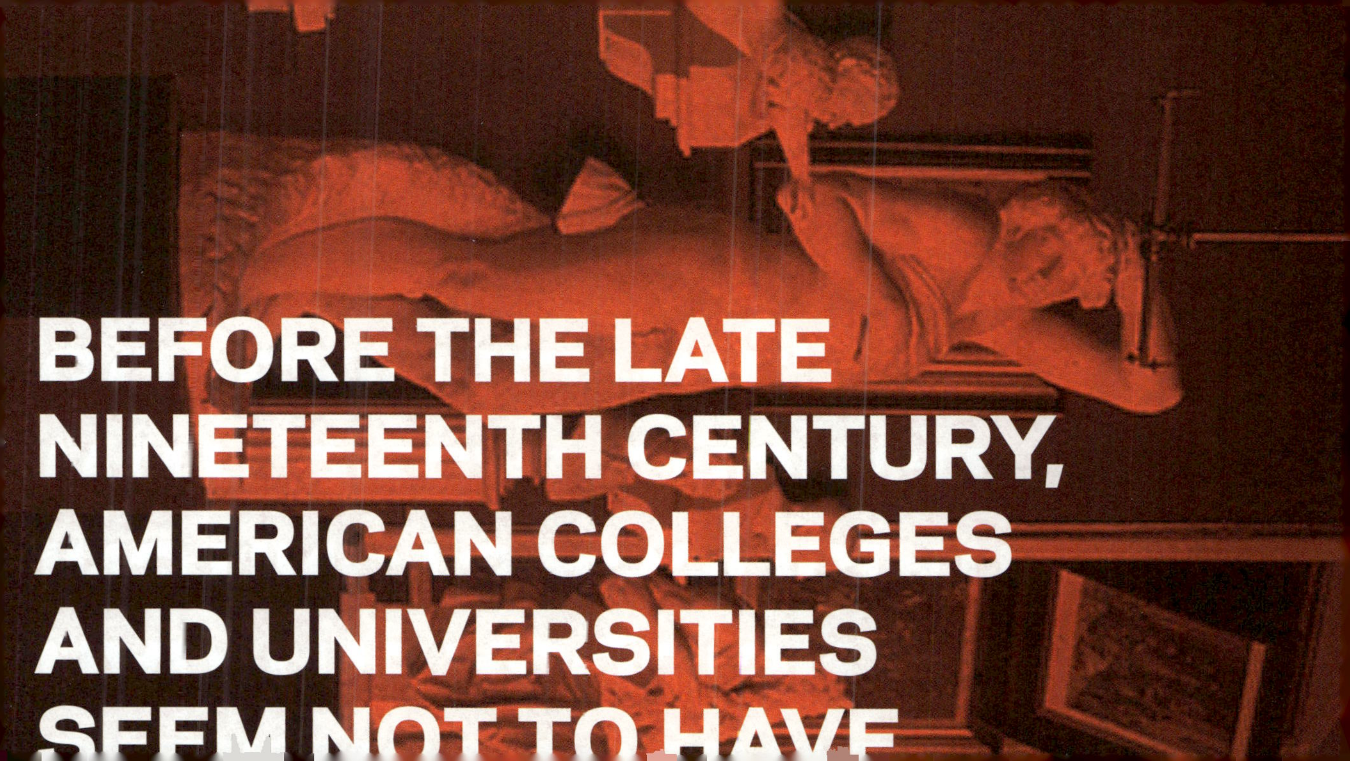

BEFORE THE LATE NINETEENTH CENTURY, AMERICAN COLLEGES AND UNIVERSITIES SEEM NOT TO HAVE

SEEM NOT TO HAVE
HAD THE ACQUISITIVE
INSTINCTS ASSOCIATED
WITH GREAT CHURCH,
GOVERNMENTAL,
CORPORATE, AND
PRIVATE COLLECTORS
OF ART.

recognition of art for its own sake developed unhurriedly and without special plan.

At Urbana, John Milton Gregory, the University's first regent, wisely did not raise the possibility of asking for state appropriations to acquire art or, for that matter, to include painting or sculpture in the curriculum. Proposals of that sort would surely have generated controversy among pragmatic legislators and trustees geared to the harsh realities of prairie life. Their chief interest lay in training Illinois youth in the most modern, efficacious methods of farming and what were known as the mechanic arts. The art department was confined to teaching basic freehand drawing and clay modeling courses to architecture and engineering students and remained a service facility well into the twentieth century.

How was it, then, that a fine arts gallery opened to the public less than a decade after the start in 1867 of the Illinois Industrial University, which became the University of Illinois?

With a profound commitment to the idea that appreciation of classical beauty enhanced life, Gregory assured trustees that the arts had played too important a part in civilization's history to necessitate "any new defense of their utility and power," and that the University would derive from the presence of an art collection "advantages and renown of no small extent." Attentive local audiences heard him tell of the incredible spread of art in New York and Boston and of how, if supporting funds could be raised, an Illinois museum would give Champaign and Urbana a "character abroad for art, genius and refinement, and in that respect [they] would stand ahead of the cities of the west." The student newspaper, the *Illini*, put it more bluntly: "The age no doubt is rapidly approaching when foreigners will no longer cry out against the supremely disgusting taste of Americans."[1]

By soliciting from area residents contributions that ultimately amounted to $3,000, and by traveling to Europe at his own expense, Gregory obtained 260 plaster casts of statues and busts, 286 photographs of famous paintings and Italian and Swiss scenes, 388 lithographed historical portraits, and an assortment of other art items.

Displayed in a large room in the west wing of the University's main building, the assemblage attracted press attention. The *Chicago Tribune*, for instance, reported that "the grand collection is now the largest west of New York," containing replicas of the best pieces in existence, while the *Illini* asserted that the gallery "will undoubtedly, in its ultimate and beneficial results, be found to be one of the most valuable" of all university facilities.[2]

sadly deteriorating remainder migrated to various campus locations. Surviving in what is now the William R. and Clarice V. Spurlock Museum are a number of small busts, photographs, photo engravings, lithographs, miscellaneous items, and ten casts, among them the *Laocoön*, *Apollo Belvedere*, and *Venus de Milo*. There are busts also in the University Library attic, the Armory, and the Modern Languages and Linguistics and Classics Libraries.

Over time, the atmosphere on campus changed. Starting in 1908, the four-member art faculty organized increasingly popular periodic loan exhibitions, often accompanied by lectures and sales, in the lobby of the newly built auditorium. These exhibitions stemmed directly from an administrative recommendation that "we might well try to do for our art interests somewhat the same kind of service which is being done for the musical interests," and the recognition that knowledge of art history and aesthetics related "to the general development of human culture."[3] In 1924, in what surely foretold increasing academic status and professionalism, the art department held its first annual faculty art exhibition. Until the nineteenth exhibition, in 1943, all members of the faculty could show their works; after that, only the College of Fine and Applied Arts members participated.

THE GRAND COLLECTION

IS NOW THE LARGEST WEST OF NEW YORK

Chicago Tribune, January 2, 1875

A phenomenal nationwide awakening in art came with 1920s prosperity. Galleries and museums grew in scope and number, American artists and regional themes gained greater recognition, and the search for an authentic modern American artistic style intensified. On campus, the impetus to collect came from a realignment of the University's aesthetic interests that culminated in a unified College of Fine and Applied Arts, the erection of a special building for "architecture and kindred subjects," and liberal appropriations (until the Great Depression hit) to purchase works for its own "small but high-class art gallery."[4] Architectural historian Rexford Newcomb, the College's first dean, did everything he could to enrich further the still modest collection. His commitment remained constant during the 23 years of his service.

With the art market developing and art collecting becoming more serious, attention everywhere turned not only to the original but to the rare, the novel, the unique, the irreplaceable.

The University's committee on art objects accepted nearly everything that came its way, even if a home for the works could not immediately be provided. Early important acquisitions included 39 Old Master and modern paintings that had been purchased during the Depression by alumni Emily N. and Merle J. Trees with a future gift to the University expressly in mind:

Far Eastern art donated by Mr. and Mrs. Spencer Ewing of Bloomington, Illinois; and the contents of Lorado Taft's Chicago studio purchased after the sculptor's death in 1936.

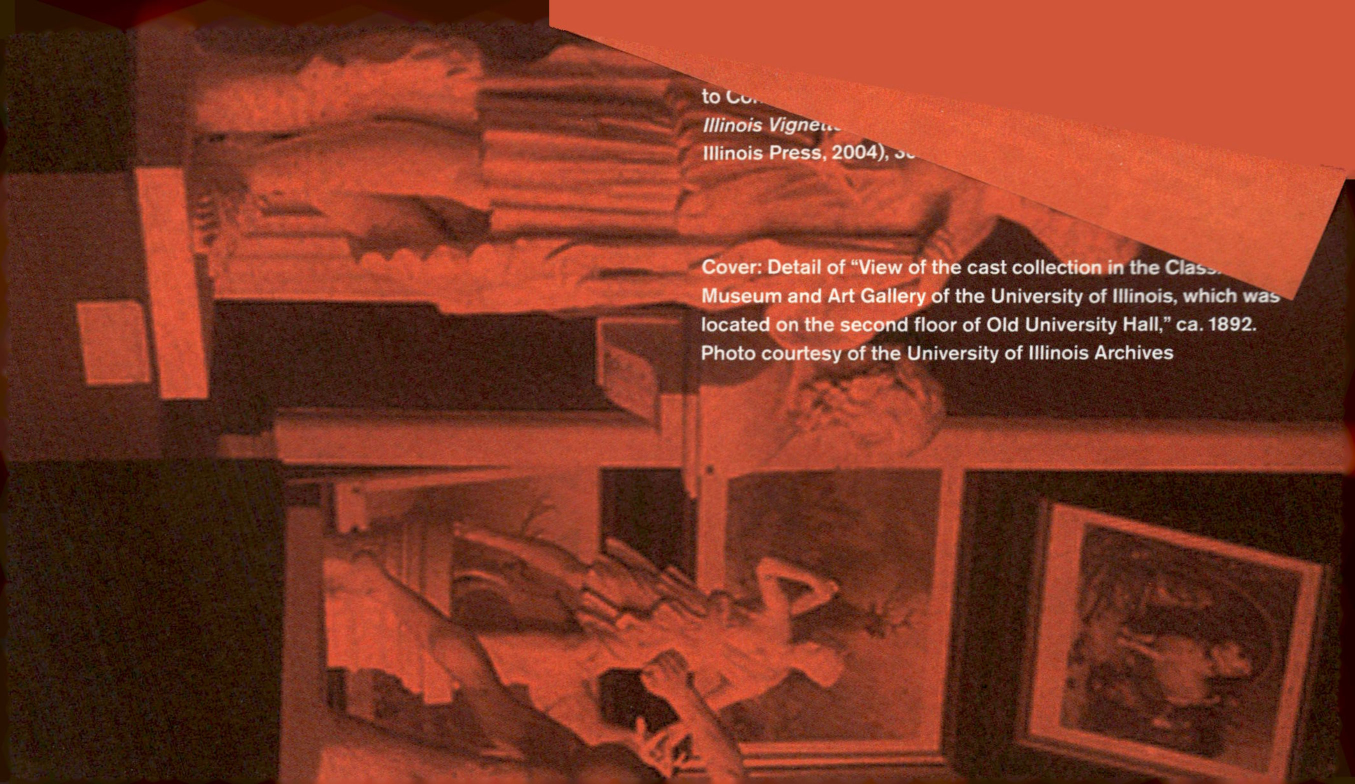

to Co…

Illinois Vignett…

Illinois Press, 2004), 3…

Cover: Detail of "View of the cast collection in the Class…
Museum and Art Gallery of the University of Illinois, which was
located on the second floor of Old University Hall," ca. 1892.
Photo courtesy of the University of Illinois Archives

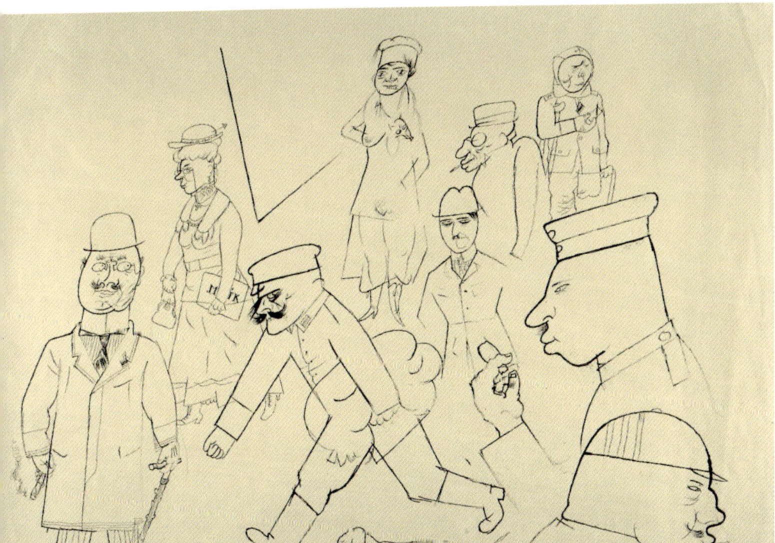

A contemporary of Juan Gris, Amedeo Modigliani, Pablo Picasso, and Diego Rivera, Jacques Lipchitz was a prominent member of the French avant-garde. Born in Druskieniki, Lithuania, in 1891 he moved to Paris, where he became the first sculptor to translate cubist principles into three dimensions.

Lipchitz's portrait of fashion designer Gabriele "Coco" Chanel (p. 180) was influenced by the neoclassical style that characterized much avant-garde art throughout Europe in the years following World War I. Critics often see French neoclassicism of the 1920s as a consequence of the war – the need to reestablish order by returning to tradition. Yet the motivations of individual artists were diverse. Lipchitz's Chanel incorporates neoclassical principles of harmony, naturalism, idealism, clarity, and simplicity, but it is not a reactionary return to classical training. The schematic modeling, for example, is indebted to cubism. Lipchitz's brief return to more naturalistic forms in the early 1920s is attributed no only to the vogue of neoclassicism but also his financial difficulties. After breaking with his art dealer, the artist turned to portraiture to secure a steady income.

Although Lipchitz always considered himself a sculptor first, he regularly made experimental drawings such as Krannert Art Museum's charcoal drawing (p. 181). The triangular shape at the top creates a frame that functions as both a window and a mirror, an ambiguity reminiscent of the work of Pablo Picasso. The figure simultaneously passes through the space and is reflected by the mirror, a doubling also found in the biomorphic compositions of Jean Arp. It is difficult to decipher the figure's attributes – elliptical forms can be read either as breasts or as eyes. This drawing underscores Lipchitz's interest in presenting complex spatial relationships in two dimensions. Eckhardt, Ritsma

(following pages)
Portrait of Mademoiselle Coco Chanel
1921
Plaster
13 1/2 × 8 1/2 inches
Gift of Jacques and Yulla Lipchitz Foundation
2001-18-1

Untitled
ca. 1927–29
Charcoal on paper
60 1/4 × 44 1/2 inches
Gift of Jacques and Yulla Lipchitz Foundation
2001-2-1

Jacques Lipchitz
France (born Lithuania)
1891–1973

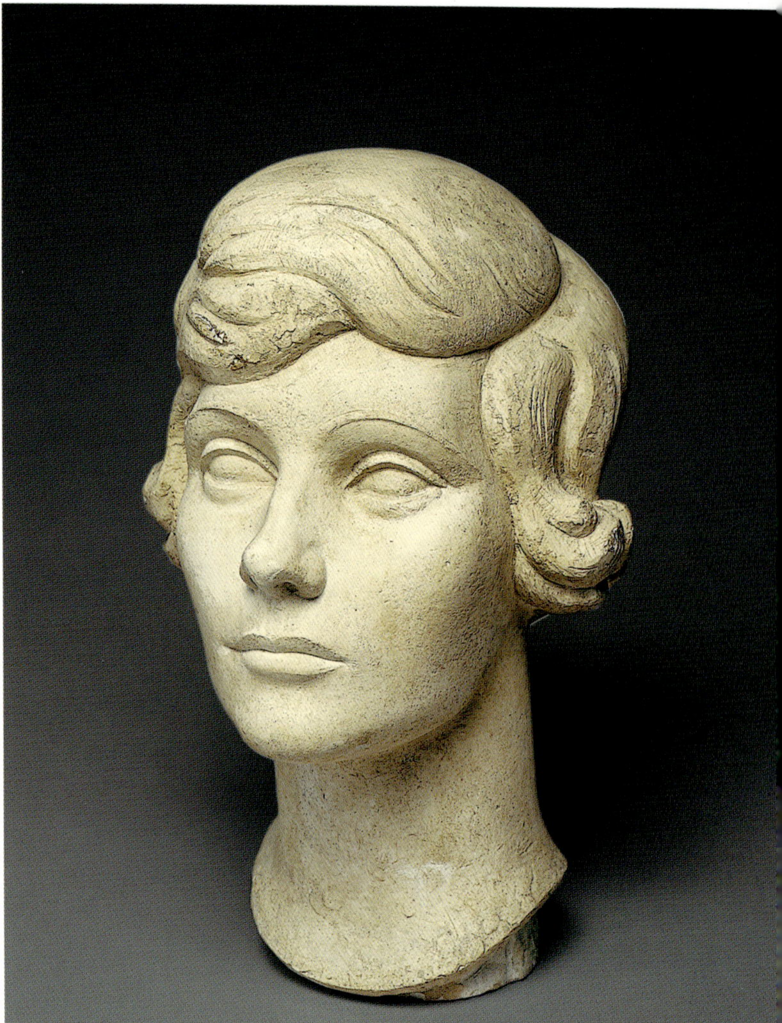

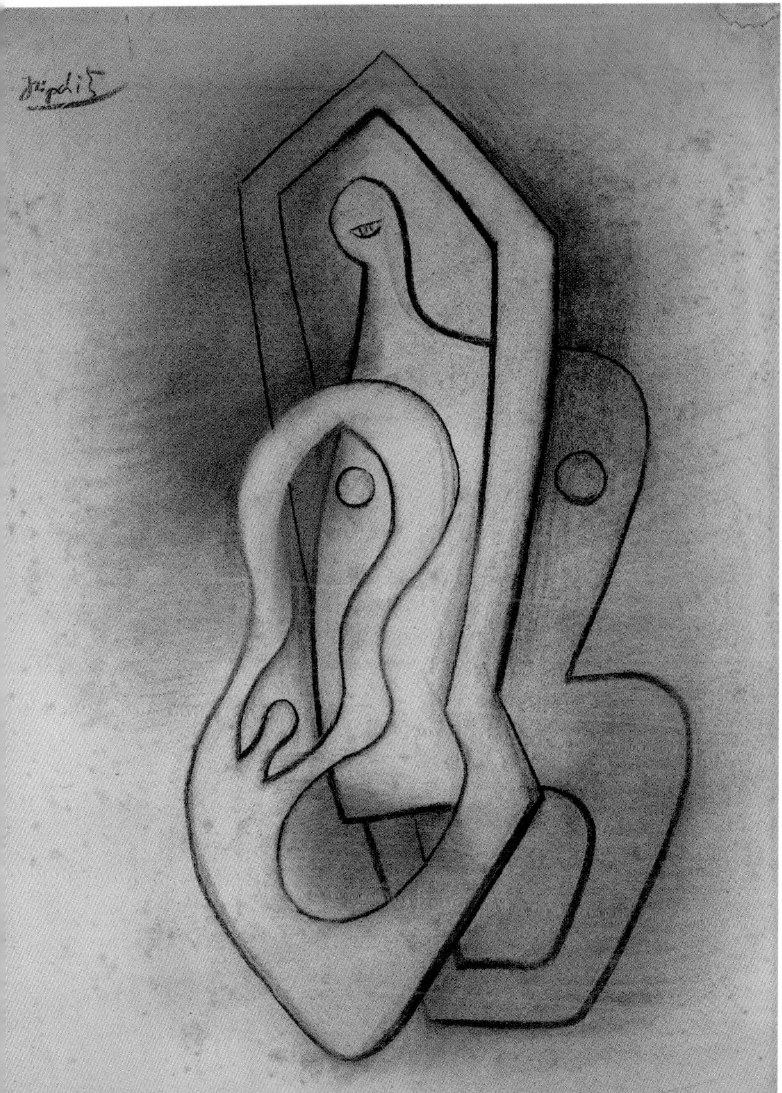

Portrait of Mademoiselle Coco Chanel
Untitled

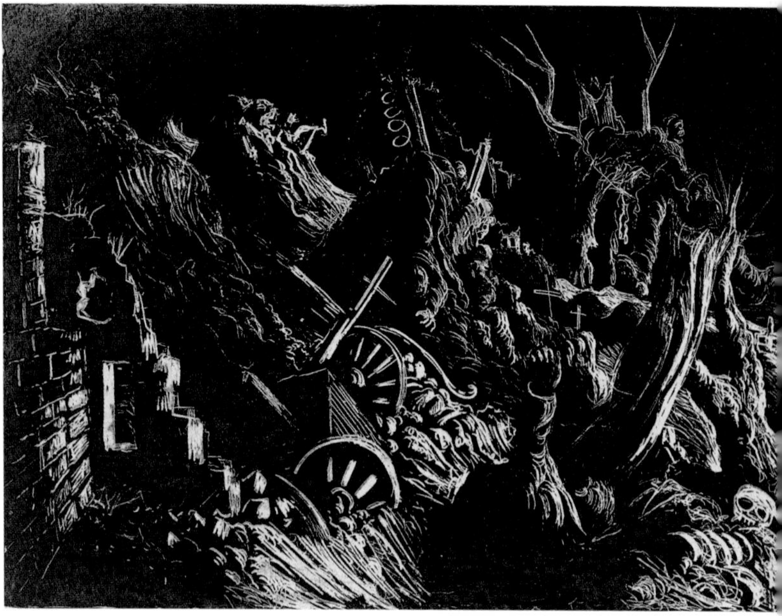

This etching is one of the 50 that comprise Otto Dix's most extensive graphic series, *The War*, produced in 1924, several years after the close of World War I. Dix had served as a machine gunner on the front and had seen and documented in drawings the horrors of war at close range. The *War* series was more detailed and realistic than his previous depictions of warfare, and more activist in intention. Along with other artists at that time, Dix was vehemently antiwar. In order to show its consequences, he studied Francisco Goya's *Los desastres de la guerra* (1863) and actual corpses and mummies to refresh his memories of six years earlier.

Known for his graphic descriptions of human suffering, in this etching Dix gives an intimate view of a post-battle landscape inspired by his own nightmares. The flare that gives the print its title illuminates the horror of a destroyed farm, the setting signified by a wooden plough. It is difficult to distinguish between the farm wreckage, bodies sprawled on the ground, and a blasted tree. Barnes

Otto Dix
Germany
1891–1969

Leuchtkugel erhellt die Monacu-Ferme
(Flare Lights Up Monacu Farm)
1924
Aquatint, etching
Image: 5 3/4 × 7 3/4 inches
Gift of Mr. and Mrs. Philip C. Goldstick
1984-43-14

Paul Klee is especially known for his reduction of people and things to evocative hieroglyphics. During the 1920s and early '30s, however, perhaps under the influence of the postwar movement in German art Die neue Sachlichkeit (New Objectivity), he made a significant number of drawings and prints of a more descriptive kind, among them *Bearded Man*. Stylistically, the lithograph reflects the artist's tenure at the Bauhaus. Klee taught at this experimental school of art, founded in Germany after World War I, from 1921 to 1931. The Bauhaus emphasis on system prompted him to give greater rigor and consistency to his works by limiting the variety of forms and techniques in each. *Bearded Man* is created entirely of short flecks, as if the figure were seen through a mist.

Except for his earliest etchings, prints were generally Klee's most inventive works. This is especially true of his lithographs, which for the most part reproduce existing drawings. Such a drawing has not been found for *Bearded Man*, but the quality of line in the short marks is similar to that of lithographs for which exact drawings exist. They suggest that the print was traced through a sheet coated with lithographic ink, either directly on the printing surface or, more probably, onto a second piece of paper that was used to transfer the image. Franciscono

Paul Klee
Switzerland
1879–1940

Bärtiger Mann (*Bearded Man*)
1925
Lithograph
Image: 8 3/4 × 6 inches
University of Illinois Purchase
1950-11-1

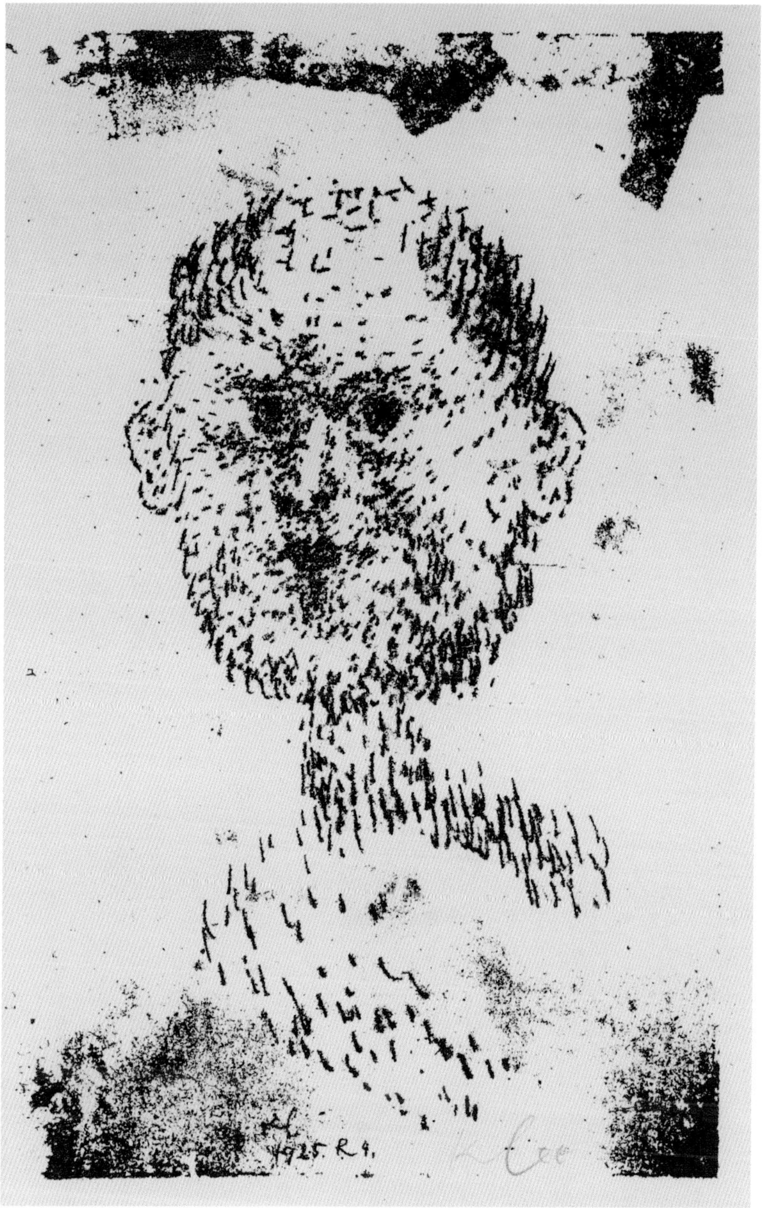
1925 R 4.
Klee

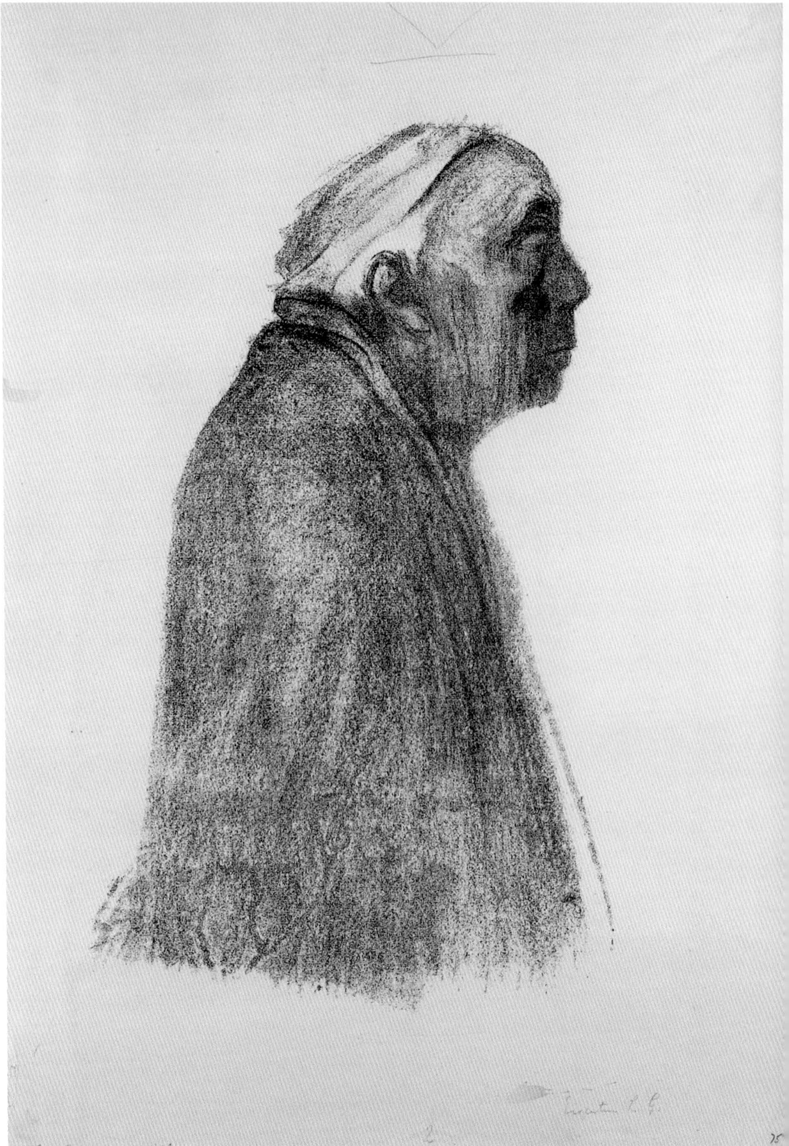
"LAST SELF PORTRAIT"

One of the best-known and most influential German printmakers of the twentieth century, Käthe Kollwitz devoted herself to the depiction of those oppressed by conflict and the affliction of war. Living most of her life in one of the poorest areas of Berlin, she was witness to the dire social and political events of the first half of the century.

Kollwitz realized early in her career that her strength was graphic, and she confined herself largely to prints and drawings in which color is absent. Her work in black and white reduces forms to essential components that heighten the dramatic gestures of her subjects. As a socialist and a mother, she identified passionately with the struggle of women to protect their children, and made it a major theme in her art. She often used herself to represent women suffering from material and emotional loss.

Kollwitz completed this self-portrait, the last in a long series spanning her career, when she was in her seventies and in poor health, and depicted herself with thinning white hair, a stooped physique, and a vacant expression. Dapper

Käthe Kollwitz
Germany
1867–1945

Self-Portrait
1938
Lithograph
Image: 18 3/4 × 11 1/2 inches
University of Illinois Purchase
1949-17-1

Max Beckmann, who is sometimes labeled an expressionist, is in some respects closer to Pablo Picasso. Like Picasso, he created a personal mythology by combining contemporary experience – private and public – with ancient myth. One of the rare landscapes in Beckmann's mature work, *Beaulieu* was painted in Amsterdam, where he had lived since fleeing Nazi Germany in 1937. We know from his diaries that the canvas, though it is small, cost him considerable effort. He began the canvas on May 24, 1947, and did not complete it until June 13.

Beaulieu is one of three paintings commemorating a vacation Beckmann and his wife took in Nice. It is based on a day trip they made by car to the village of Beaulieu-sur-Mer, east of Nice. The artist recalled that the outing was pleasant, yet characteristically he filled the scene with import. The picture includes glimpses of palms, an arcade, and the Mediterranean, but it provides little to identify the village. It is as much still life as landscape, and it has many of the characteristics of Beckmann's more overtly allegorical or symbolic paintings: a dense, compacted space; deeply saturated colors and dark shadows that belie the dazzling light of the Riviera; bold, free brushwork; and the massing of objects in such a way that their shapes and positions are obscured. This treatment gives common objects an air of mystery. On the table in the foreground are a cat, a flask of wine, and a plate with two red fish. These common motifs in Beckmann's paintings may have represented for him the life of the senses. Franciscono

Max Beckmann
Germany
1884–1950

Beaulieu
1947
Oil on canvas
31 3/4 × 39 1/2 inches
Festival of Arts Purchase Fund
1950-2-1

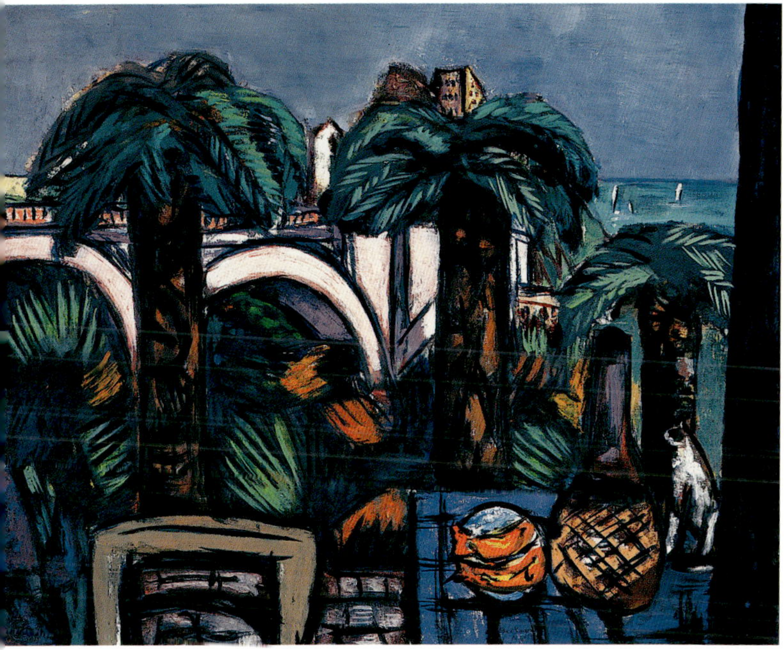

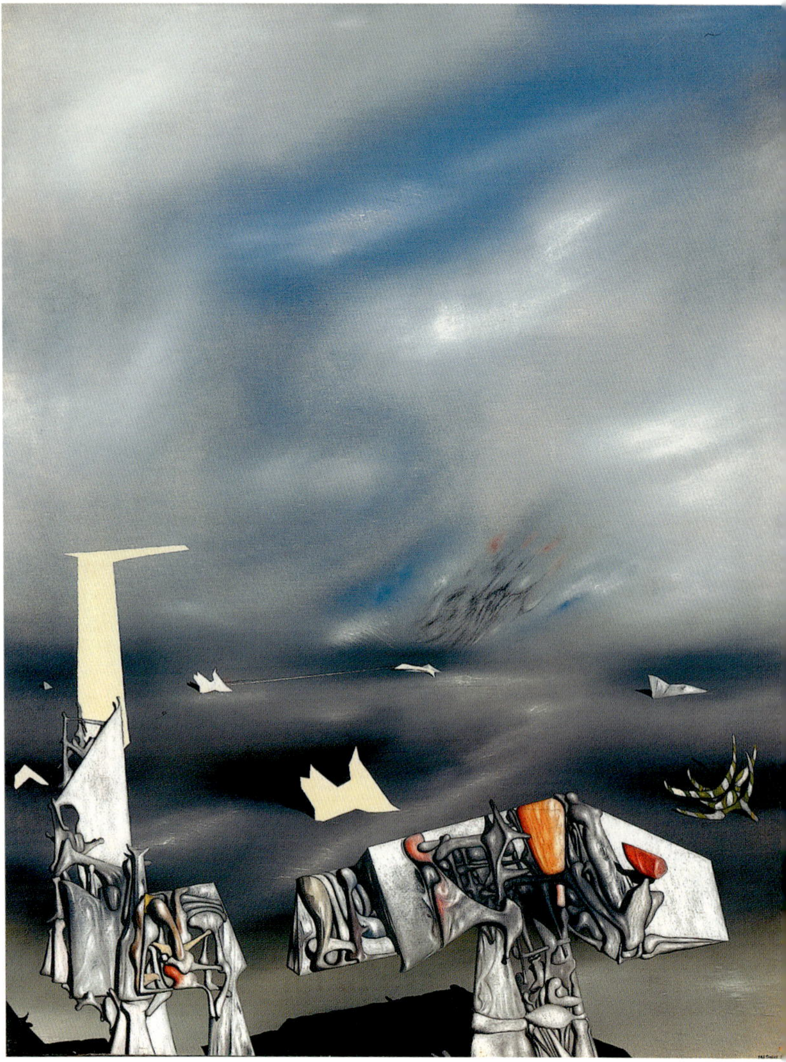

Yves Tanguy had no formal training, but was inspired to pursue art after seeing metaphysical work by Giorgio de Chirico in the window of Galerie Paul Guillaume in Paris. Responding to the eerie and dreamlike qualities of de Chirico's painting, Tanguy began conceiving his own mysterious pictorial worlds. In 1925 he met André Breton, leader of the surrealist group, and officially became a member. The surrealists sought to express in art their unconscious thoughts and desires. By the time of his first one-man exhibition at the Galerie Surréaliste in 1927, Tanguy had developed a distinctive vocabulary of mutating biomorphic forms and vaporous landscapes. He focused on landscape perhaps more than any of his surrealist contemporaries and, although his style changed throughout his career in Europe and after his immigration to the United States in 1940, his interest in the genre persisted.

In *Le malheur adoucit les pierres*, Tanguy presents the imaginings of the unconscious mind through a remote and peculiar landscape inhabited by unidentifiable geometric and amorphous forms. With a predominantly gray palette, the artist created an environment of indeterminate depth, vaguely delineated by a soft horizon line. A shape with a humanlike aura confronts the viewer in the central foreground, as if displaying outstretched limbs. The form suggests a menacing gatekeeper barring entrance to the realm beyond. Ominously pointed objects in the background intensify the atmosphere. The artist often generated his titles based on his research of subjects such as telepathy, clairvoyance, levitation, and other unexplainable spiritual phenomena. Although the title of this work cannot be construed literally, the artist evokes mental suffering and unconscious fears through the barren, seemingly post-apocalyptic landscape. Wolfskill

Le malheur adoucit les pierres
(*Suffering Softens Stones*)
1948
Oil on canvas

Yves Tanguy
France
1900–1955

36 × 28 inches
Festival of the Arts Purchase Fund
1949-9-1

Jacob Epstein began to study art while working at a bronze foundry in New York City. In 1902 he moved to Paris, enrolling at the École des Beaux-Arts. In Paris he took a particular interest in the ancient and primitive sculptures he saw at the museums, which were to influence his mature work. His later work was also indebted to the romantic sculpture of Auguste Rodin, whose studio he visited.

The artist launched his career in London, where his early public sculptures were controversial for their depictions of nudity and sexuality. For example, the 18 he created for the British Medical Association building were later removed and destroyed. Epstein's major works include the tomb of Oscar Wilde in Paris and several projects in England, including *St. Michael and the Devil*, a monumental bronze for the façade of Coventry Cathedral, which was rebuilt after the medieval edifice was destroyed by bombs during World War II.

Epstein is most highly regarded for his bronze portrait heads, executed with roughly textured surfaces reminiscent of those of Rodin. They include representations of Joseph Conrad, Albert Einstein, Jawaharlal Nehru, and Paul Robeson. This head of Wynne Godley, Epstein's son-in-law, is not only a portrait bust, but also a maquette, or study, for the head of St. Michael in the large bronze depicting the victory of the saint over the devil on the outer wall of Coventry Cathedral. Smith

Jacob Epstein
England
(born United States)
1880–1959

Head of Wynne Godley
1956
Bronze
20 × 12 inches
Festival of Arts Purchase Fund
1957-7-1

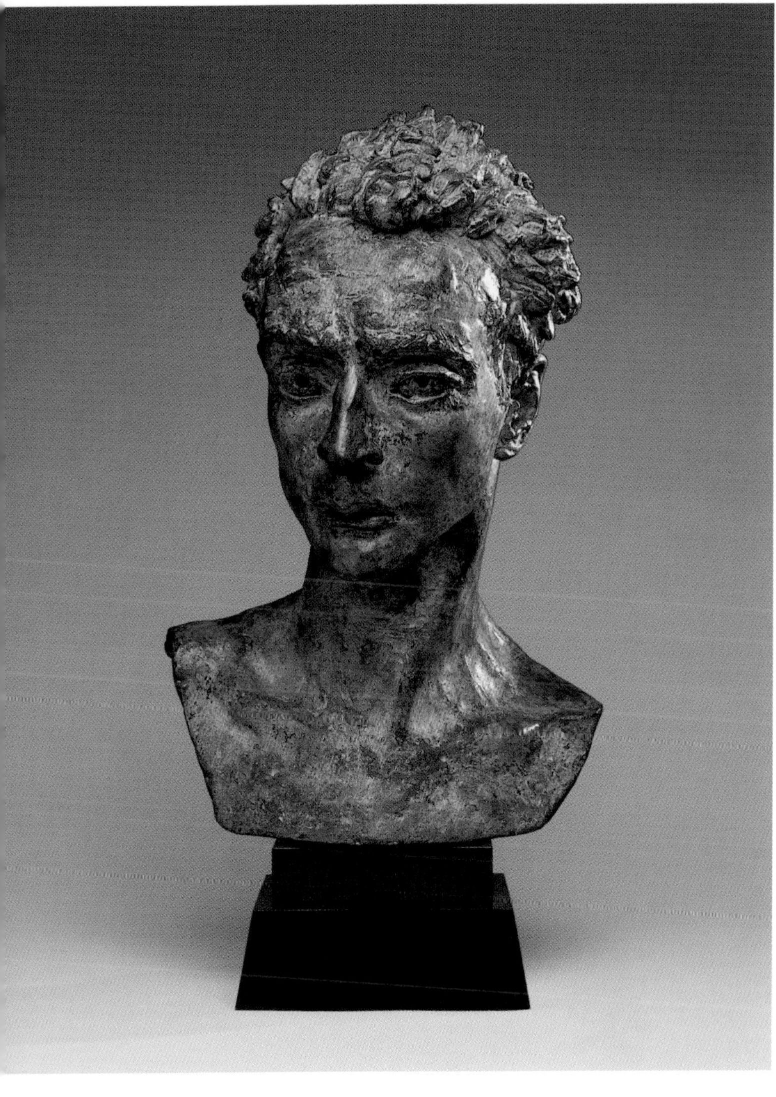

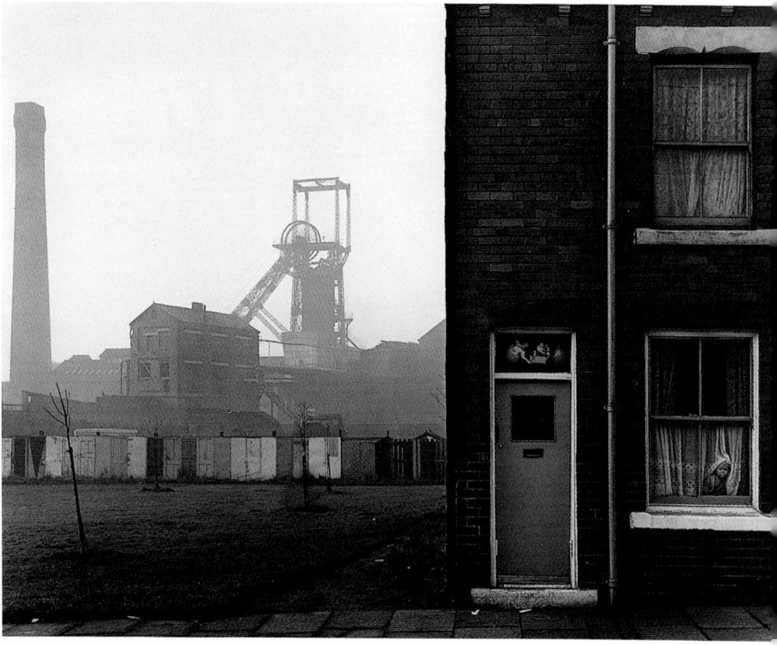

Castleford, in West Yorkshire, England, is an industrial town known for its collieries, bottle companies, and earthenware jar works. These industries dominate the lives of its inhabitants; fluctuations in the economy regularly put workers out of work. An effort is made to relieve the bleakness through gestures such as the planting of trees in side lots. The Christmas holiday is marked with a cutout of Father Christmas and a few balloons above the door.

Born on the Isle of Man, Chris Killip captured the daily existence of the sea coalers and miners, with whom he lived in the late 1970s and mid-'80s. Theirs is a life in which items are scrounged and recycled until they have no further use. The theme of survival in hostile environments pervades Killip's oeuvre.

As seen in the two series held by Krannert Art Museum, Killip functions as a biographer of his subjects. Images of such simple acts as eating, playing, or pursuing daily work produce a feeling of familiarity in the viewer. Many of his works contrast crisp lines in the foreground and the misty background seen here. By capturing, in this case, a child's longing and curiosity, Killip creates sympathy for the subject. Connelly

Chris Killip
England
born 1946

XMAS, Castleford,
N. E. England, 1976
1976
Silver gelatin print
Image: 11 × 13 1/4 inches
Art Acquisition Fund
1985-25-4

The child of Ukrainian Jews, Ilya Kabakov fled the Nazi invasion of the Ukraine in 1941 and began a life of displacement, exclusion, and exile. In the 1950s he studied graphic art and worked as a book illustrator under official Soviet patronage. During the 1960s and '70s he became a leader of a group of censored underground artists in Moscow that included Vitali Komar and Alexander Melamid, who also achieved recognition in the West. Kabakov moved to Paris in the late 1980s and to New York several years later, where he became known as the "father of Russian conceptualism."

Kabakov's works reflect his experience in the former Soviet Union, a modern superpower founded on the utopian ideals of Marxism, which eventually disintegrated. Absurdity and disjunction characterize his paintings and installations. He explores the distance between public and private life under Soviet rule; the disparity between Marxist ideals and the drab reality of daily life; the unique space in which "underground" artists existed, simultaneously cut off from official Soviet socialist realism and emerging postmodernism in the West; and the gap between the imagined Western audience and the disappointing first encounters with it.

Drawing on his own earlier graphic work as well as reflecting the ironic contradictions of Dada artists such as Marcel Duchamp and Man Ray, Kabakov in *Woman as Fountain: Courtyard Sculpture Project* proposed a waterless fountain in the shape of a woman for a future public sculpture. Mitchell

Ilya Iosifovich Kabakov
Ukraine
born 1933

Woman as Fountain:
Courtyard Sculpture Project
1998
Etching
24 × 18 inches
Sheldon Good Family
Charitable Foundation
2000-9-1

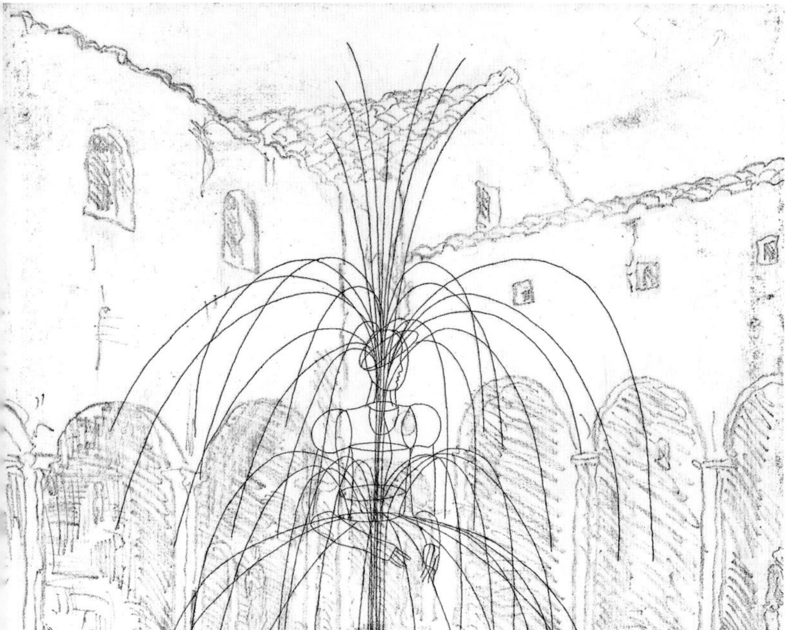

„Женщина-Фонтан" /фонтан из металлической проволоки/ /проект для двора./

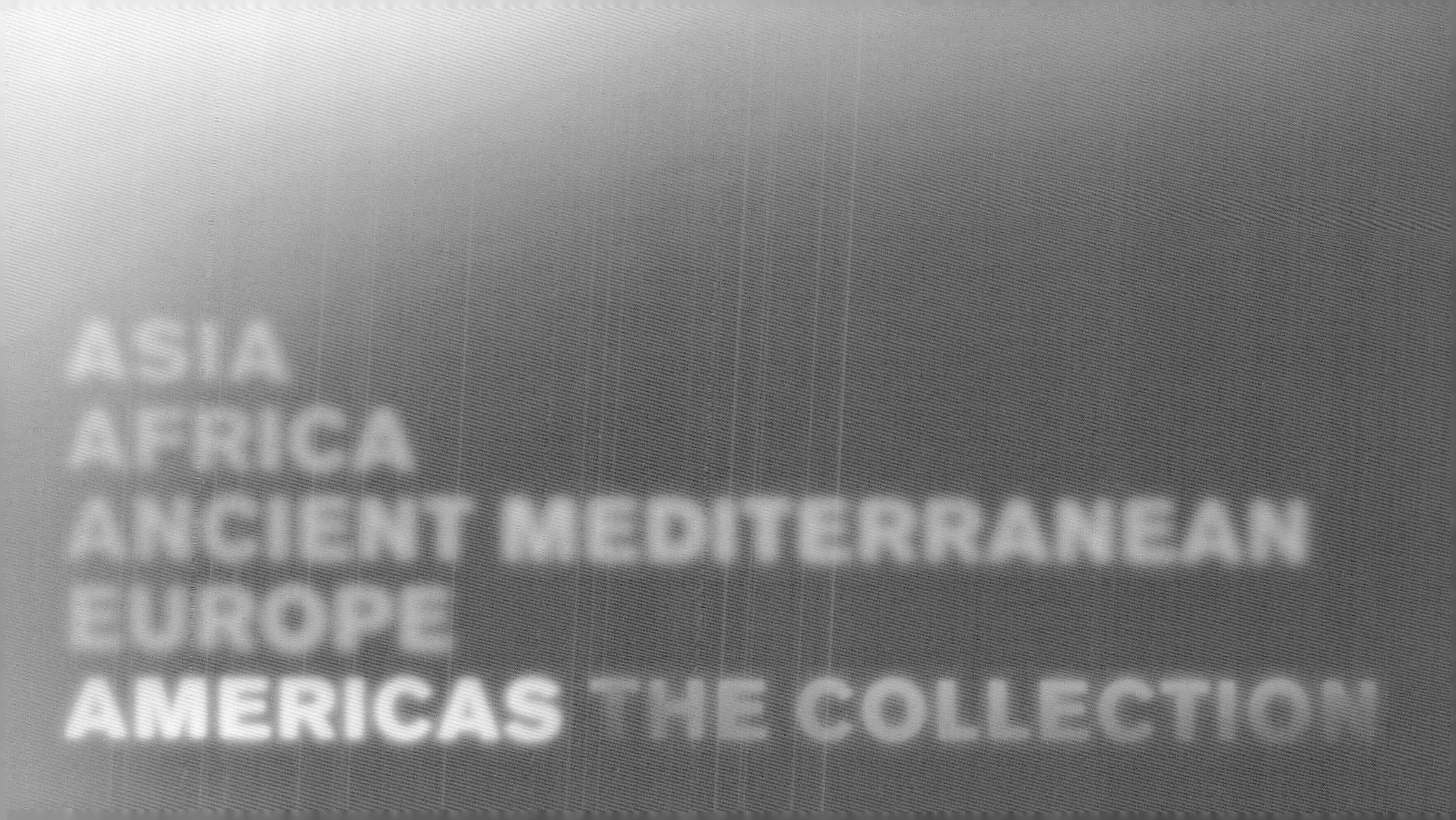
ASIA
AFRICA
ANCIENT MEDITERRANEAN
EUROPE
AMERICAS THE COLLECTION

The Nasca people, heirs to the South Coast Peruvian textile tradition, continued the well-established practice of wrapping and burying their dead in multiple large woven mantles. Mantles such as this, which is believed to date from early in the Nasca period (ca. 400 BCE–ca. 800 CE), demonstrate a high degree of technical skill and investment of labor. One can infer a strong connection between the number and quality of a deceased individual's burial shrouds and the status or social role that person had in life. Although little is known of the exact origin of this particular textile, its former owner was most likely a fairly high-ranking member of Nasca society.

The arid climate of the region accounts for the preservation of the textile's vivid color scheme. Embellished with a wool border of intricately detailed and alternately colored hummingbirds, the main body of the piece is composed of a single expanse of dark blue plain-weave cotton cloth. The hummingbirds were fashioned in a difficult embroidery technique sometimes referred to as needle-knitting or cross-knit looping. The cross-knit looping technique is indicative of the early Nasca stylistic phase.

The hummingbird design may have symbolic meaning. In nature, the birds are fast, agile, and very territorial; they will not hesitate to attack much larger birds that stray into their territory. Several ancient Peruvian artistic traditions draw an analogy between warriors and hummingbirds, and it may be that this mantle shrouded an important member of the warrior class. Jackson

Peru, Nasca
ca. 100 BCE

Detail of mantle with
hummingbird design
Cotton, alpaca wool
73 1/4 × 56 3/4 inches
Gift of Fred Olsen and
the Art Acquisition Fund
1967-29-56

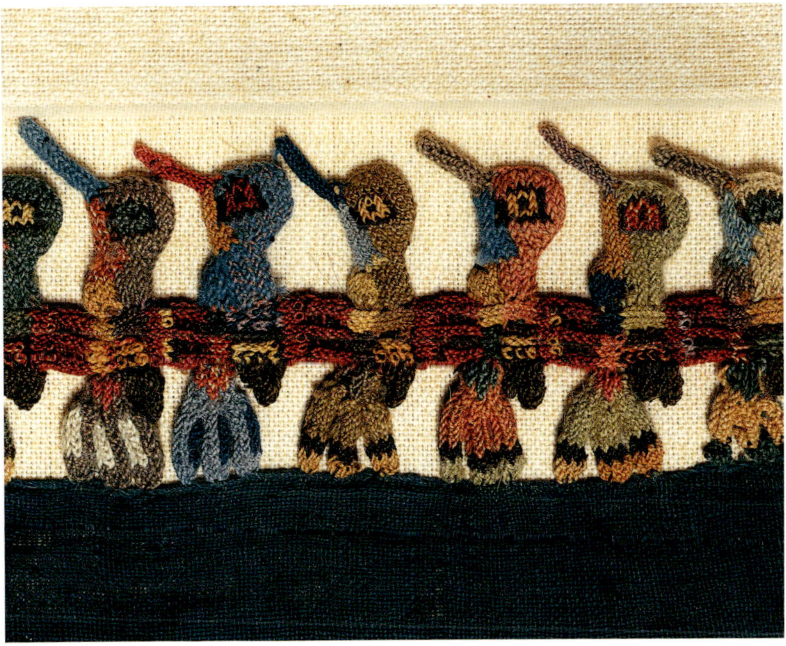

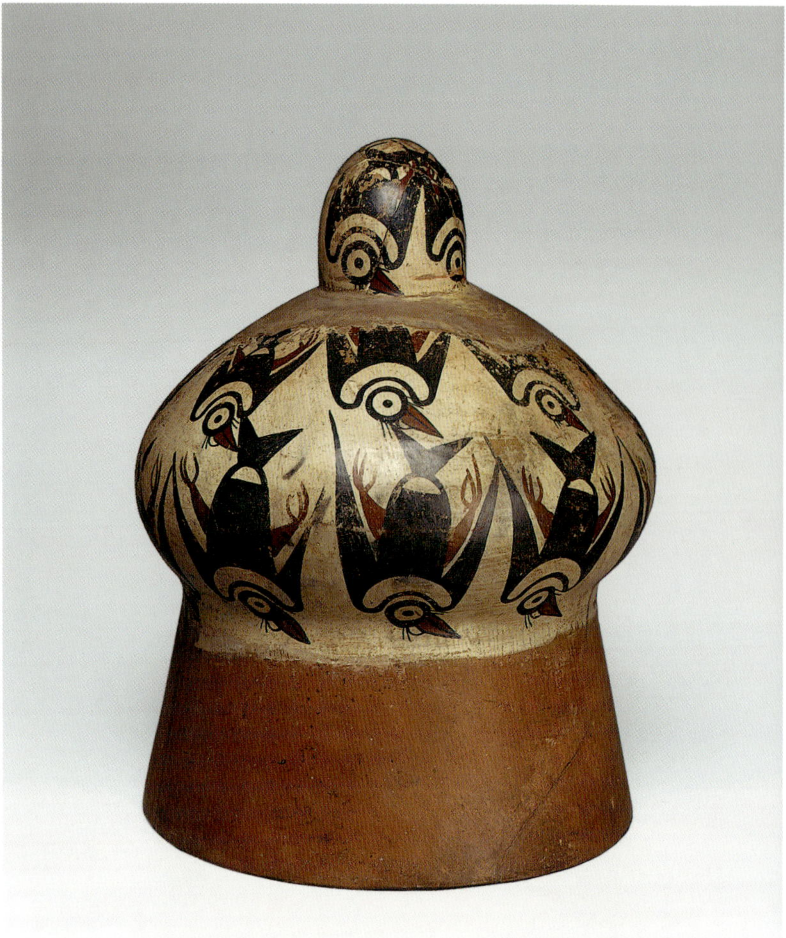

In ancient Peru, it was believed that the sound of flutes, songs, and drums drew the attention of the gods. Special ceremonial drums played a key role in the success of religious events among the Nasca people of the South Coast. This drum would originally have had a membrane stretched across its open end and, it seems, would have been played while being carried under the arm. Such easy portability would make the drum an ideal instrument for use during active ceremonial processions at sites like Cahuachi, the major site and capital of early Nasca culture, or out on the flat pampas, or lowlands, where the famous Nasca geoglyphs are located.

This ceremonial drum is decorated with a heavy layer of polychrome slip, or watered-down clay, and was originally burnished to a high sheen. The design is a pattern of white-collared swifts, migratory birds associated with the annual growing cycle. Agriculture in the arid Nasca region was crucially dependent on water flowing from the highlands during the rainy season. The appearance of the swifts heralded the coming of the growing season. Thus, their image on a ceremonial drum of this type is undoubtedly significant, suggesting the natural associations the drum may have had and the kind of ceremonies for which it may have been used.

Apart from its intrinsic value as a work of art, this drum is interesting for its unusual conservation history. At some point prior to its acquisition by Krannert Art Museum, the drum was broken and heavily restored. When layers of color began to separate from its surface, University of Illinois scholars, scientists, and conservators conducted extensive analyses to discover the extent of the reconstruction and to reverse its unnatural effects. The results of their work yield a more accurate view of how the artwork originally looked. Jackson

Peru, Nasca
ca. 100 BCE

Ceremonial drum
Terracotta, polychrome slip
18 3/4 × 15 inches in diameter
Gift of Fred Olsen and
the Art Acquisition Fund
1967-29-110

The Moche of the north coast of Peru are known for their monumental pyramids, temple complexes, murals, textiles, and metalwork. They are most famous, however, for their skill at creating elaborately modeled and painted ceramic vessels. Moche ceramics exhibit a realism, a succinct style of depiction, and well-developed artistic canons governing complex iconography in both sculptural and painted forms.

Moche artists favored sleek, volumetric forms that were finished by smoothing and polishing. Color was achieved through the application of cream- or terracotta-colored slip, or watered-down clay, and the very occasional use of black accents. This type of vessel is known as a stirrup spout because of the form of the looping spout. Although the precise origin of this particular bottle is unknown, it was probably part of a funerary offering in a tomb. Such vessels were reserved for special occasions and were most likely used to make ritual libations at Moche gatherings and ceremonies.

This piece combines sculptural modeling and abstract painted symbols. It not only depicts the shields and war clubs of Moche warriors but itself mimics the form of a round shield with a war club emerging from the top. Warfare appears to have been endemic to Moche society. Leadership was tied to prowess at handling arms and taking prisoners, and receiving rewards from offerings to various deities. Thus, warriors and warfare are often shown in close association with obviously religious activities. Such activities were often described in detail as pictorial narratives, but could also be shown in a more abbreviated, iconic manner, where the main protagonists are referred to by symbols alone. This example, with its images of shields and war clubs configured as animated bundles of weapons, references a more elaborate account of warfare, prisoner capture, sacrifice, and political legitimation through religious practice. Jackson

Peru, Moche IV
ca. 400

Stirrup spout bottle
Earthenware, pigment
9 3/4 × 8 3/4 inches
Gift of Fred Olsen and
the Art Acquisition Fund
1967-29-72

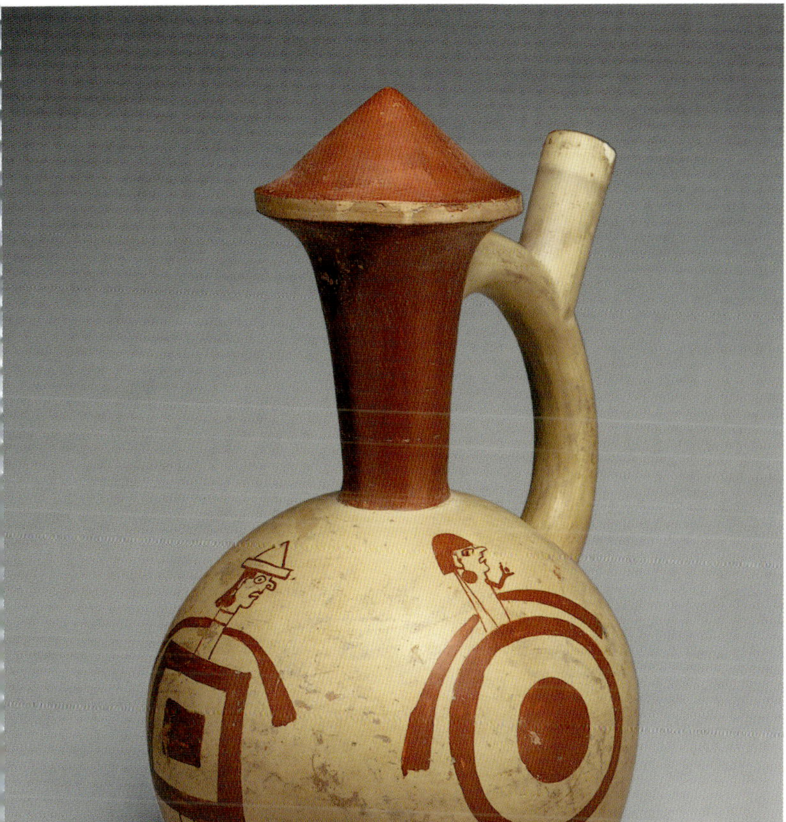

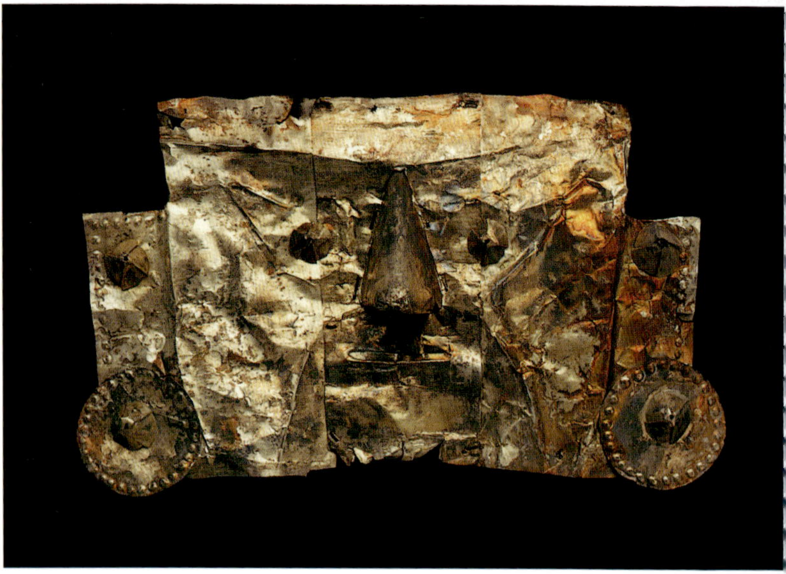

Like many ancient Andean cultures, the Chimú of the north coast of Peru typically buried their dead in an upright seated position wrapped in layers of textiles. Once wrapped, the deceased took on the aspect of a large bundle. Such bundles seem to have been the honored focal points of public ceremonies and rituals. As such, they were often decorated with paint, a funerary mask, and sometimes a headdress, garments, or jewelry. More humble burials employed ordinary textiles and simple decorations, which might have included a mask made of painted wood. High-status individuals, by right of wealth and birth, could claim the use of more precious materials, as in this gold mask.

Such masks were usually painted with red cinnabar, a mineral associated with funerary rites, though it is absent from this example. Feathers or textiles were often attached. Chimú artists were skilled in the gold *repoussé* technique, whereby a single piece of metal was hammered over a flat or textured form until it was uniformly transformed into a thin sheet bearing the impression of whatever surface was under it. In many cases, additional ornament was added in the form of dangling medallions, either tabbed or slotted into place, as is seen in the nose, eyes, and ear spools of this example.

This mask is clearly part of the larger Chimú tradition, the artistic canons of which include the use of flattened geometric shapes for the overall composition of the human face. The mask also exhibits the distinctive upturned teardrop eyes associated with the northern sphere of Chimú influence. The presence of this stylistic trait, closely related to the Lambayeque culture now known as Sicán, marks this mask as having originated within the Lambayeque region. Jackson

Peru, Chimú Lambayeque (Sicán)
ca. 700–1200

Mask
Gold
6 × 10 1/4 inches
Gift of Fred Olsen and the Art Acquisition Fund
1967-29-179

Among the most enigmatic of ancient Andean textile creations are three-dimensional textile sculptures like the central coast Chancay fruit tree shown here. The basic structure of the tree is made of cane, the trunk is wrapped in yellow cloth, and the branches are wound in yellow thread. Nine small needle-knit birds perch among the branches, whose tips have blossoms of red and yellow yarn. Green leaves and native beanlike fruits dangle from the branches. A figure stands at the top of the tree, holding a hooklike stick. Its face and eyes are made of tapestry weave and embroidered fabric, its body is stuffed with vegetable fiber, and its clothing is unadorned. Krannert Art Museum's collection also includes four additional figures that supposedly were originally attached, along with the tree, to a woven, padded base. The assembled group would have reenacted an event at a miniature scale. Three of the four figures seen here play Pan pipes, suggesting that the scene originally showed musicians playing while the tree was being harvested. Such an interpretation is in keeping with modern Andean harvest practices, which are sometimes marked by music and ritual offerings.

This model tree probably served as a funerary offering. Although its context is unknown, miniature tableaux made of wood, ceramic, and precious metal have been recovered from other late-period burials. In most cases, such miniatures depict ritual gatherings of individuals dancing, playing instruments, and engaged in other activities. As an object of funerary significance for those involved in ancestor worship, the gathering around the cultivated fruit tree may have symbolized the *ayllu*, or "extended clan," of the deceased, or possibly a future harvest in the afterlife. Jackson

Peru, Chancay
ca. 1000–1470

Model tree
Plain weave textile, thread,
yarn, cotton, reed
30 × 21 1/4 inches in diameter
Gift of Fred Olsen and
the Art Acquisition Fund
1967-29-309

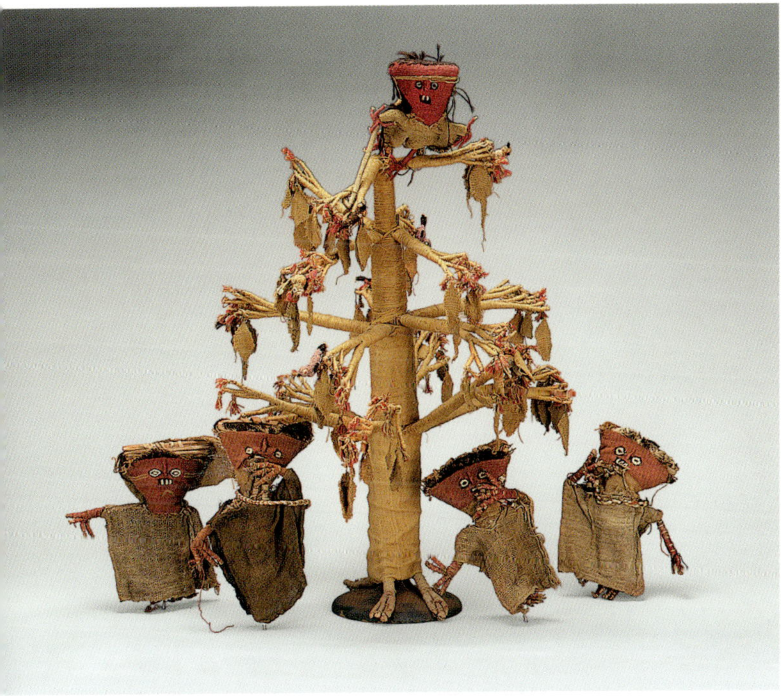

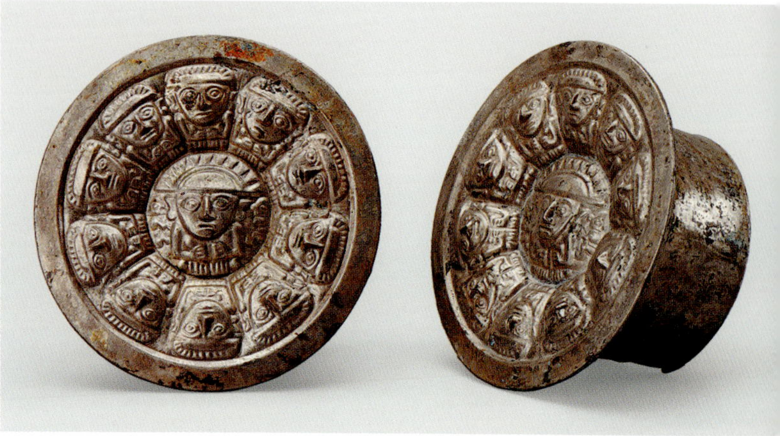

The Chimú elite expressed their wealth and status with elaborate personal adornment and jewelry, such as this pair of silver ear spools. The most extravagant examples of personal embellishment are associated with men, making it likely that these ear ornaments were owned by a nobleman. Such ear spools were still in use by Inca rulers at the time of the Spanish conquest in the early sixteenth century.

These large ear ornaments are made of lightweight silver. The metal received its detailed pattern by the *repoussé* technique, whereby a single piece of metal was hammered over a flat or textured form until it was uniformly transformed into a thin sheet bearing the impression of whatever surface was beneath it. The spools would have been held in the ears with cotton plugs inserted from behind.

Typical of Chimú art, the imagery here is stylized. Ten figures surround a larger central figure. The emphasis is on the face, headdress, and pose of the figures, as these hold the principal meaning. Each figure wears a distinctive rounded headdress topped by a variegated crescent, and ear spools. The remainder of the body is radically diminished. Nevertheless, the figures can be read as seated cross-legged, with their hands resting on their stomachs in a standardized gesture associated with veneration and ritual practice. The indication of breasts suggests that the figures are female. The central figure is flanked on either side by a crouched attendant, suggesting that she is of high rank. But since all wear essentially the same costume, it is equally possible that the figures represent the same person, social role, or entity. The Chimú venerated a moon goddess named Si, and had priestesses, some of whom wore ear spools like those worn by these figures. Females of high rank were sometimes the objects of Chimú veneration as well. Thus, the imagery may refer to the Chimú moon deity, the women who served her, or some other honored ancestor. Jackson

Peru, Chimú
ca. 1000–1470

Ear spools
Silver
Each 4 3/4 inches in diameter;
2 3/4 inches in depth
Gift of Fred Olsen and
the Art Acquisition Fund
1967-29-274a, 1967-29-274b

This silver miniature, identified as a funerary procession, depicts six human figures carrying a sedan chair and an oval casket. Although the chair and casket are vacant, we know from other works of art that even in death, high-status individuals were carried in sedan chairs like the one shown here.

The figures were constructed of multiple pieces of sheet silver joined through slotting, soldering, and crimping. They are sewn onto a fabric base that appears to be original, suggesting that the figures are still arranged in their intended configuration. Included in this arrangement is a small vase that today holds a single feather, raising the likelihood that the piece may have included other, more delicate materials now lost.

This type of tableau is tied to a larger tradition of commemorating ritual events in miniature. The custom is found in many cultures along the Peruvian coast. Funerary scenes found in the Chimú area tend to be made of ceramic or wood, while the central-coast Chancay are better known for their textile miniatures, the subject matter of which includes a wide variety of special events. Both cultures are known for their skill at metalworking. Elaborate miniature sculptural scenes found in context at the Huaca de la Luna (Temple of the Moon) in the Moche Valley in northern Peru suggest that Krannert Art Museum's silver funerary cortege may originally have been one of several scenes inside a single tomb.

The exact function of such artwork is not well understood. However, pictorial arrangements give an idea of how coastal Chancay and Chimú funerary rituals may have been conducted. It seems that the deceased would have been accompanied to the afterlife, at least symbolically, by an entourage engaged in the perpetual enactment of religious ritual. Jackson

Peru, Chimú-Chancay
ca. 1400

Model funerary cortege
Silvered copper, cloth-covered reed mat, silver gilding, feather
23 1/4 × 10 1/4 inches
Gift of Fred Olsen and the Art Acquisition Fund
1967-29-303

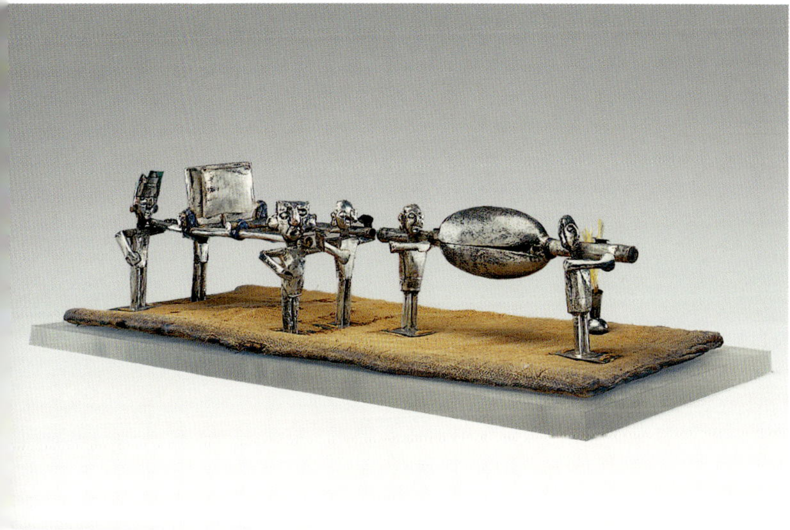

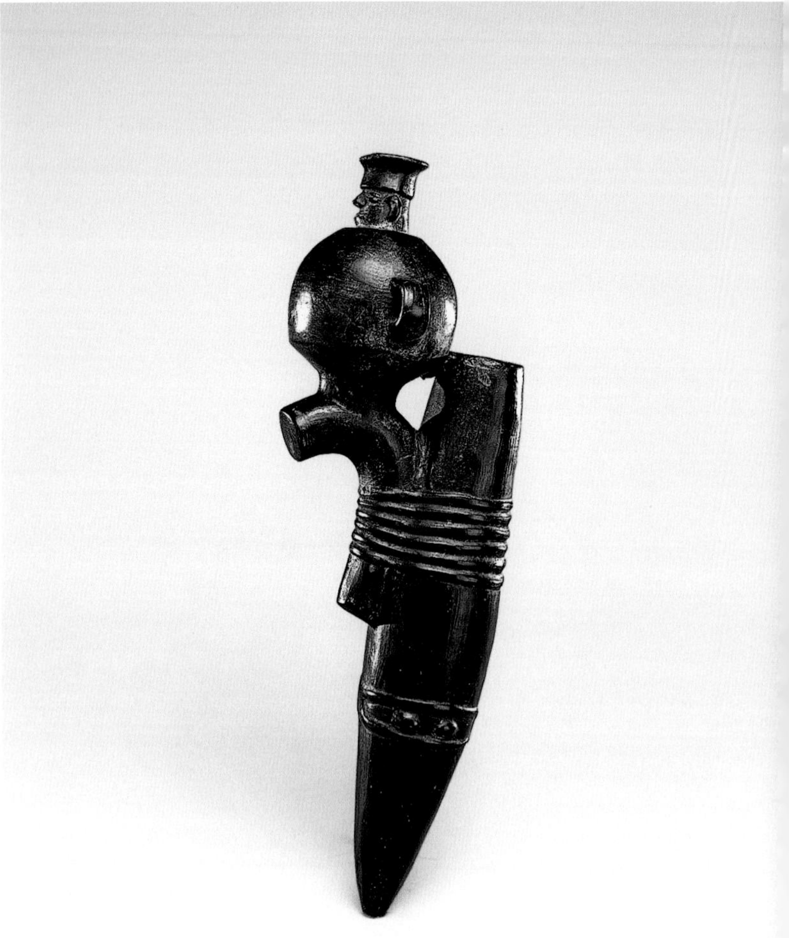

A true hybrid, this object unites the Peruvian north coastal Chimú ceramic style with particular forms associated with the highland Inca empire. It features a miniature globular vessel, known as an *aryballo*, perched atop a representation of a foot plough or *taklya*. This tool is still widely used in the highlands to break the soil for planting. Here it symbolizes the larger concept of planting and agricultural fertility. The *aryballo* is modified by the addition of a face press-molded onto the vessel's neck. The anthropomorphization of large-bodied vessels and the surface treatment of burnished blackware forms are coastal traditions of great antiquity.

Although this vessel was probably found in a funerary context, it is likely that the piece was originally used in a ritual or ceremonial context related to agriculture. A suggestion of the age-old custom of offering ritual libation to *Pachamama* (a fertility goddess called "Mother Earth") is implicit in this vessel. The miniature *aryballo* on top received liquid while a small hole in the tip of the foot plough released it, allowing the celebrant to easily distribute a small stream in any direction. Planting ceremonies, which are known to have been widespread in Inca culture and continue today in some regions, typically included playing music, drinking *chicha* (corn beer), and making offerings to *Pachamama* in hopes of a good harvest. Thus, in its function and meaning, the vessel's imagery is clearly self-referential. Jackson

Peru, Chimú
ca. 1470–1532

Digging vessel
Earthenware
16 1/2 × 6 1/2 inches
Gift of Fred Olsen and the Art Acquisition Fund
1967.20.223

As he set sail for England just before the American Revolution, John Singleton Copley was the most popular portrait painter in the American colonies. He quickly became one of the most respected painters in England as well, and was elected to the Royal Academy in 1776. This painting shows the artist's striking stylistic transition from his American work, such as the famous portrayal of Paul Revere (1768–70) at the Museum of Fine Arts, Boston. Squire Nathan Hyde's pose is relaxed and is described in softer lines. The classical allusions, such as the column in the background, reflect Copley's exposure to late-eighteenth-century neoclassicism, while the lighter colors and more fluent brushwork may show the influence of Sir Joshua Reynolds.

The sitter is attired in a richly trimmed green jacket and posed before a background of rose brocade, the base of a column, and a distant landscape. Perhaps, as has been suggested, the clothing and cloth backdrop served as an advertisement for the gentleman's textile company. The face and hands are painted in meticulous detail by means of glazing – the application of transparent color over a base color.

Copley's paintings of the Hyde family later traveled to the United States. Krannert Art Museum's portrait of Nathan Hyde was originally purchased for the Art Institute of Chicago. It was later sold, and Copley's portrait of Robert Hyde, Nathan's older brother, was bought as a replacement. Copley's portrait of Mrs. Robert Hyde is now in the collection of the Yale Center for British Art in New Haven. Smith

John Singleton Copley
United States
1738–1815

Squire Hyde of Hyde
1777
Oil on canvas
30 1/2 × 25 1/4 inches
Gift of Mr. and Mrs. Merle J. Trees
1945-1-1

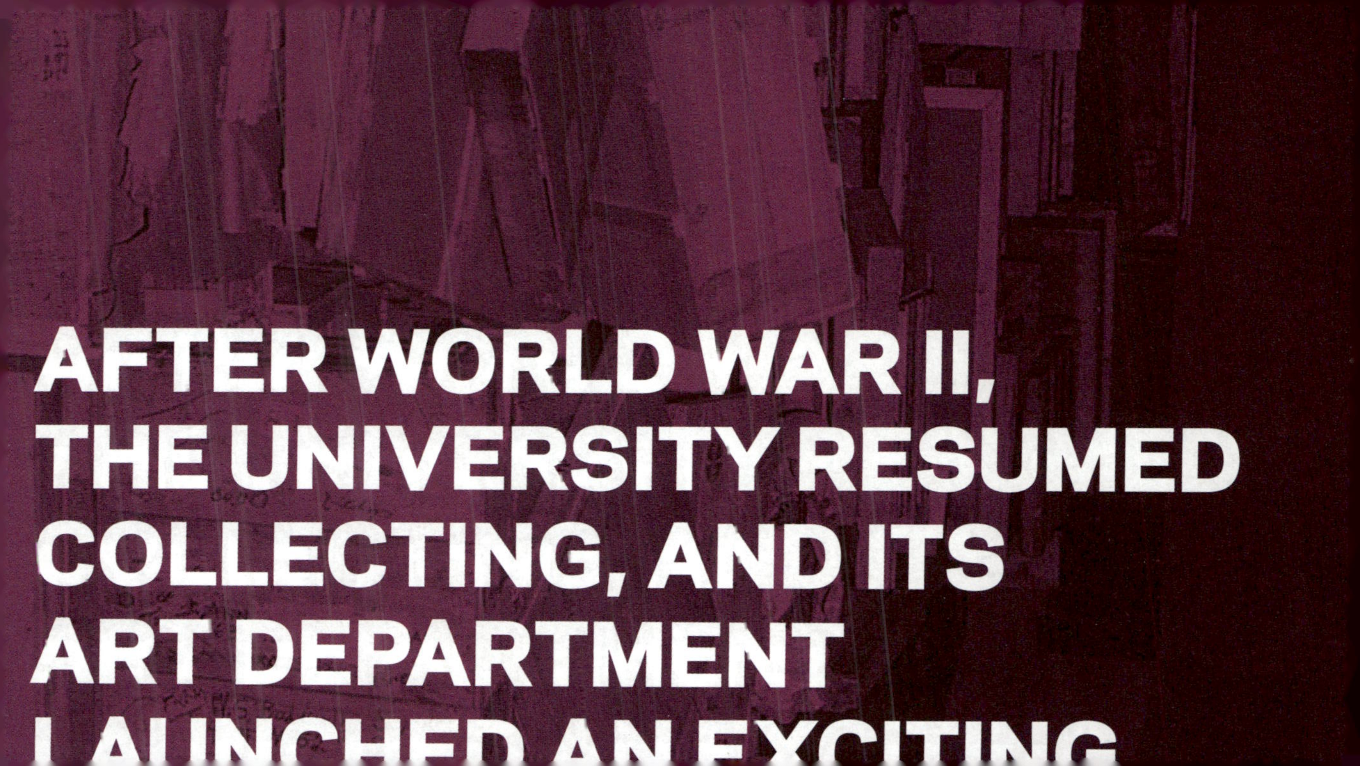

AFTER WORLD WAR II, THE UNIVERSITY RESUMED COLLECTING, AND ITS ART DEPARTMENT LAUNCHED AN EXCITING

LAUNCHED AN EXCITING
SERIES OF PIONEERING
EXHIBITIONS OF
CONTEMPORARY
AMERICAN ART.

a general, nationwide movement toward collecting and showing professional art at universities and colleges, the 30-member art faculty in 1947 urged resumption of its annual purchases of art. The distance from Chicago deterred students from seeing original current art except at infrequent intervals, department head Frank Roos pointed out to the dean, Rexford Newcomb. Proposing that the University run competitive annual or biennial exhibitions, on a grand scale, with sizable purchase awards, Roos noted that since no other university was mounting such a show, it would bring national attention in the art press and in the news columns as well. "We could, through such an exhibition," he asserted, "let the country know not only that we are here, but that we have a contribution to make in the development and knowledge of American culture. The mid-west State University has too long let the eastern endowed schools lead the way in such matters."[1]

Roos recommended that representative work from all phases of recent art should be shown, and the jury should be composed of "three top-notch men in the art field." An illustrated catalogue would list painters and prize winners and would include a historical essay on the relationship of art to higher education. "It would be desirable that the catalogue be regarded by the public at large, by those interested in art and by librarians, as a book," Roos wrote. Outstanding scholars and artists might be brought to campus to participate in roundtable or workshop discussions on American art. If they disagreed with one another about abstract art, so much the better. "The resultant publicity," according to Roos, "would again tell the country we are here."[2]

Funds would be obtained by putting to different use monies already requested for the 1947–48 budget: with the consent of the Carnegie Corporation, transferal of $4,000 it had given for a visiting artist; curtailment of programs and cutting of operational costs for the gallery by $2,800; and reduction of the $10,000 previously requested for the restitution of annual purchases in order to have $7,500 for purchase awards. "If we knew, sometime in May, that we could have the greenlight for the show," Roos added, "it could be held in November, next. If not, it would have to be postponed [until 1948]. Several members of the staff are so enthusiastic about the project that they have offered to curtail their vacation time to work on it, should it be approved."[3]

As might be expected, Newcomb found the proposals constructive, and good for students, staff, and the community in general. The new University president, George D. Stoddard (who in his former capacity as dean of the Graduate School of Iowa had closely supported the innovative programs of showing sponsored series of month-long "Festivals of Contemporary Arts" was initiated, for presentations (as it developed) in the fields of music, dance, theatre, film, architecture, landscape architecture, and urban planning, as well in the fine arts.

The first *University of Illinois Competitive Exhibition of Contemporary American Painting* was held February 29 through March 28, 1948.

Two thousand notices were sent out announcing the nationwide competition and calling for oil, egg tempera, or encaustic painting executed within the past three years; no watercolors, gouaches, or pastels would be considered. All works were to be framed and only one painting could be submitted by each artist. A three-man faculty jury visited New York City galleries and solicited 71 works by recognized artists. Because of the large purchase prizes, dealers had their best paintings out for examination. Another 73 acceptances came after winnowing by the faculty from an astonishing 953 entries.

As space was limited and the Krannert Art Museum did not materialize until 1961, the 144 works were hung in the Hall of Casts, in Room 120, and in the East Gallery of the Architecture Building. Thirty art professors and fifteen student volunteers became carpenters and clerks and attended to jobs of correspondence,

ACQUIRED: WORKS BY

BERENICE ABBOTT

LEONARD BASKIN

WILLIAM BAZIOTES pp. 280–82

MAX BECKMANN pp. 188–89

storage, hanging, and publicity. Newcomb later recalled the difficult logistics, telling Stoddard that "the first year we had 953 entries which nearly killed us off as each had to be uncrated, judged, recrated and shipped. We can accommodate only about 150 canvases at most."[4] From then on, all shows were invitationals.

Subjects extended to laborers and minorities; landscapes, seascapes, and urban scenes; portraits, nudes, and still lifes; the devastation of war and its aftermath; social, mythical, and religious images; and the inexplicable. Styles reflected tendencies then current or just beginning to emerge, from the naturalistic to the abstract, the cubist, the surrealistic, the nonobjective, and the expressionistic. Among better-known artists whose works appeared were Max Ernst, Phillip Evergood, Adolph Gottlieb, Hans Hofmann, Edward Hopper, Alexander Brook, Walt Kuhn, Yasuo Kuniyoshi, Jack Levine, John Marin, Lázló Moholy-Nagy, I. Rice Pereira, Philip Guston, Abraham Rattner, Karl Knaths, Eugene Speicher, Andrew Wyeth, and Max Weber.

The costs for the entire venture amounted to $14,137.49. Purchase awards totaling $7,500 made it possible for the University to acquire ten paintings constituting a cross-section of prevailing major trends.

An outside jury selected the winners, a practice that ended

EUGENE
BERMAN

JAMES
BROOKS

CHARLES
BURCHFIELD pp. 278–79

JACOB
EPSTEIN pp. 192–93

Hofmann's *The Third Hand*, an early manifestation of the abstract expressionistic style and probably the most controversial object in the first show, was not chosen. The University acquired one of his important and valued paintings, *Apparition*, in the third show.

A slightly defensive note, perhaps anticipating public misunderstanding or rejection of the more extreme works, can be discerned in statements written for the first exhibition catalogue. President Stoddard maintained that "a work of art, however unique, possesses qualities related to the time and place in which it was produced. [Artworks] are the product of the artists and the times – and either (or both) may be out of joint. They carry psychological and sociological meaning. They may well arouse visitors to a degree of self-analysis, or even revolt. In this way the spectator becomes, in a measure, creative in his own right. In short, we trust that the paintings in their total impact will enlarge the insight and experience of all concerned."[5]

Dean Newcomb spoke of the sampling process necessary to put together a varied and thought-provoking exhibition, and noted how appropriate it was that the University should recognize not only "established reputations, but that it should also encourage and acquire for its permanent collection the work of new and vigorous talents."[6]

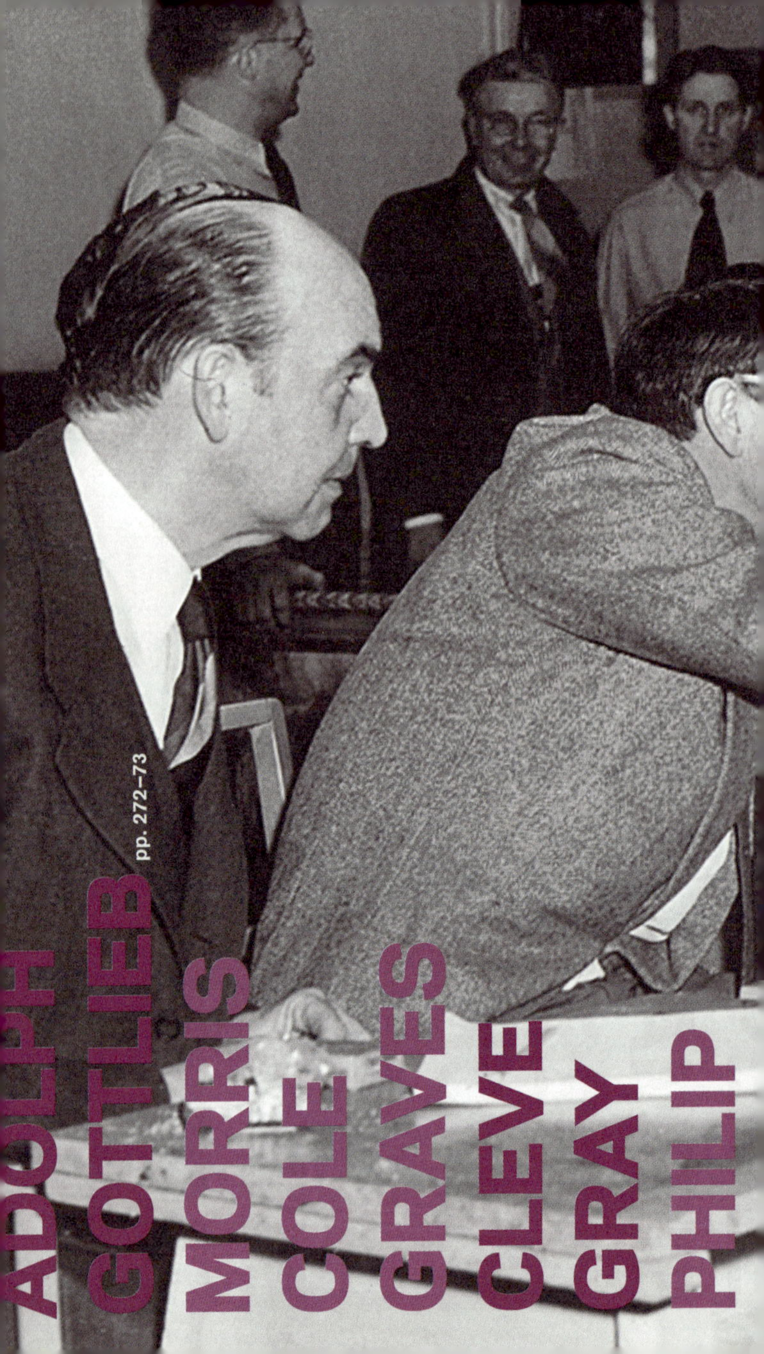

pp. 272–73

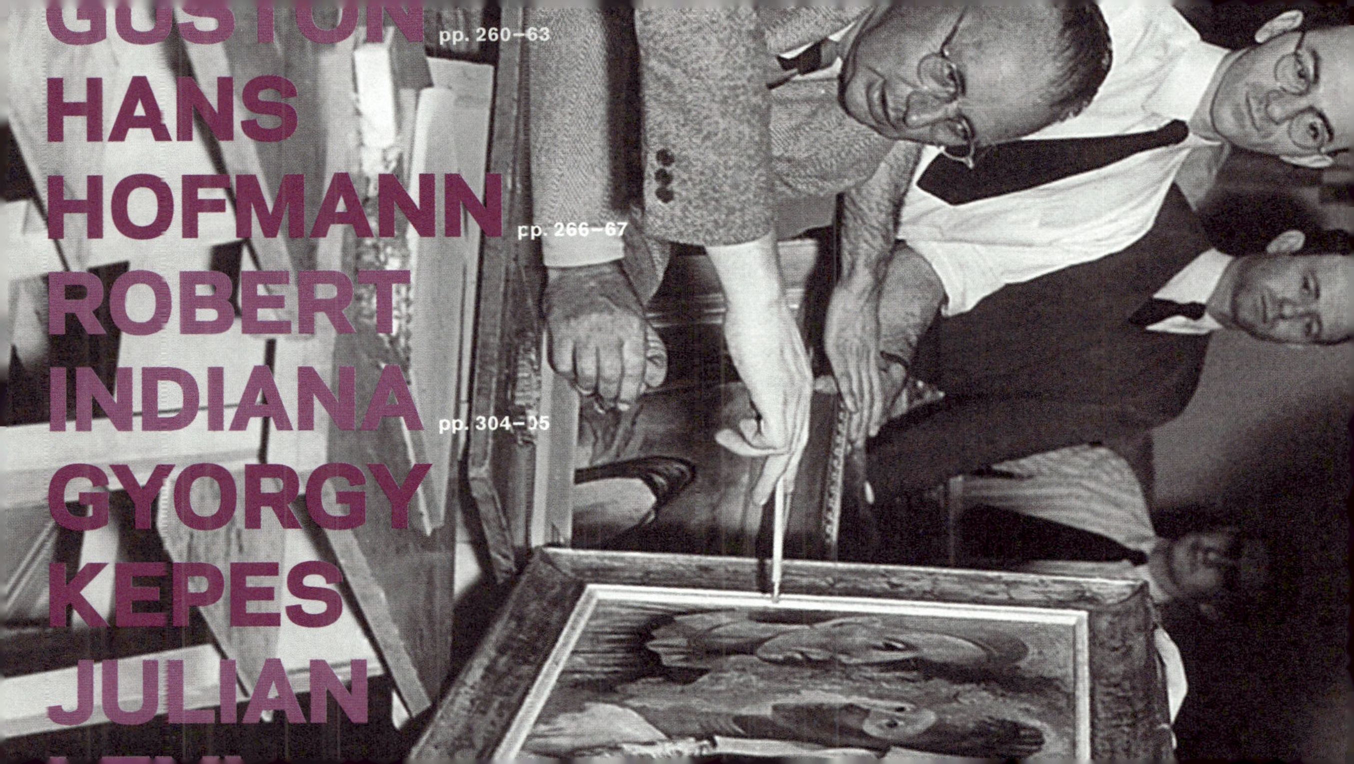

LEVI
SOL
LEWITT pp. 312–13
MATTA pp. 280–81, 283
DAVID
PARK pp. 292–93
THEODORE
ROSZAK

Frank Roos and Allen Weller (who prominently figured in all the shows and served as dean after Newcomb retired) placed the selections in context, reminding the reader of the University's emergence as a special kind of art collector, one that could illuminate technical and humanistic teaching and display for a larger audience the vital and experimental directions of current art. "Progress can only be achieved through change and evolution," they proclaimed. "Controversy is inherent in the idea of change. This exhibition should give rise to much healthy controversy."[7]

How times had changed since Regent Gregory assembled – for a not very enduring public – his carefully chosen collection of authenticated ancient masterpieces in plaster casts, which he believed would suffice in every way to educate in as good stead as the originals. Organizers of the 1948 show, by contrast, put up works they knew might seem "disjointed and lacking in clarity," reflecting chaotic conditions and unresolved "conflicts of existence."

Whether one regarded the paintings as conservative or radical, the exhibition guaranteed that a range of styles and art movements would reach a diverse audience.

Journalists, professionals in the art field, and the public came to

PETER SAUL pp. 314–17

KURT SELIGMANN pp. 284–85

BEN SHAHN pp. 290–91

AARON SISKIND

exhibition was the second most lucrative show (after Pittsburgh's Carnegie) in the nation. Peyton Boswell of the *Art Digest* said the exhibition "attained in its initial presentation the status of national importance," adding that "within the state's borders, it gives the Chicago Art Institute its first serious competition." By the time of the 1952 festival, the *Chicago Herald American* critic Copeland Berg noted that Urbana "now not only lead[s] all universities surpassing even Iowa and Nebraska, which formerly held top honors, but is rated above the exhibitions of all museums in the country." He also wondered why the Illinois president and trustees willingly spent "thousands and thousands of dollars on art, while the University of Chicago and Northwestern University, both richer than rich, spend practically nothing and neither has had any exhibitions of any consequence compared with the Illinois show."[8]

The jury of the initial exhibition thought the pictures would prove a good financial investment and that students would find the exhibition of tremendous cultural value. Roos told reporters that "if any part of the exhibit gives anyone 'aesthetic indigestion,' it is the same reflection of life as that which will give anyone indigestion over a third or fourth political party." Fran Myers of the *News-Gazette* observed that some paintings belonged to the old school, while others were the latest in abstraction. Still other

HEDDA STERNE pp. 286–87
RUFINO TAMAYO
YVES TANGUY pp. 190–91
BRADLEY WALKER

works left the layman asking, "What is it?" Myers wondered if another visit would make the art more comprehensible. "The show is the 'new look' in art," she concluded. The art critic of the *New York Times*, Howard Devree, who came to campus to lecture, labeled as "utterly absurd" the condemnation of a work not understood, and said that the show was a good example of experimental "and therefore the healthy" aspects of contemporary art. But a student, Bob Wilbert, writing in the *Daily Illini*, disagreed: "Representative to the point of being wishy-washy, the show should make enemies of no one. By the same token, the exhibit cannot be heralded as the champion of the art 'isms' and will make no real friend in the art world."[9]

Attendance was recorded as high: Nearly 10,000 persons viewed the first show during its month of display; 35 groups of from 20 to 120 people came from all over the state and the region. Faculty members and prominent visiting artists and critics gave lively gallery talks and illustrated lectures. The public voted for their favorite paintings (it made no difference; all choices for purchase had been made before opening day). Speicher's stalwart *Farmer* proved most popular. Trailing closely behind was Wyeth's standing figure of a woman in the painting, *Afternoon*. Art students preferred two of the more avant-garde works, Hazel Janicki Tovrel's

TOMLIN
PETER
VOULKOS

biomorphic fantasy, *Labyrinth*. Of these four, only the Teyral was among the ten bought for the permanent collection.

In all, the University held 15 Contemporary Arts Festivals over a period of 26 years, the first six annually.

Starting in 1953 (when sculptures began to be shown too), shows were held biennially because of the extraordinary amount of time required to organize them and because of financial inadequacies. Prohibitive insurance costs in the early 1970s and the realization that it no longer seemed imperative to mount special shows of vanguard art – such exhibitions were held routinely by then – brought the series to a close in 1974.[10]

What had been accomplished? Comprehensive illustrated exhibition catalogues containing artists' statements, biographical information, and insightful introductory essays by Dean Weller reached an even wider audience than those actually attending the shows through dissemination by galleries, collectors, and later the Krannert Art Museum. Even the U.S. Department of State, on several occasions, distributed them overseas. Over the years, a curious, receptive public had enjoyed not only a series of provocative art exhibitions and lectures, but a variety of entertaining modern dance recitals, new music concerts, film screenings and theatrical presentations, and special events in literature, radio, and television.

Over one thousand different artists exhibited a total of 2,036 works. From the first nine shows, the $7,500 allotted for each was sufficient to obtain a total of 76 paintings and sculptures for the collection.

After that, supplementary nonrecurring funds frequently became necessary to balance the budget. A record high of $20,280 in 1963, for example, could buy only four now price-inflated art objects. The last exhibition yielded just two: James Prestini's nickel-plated steel *Construction #216* and William Wiley's large-scale abstract acrylic and watercolor canvas *Spirit Line*.

In all, 98 notable works of art swelled the University's holdings. Eminent artists, many of whose works accrued significantly in value since being acquired, include Kurt Seligmann, Hans Hofmann, Yves Tanguy, Ben Shahn, Max Beckmann, Abraham Rattner, William Baziotes, Adolph Gottlieb, Rufino Tamayo, Morris Graves, Leonard Baskin, Charles Burchfield, Loren MacIver, Philip Guston, David Park, Matta, Stuart Davis, James Brooks, Robert Indiana, Peter Saul, and Sol LeWitt.

Controversial art given public exposure by a prestigious educational institution engendered a serious interest in a rich credibility to the worth of American artistic production. Greater numbers of prospective art students nationwide applied for admission to the art department's graduate programs. The idea of universities as legitimate, active patrons of art gained momentum.

In his last report as dean (1970–71), Weller summed up the benefits of the University's support of the arts. He noted that it had been his great good fortune to serve "during a period of expansion, when new ideas and programs were welcomed by the sympathetic attention of the central administration, when new facilities were provided for parts of the College, and when funding was granted for some of the many requests and programs which originated within the departments. At times it seemed as if all we could was to simply keep up with the burdens imposed by increased enrollments, but important educational developments and innovations were also accomplished."[11]

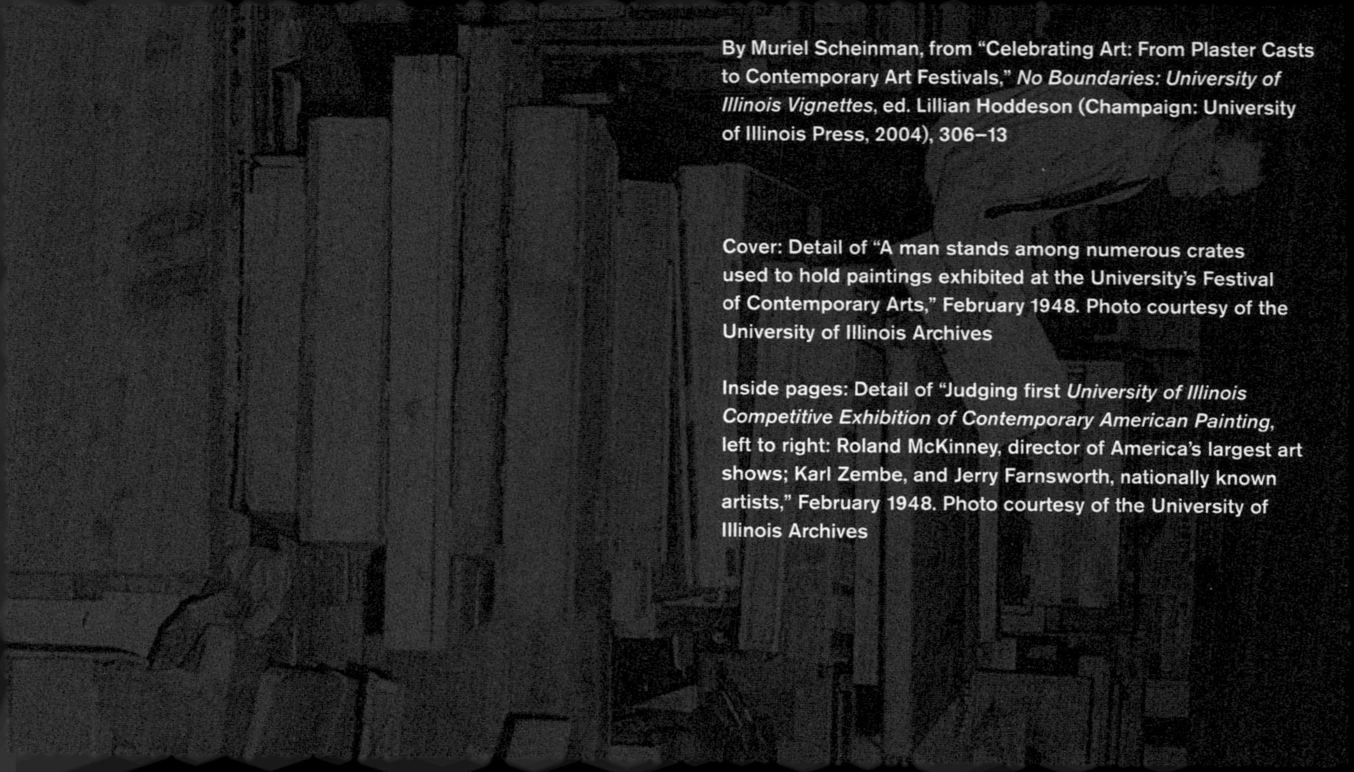

By Muriel Scheinman, from "Celebrating Art: From Plaster Casts to Contemporary Art Festivals," *No Boundaries: University of Illinois Vignettes*, ed. Lillian Hoddeson (Champaign: University of Illinois Press, 2004), 306–13

Cover: Detail of "A man stands among numerous crates used to hold paintings exhibited at the University's Festival of Contemporary Arts," February 1948. Photo courtesy of the University of Illinois Archives

Inside pages: Detail of "Judging first *University of Illinois Competitive Exhibition of Contemporary American Painting*, left to right: Roland McKinney, director of America's largest art shows; Karl Zembe, and Jerry Farnsworth, nationally known artists," February 1948. Photo courtesy of the University of Illinois Archives

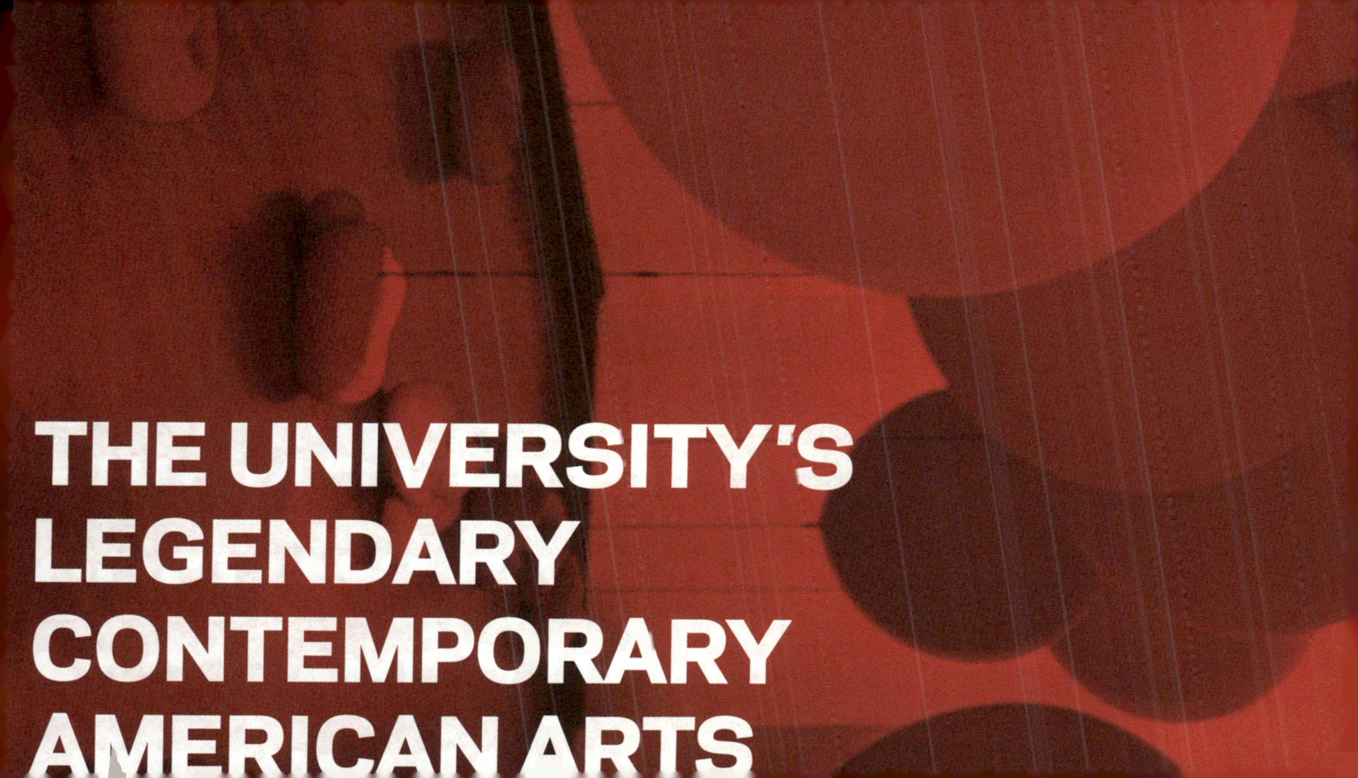
THE UNIVERSITY'S
LEGENDARY
CONTEMPORARY
AMERICAN ARTS

AMERICAN ARTS
FESTIVALS (1948–74)
CULTIVATED A DIALOGUE
AMONG ARTISTS,
CURATORS, AND
COLLECTORS AND LAID
THE FOUNDATION FOR THE
ONGOING COMMITMENT
OF KRANNERT ART

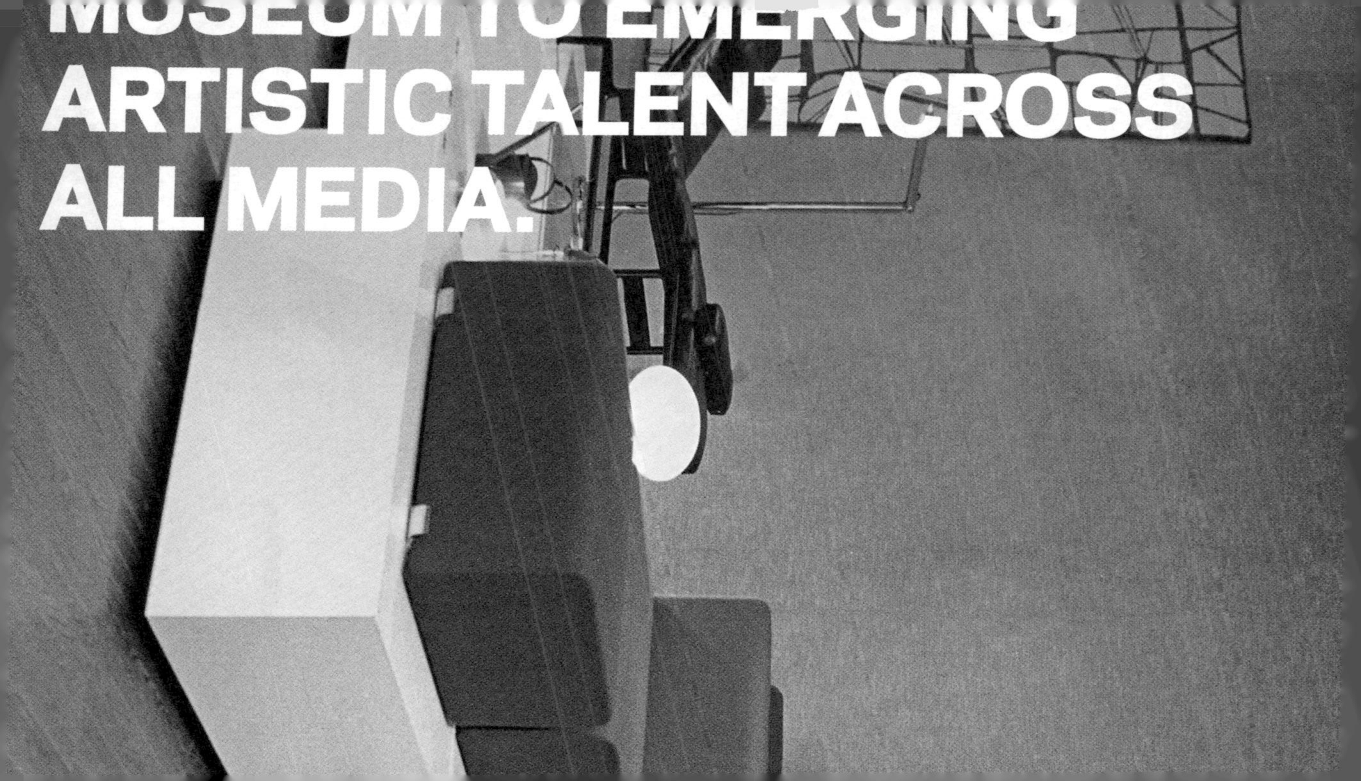
MUSEUM TO EMERGING
ARTISTIC TALENT ACROSS
ALL MEDIA.

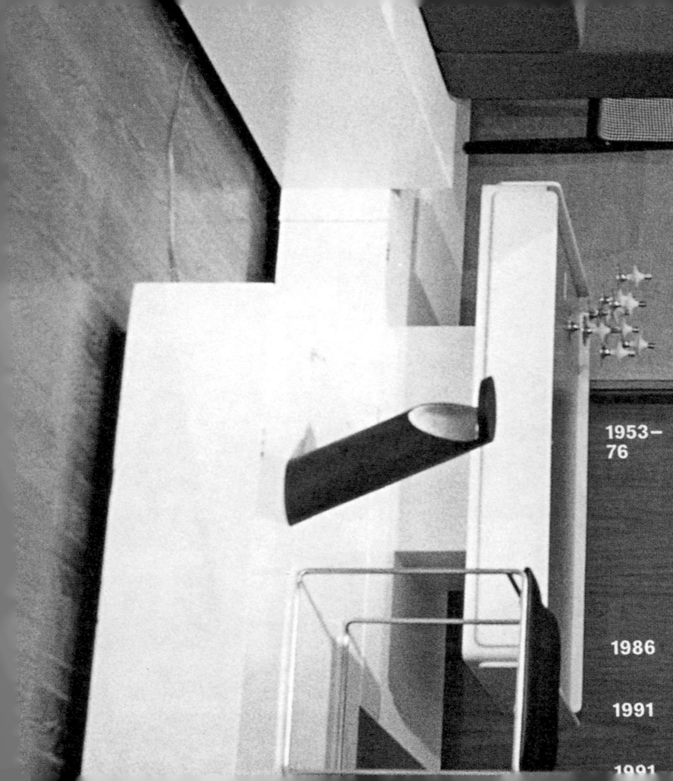

Just as acquisitions were a significant outcome of the festivals, over the last decade Krannert Art Museum (KAM) has again made it a priority to purchase objects from the exhibitions it organizes.

Through its active exhibition and acquisition programs, the museum has grown from a small collection of plaster casts into a breathing, evolving arts institution with a vision focused on the contemporary moment.

Selected Exhibitions

* KAM-organized

1953–76 "For Your Home" / "The New Environment"* introduces innovative approaches to form and function in the American home by leading regional and national designers and design studios.

1986 *Peter Eisenman: Transformation Drawings for House IV**

1991 *Drawings and Objects by Josef Hoffmann*

1991 *The Alexander Collection of*

Organized by the College of Fine and Applied Arts, the semi-annual design series "For Your Home" (in 1973 renamed "The New Environment") sparked KAM's interest in exhibiting and collecting design; since the 1980s, the museum has continued to organize a number of significant design exhibitions.

EXHIBITING AND COLLECTING DESIGN

the University of Illinois's School of Architecture. The collection comprises a survey of furniture created between 1860 and 1974 by designers from Gustav Stickley to Harry Bertoia.

1995 *William Stumpf: Chairs (and Other Ideas)** presents the work of Illinois alumnus and designer William Stumpf.

2005 *Design Excellence Collection**

2006 *Designing Experiences: How Graphic and Industrial Design Shape Daily Life** offers perspectives on graphic and industrial design as they relate to the market economy.

Upcoming

2009 *WOW Design: Marloes ten Bhömer** is the first in a series focusing on outstanding contemporary designers.

TWENTIETH-CENTURY PHOTO-GRAPHERS

1975 *Photographs by Diane Arbus* and *New Japanese Photography*

1979 Presentation of the landmark *Mirrors and Windows: American Photography since 1960*, organized by the Museum of Modern Art, New York

1980 KAM hosts the Museum of Modern Art exhibition *Ansel Adams and the West*

1981 *Harry Callahan: Photographs in Color**

1984 *Photographs by Art Sinsabaugh** and *Photographs by Walker Evans**

1985 *The New Spirit in American Photography: Experiment and Innovation at the New Bauhaus and School of Design, Chicago** merges KAM's interests in photography and design.

1986 *Alexander Rodchenko*

KAM demonstrated its ongoing

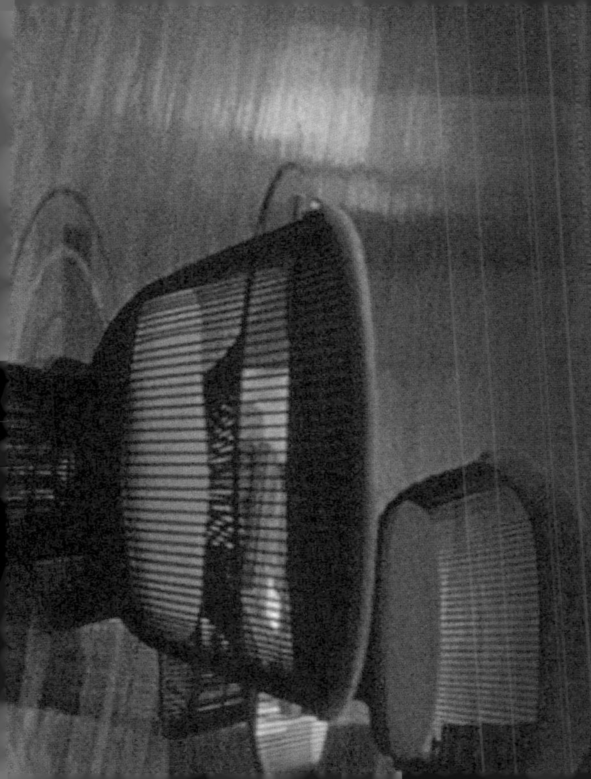

Photographs, 1969–1983

1990 *Couplings: Photographs of Edward Weston**

1991 *Hans Bellmer: A Photographic Retrospective**

1993 *Hiroshi Sugimoto: Seascapes*

1995 *Garry Winogrand: Photographs from the Women Are Beautiful Series**

2001 *Edward Weston: The Point Lobos Photographs**

Upcoming

2009 *Polaroids and Portraits: A Photographic Legacy of Andy Warhol** showcases a recent gift of 152 images from the Andy Warhol Photographic Legacy Program.

1970s by hosting important exhibitions of the work of artists such as Diane Arbus, William Eggleston, Edward Ruscha, Jerry Uelsmann, and, in 198[illegible], Ansel Adams. These shows inspired KAM to conceive solo exhibitions of influential and innovative twentieth-century American photographers over the course of the next three decades.

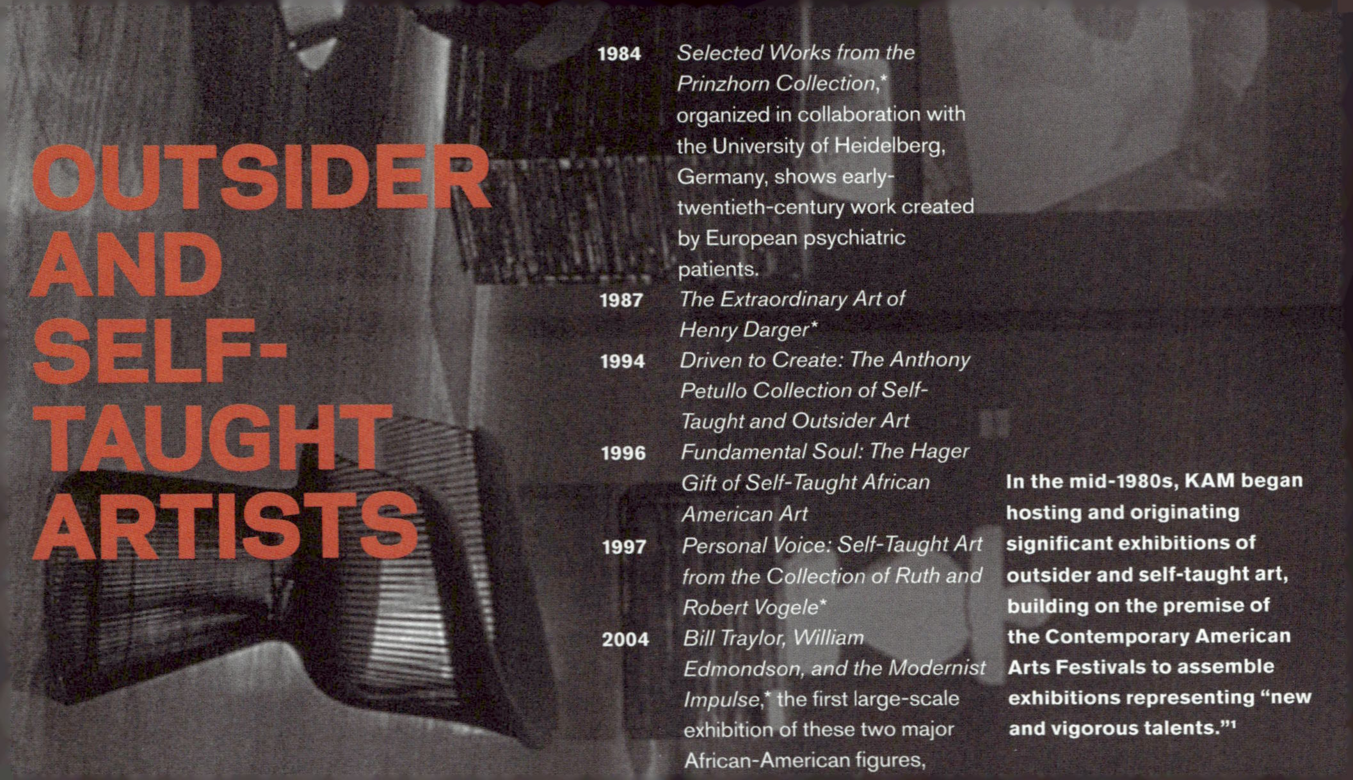

OUTSIDER AND SELF-TAUGHT ARTISTS

1984 *Selected Works from the Prinzhorn Collection,** organized in collaboration with the University of Heidelberg, Germany, shows early-twentieth-century work created by European psychiatric patients.

1987 *The Extraordinary Art of Henry Darger**

1994 *Driven to Create: The Anthony Petullo Collection of Self-Taught and Outsider Art*

1996 *Fundamental Soul: The Hager Gift of Self-Taught African American Art*

1997 *Personal Voice: Self-Taught Art from the Collection of Ruth and Robert Vogele**

2004 *Bill Traylor, William Edmondson, and the Modernist Impulse,** the first large-scale exhibition of these two major African-American figures,

In the mid-1980s, KAM began hosting and originating significant exhibitions of outsider and self-taught art, building on the premise of the Contemporary American Arts Festivals to assemble exhibitions representing "new and vigorous talents."[1]

taught" art to the broader realm of modern art and culture.

2006 *Cosmic Consciousness: The Work of Robert Bannister**

Upcoming

2010 *Stranger in Paradise: The Works of Reverend Howard Finster**

CONTEMPO-RARY

1985 *Judy Chicago: The Birth Project*

1986 *Slices of Life: The Work of Barbara Kruger** and *Robert Arneson: Nuclear Visions**

1990 *Leon Golub: Figurative Paintings**

1991 *Jay DeFeo: Works on Paper,** *Peter Saul: The Political Paintings*, and *Karl Wirsum: A Retrospective**

1992 *Adrian Piper: What It's Like, What It Is, #2*

ART SCULPTURE, DESIGN, PERFORMANCE

Contemporary exhibitions from the mid-1980s through the '90s presented the work of individual artists in sculpture, design, and performance, including several associated with Chicago-based imagism (Leon Golub, Peter Saul, and Karl Wirsum).

1993 *Another Song: A Susan Barron/John Cage Collaboration**; *Meredith Monk: Silver Lake and Dolmen Music**; *The Black Woman in America: Prints by Elizabeth Catlett**; and *Out of Town: The Williamsburg Paradigm**

1994–98 In the "Contemporary Art Series," reminiscent of Illinois's Contemporary American Arts Festivals, four artists are featured in solo exhibitions each year, while a summer exhibition showcases contemporary objects from the permanent collection. The series has featured 20 artists over five years, including Tom Otterness,* Jean-Michel Basquiat, Yong Soon Min,* and Bill Viola.*

1996 *Carrie Mae Weems: Sea Islands and Africa Series**

1997 *The Body and the Object:*

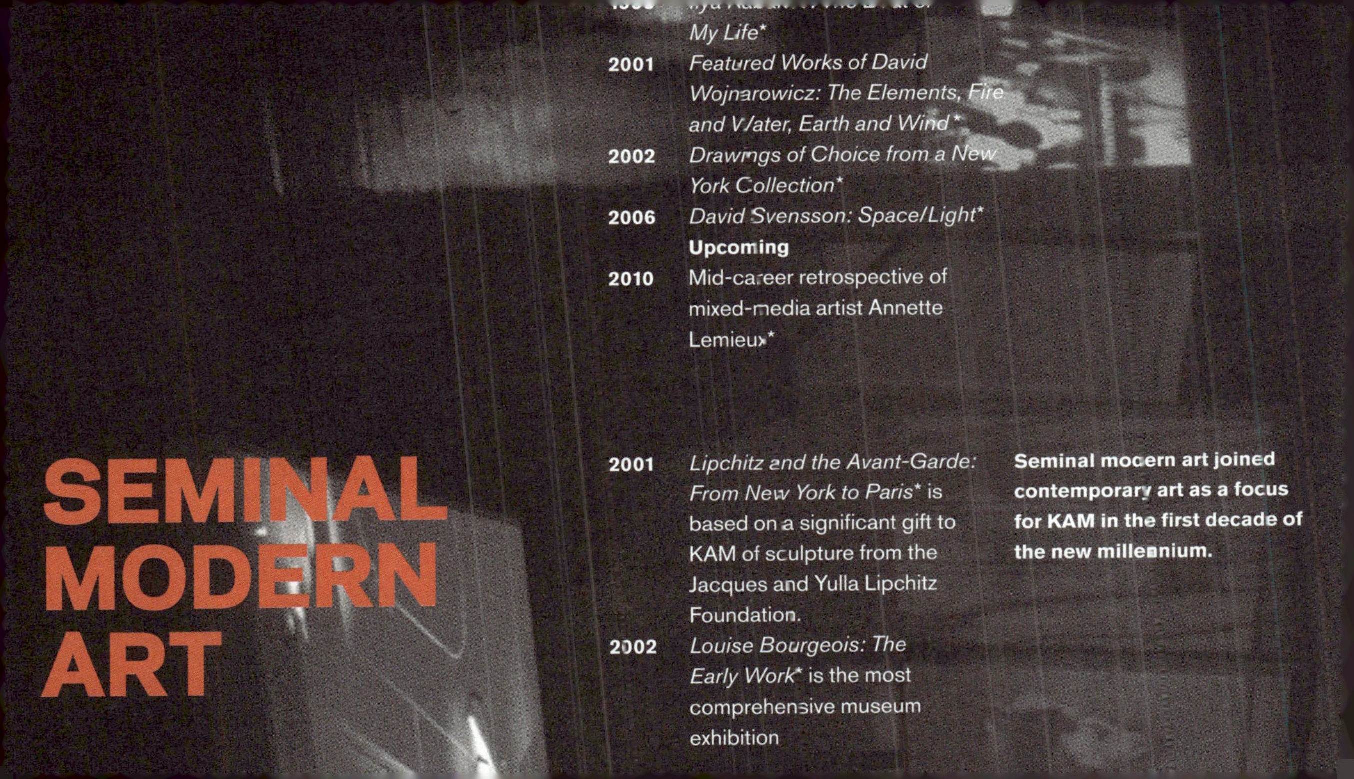

SEMINAL MODERN ART

*My Life**

2001 *Featured Works of David Wojnarowicz: The Elements, Fire and Water, Earth and Wind**

2002 *Drawings of Choice from a New York Collection**

2006 *David Svensson: Space/Light**

Upcoming

2010 Mid-career retrospective of mixed-media artist Annette Lemieux*

2001 *Lipchitz and the Avant-Garde: From New York to Paris** is based on a significant gift to KAM of sculpture from the Jacques and Yulla Lipchitz Foundation.

2002 *Louise Bourgeois: The Early Work** is the most comprehensive museum exhibition

Seminal modern art joined contemporary art as a focus for KAM in the first decade of the new millennium.

of Bourgeois's early work since her retrospective at the Museum of Modern Art in New York in 1982.

2006 *Uninterrupted Flux: Hedda Sterne, A Retrospective** includes almost one hundred works from museums across the country, as well as selections from the artist's collection.

2007 *An Architect Collects: Robert D. Kleinschmidt and a Lifetime of Fine Arts Acquisitions** presents over one hundred cutting-edge modernist works by Joseph Albers, Harry Bertoia, Helen Frankenthaler, Jasper Johns, Sol LeWitt, Brice Marden, László Moholy-Nagy, Robert Motherwell, Frank Stella, Mark Tobey, and Ulfert Wilke. Each year, Kleinschmidt donates key works from his collection to Krannert Art Museum.

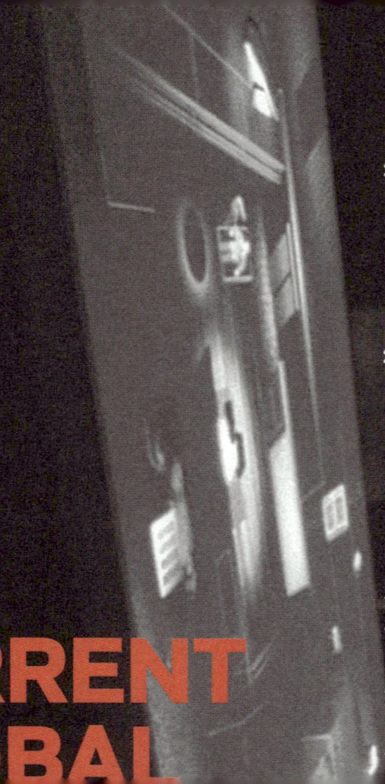

CURRENT GLOBAL

1987 *The Art of Jin Soo Kim**

1988 *Contemporary Chinese Painting**

1992 *Contemporary Japanese Calligraphy**

1998 *Concerned Theatre Japan:*

KAM's commitment to modern and contemporary art reaches beyond European-influenced or originated work to connect current global perspectives with strengths in the museum's

PERSPEC-TIVES

2000 *Rivers of Spirit: Art Women in the African Diaspora**

2001 *An Early Nasca Hummingbird Mantle and the Work of Josef Albers**

2008 *Collecting East Asia: The Lee Wonsik Collection**; *The Rise of Abstraction in Post-War Japan:* Sosaku Hanga *Woodblock Prints**; and *The World of Yugen: The Japanese Paper Artworks of Kyoko Ibe**

THEMATIC EXHIBITIONS

In recent years, KAM has become identified with exhibitions of work by living artists who shed light on complex and compelling issues of contemporary society and cultural psychology.

2004 *Beyond East and West: Seven Transnational Artists** features the work of Jananne Al-Ani, Ghada Amer, Mona Hatoum, Y. Z. Kami, Walid Raad, Michal Rovner, and Shahzia Sikander and *Social Studies: Eight Artists Address Brown v. Board*

EXHIBITIONS ABOUT CONTEMPO-RARY SOCIETY

*of Education** includes works by Dawoud Bey, Sanford Biggers and Jennifer Zackin, Brett Cook-Dizney, Virgil Marti, Gary Simmons, Pamela Vander Zwan, and Carrie Mae Weems.

2005
*Balance and Power: Performance and Surveillance in Video Art** includes Vito Acconci, Antenna, Sophie Calle, Jim Campbell, Peter Campus, Jordan Crandall, Harun Farocki, Subodh Gupta, Kevin Hamilton, Tiffany Holmes, Tim Hyde, Paul Kaiser and Shelly Eshkar, Kristin Lucas, Steve Mann, Jenny Marketou, Jill Magid, Jonas Mekas, Muntadas and Marshall Reese, Bruce Nauman, Martha Rosler, Julia Scher, and Kiki Seror; *OVER + OVER: Passion for Process** features the work of Chakaia Booker, Juliann Cydylo, Tom Freidman, Christopher Rauschenberg, Joel Ross, Do-Ho Suh, Rick Valentin, and Michael Wolf; and *Branded and On Display** includes work from Ai Weiwei, Amy Barkow, Conrad Bakker, Ashley Bickerton, Michael Blum, Louis Cameron, Diller + Scofidio, Terence Gower, Laurie Hogin, Pierre Huyghe, Clay Ketter, Ryan McGinness, Amelia Moore, Donna Nield, Haim Steinbach, Tempi & Wolf, Yuken Teruya, Hank Willis Thomas, Brian Ulrich, Siebren Versteeg, and Zhao Bandi.

2008
*Landscapes of Experience and Imagination: Explorations by Midwest Latina/Latino Artists** features the work of Miguel Cortez, Gisela Insuaste, Alejandro Lugo, Paul Sierra, Edra Soto, and Gabriel Villa,

Lou, Jennifer Maestre, Elizabeth Simonson, Devorah Sperber, Fred Tomaselli, and Rachel Perry Welty.

2006 *When We Were Young: New Perspectives on the Art of the Child** juxtaposes selected childhood works of preeminent historical artists, including Paul Klee and Pablo Picasso, with modern and contemporary children's drawings.

2007 *FACADES** includes work by Anna Nordquist Andersson, Janine Antoni, Luke Batten and Jonathan Sadler, Vanessa Beecroft, Francis Cape, Jordi Colomer, Olafur Eliasson, Maria Friberg, Terence Gower, Huang Yan, IngridMwangiRobertHutter, Wendy Jacob, Robert Lazzarini, Iñigo Manglano-Ovalle, Gordon Matta-Clark, Jillian McDonald, Boym Partners Inc., Adam Cvijanovic, E. V. Day, Heide Fasnacht, Barnaby Furnas, Carlos Garaicoa, John Gerrard, Penelope Gottlieb, Fabrice Gygi, Jone Kvie, Pia Lindman, Stefana McClure, Cornelia Parker, Sarah Pickering, Michael Rakowitz, Gerhard Richter, Thomas Ruff, Charles Sandison, Eduardo Santiere, and David Svensson, and *Out of Sequence: Underrepresented Voices in American* Comics* features the work of 74 practitioners of sequential art.

Upcoming

2010 *Under Control**

2011 *Passing Time**

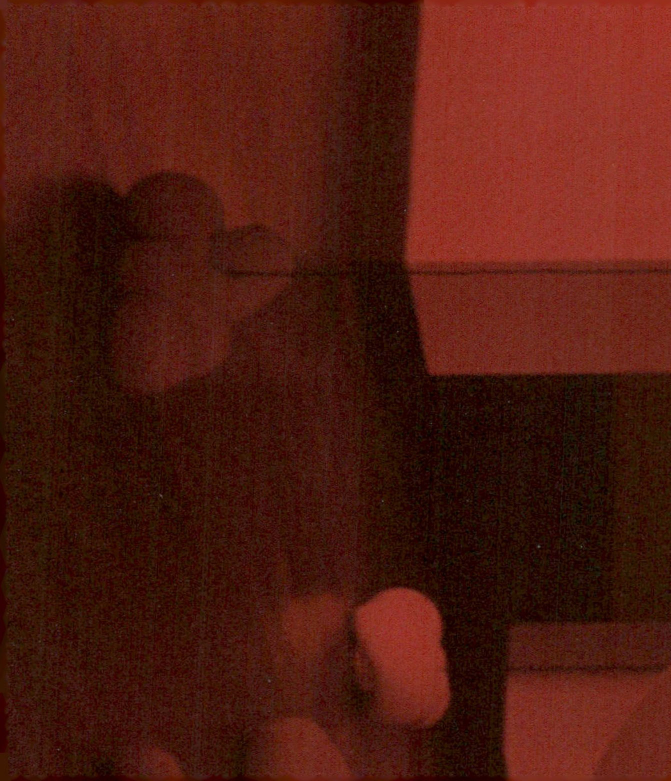

By Dana Burchfield (with assistance from Kathyrn Koca)

Cover: View of Jenny Marketou, *99 Red Balloons: Be Careful Who Sees You When You Dream*, 2005, in *Balance and Power: Performance and Surveillance in Video Art*, organized by KAM and presented October 22–December 31, 2005. Photo courtesy of Wilmer Zehr

Inside pages: Installation view of *For Your Home*, organized by KAM and presented March 15–April 19, 1970. Photo courtesy of Krannert Art Museum

Installation view of *Bill Traylor, William Edmondson, and the Modernist Impulse*, organized by KAM and presented October 22, 2004–January 2, 2005. Photo courtesy of Wilmer Zehr

Installation view of *Balance and Power: Performance and Surveillance in Video Art*, organized by KAM and presented October 22–December 31, 2005. Photo courtesy of Wilmer Zehr

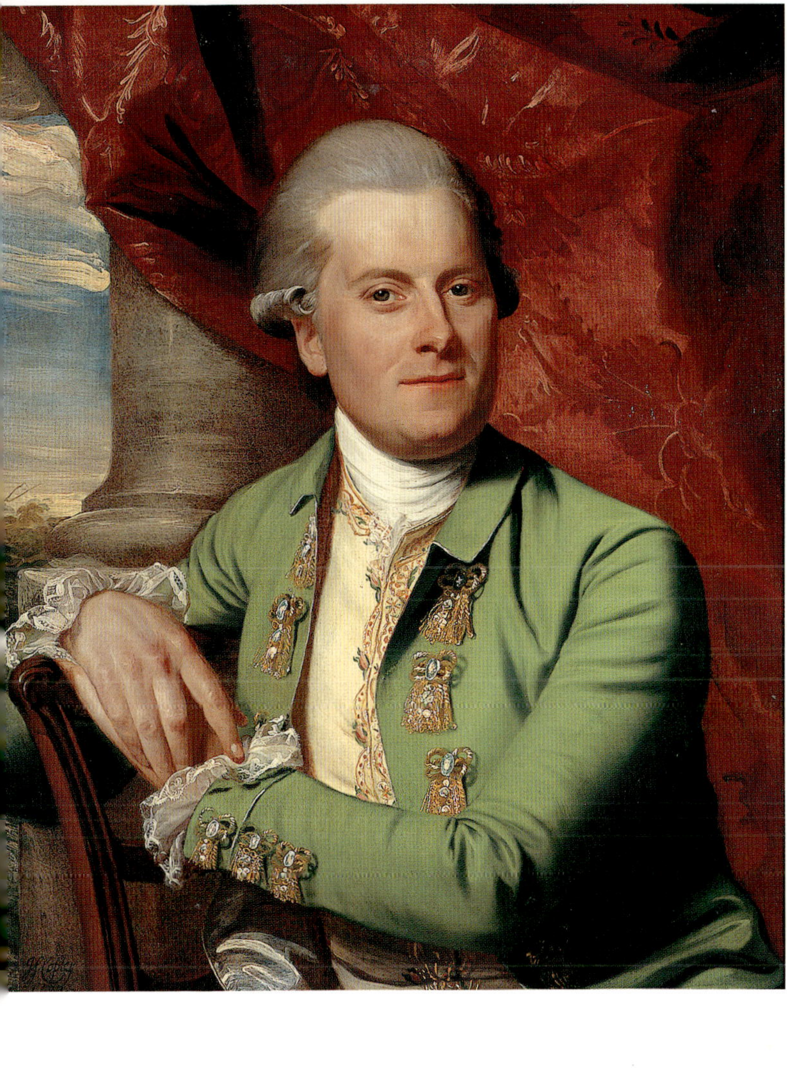

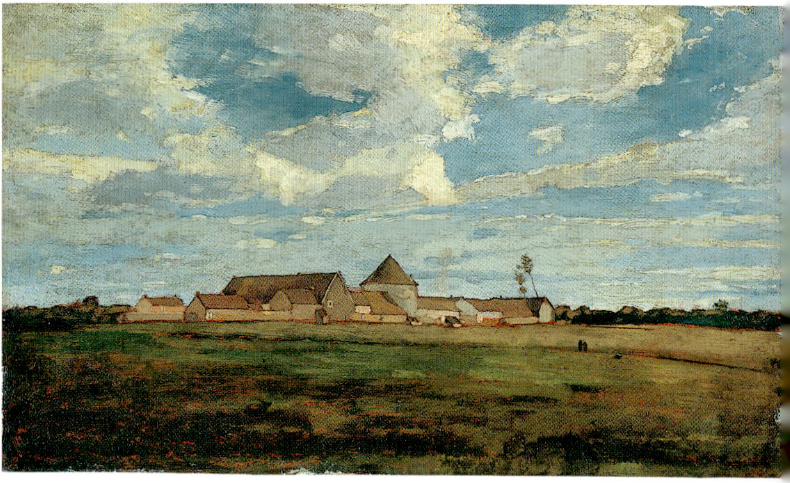

Winslow Homer's sole artistic training was an apprenticeship to a Boston lithographer. He then worked as a freelance illustrator, first for *Ballou's Pictorial Drawing Room Companion*, and then documenting the Civil War for *Harper's Weekly*. After the war, Homer began painting and was soon made a member of the National Academy. He made his first trip abroad from 1865 to 1867, when his *Prisoners from the Front* (1866) and *The Bright Side* (1865) were shown at the 1867 Exposition Universelle in Paris. While in France he executed 19 paintings, *Cernay-la-Ville – French Farm* among them, and three illustrations. Homer's stay abroad, however short, presents a problem in art-historical scholarship. His susceptibility to European art has largely been dismissed in the critical literature, which has favored a narrative in which Homer is a uniquely American master untainted by foreign influences.

Cernay-la-Ville – French Farm is a small oil painting on a mahogany panel. The composition is simple and balanced. A cluster of distant buildings, reduced to geometric essentials, sits on a low horizon within the landscape. The scene is generalized, with very few details, and there is a certain hardness in the delineation of forms. Homer's brushstrokes are quick and active, suggesting rapid execution, perhaps *en plein air*, or "in the open air." They draw attention to the process of painting itself. The painting lacks conventional finish and patches of the mahogany show through in places. Although Homer has painted a rural landscape, he gives it none of the sentimental or emotional content common in landscapes of the nineteenth century. Fuessle

Winslow Homer
United States
1836–1910

Cernay-la-Ville – French Farm
1867
Oil on panel
10 3/4 × 18 1/4 inches
Gift of Mr. and Mrs. Merle J. Trees
1940-1-3

Born in New York City, Ralph Albert Blakelock studied at the Free Academy and at the Cooper Union, where he was schooled in the techniques and theories of the Hudson River School. After his first exhibition at the National Academy of Design in 1868, he spent the greater part of three years in the West, painting the grandeur of nature and the life of American Indians. He gradually abandoned the realism of the Hudson River painters for a more interpretive and introspective style related to the work of George Inness, Albert Pinkham Ryder, and John H. Twachtman.

In Blakelock's later paintings, such as *Moonlight on the Brook*, the dark foliage of trees creates a lacy pattern over a distant, nocturnal landscape. The lighting is complex, with the sky faintly glowing, the moon partially obscured by a large tree at the center left, and its reflection in the water cut off by the sloping bank. A close examination of the canvas reveals a surprising degree of detail extending to the bluish horizon.

Blakelock was perhaps the best-known American painter in the late nineteenth century, in part because one of his canvases sold for $30,000, at the time the largest sum ever bid at auction for a painting by a living American artist. He was also known for his widely publicized mental illness. The pressures of his futile attempts to support a large family, the intense criticism of his later paintings, and his lack of business acumen, combined with mental illness, led to a long hospitalization and his eventual suicide. Smith

Ralph Albert Blakelock
United States
1847–1919

Moonlight on the Brook
1868
Oil on canvas
26 3/4 × 21 1/2 inches
Gift of Mr. and Mrs. Merle J. Trees
1940-1-2

In 1859, Cornwall Kirkpatrick (1814–1890) and his brother Wallace (1828–1896) founded Anna Pottery in the southern Illinois town of Anna. Krannert Art Museum owns two of the brothers' best works – a snake jug (one of about two dozen known examples) and a directory jug (one of about ten) (pp. 225, 226). The whiskey (snake) jug bears 12 finely articulated timber rattlesnakes and three men. The snakes slither out of the jug and sprawl in tangles across most of its surface. Two young men dive into it through its sides and, in front, the head of an aged bearded man emerges, bedraggled. Five snakes are poised to attack the revenant from below; a sixth, striking from above, already has the crown of his head between its jaws.

Almost nothing is known of the reception of the Kirkpatricks' figural works in their own time. In the twentieth century, scholars saw the Kirkpatrick snake jugs as temperance warnings against the evils of drink. More recent interpreters, however, draw attention to the jugs' grotesque, macabre, sexual, and scatological aspects, their humor, and their self-consciously extravagant style, and argue that they are an ironic debunking of Victorian values. According to this reading, the Kirkpatricks were, like their contemporary Mark Twain, misanthropic liberals.

Cornwall's directory wares elaborate on a folk tradition and stand somewhat apart from the rest of the Kirkpatrickian corpus. Most of the directories were made for particular occasions, usually local or regional fairs. In these cases, they record the names of the fair's officers, prize categories, judges for each category, and frequently town and county officials as well. The number of names runs into the hundreds. Typically, directories were presented as gifts to the fairs' organizers, presumably for publicity purposes, and were a frequent subject of comment in local newspapers.

Krannert Art Museum's jug is unusual in that it is a business directory. Incised on its surface, in facsimile, are about 140 business cards for Chicago newspapers and periodicals, some with titles in German, Polish, or Swedish. Each card presents the title and address of a publication, usually the name of its editor, and sometimes that of its publisher. Cornwall, apparently as a joke, sneaked in a card for Anna's liberal newspaper, the *Union County News*. All data was taken directly and completely from the *Lakeside Directory of the State of Illinois* (1875). The cards are strewn across the top of the jug like confetti, but gradually solidify into contiguous blocks of text toward the bottom. The jug was made as a complement to an officers' directory Cornwall made for the 1879 run of Chicago's annual Inter-State Industrial Exposition (1873–92). In the outlandishness of their concept, their iterative style, the use of words as elements, the obsessiveness of execution, and the manifest *horror vacuui*, Cornwall's directory wares are harbingers of twentieth-century outsider art. Mohr

(following pages)
Snake jug
ca. 1875–90
Albany slip-glazed stoneware
11 × 10 inches in diameter
Gift of the Department of Ceramic Engineering,
University of Illinois
1980-5-54

Directory jug
1879
Salt-glazed stoneware
22 × 12 inches in diameter
Gift of the Department of Ceramic Engineering,
University of Illinois
1980-4-224

Anna Pottery
United States
flourished 1859–90

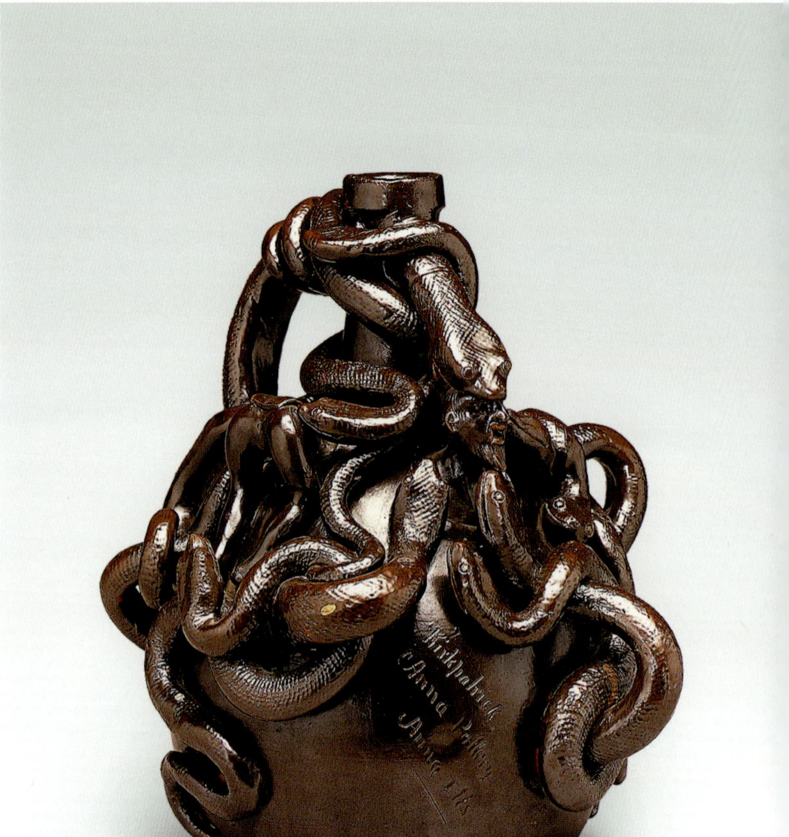
Kirkpatrick
Anna Pottery
Anna Ills

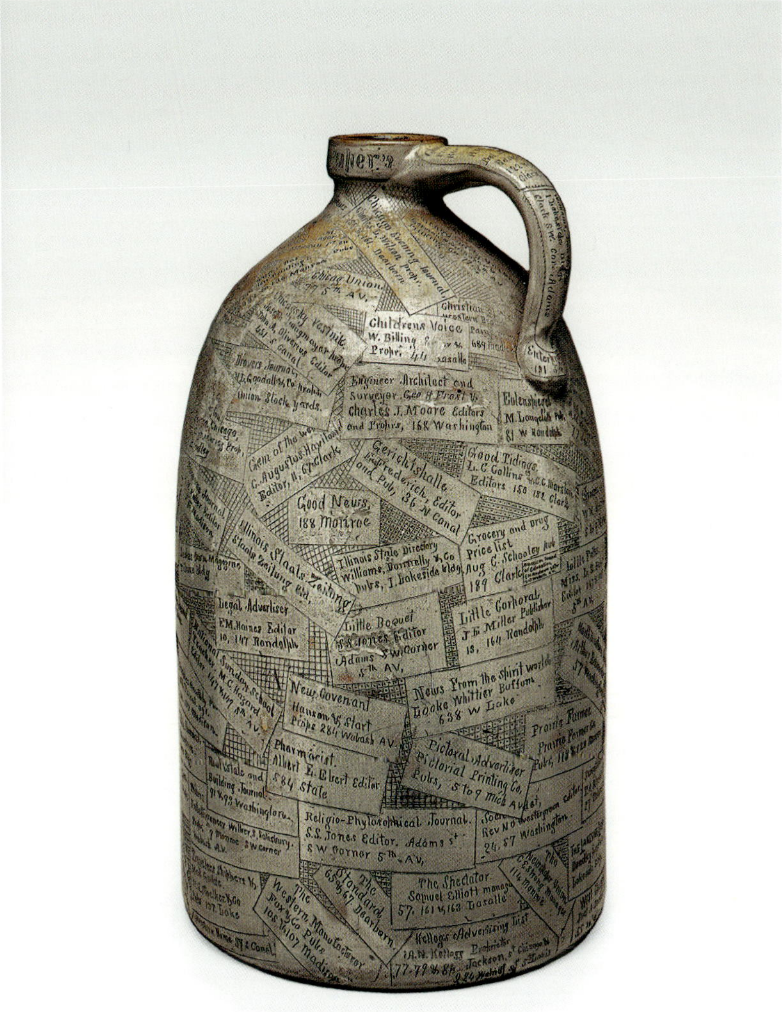

Snake jug
Directory jug

Born in Florence to American parents, John Singer Sargent belonged to a generation of American expatriates who shared a fascination with Europe and were attracted to the "exotic" cultures of Spain and North Africa. Sargent's art helped to both shape and satisfy that taste, as did the work of Europeans such as Édouard Manet and Jean-Léon Gérôme. Sargent's greatest success at the Paris Salon was his *El Jaleo* of 1882, a large, exuberant canvas that captured the dramatic movements of a flamenco dancer in a dark, atmospheric Spanish cantina. *El Jaleo* resulted from Sargent's first trip to Spain and North Africa in 1879–80. Most likely, this trip also provided the occasion for Krannert Art Museum's undated watercolor study of a North African man. Sargent found Morocco picturesque, and he wrote to a friend from Tangier that "the aspect of the place is striking, the costume grand and the Arabs often magnificent."

Sargent cultivated a serious interest in watercolor early in life, culminating in the virtuosity of the well-known works he made after 1900, in which he made free and bold use of transparent washes. Early successes include two watercolor views of Venice exhibited at the Paris Salon of 1881. Krannert Art Museum's watercolor has the look of a study rather than a work intended for display. Limiting his palette to earth tones and applying opaque pigment to the figure's face, Sargent placed less emphasis on the display of brushwork than the careful delineation of features.
Gaudio

John Singer Sargent
United States
1856–1925

Untitled
ca. 1880
Watercolor
11 1/4 × 11 1/4 inches
Gift of the School of Art + Design, University of Illinois
1982-9-2

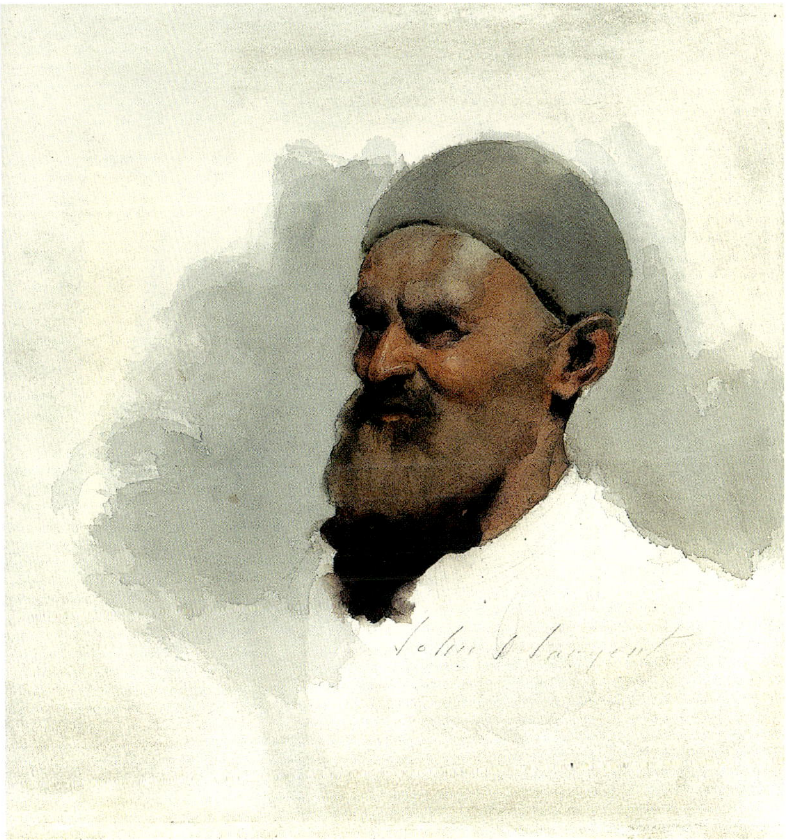
John S Sargent

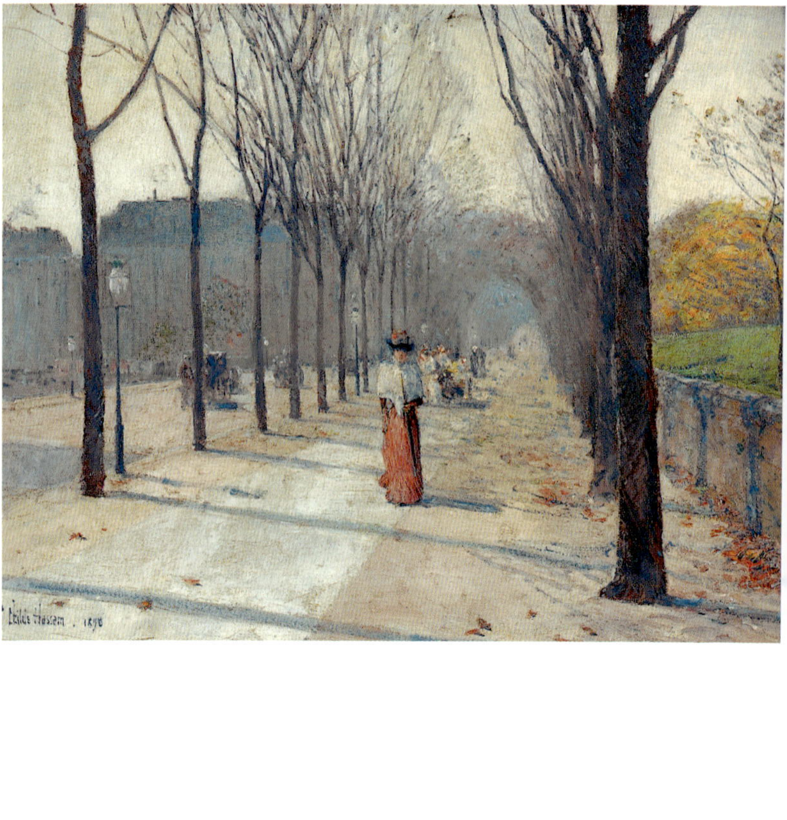
Childe Hassam

Like Winslow Homer, Childe Hassam began as an illustrator for magazines, including *Harpers* and *Scribners*. His early paintings reflect contemporary styles: the realism of Winslow Homer, the tonalism of George Innes, and the romanticism of the Hudson River School. In the spring of 1886, Hassam moved to Paris to study impressionism.

Hassam and other American artists sought to reconcile the realist tradition with impressionistic color and light, which made their work generally quite different from that of their French sources. Hassam's paintings after his stay in Paris are typical of American impressionism in the restraint of their color and brushwork. He was one of the American painters included in the celebrated and, by some accounts, notorious *International Exhibition of Modern Art* of 1913 (later referred to as the Armory Show).

Lady in the Park, painted after Hassam's return to New York in 1890, shows a woman approaching the viewer on a wide, tree-lined walk along an urban park, the pink of her slim skirt echoing the roses on her hat. In the sun-filled scene, the bright sidewalk and street recede to a hazy background of aqua-blue buildings and carriages. The composition is paced out by the diminishing verticals of streetlamps and the trunks of slender, leafless trees, and balanced by diagonal blue shadows. Smith, Sprugel

Childe Hassam
United States
1859–1935

Lady in the Park
1890
Oil on canvas
14 1/4 × 18 inches
Gift of Katherine Trees Livezey
1973-3-1

Born near Newburgh, New York, American landscape painter George Inness grew up in and around New York City and Newark, New Jersey. He had received little formal training as an artist when he began exhibiting publicly around 1844. He made several trips to Europe, spending most of his time in Italy and France. In 1878, he moved to Montclair, New Jersey, where he lived and painted until his death in 1894.

Inness was known by his contemporaries as a painter of storms: approaching and passing tempests, lowering steel-gray skies, sun-streaked thunderheads, wind-tossed trees, and rainbows. Like the French impressionists, whose work caused a stir when exhibited in New York in 1886, Inness delighted in rendering the fleeting effects of weather. In numerous paintings, he described the visual effects on the landscape of whipping wind and dark, rain-soaked skies. In *The Approaching Storm*, a thick dark-gray cloud cover at the horizon slowly overtakes the clear sky still visible at upper left, as glowing orange clouds roll over the landscape, their turbulent progress manifested in swift and multidirectional brushwork. A cluster of trees to the right reflects the sunlight that pierces the clouds to illuminate the fore- and middle ground with a brilliant green-yellow gleam.

Exemplary of Inness's later work, *The Approaching Storm* was most likely inspired by the landscape of Montclair. Inness generally painted from memory, and late landscapes such as this one are usually evocations of his subjective experience of the inexorable forces of the natural world rather than exact renderings of place.
DeLue

George Inness
United States
1825–1894

The Approaching Storm
1893
Oil on canvas
25 × 30 inches
Gift of Mr. and Mrs. Merle J. Trees
1942-1-3

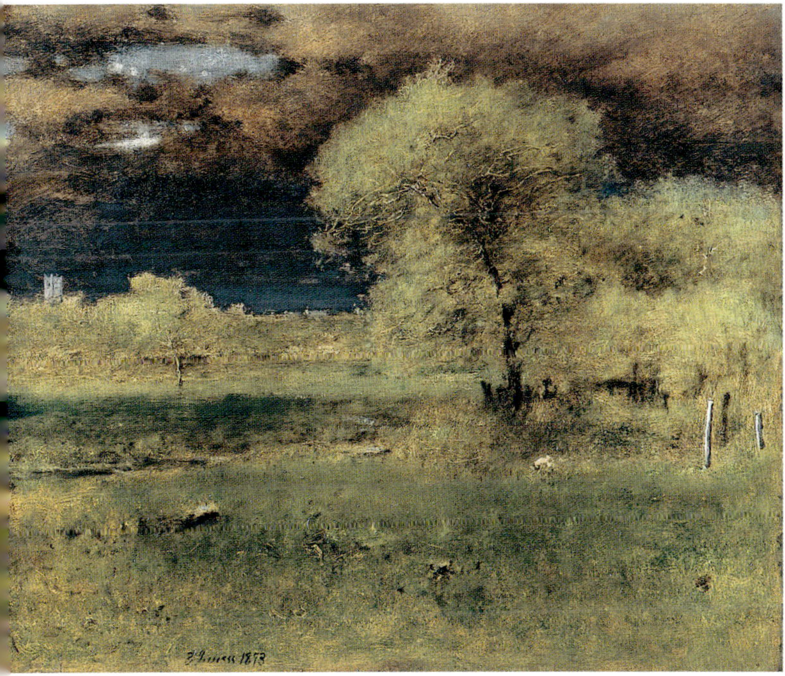

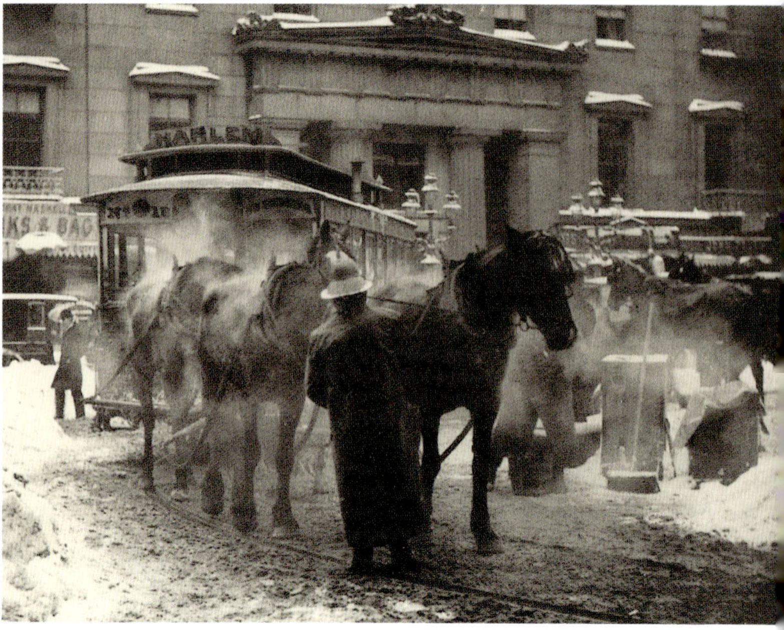
HARLEM

On his return to New York City in 1890 after living and studying in Germany for nine years, Alfred Stieglitz sensed a "spiritual emptiness" that left America lagging behind Europe in its cultural and artistic vitality. He shot *The Terminal* shortly after his arrival, and it embodies his loneliness in this familiar yet foreign country. He later remarked that:

> The New York that I had come back to was not my old New York. I used to wander around the streets disconsolately, until one night during a blizzard, I happened to see a man watering a couple of steaming horse-car horses, and I thought, "well, there at any rate is the human touch." That made me feel much better.

The Terminal is an early example of the expressive pictorialist style Stieglitz promoted in the United States. The smoky, romantic atmosphere created by the horses' warm breath mixing with the cool air transforms the ordinary urban scene at the southern end of the Harlem streetcar line. Stieglitz shows his technical proficiency in the use of a hand-held camera, achieving great clarity of detail despite the challenging photographic conditions.

Stieglitz vehemently believed in photography as a fine art and in 1902 organized the Photo-Secession group as a way of raising the medium's artistic standards. In 1905, he established the elite gallery "291," where photographs were framed and displayed like paintings, and founded and edited the quarterly publication *Camera Work* (1902–17). *The Terminal* was published in the October 1911 issue and is one of Stieglitz's best-known works. Kuechler

Alfred Stieglitz
United States
1864–1946

The Terminal
1893
Photogravure
4 3/4 × 6 1/4 inches
Art Acquisition Fund
1990-3-1

After the Great Fire of 1871, Chicago immediately began rebuilding; by the 1890s the city was renowned for its architecture, including the new phenomenon of the skyscraper. Steel framing made it possible to build upward on small, expensive city lots without massive areas of masonry for support. Easy and rapid access to the upper floors of tall vertical architecture became practical with the development of elevators. This handsome screen was designed by Louis Sullivan to close off the elevator shafts from the third to the top floor of the 13-story Chicago Stock Exchange. Some of the screens also served as elevator doors. The elevators were replaced in 1960 with high-speed mechanisms, and the building itself was razed in 1972.

The screens were made of wrought, or strap, iron with cast-iron details. The original finish was a blue-black Bower-Barff framed by bronze-plated casings. The kick plates were incised with geometric borders. Although Sullivan is known for exuberant surface ornamentation, the museum's screen is relatively austere and abstract. The design repeats circles and ovals horizontally pinned together. Groups of four "stamens" are attached diagonally to vertical supports. Sullivan's biographer Robert Twombly suggests that the forms represent seed germs giving birth to an eternal circle of life. Sullivan often used metaphorical language in his designs and wrote numerous prose poems about nature's cycles.

In his decorative elevator screens, Sullivan applied to functional objects the deeply felt values he expressed to such perfection in his architecture. Architectural styles and times change, however, and the famed "prophet of modern architecture" died penniless in 1924. Huck

Louis Henri Sullivan
United States
1856–1924

Elevator gatescreen from
Chicago Stock Exchange Building
1894
Cast iron with bronze plating
84 × 31 1/4 inches
Gift of the City of Chicago
1963-42-2.2

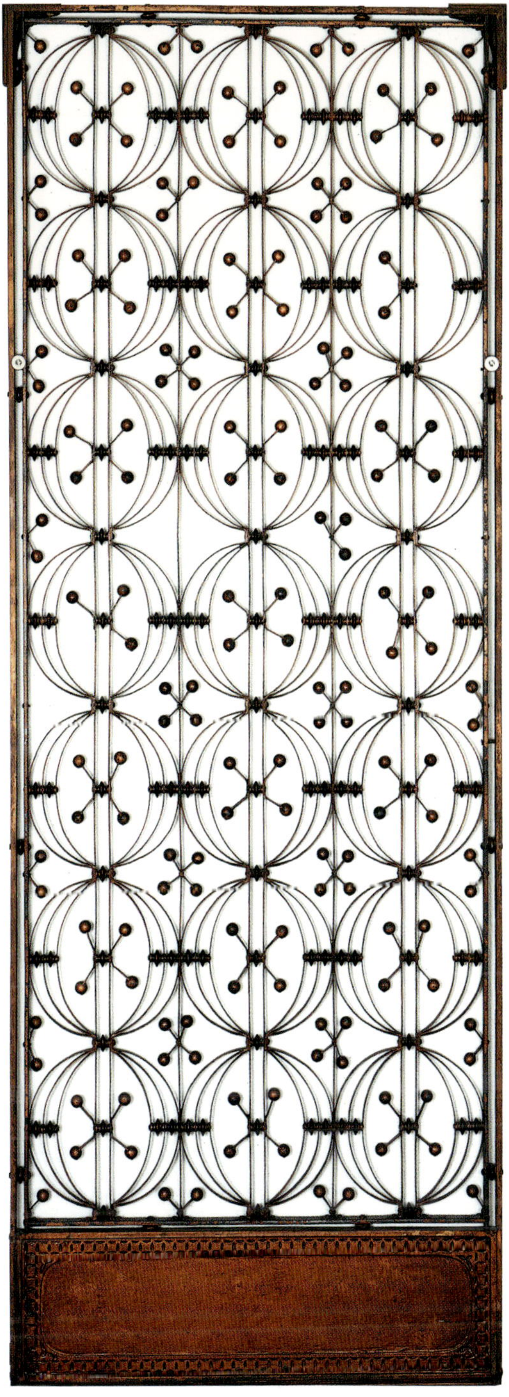

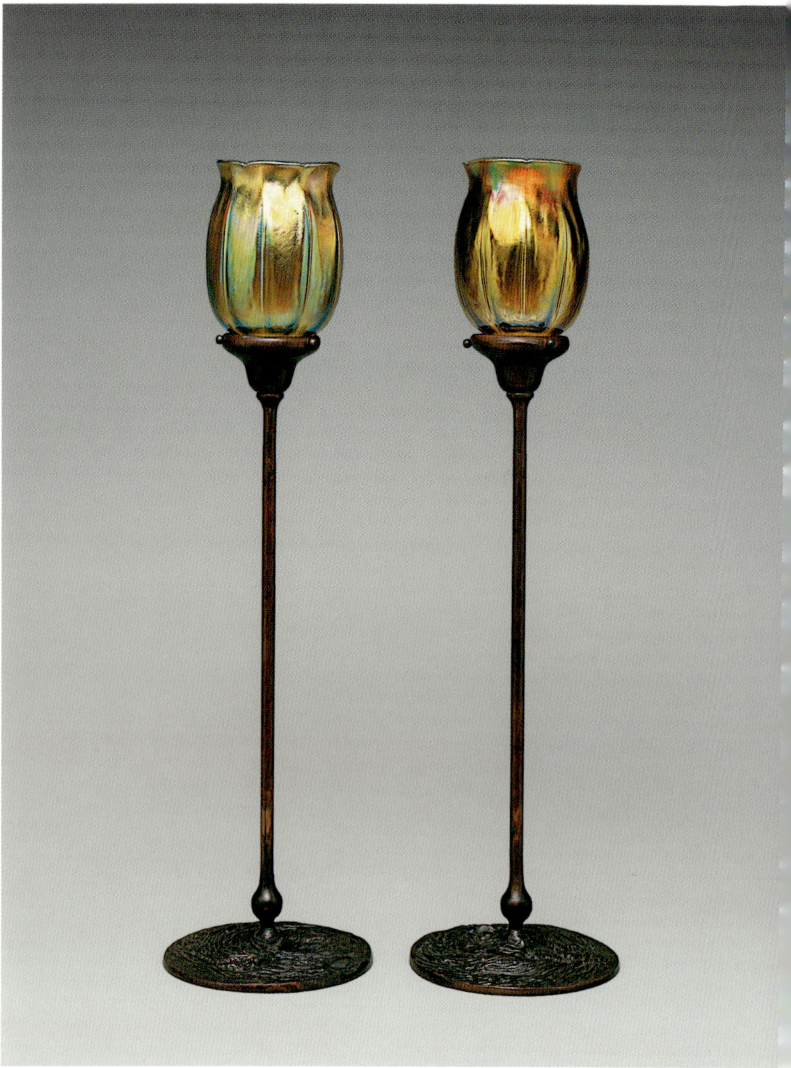

These candlesticks consist of tall slender bronze shafts capped by tulip-shaped glass shades. The swirling organic motif of the wide circular bases offers a rough texture that balances the smooth finish of the shafts' simple geometric ornamentation. A cup at the top of the shafts conceals a cylindrical hollow for holding candles, and screws secure the glass shades. Both candlesticks preserve their original brown patina. Three identifying marks are inscribed on the underside of each base: the phrase "Tiffany Studios" in block letters, the Tiffany monogram, and the item number (30388 and 30353, respectively). The shades are made of Tiffany Studios' patented hand-blown Favrile glass. Both shades are amber-colored with an iridescent sheen vacillating between red and gold. One also features blue iridescence. The initials "L. C. T." are incised on the bases.

In 1898, Louis Comfort Tiffany added a foundry to his decorative-glass business, creating the Tiffany Studios. Tiffany was influenced by the hand-crafting principles of the Arts & Crafts movement and the organic forms of Art Nouveau, while remaining a pragmatic citizen of the industrial age. Thus, Tiffany Studios produced both unique decorative-arts pieces and handmade, albeit mass-produced, items for commercial sale. These candlesticks belong to the latter category, in which hand-worked elements are combined with mold-made forms. Hand-production is evident in the shades' variation of coloration and silhouette, while the uniform bases signal the use of molds. Components of these candlesticks resemble other objects produced by Tiffany Studios, but the pairing of a single tulip shade with a long, slender shaft is unparalleled. These objects are rare among Tiffany's output, with no known identical examples. Sienkewicz

Louis Comfort Tiffany
United States
1848–1933

Candle lamps
ca. 1906–18
Bronze, Favrile glass
16 × 5 inches each
Gift of Mr. and Mrs. Willis Bruce
1982-16-6, 1982-16-7

Lorado Taft was best known during his lifetime as a designer of complex, heroic public monuments. He graduated from the University of Illinois in 1879 at nineteen, and went to Paris to study at the École des Beaux-Arts, the official stronghold of academic art education. After a brief return to Champaign in 1883, Taft completed a final year of independent study in Paris. On his return to the United States, he founded a sculpture studio at the School of the Art Institute of Chicago.

The monumental *The Blind* probably did more than any other single work to establish Taft's national reputation. The ensemble is based on the symbolic one-act play *Les Aveugles* (*The Blind*) (1891) by Belgian poet Maurice Maeterlinck. Taft's sculpture depicts the final scene, in which a group of sightless people of different ages and one sighted child are lost in a forest. One of the women holds aloft the child who can see, in hopes that he will lead them all to safety. Taft conceived of the sculptural group in 1906 when he and fellow members of the Eagle's Nest colony near Oregon, Illinois, performed the play. A small clay model was displayed in Chicago later that year, and in 1908 a full-scale plaster model was exhibited at the Art Institute of Chicago. The large model was also on view that year at the National Sculpture Society in Baltimore and at the National Academy of Design in New York. Although Taft had wanted to have the plaster cast in bronze, it remained in his Midway Studios in Chicago until his death in 1936. At that time, the University of Illinois purchased the contents of his studio, and *The Blind* was brought to Urbana. Not until 1988, however, was the sculpture finally cast into bronze and installed in the newly built Kinkead Pavilion at Krannert Art Museum. Morgan

Lorado Zadok Taft
United States
1860–1936

The Blind
1908 (cast 1988)
Bronze
9 × 10 1/2 feet
Estate of William S. Kinkead
1988-7-1

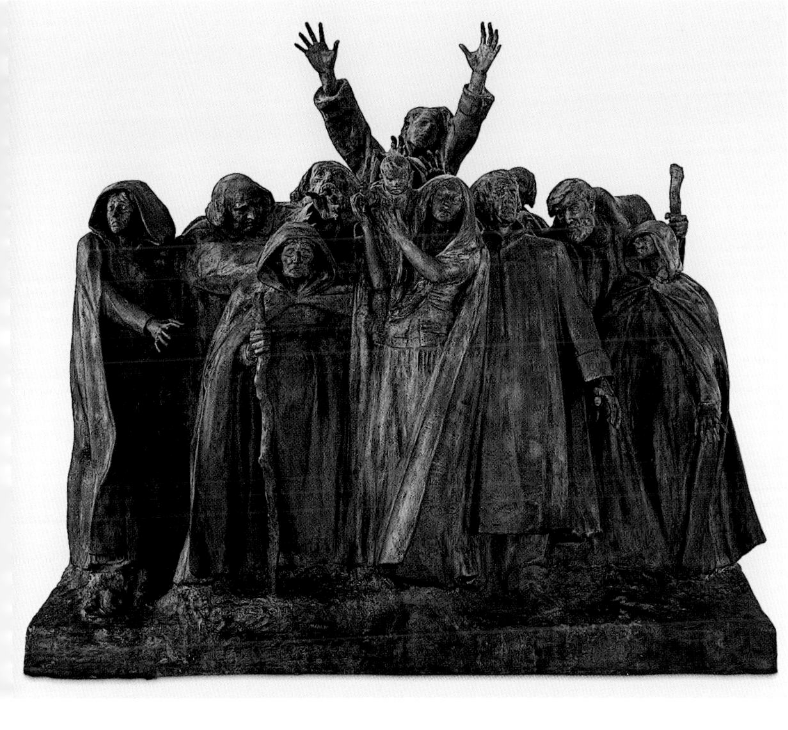

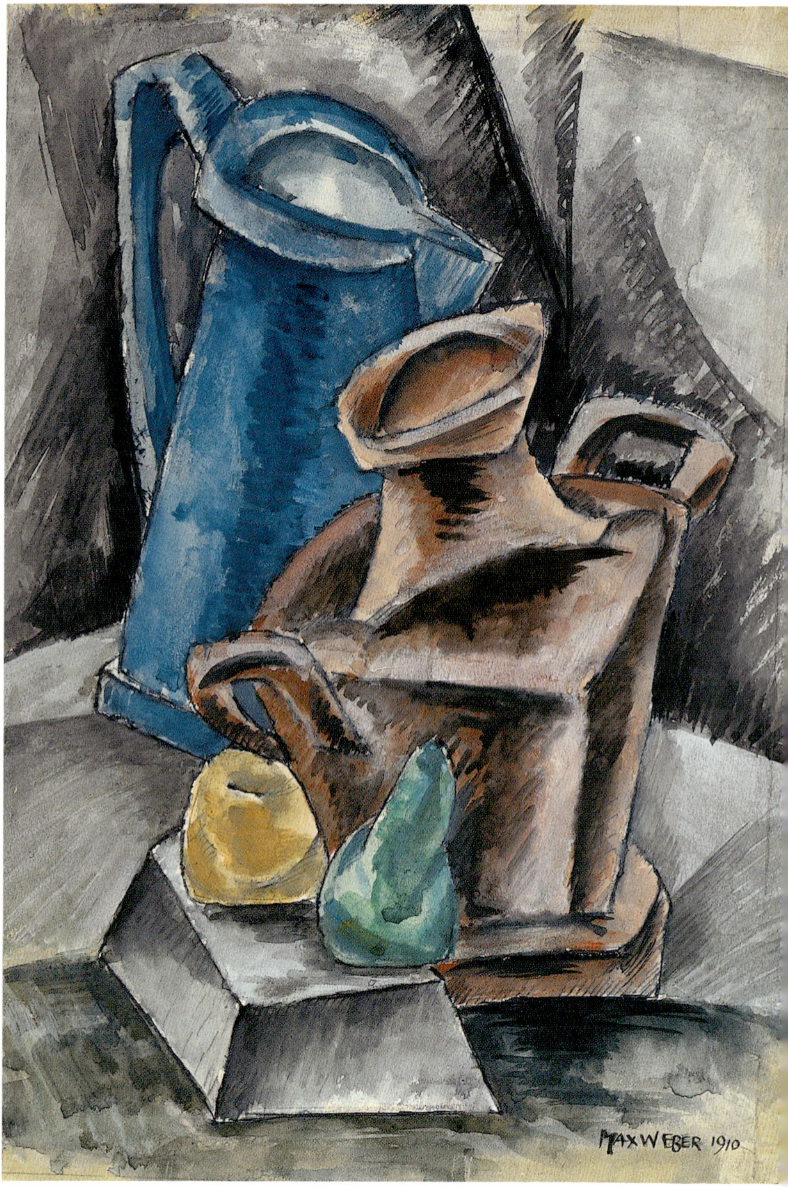
MAX WEBER 1910

Still Life with Orange and Pear was included in the January 1911 retrospective of Max Weber's work at Alfred Stieglitz's gallery "291" in New York. Stieglitz wrote ambivalently about the exhibition in *Camera Work*: "His compositions are logical and forceful, his mind is creative, his color is pleasing – and yet his work worries one. It appeals so much to the mind that it challenges criticism, and one cannot quite relax in front of it." Having been influenced in Europe by such artists as Paul Cézanne, Henri Matisse, Henri Rousseau, Georges Braque, and Pablo Picasso, Weber, who arrived in the United States in 1909, created experimental work with which the viewing public was unfamiliar and uncomfortable. Weber articulated his approach in *My Aim*, an unpublished essay written to accompany his 1911 exhibition: "I feel I can best explain myself … when I employ forms made up of intersecting planes." This watercolor in a cubist style is an early step in Weber's progression toward abstraction.

In Krannert Art Museum's still life, Weber defined depth by placing light edges against dark grounds, while organizing the elements in independent, often contradictory spatial planes. Objects are reduced to geometric forms: the central jug, for example, is the sum of disparate shapes stacked at odd angles – an oblong mouth and triangular neck sit on a cubical body, which ends in a rounded foot. The work communicates something of the tension on which Stieglitz remarked in his critique, but its angularity and skewed space also lend it energy.
Donovan

Max Weber
United States
(born Russia)
1881–1961

Still Life with Orange and Pear
1910
Watercolor
10 1/4 × 7 1/2 inches
Purchased with the support
of Alice and Donald Dodds,
Eva Maria Worthington
(in honor of Dr. Maglione),
and the Art Acquisition Fund
2003-1-1

A native of Saint Louis, Missouri, Albert Bloch began his artistic career as an illustrator, cartoonist, and caricaturist for the Saint Louis *Mirror* and other periodicals. In 1909 he moved to Munich, Germany, where he taught himself to paint by studying the old masters and modern French and German artists. In the fall of 1911, Bloch met Franz Marc and Wassily Kandinsky, who invited him to participate in the first exhibition of *Der Blaue Reiter* (The Blue Rider), which opened in Munich that December. The only American to participate in this landmark modernist exhibition, Bloch is often referred to as "the American Blue Rider." He remained in Germany until 1919, and later served as head of the art department at the University of Kansas (1923–47).

In the years leading up to World War I, Bloch's painting became increasingly abstract as he assimilated the influences of cubism and Kandinsky's colorful abstract expressionism. *Die Höhen* dates to the period of Bloch's closest stylistic affinity with Kandinsky and shares the Russian's bold and simple palette, energetic paint handling, and the subject matter of a mountainous landscape that appears to quake with spiritual energy. In a departure from Kandinsky, who had by this time abandoned figuration, Bloch includes in *Die Höhen* a yellow figure reclining at the lower right and a red one slumped over a rock at the upper left center. They appear out of scale yet in harmony with the surrounding landscape.

Bloch's inscription on a preparatory drawing (private collection, Kansas City, Missouri) specifies the mood he sought to create: "Lyrical note strictly to be avoided. Contrasts harsh and discordant – Forbidding – gloomy – 'cold.'"
Cateforis

Albert Bloch
United States
1882–1961

Die Höhen (*The Heights*)
1914
Oil on canvas
53 1/4 × 39 1/4 inches
Gift of Herman Spertus
1961-20-1

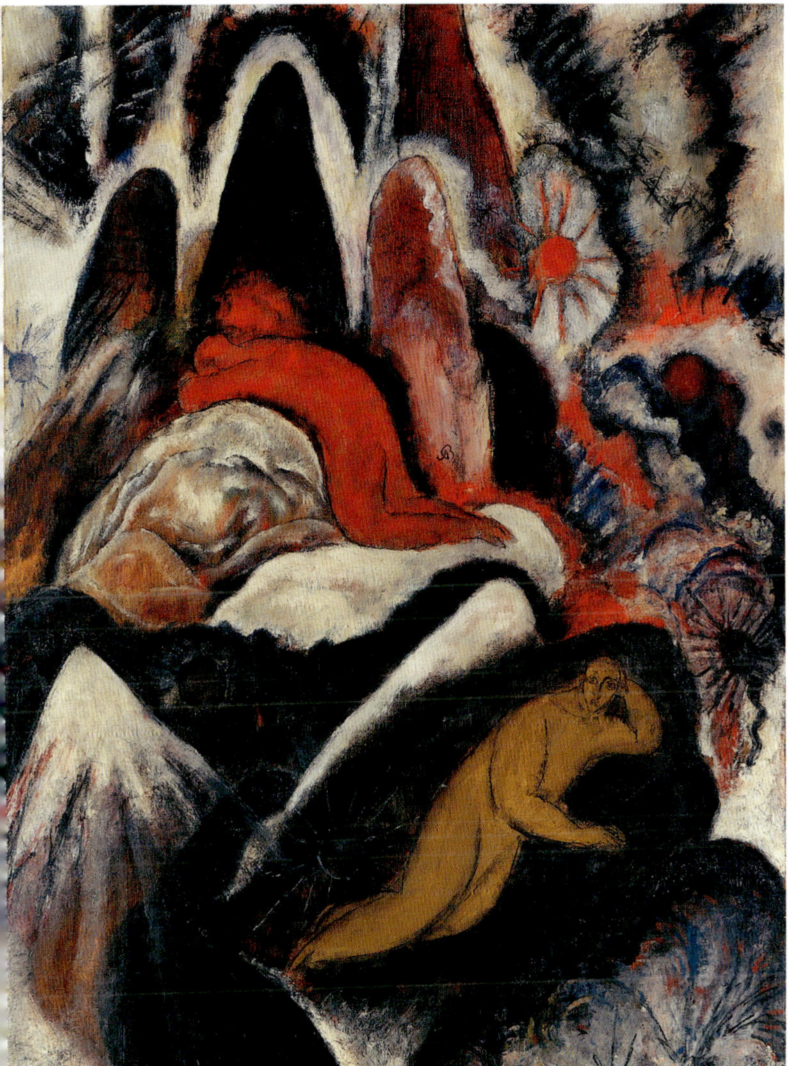

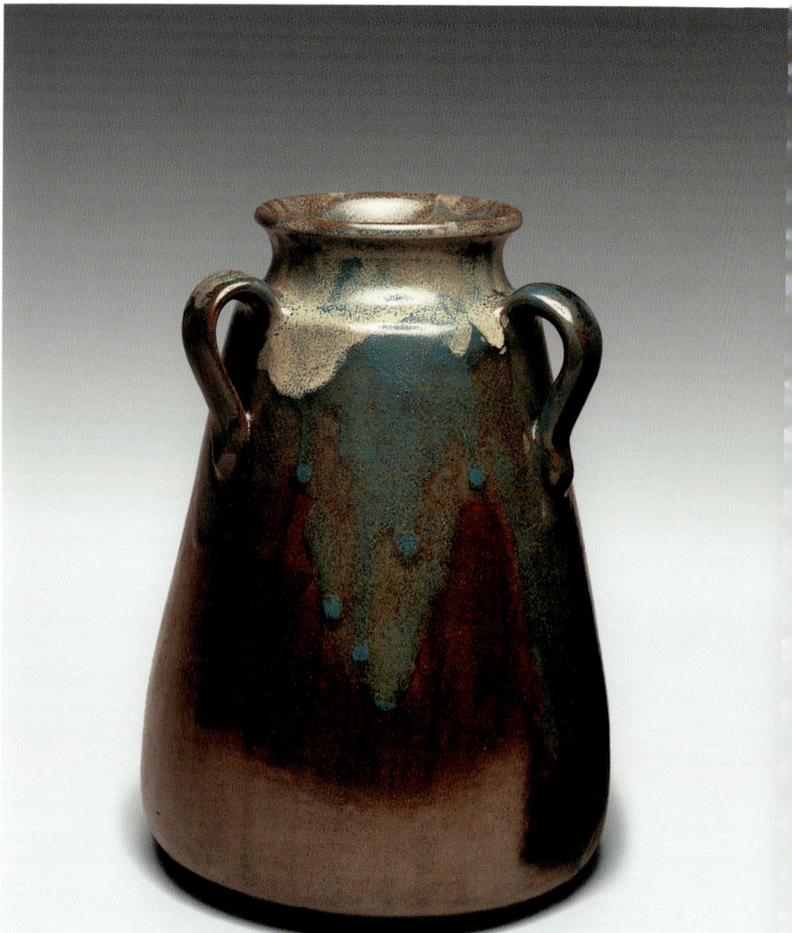

In contrast to other American art pottery vases held by Krannert Art Museum, this one is marked on the bottom with the initials "L. S.," indicating that it was designed, formed, glazed, and fired by a single person. The unidentified woman was part of a program created in 1906 at the Boston Library Club House by a group of immigrants known as the Saturday Evening Girls. The association, which the girls first joined as an educational pastime, grew into a profitable enterprise in which they could earn their living as potters. In 1908 the group moved to a location on Hull Street near the Old North Church, where Paul Revere had famously seen the signal lanterns. After the move, the Saturday Evening Girls began to use the name Paul Revere for their pottery works.

This vase departs from most Paul Revere examples, which were customarily decorated with large incised flower shapes filled with color. Typically, glazes were solid colors with matte or reflective surfaces. The base color of this vase, however, is a mottled brown, and a thin green glaze flows between three evenly spaced handles on the shoulder to form an irregular pattern on the body. An oyster-gray glaze washes over the lip and into the green glaze on the shoulders. There are no applied decorative details. Hixon, Smith

Paul Revere Pottery
United States
(ca. 1908–42)

Vase
1915
Ceramic
11 × 7 1/2 inches
Harlan E. Moore Charitable Trust
1987-14-1

André Kertész was born in 1894 in Budapest, where he taught himself photography while earning a business diploma and working in the stock exchange. During World War I, he began to develop the photo-reportage approach that made him a seminal figure in the field of photojournalism. Unfortunately, nearly all of these early images were lost in the war, a calamity that would be repeated during World War II, when Kertész would lose another extended period of his oeuvre.

The modest attention accorded Kertész's photographs in Budapest encouraged him to move to Paris in 1925. He lived in Montparnasse, where he frequented the Café du Dôme along with other writers, artists, and collectors. It was there that the photographer met Jan Slivinsky, who offered him his first one-man show in 1927. As a result, Kertész's international reputation grew and his work was included in other major presentations, notably the 1928 *Salon Indépendant de la Photographie* in Paris and the 1929 exhibition *Film und Foto* in Stuttgart. Kertész spent World War II in New York, where he worked on the staff of several publications and as a freelance journalist. He had difficulty gaining recognition in America until 1965 when the late curator and photographer John Szarkowski organized a one-man show at the Museum of Modern Art.

The subject of *Dumaharaszti* – a nude male sitting in a romantic landscape – is unusual within the photographer's oeuvre, but its personal, expressive, and intimate style is characteristic. Kertész made the image during a country sojourn in the spring of 1920. Fuessle

André Kertész
United States
(born Hungary)
1894–1985

Dunaharaszti
1920
Silver gelatin print
8 × 10 inches
Art Acquisition Fund
1972-3-1

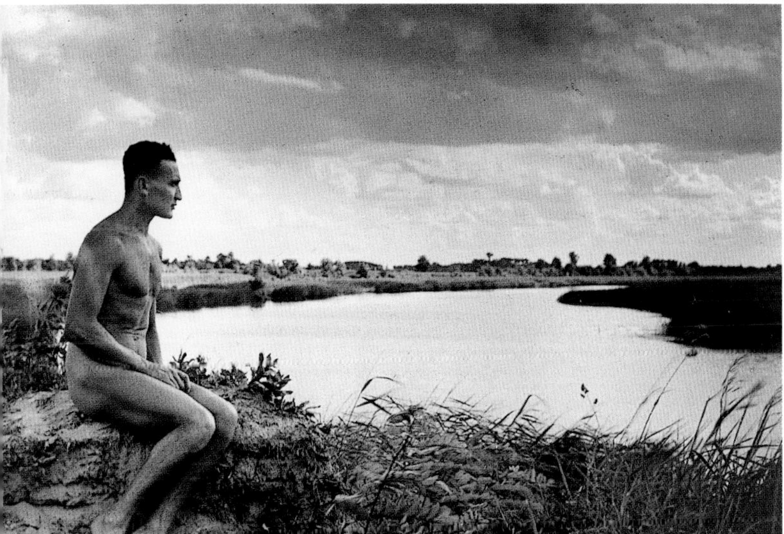

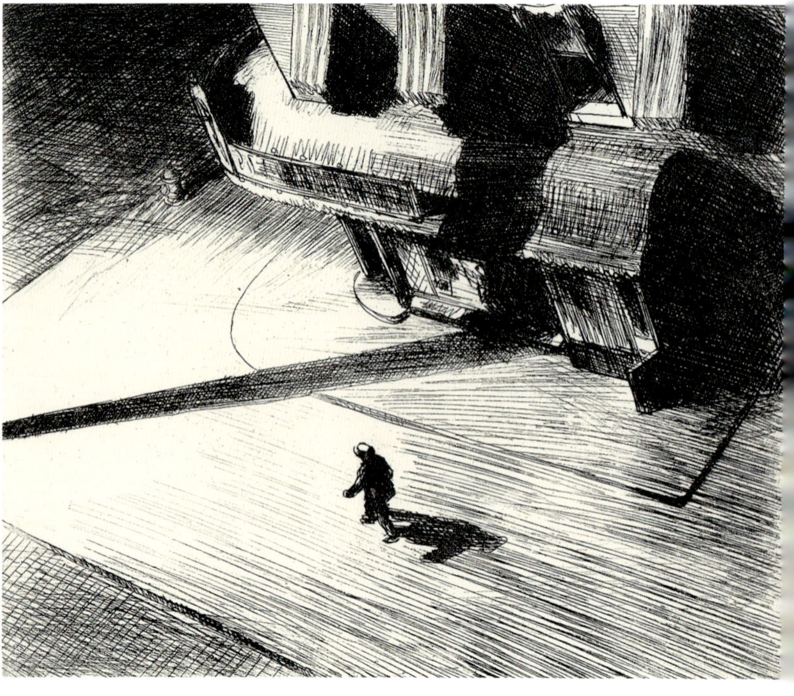

Night Shadows was one of four etchings Edward Hopper showed in 1921 at the National Academy of Design in New York. By this time, the artist had enjoyed only limited success with his paintings, and his modest income was based on intermittent work as an illustrator and commercial designer. Printmaking was something of a sideline for him. Though his friend and fellow artist Norman Lewis had given him some technical advice on the etching process, Hopper was a largely self-taught printmaker who gained confidence through trial and error. The National Academy of Design presentation won Hopper praise from a *New York Times* critic who characterized him in 1921 as "a genius for finding beauty in ugliness," and initiated an upswing in his career.

Night Shadows illustrates pictorial elements that would define Hopper's art for decades to come. The combination of unorthodox perspective, raking shadows, and a looming architectural façade combine to engulf the isolated figure in tension. The mood of estrangement would typify the majority of his later paintings.

Though Hopper's interest in the etching process waned by the mid-1920s, it had a pivotal and lasting effect on his paintings. Late in his life he commented, "After I took up etching, my painting seemed to crystallize." With his experience in printmaking, Hopper continued to make sketches from life for paintings, but he also began to rely more and more on memory and imagination. Atterberry

Edward Hopper
United States
1882–1967

Night Shadows
1921
Etching
7 × 8 1/2 inches
Art Acquisition Fund
1985-15-1

Edward Weston kept meticulous records of his work throughout his long career, and in a daybook entry of 1925 wrote that he had created "the finest series of nudes I have ever done." The model for the series was his friend Anita Brenner, who posed for a single sitting in November of that year. The female form is difficult to decipher in photographs from the series on Brenner. The figure in Krannert Art Museum's print (p. 252) is more legible than others – the model is seated with her back to the photographer and her arms raised around her drawn-up legs. In another example, where the model's arms and legs are tucked in completely, the form resembles that of Weston's iconic pepper print. Weston wrote of the series that he was "not prepared to say that this is a finer use of photography than the rendering of realism or the grand statement of fact, the capturing of fleeting moments from life, as I have done," but that "at present my tendency seems entirely toward the abstract."

A comparison of Weston's nude with the work of his student Ruth Bernhard shows his influence. Born in Germany, Bernhard moved in 1927 to New York, where she began a career in photography. In 1953 she moved to Carmel, California, to study with Weston. She eventually settled in San Francisco, where she worked as a commercial photographer while pursuing her artistic work. Like Weston, Bernhard photographed the female nude throughout her career. The year after making *Two Forms*, she wrote in the *History of the Nude in Photography*:

> Down through the centuries, poets, sculptors, painters and now photographers have also been striving to grasp and immortalize the beauty of the human body, both male and female. I see in these forms the elemental relationship to the large forms of nature.... If I have chosen the female form in particular, it is because beauty has been debased and exploited in our sensual twentieth century.... To raise, to elevate, to endorse with timeless reverence the image of woman has been my mission – the reason for my work which you see here.

Unlike Weston, Bernhard experimented with the camera and darkroom techniques. Her hallmark is the treatment of light, which she manipulated in the studio. She is quoted as saying, "Light is my inspiration, my paint and brush. It is as vital as the model herself. Profoundly significant, it caresses the essential superlative curves and lines." Stanulis

Edward Weston
United States
1886–1958

(following pages)
Untitled (*Nude*)
1925
Platinum print
8 3/4 × 7 1/2 inches
Art Acquisition Fund
1964-3-51

Ruth Bernhard
United States
(born Germany)
1905–2006

Two Forms
1963
Silver gelatin print
13 1/2 × 10 1/2 inches
Art Acquisition Fund
1965-4-4

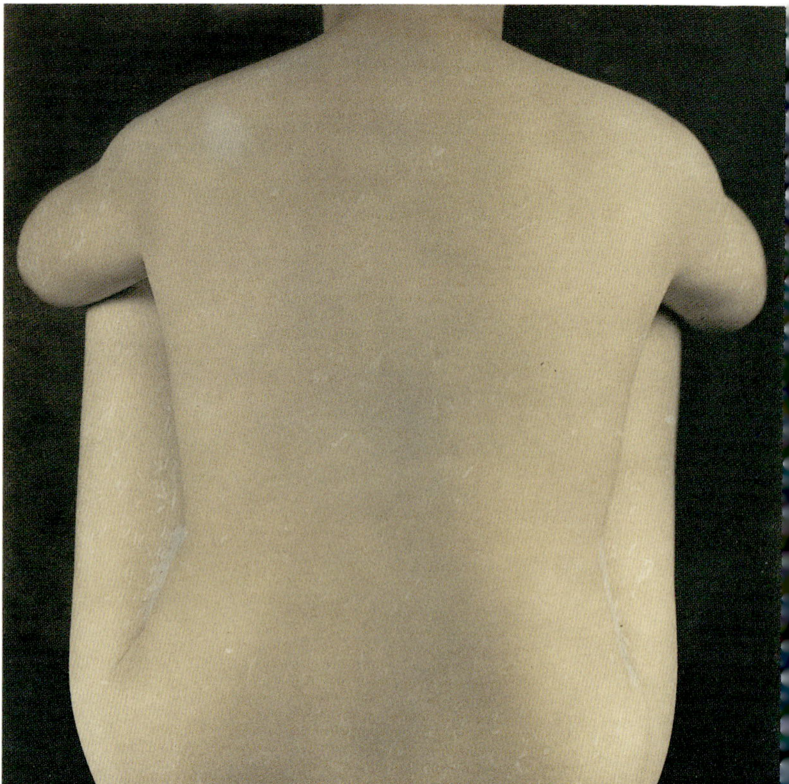

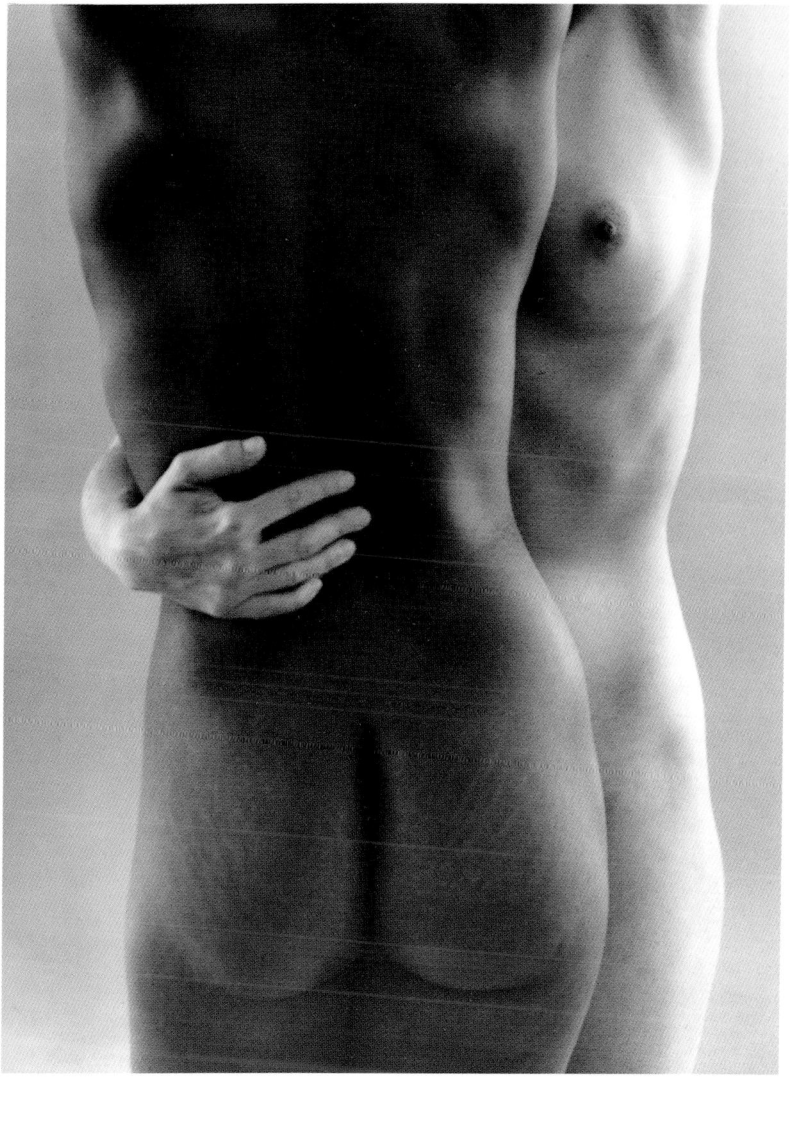

Untitled (*Nude*)
Two Forms

New York City and its landmarks were a popular subject with early-twentieth-century American artists. In this canvas, the impressionist Guy Carleton Wiggins has painted Wall Street during a heavy snowfall. Lightly obscured by the snow, taxicabs, people, and buildings line the street, which creates a strong diagonal thrust up to the hazy silhouette of Trinity Church. In the foreground, to the immediate right, is the old Sub-Treasury Building with its monumental statue of George Washington. The falling snow is blown by the wind to create a dizzying pattern at the center of the composition.

This work, which probably dates from the late 1930s, suggests key American values of the period: the church symbolizes faith, the statue of George Washington embodies patriotism, and the old Sub-Treasury Building (site of Washington's inauguration) represents finance and trust in capitalism.

Although Wiggins is best known for his winter scenes of New York, which often included Wall Street, he traveled widely and painted in many different locales throughout the United States and Europe. Kriz

Guy Carleton Wiggins
United States
1883–1962

Wall Street, New York
(Winter, New York)
n.d.
Oil on canvas
24 × 20 inches
Gift of Mr. and Mrs. Merle J. Trees
1943-1-5

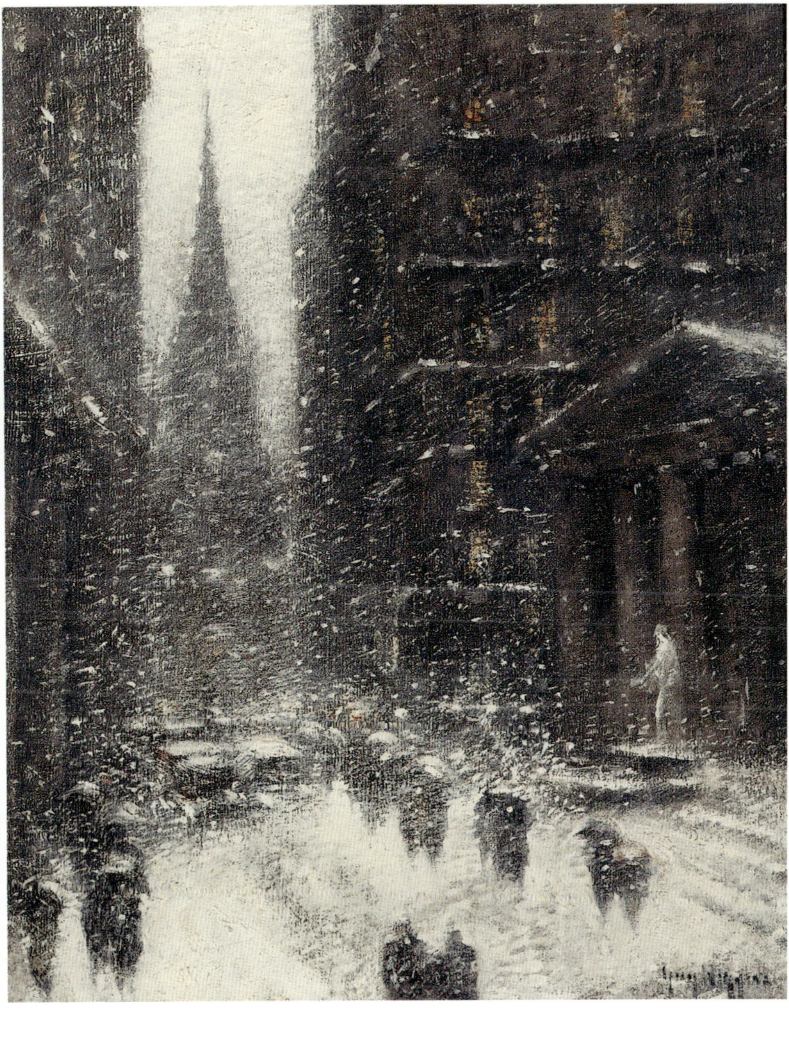

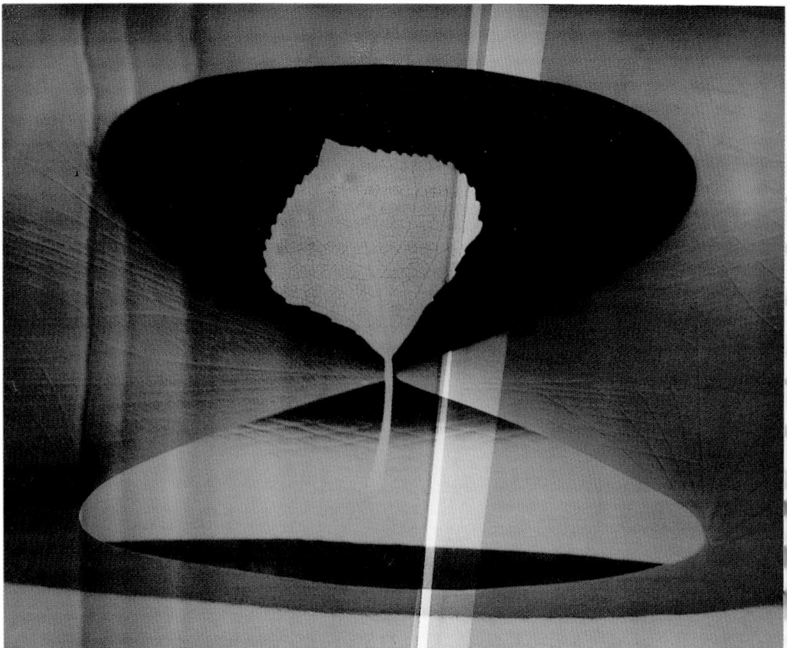

Trained at the Academy of Fine Arts in Budapest, György Kepes was a leading teacher of visual literacy, maintaining throughout his career that vision was key to understanding the formal, social, and cultural realities of the twentieth century.

In his photograms, in which objects and materials are exposed to light over sensitized paper, Kepes transformed cast shadows and solid forms into luminescent figures and designs. Many artists made camera-less photograms during the 1920s and '30s, but Kepes was unusual in ascribing social meanings to the formal qualities of transparency, overlay, and structure. He felt that art played an important role in envisioning the interdependence of natural and manmade structures and the interrelationship of art, science, and technology. He described these conditions in overlapping registers of white, gray, and black.

Kepes promulgated his aesthetic and moral philosophy in pedagogical activities, in the manner of his friend and fellow Hungarian artist László Moholy-Nagy, who hired him as an assistant in Berlin and London, and in 1937 invited him to the United States to head the department of light and color at the New Bauhaus in Chicago. In 1945 Kepes began teaching at the Massachusetts Institute of Technology, where in 1967 he established the Center for Advanced Visual Studies, which continues to support innovative research in the creative applications of art and science. Kepes's most important work as an educator and theorist appears in books such as *Language of Vision* (1944) and the numerous anthologies he edited as part of the *Value + Vision* series. Mendelson

Untitled
1939
Photogram
16 × 19 inches
Art Acquisition Fund
1985-4-1

György Kepes
United States
(born Hungary)
1906–2001

Walker Evans was born into wealth in St. Louis and pursued his education at Andover Academy and Williams College. He moved to New York in the 1920s and lived for a year in Europe, studying at the Sorbonne in Paris. On his return to the United States, Evans took up photography. His work was nearly always commissioned by magazines or by federal programs designed to assist poor farmers during the Great Depression. Despite, or perhaps because of, Evans's privileged background, his best-known photographs are of destitute southern sharecroppers during the height of the Depression. Several were published in Evans's experimental book collaboration with writer James Agee, *Let Us Now Praise Famous Men* (1941). Evans was also known for his photographs of African sculpture and regional American architecture, such as antebellum plantation houses in the Deep South and Victorian buildings in the Northeast.

Like most of his previous work, *Negroes, Tallahassee, Florida* was part of a series produced in collaboration with a writer, in this case Karl Bickel, the former head of United Press International. Having retired to Florida, Bickel wanted to prepare a book on the history of the west coast of the state, to be called *The Mangrove Coast*. For the project, Evans did not photograph Florida's beaches but instead concentrated on the idiosyncrasies of local culture – Greek sponge divers in Tarpon Springs, retirees in Tampa, tourists, postcard displays, camper trailers, and, especially, images of the circus such as dancing elephants, posters, and circus-train cars. During his six-week stay, Evans made a side trip to Tallahassee to photograph views such as this one. The image of the milling crowd on the sidewalk recalls Evans's street scenes in Havana and New Orleans, and harkens to his time recording the street life of Paris years before. The photographer's powers of observation during his nearly fifty-year career earned him a reputation as one of the most influential American photographers of all time. Mitchell

Walker Evans
United States
1903–1975

Negroes, Tallahassee, Florida
ca. 1941
Silver gelatin print
7 1/2 × 7 1/2 inches
Gift of Arnold H. Crane
1982-28-18

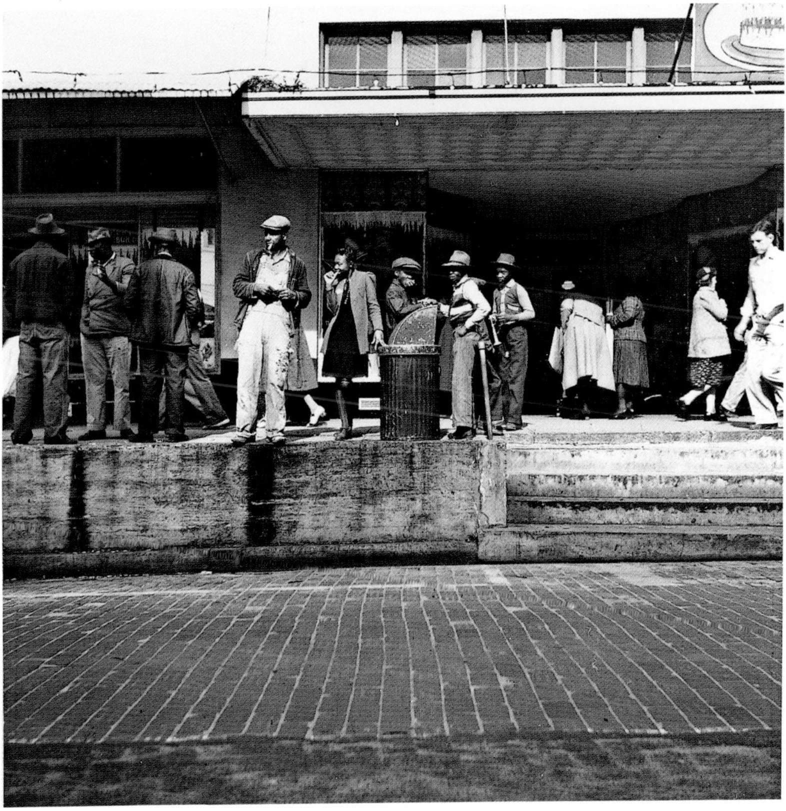

Philip Guston's formative years in Los Angeles provided the themes of his paintings for nearly fifty years: combat and struggle, political and social awareness, depression and melancholy. When he was ten years old, his father hanged himself. Guston discovered the body and cut it down. The first images he began making as a teen were of hooded figures evoking the Ku Klux Klan, which was burning crosses and breaking labor strikes in Los Angeles during his youth. In the 1930s, the artist moved to New York, where he painted Works Progress Administration (WPA) murals sponsored by the federal government as part of the New Deal. At that time, he changed his name from Goldstein to Guston.

In addition to the work of the Mexican muralists (particularly José Orozco and David Siqueiros), Guston responded to Italian Renaissance painting (especially that of Piero della Francesca) and the work of European modernists such as Giorgio de Chirico, Pablo Picasso, and Max Beckmann. In 1945 Guston began teaching at Washington University in St. Louis, where he had the opportunity to study Beckmann's paintings firsthand. After World War II, he spent time in an artists' colony in Woodstock, New York, and traveled to Europe on a Prix de Rome fellowship. He returned to New York City in the 1950s and became a key member of the abstract expressionist group, which included his long-time friend Jackson Pollock.

All of Guston's early influences are woven into the composition and style of *The Porch* (p. 262), which depicts a group of children dressed as street performers playing musical instruments. The figures occupy a compressed cubist space divided by two white lines forming a cross. Italianate architecture appears in the background at the upper left. Figures at the left play cymbals and a horn, while to the right a masked harlequin lifts the sole of his shoe to the viewer. In the foreground are two children, one with a paper hat and another playing a drum. The palette and the nature of the architectural forms recall both Piero della Francesca and de Chirico. The stylistic treatment of the theme of performers, musicians, and harlequins evokes the work of Picasso and Beckmann, both of whom often used performers as surrogates of the artist.

Beginning in the late 1960s, Guston returned to figurative painting with a series of hooded figures representing both himself and the Ku Klux Klan. He also began making cartoonlike images similar in style to the comic strip *Krazy Kat* and the work of illustrator Robert Crumb, which he infused with ironic social commentary. Shoe soles, trashcan lids, paintbrushes, fingers with cigarettes, clocks, body parts, and hooded figures populated his canvases during his later years.

Combat II (p. 263) continues the theme of struggle Guston began addressing early in his career, and it draws on the visual vocabulary he developed in the late 1960s and '70s. Painted with his trademark thick strokes of pink, red, and powder blue colors, *Combat II*, like *The Porch*, is spatially ambiguous. What at first appears to be a flat image takes on three-dimensional depth the longer one looks at it, a subtle reminder of Guston's early interest in cubism. *Combat II* reflects the artist's preoccupation with conflict and horror, which undoubtedly arose from his own family history, his awareness of social and political injustice, and the climate of violence generated by current events. At first, Guston was harshly criticized for abandoning abstraction, but he was later recognized by critics, scholars, and painters as being ahead of his time and an influential figure for the "new image" and "neo-expressionist" painting of the late 1970s and '80s. Mitchell

(following pages)
The Porch
1945
Oil on canvas
56 1/4 × 34 inches
Festival of Arts Purchase Fund
1948-10-1

Combat II
ca. 1978
Oil on canvas
42 1/4 × 48 1/4 inches
Estate of Musa Guston
1992-2-2

Philip Guston
United States
(born Canada)
1913–1980

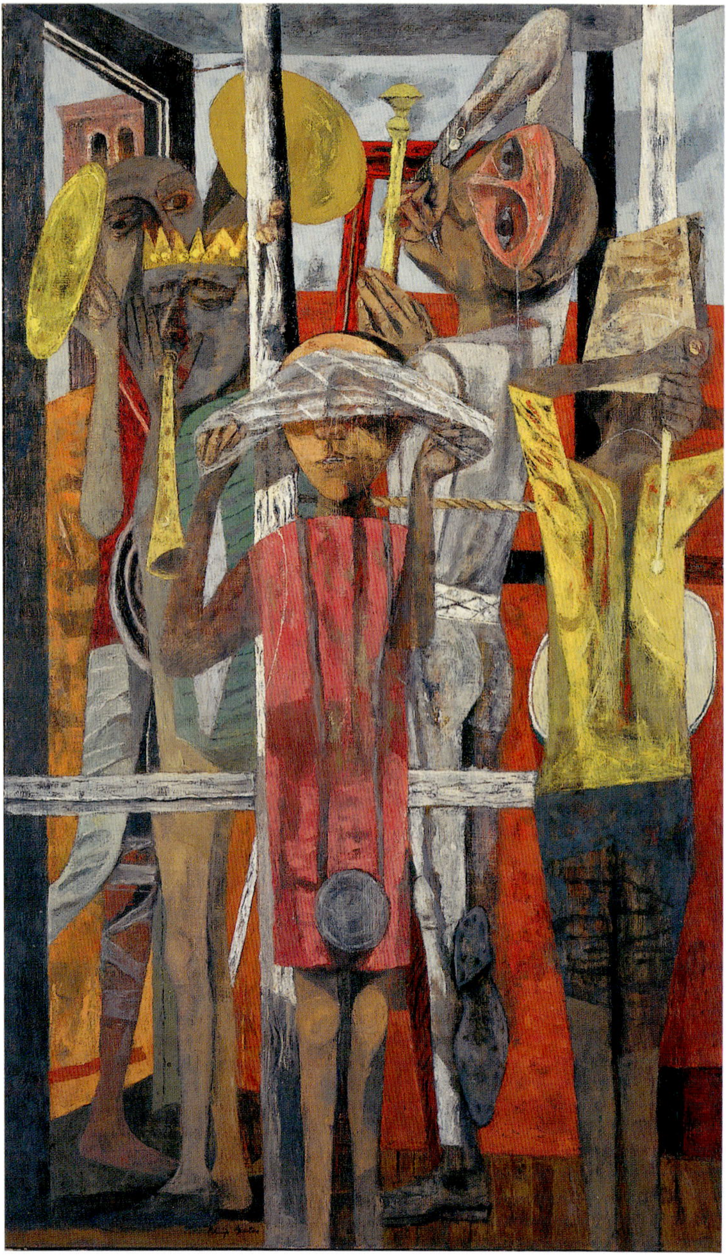

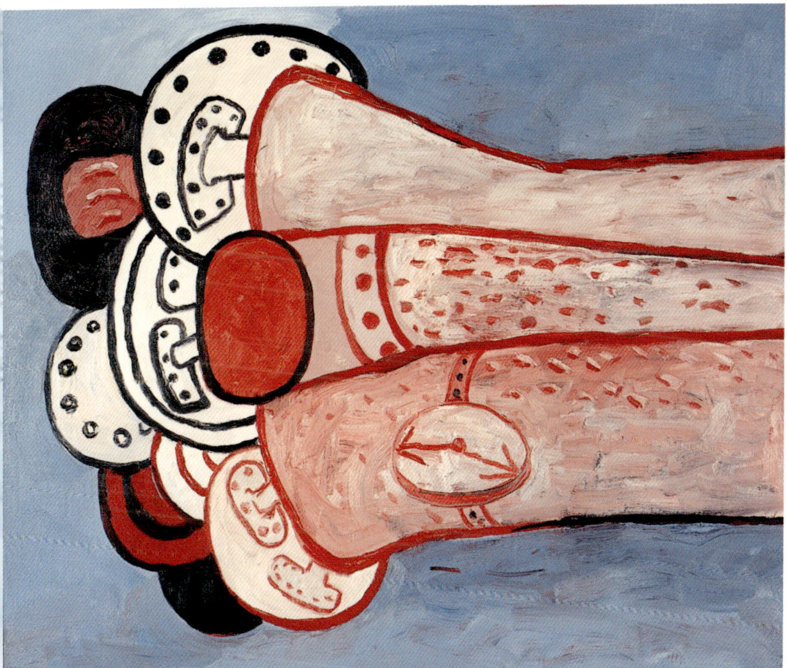

The Porch

Combat II

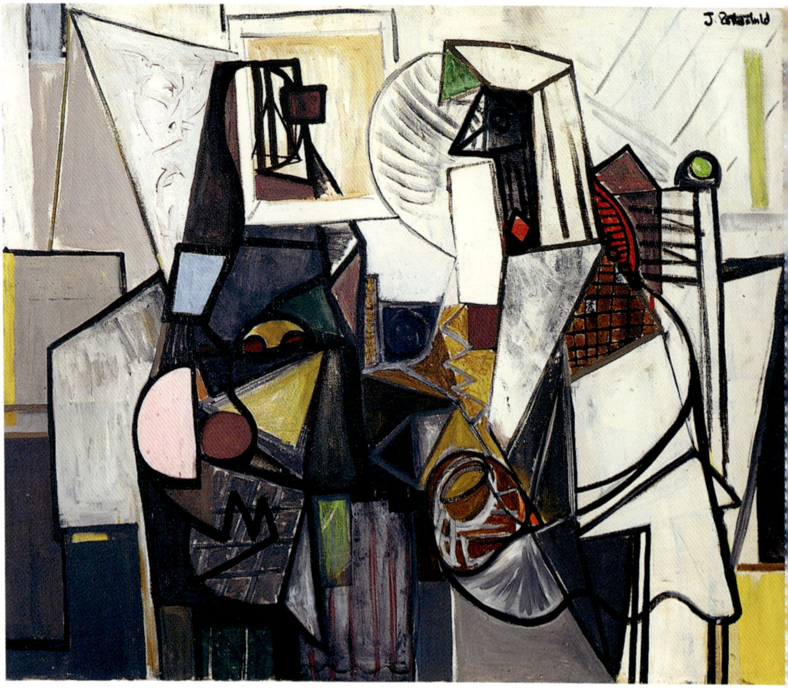

After graduating from Wellesley College, Judith Rothschild studied briefly at the Art Students League before seeking instruction from the German-born painter and teacher Hans Hofmann in the fall of 1943. Rothschild's early work reflects Hofmann's European modernist abstraction as well the influence of the paintings of Piet Mondrian and Pablo Picasso. At age twenty-two, Rothschild had her first solo exhibition, at the Jane Street Gallery in New York. Subsequently, she was elected to join the avant-garde American Abstract Artists. Despite its factions, the group was unanimously and passionately dedicated to abstraction, in strong contrast to the approaches of American Scene painting and social realism.

Personnages was exhibited in Rothschild's widely praised second solo exhibition in 1946 at the Luyber Galleries. The French title, which can be translated as "characters" or "individuals," suggests the reverberations of figuration in the work.
Stanulis

Personnages
1946
Oil on canvas
40 1/4 × 48 inches
Gift of The Judith Rothschild Foundation
and Knoedler & Company
2002-13-1

Judith Rothschild
United States
1922–1993

Well-known as both a teacher and a painter, Hans Hofmann was grounded in theory, and often quoted the writer Johann Wolfgang von Goethe, the philosopher G. W. F. Hegel, and the art historian and theorist Heinrich Wolfflin. Between 1915 and 1939, Hofmann developed and taught his own approach to painting. He studied the ways in which two-dimensional forms could create an effect of three dimensions. To produce the effect he described as "push and pull," he applied particular colors in carefully calibrated relationships to cause some areas to advance while others dramatically recede.

Hofmann has sometimes been seen as the preeminent colorist among the abstract expressionists. He was inspired by Paul Cézanne's expressive brushwork and preference for planes of color as opposed to line. The gestural swirls of colors and biomorphic shapes in *Apparition* evoke some of the movement and brilliance of the early paintings of his contemporary, Wassily Kandinsky. However, Hofmann's work displays a unique tension between contrasting colors and planes. Here he used opulent hues and dynamic brushstrokes to create a "push and pull" of colors. Undefined images float over the picture plane against the green and yellow colors of the background, freed from the confines of representation. Barnes

Hans Hofmann
United States
(born Germany)
1880–1966

Apparition
1947
Oil on reinforced plywood
48 × 58 inches
Festival of Arts Purchase Fund
1950-6-1

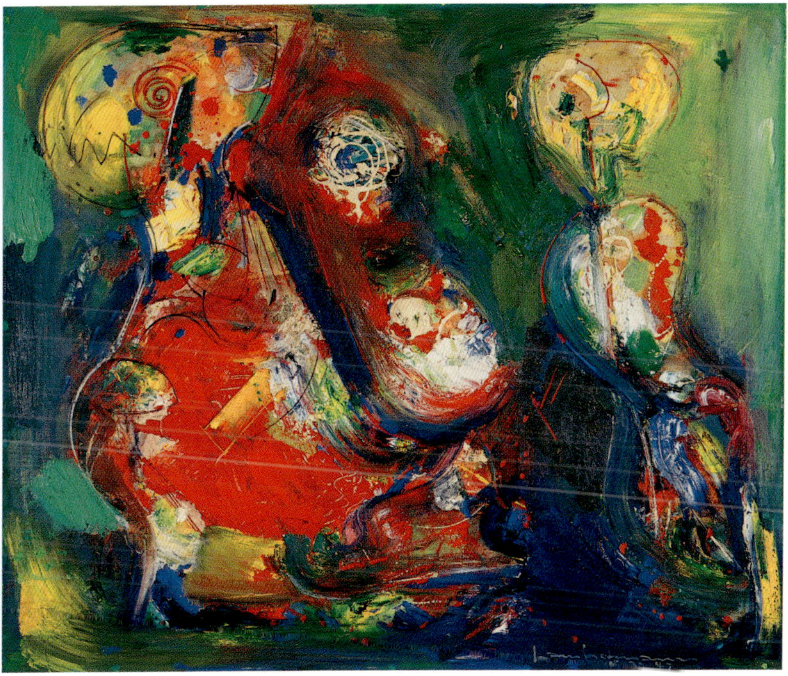

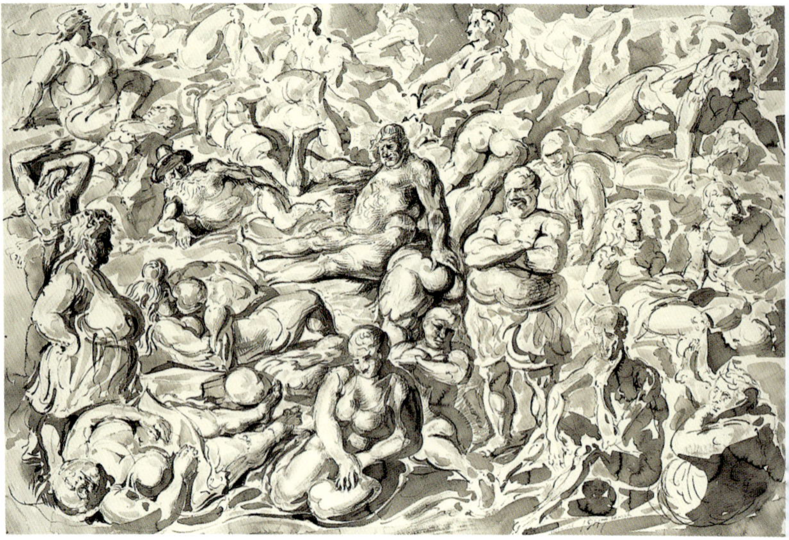

Reginald Marsh, whose artist parents encouraged him to pursue a career as a painter, always considered himself primarily a draftsman. Born in Paris to American parents, Marsh grew up in the suburbs of New York City and in New Jersey. At Yale Art School, Marsh was an art editor and cartoonist for the *Yale Record*. He later worked in New York as a freelance illustrator for prominent newspapers and magazines. There he began a lifelong association with the Art Students League, where he was first a student of artists John Sloan, George Luks, and Kenneth Hayes Miller, and from 1935 on, an instructor. Marsh's travels to Europe in the 1920s introduced him to the bold figural compositions of Michelangelo and Peter Paul Rubens, artists who had a lasting influence on his work.

Marsh's love of graphic media served his journalistic inclination to roam the streets of New York with a sketchpad. In etchings and engravings, as well as in tempera paintings and watercolors, he captured the noisy, bustling life of the city's streets, parks, movie palaces, burlesque houses, and beaches.

Coney Island Beach anticipates Marsh's large-scale experimentation with Chinese ink. A chaotic mass of monumental, partially clad bodies fills the scene. Nothing but bulging flesh demarcates space – there are no buildings or signs of water or beach. The figures are linked in fluid rhythms and tonal harmonies, but – with the exception of an occasional embracing couple – there is little interaction among them. As with his other late works, Marsh imbued natural forms with a sense of the grotesque. Morgan

Reginald Marsh
United States
1898–1954

Coney Island Beach
1947
Ink on paper
26 × 39 1/2 inches
Estate of Felicia Meyer Marsh
1979-16-3

Much of Milton Avery's subject matter was derived from his prolific sketches of the people in his life engaging in their daily activities. He frequently painted his daughter March, tenderly chronicling her youthful pastimes. His style and handling of color show fauve influences, specifically Henri Matisse's non-mimetic use of color. In a 1951 interview, Avery explained, "I try to construct a picture in which shapes, spaces, colors, form a set of unique relationships, independent of any subject matter. At the same time I try to capture and translate the excitement and emotion aroused in me by the impact with the original idea."

In *Bouquet with March*, Avery portrays his daughter engaged in her own artwork. The red blossoms in the bouquet dominating the center of the composition are delineated by scratches made in thinly applied paint. March appears at the extreme right, her face, her body, and some of her art implements forming sharply angled geometric shapes. Unlike many of Avery's color arrangements, this painting reflects the actual hues of the scene: the vibrant red of the plant and the orange of March's hair.

Avery's work inspired his painter friends Mark Rothko and Adolph Gottlieb. At Avery's memorial service in 1965, Rothko spoke of him as "a great poet-inventor who had invented sonorities never seen or heard before. From these we have learned much and will learn more for a long time to come." Donovan

Milton Avery
United States
1885–1965

Bouquet with March
1948
Oil on canvas
34 × 38 inches
Gift of Mr. and Mrs. Roy R. Neuberger
1953-12-1

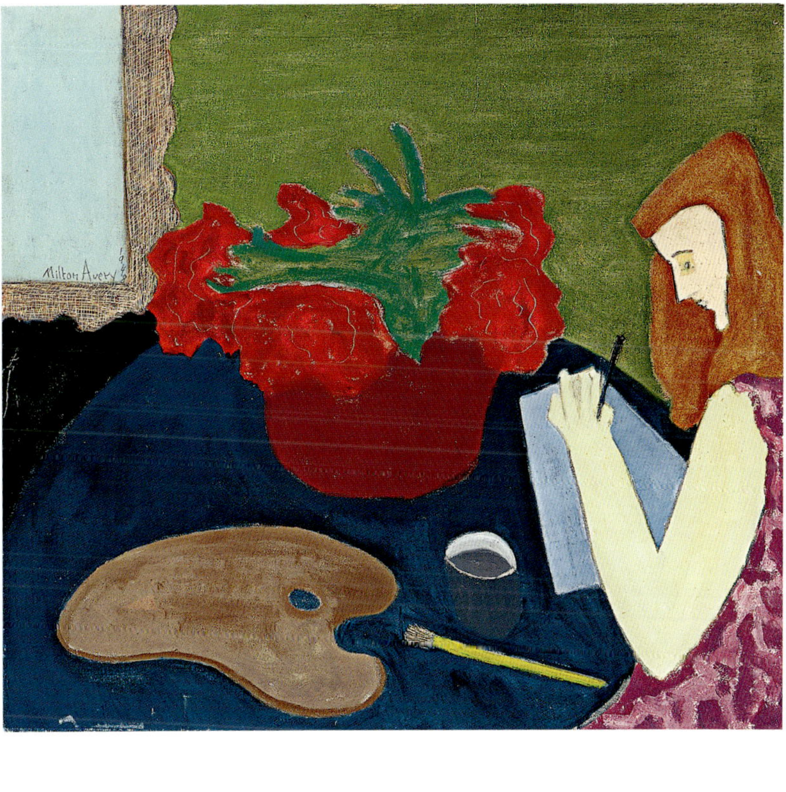
Milton Avery

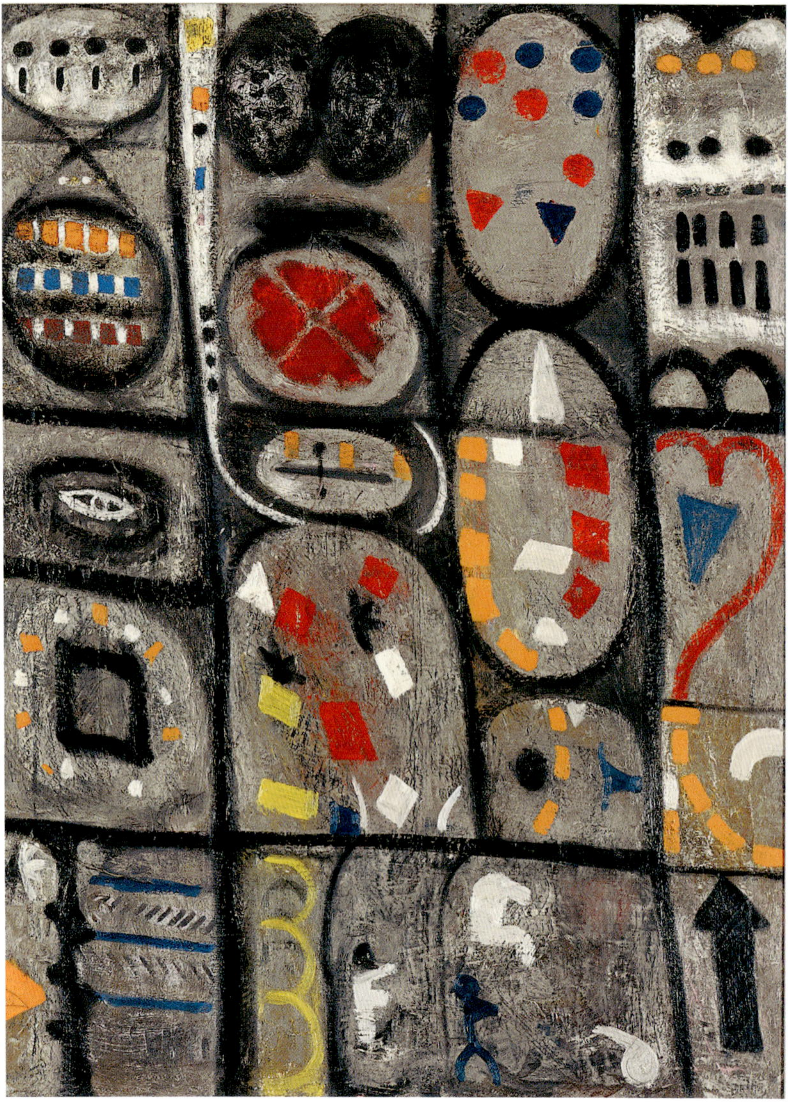

The wide stylistic range of Adolph Gottlieb's pictographs of 1941–53 distinguished them in the American art world of the 1940s. At a time when many looked to Europe as the pinnacle of artistic production, Gottlieb and a small group of New York artists influenced by the thinking of Carl Jung drew inspiration and imagery from global sources. Jung, a psychoanalytical theorist, introduced the notion that the unconscious mind stored images and symbols that connected cultures throughout history. Gottlieb had an extensive collection of African, Native-American, prehistoric, and Oceanic art. With Mark Rothko, Milton Avery, and others, he often added titles to his work that reflected an interest in mythological and medieval themes.

The grid that compartmentalizes the imagery in *Romanesque Facade* is typical of Gottlieb's pictographs. However, the painting is unusually representational: the compartments containing red and black dots, squares, and triangles bear a resemblance to the stained-glass windows of a cathedral's facade. Barnes

Romanesque Facade
1949
Oil on canvas
48 × 35 3/4 inches
Festival of Arts Purchase Fund
1951-6-2

Adolph Gottlieb
United States
1903–1974

Mark Rothko painted *No. 13* during a dynamic period in the evolution of abstract expressionist art. While Jackson Pollock was working with gestural drips and splatters of paint, Rothko by 1949 had replaced symbolic and surrealistic imagery with layers of pure color. The artist reduced color to its essence and allowed it to communicate form on its own. Rothko called his paintings from 1948 to 1949 "multiforms" because of the proliferation of patches of color. By 1949–50, he had replaced the multiple areas of color and intimate scale with large horizontal expanses of bounded color on mural-sized canvases.

In *No. 13*, Rothko used thin sponges, rags, and cloth to build up veils of color. The layers of paint have bled into their support, all but eliminating surface texture and evidence of the artist's gesture. Hazy blocks of color dispersed throughout the painting are activated by intermittent opaque strokes of purple and red paint. The soft, uneven segments seem to float on the support. Rothko eliminated perspectival illusionism, but the relationships of color create a sense of depth in the flat composition. The solid orange block at the lower left, for example, pushes forward, while the neighboring purple pulls back. Using abstract form to make an immediate and, to his mind, universal artistic statement, Rothko's simplified visual vocabulary was intended to evoke elemental human emotions and to prompt contemplation. Wolfskill

Mark Rothko
United States
(born Russia)
1903–1970

No. 13
1949
Oil on canvas
56 × 28 inches
Gift of Walter Bareiss
1955-16-1

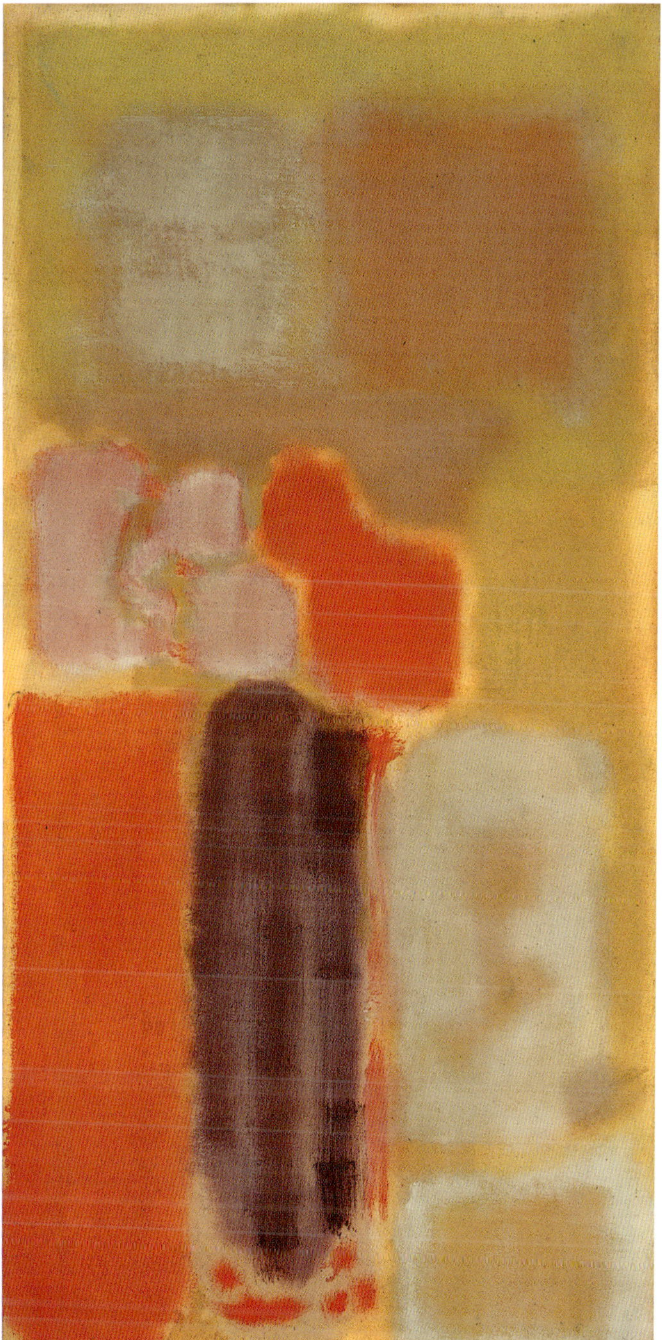

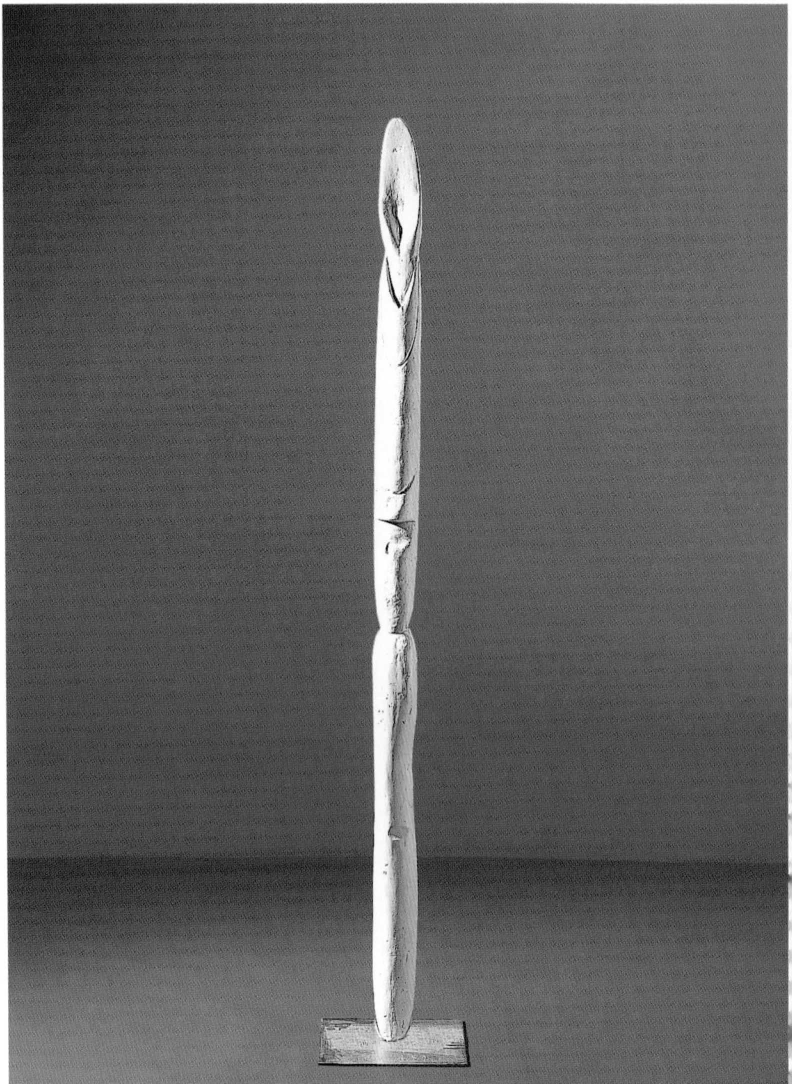

Louise Bourgeois began working in three dimensions with her *Personages* – the series to which *Depression Woman* (previously *Spoon Woman*) belongs – in New York in the late 1940s and early '50s. These thin vertical sculptures, carved in wood and then cast in bronze, were first displayed in the artist's home and at the Peridot Gallery in New York in groups of two or three, and later were occasionally grouped close together in larger clusters. Many have been dispersed as single objects in galleries, museums, and private collections throughout the world.

In an interview published in 1976 in *Art Journal*, Bourgeois stated that "these pieces were presences – missed, badly missed presences." Except for rare examples named for specific people, such as her son, Jean-Louis, the identities of the portraits are unknown. Their life-size forms evoke human bodies, with suggestions of head, neck, and waist, but their rough-hewn abstraction de-individualizes them to suggest more general human conditions and emotions.

Bourgeois has described the *personages* as representing isolation within a group. Each sculpture is self-contained, with no means of engaging with the sculptures around it. Scholars have suggested that this expression of remoteness in her work may have resulted from her status as a recent immigrant and as a woman in a profession then overwhelmingly dominated by men. Donovan

Louise Bourgeois
United States
(born France)
b. 1911

Depression Woman
1949–50
Painted bronze
74 1/2 × 4 inches
John Needles Chester Fund
2002-16-1

In an entry in his journal in 1916, Charles Burchfield scribbled an idea for painting "a tree showing winter at the bottom, Spring in the lower branches, summer in the upper with Autumn crowning the top with fruit." He was long fascinated by the subject of seasonal change, but the late watercolor *The Four Seasons* is the closest he ever came to realizing the ambition of representing it. The foreground of this wooded scene is a shadowy winter landscape. A rich autumnal passage between the two foremost trees marks not only seasonal transformation but also a transition from the exterior to a bright, cathedral-like interior space and a spring landscape of yellows and greens. In the middle ground, a screen of trees forming pointed Gothic arches opens onto a summer landscape in the distance. The arches also point toward a life-giving sun that imbues the interior space with warmth and energy. As rays of light fall on the foreground trees, their branches fairly burst into orange flame. Burchfield's pictorial language of semi-abstract, calligraphic brushstrokes lends a sense of animate presence to this pictorial meditation on seasonal and spiritual metamorphosis.

In his early work in watercolor, Burchfield's preferred medium, he explored natural subjects around his hometown of Salem, Ohio. While his work of the 1920s and '30s focused on urban subject matter and the "American scene," in the 1940s he returned to painting the natural world, often reworking landscapes he had begun early in his career. The spiritual intensity of these late works places them in a romantic tradition extending back to the nineteenth-century landscapes of painters such as Casper David Friedrich and Thomas Cole. Gaudio

Charles Burchfield
United States
1893–1967

The Four Seasons
1949–60
Watercolor
56 × 48 inches
Festival of Arts Purchase Fund
1961-2-1

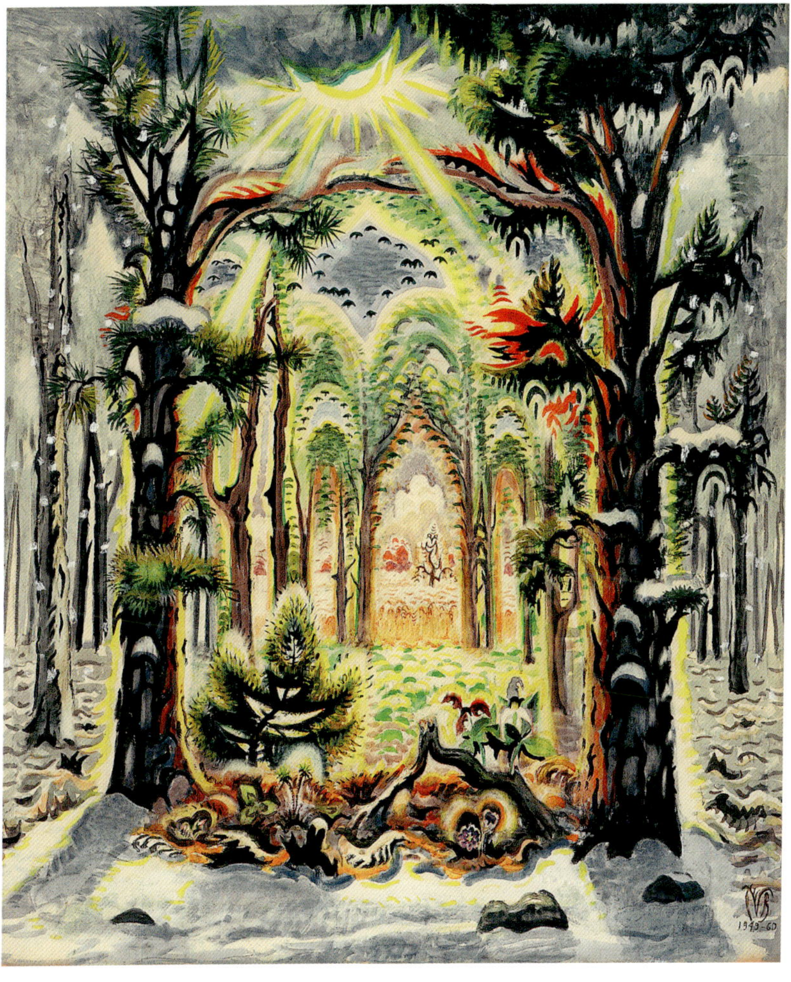

In his *Manifesto of Surrealism* of 1924, André Breton defined the creative method of automatism as the use of free association to elicit literary imagery from the unconscious mind. In the 1930s and '40s, surrealists such as William Baziotes and Matta applied the approach to the visual arts in both their subject matter and style. Baziotes and Matta met in New York in 1940 and in the early part of the decade experimented with automatism, allowing paint to drip onto their canvases to create unguided forms. Their practices were to have an impact on a group of American artists that included Robert Motherwell and Jackson Pollock.

Automatism allowed Baziotes to become freer in his compositions, to use a more fluid line, and to engage the mythical and fantastical images of surrealist art and writing. He derived his imagery from Carl Jung's philosophy of unconscious archetypes, the representations of transhistorical and transcultural experiences. Such archetypes include the sun, the moon, and various animals. In Baziotes's *Moon Animal* (p. 282), a biomorphic animal stands in the blue night before a small sun form that radiates a rectangle of light over a larger, glowing white moon.

Matta was a strong proponent of the use of automatism in the early 1940s. By the late 1940s and early '50s, his art began to diverge from that of painters such as Baziotes. Rather than painting mythical archetypes, Matta dispassionately painted his response to the social and political world. After World War II, the artist emphasized the role of science in the destruction caused by war, painting totemic machines locked in battles of epic scale. Krannert Art Museum's *L'horreur du mal, l'ultime, l'ennemi intérieur, la memoria cósmica* (p. 283) shows such warring figures, which strike out at each other with bladelike appendages in a scene suggesting universal conflict. Donovan

(following pages)
Moon Animal
1950
Oil on canvas
43 × 36 1/4 inches
Festival of Arts Purchase Fund
1951-6-1

William Baziotes
United States
1912–1963

L'horreur du mal, l'ultime, l'ennemi intérieur, la memoria cósmica (*The Horror of Evil, the Ultimate, the Internal Enemy, Cosmic Memory*)
1951
Oil on canvas
59 × 70 1/2 inches
Festival of Arts Purchase Fund
1951-5-1

Matta (Roberto Sebastián Antonio Echaurren)
France (born Chile)
1911–2002

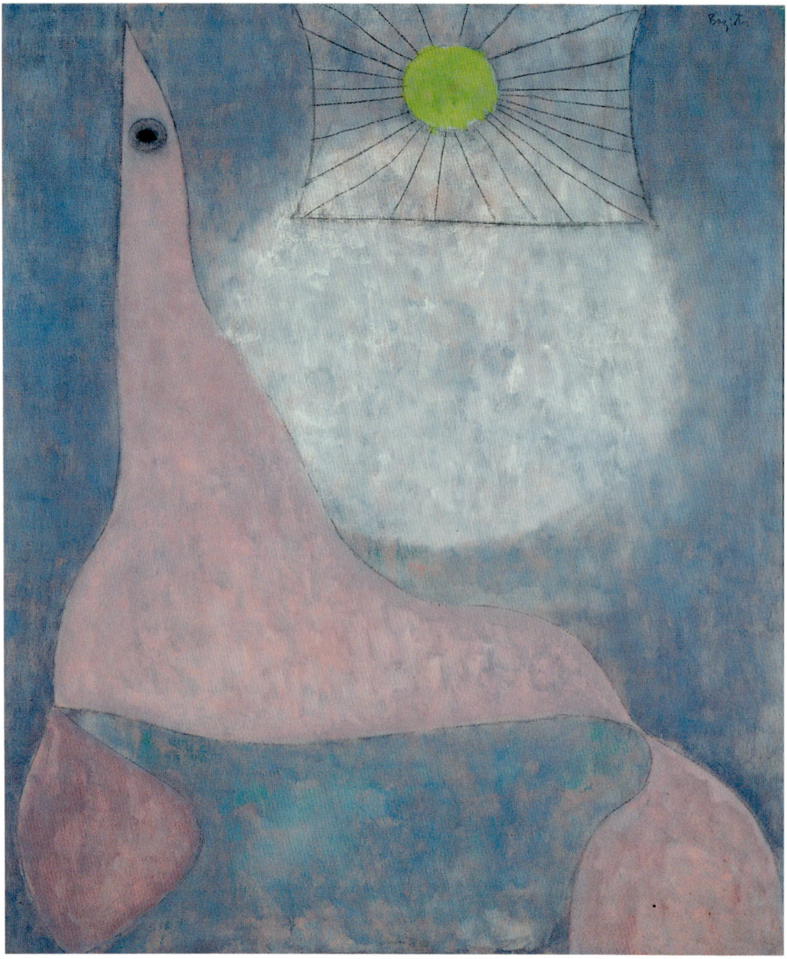

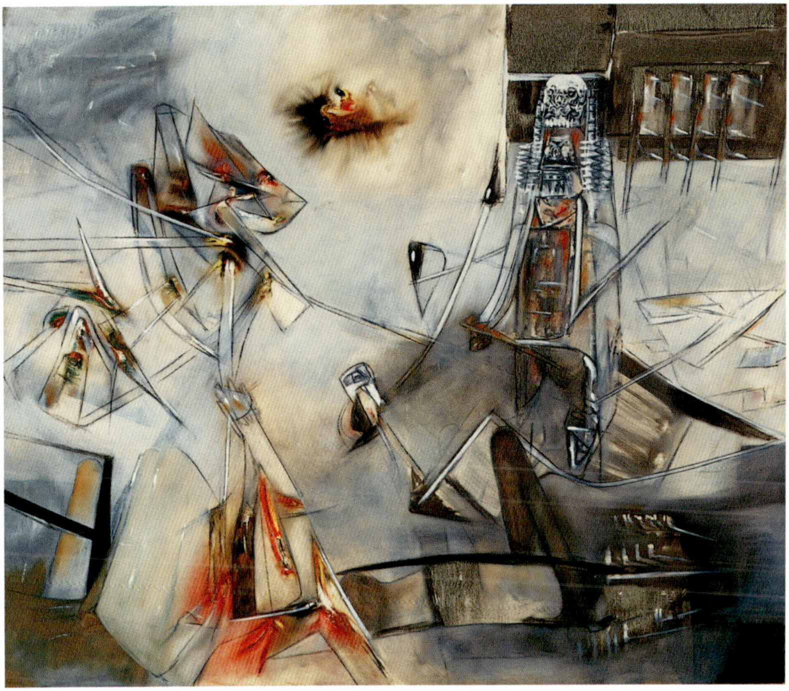

Moon Animal

L'horreur du mal, l'ultime,
l'ennemi intérieur, la memoria cósmica

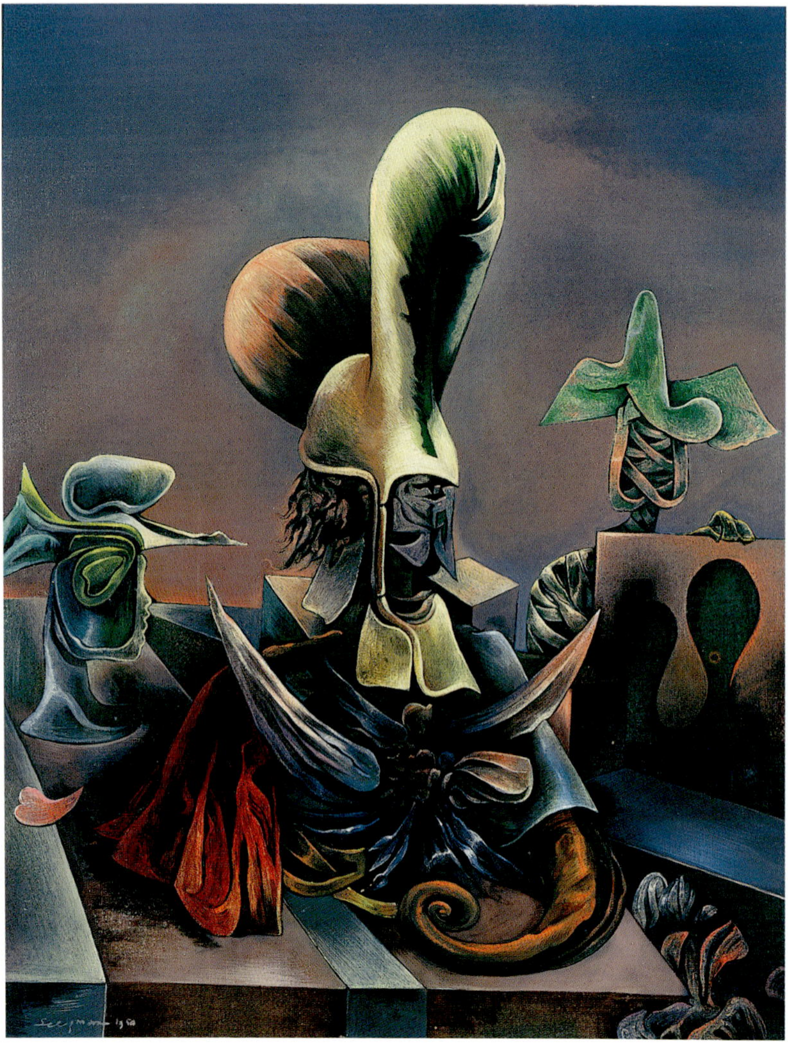

Kurt Seligmann studied art in Geneva with Alberto Giacometti before immigrating in 1939 to the United States, where he acquired citizenship in 1948. On his arrival, he joined the surrealist movement, but was expelled in 1943 by its capricious founder and high priest, André Breton.

Seligmann was proficient in a variety of media, including engraving, etching, and painting in oil and tempera on canvas and glass. Throughout his life, he oscillated between his earliest approach of abstracted two-dimensional form and the hermetic imagery of his later surrealist vocabulary. As a scholar, he became an authority on magic and occultism, and published a book on the subject in 1948. As an artist, he sought inspiration from a wide range of sources: the paintings of his fellow surrealist Max Ernst, indigenous magic, traditional Swiss painting, and childhood memories. *High Priest* shows three anthropomorphic figures composed of geometric and abstract shapes. They are set in a fantastic desert landscape that pulls the viewer's gaze into a diffused greenish-pink sky. The fantastic headgear of the high priest is based on the artist's memory of carnival costumes.

Seligmann's talent as a draughtsman manifests itself in the strong contours and lines of the figures. This skill is also evident in six etchings from the *Oedipus* series he made for his close friend, art historian Meyer Schapiro, also in Krannert Art Museum's collection. Tallone

Kurt Seligmann
United States
(born Switzerland)
1900–1962

High Priest
1950
Oil on canvas
43 1/4 × 34 inches
Festival of Arts Purchase Fund
1951-3-1

Hedda Sterne was trained in Bucharest, where she was born, and later in Vienna. In the 1930s, her compatriot and fellow artist Victor Brauner introduced her to the surrealists in Paris, and late in the decade she began exhibiting with them. In 1941, Sterne narrowly eluded a roundup of Jews in German-occupied Bucharest and escaped to New York, where art patron Peggy Guggenheim introduced her to a vital community of émigré artists, including Max Ernst, Marcel Duchamp, and Piet Mondrian. After her first solo exhibition in New York in 1943, Sterne joined the roster of the Betty Parsons Gallery, which included Jackson Pollock, Mark Rothko, and Ad Reinhardt, and became a significant presence in New York.

Machine 5 is an outstanding example of what Sterne has called her "anthropographs," images of machines with human-like qualities that she painted from the late 1940s through the early '50s. The concept of the anthropographs stemmed from Sterne's observation on arriving in the United States that the American landscape was more surreal than any surrealist invention. She was intrigued by the idea that human beings, possessing an insatiable desire for consumption, make machines that unconsciously serve as portraits of their own inner needs. Most likely inspired by a New York City construction site, the abstract and impossibly top-heavy industrial equipment in *Machine 5* undermines any notion of conventional function. The vibrant red background detaches the machine from any setting. At once whimsical and frightening, it has come to life, with multiple eyes wide open and jaws ready to devour. Eckhardt

Hedda Sterne
United States
(born Romania)
b. 1916

Machine 5
1950
Oil on canvas
51 × 38 1/4 inches
Festival of Arts Purchase Fund
1950-7-1

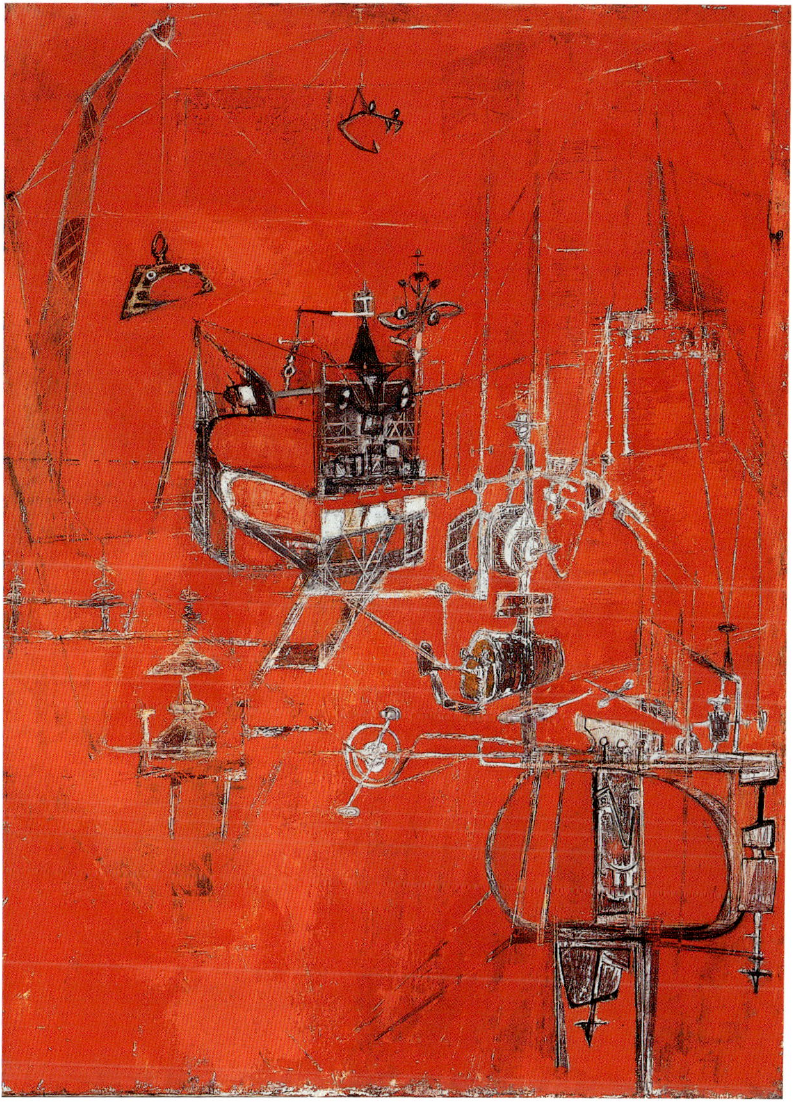

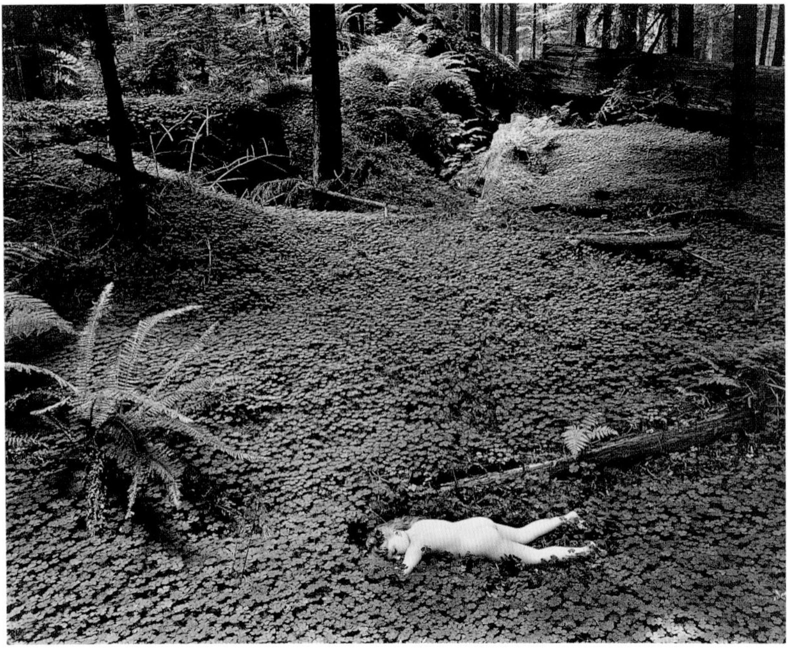

Wynn Bullock was born Perry Wingfield Bullock in Chicago and worked as a professional singer before turning to the visual arts. Photographs by Man Ray and Lászlo Moholy-Nagy sparked Bullock's interest in photography, and in his thirties he began seriously pursuing photography. He was later influenced by the work of Edward Weston.

In the 1950s, Bullock turned to the depiction of the nude. A prolific writer who considered his philosophy and photography inextricably linked, he became increasingly interested in the relationship between the human figure – especially the nude – and nature. He stumbled on the location shown in *Child in Forest* while picnicking by a highway, and combined the element of chance with straight photography to create a striking image. The body of his sleeping daughter Barbara complements the "virginal" forest while contrasting with the history implicit in it. Visually, the figure provides a rest point for the viewer, whose eye is stimulated by the overall pattern of vegetation.

Child in Forest was one of the most successful and well-received works of Bullock's mature period. Curator and fellow photographer Edward Steichen included it in his landmark *Family of Man* exhibition at the Museum of Modern Art in 1955. Kuhl Cox

Wynn Bullock
United States
1902–1975

Child in Forest
1951
Silver gelatin print
7 1/2 × 9 1/2 inches
Festival of Arts Purchase Fund
1967-14-1

In 1906, Ben Shahn immigrated to the United States from Kovno, Lithuania, and settled in New York City. He is best known for his socially conscious images from the New Deal era of the 1930s and '40s. *Second Allegory* reflects his transition in the early 1950s from subjects that literally describe social injustice to symbolic imagery that concerns more universal experience.

In this painting, a male figure appears to be pinned down by a hand descending from fiery clouds in a sky rendered with the palimpsests that began to appear in Shahn's work after 1951. The painting can be interpreted as an allegory of contemporary political persecution, representing the accusing finger of Joseph McCarthy or the underlying presence of the atomic bomb, which was detonated by the United States in 1952. But it is more probably tied to Shahn's emerging interest in the universal balance of spirituality, science, and philosophy, ideas he was deeply involved with from 1950 until his death. The red molecular forms floating above the knee of the fallen figure evoke Shahn's concern about science. The artist felt that scientific advances, coupled with the nation's growing materialism, would lead to what he considered a degeneration of man's spiritual forces, an attitude he expressed in his 1951 essay "How Can Art Contribute to an Industrial and Scientific Age?"

Shahn may also have had in mind the mystical teachings and imagery of the Kabbalah, specifically the diagrammatic tree of life whose shape resembles the cluster of molecular forms. The celestial tree of life is a central feature of Jewish mystical speculation about the harmonious balance of the universe. Cox

Ben Shahn
United States
(born Lithuania)
1898–1969

Second Allegory
1953
Tempera on Masonite
53 1/2 × 31 1/2 inches
Festival of Arts Purchase Fund
1953-7-1

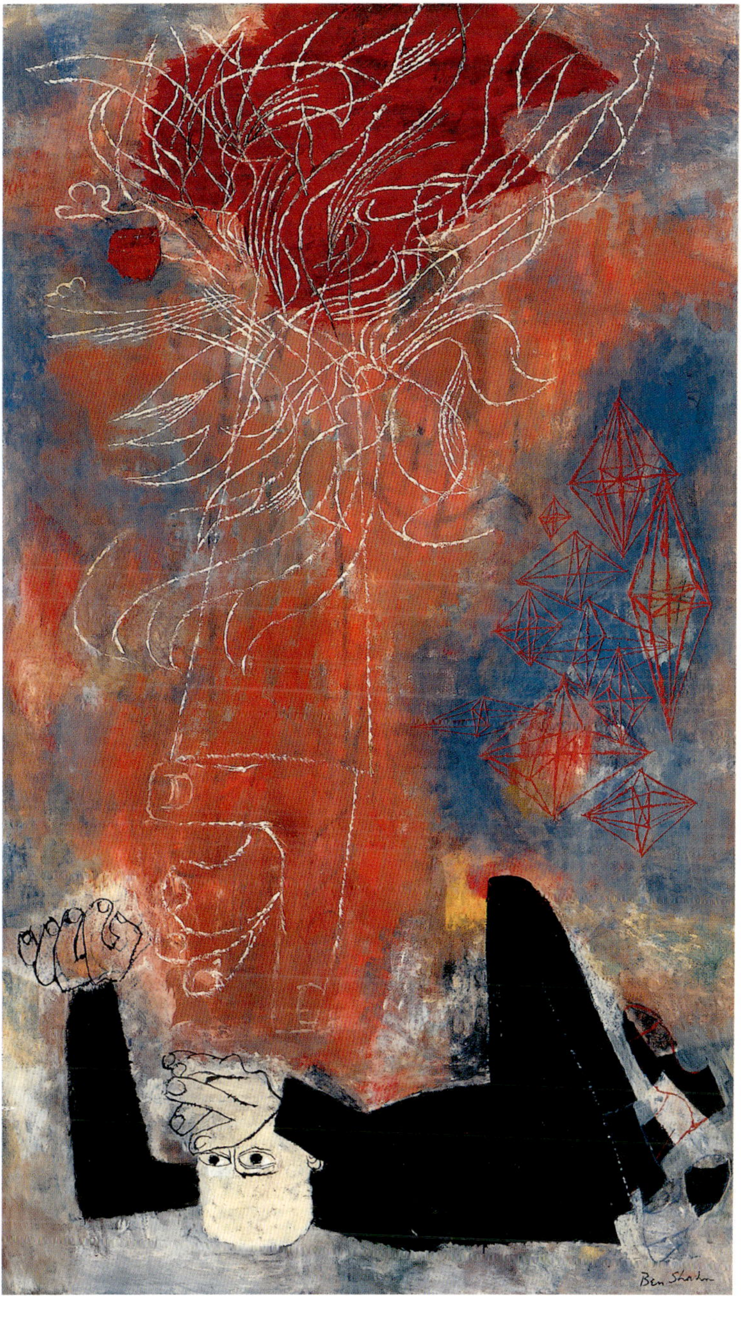
Ben Shahn

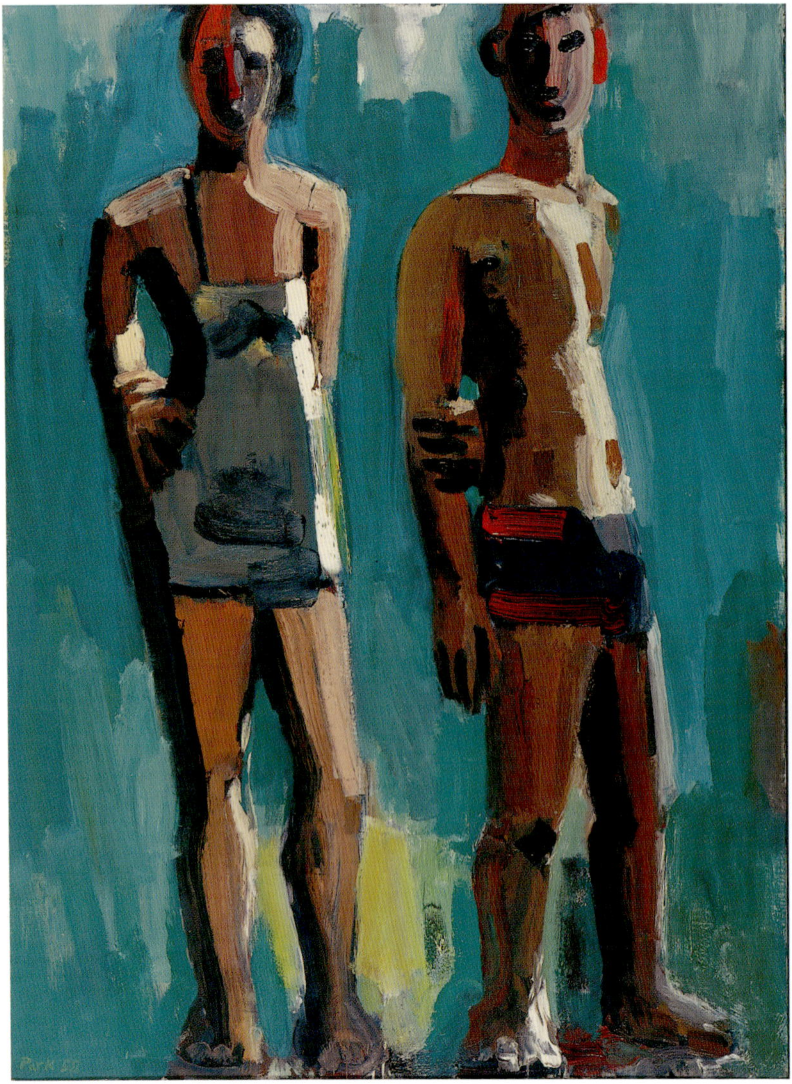
Park

David Park's expressionistic brushwork reflects the influence of artists of the New York School, particularly Robert Motherwell, Mark Rothko, and Clifford Still; from 1945 to 1947 Park visited exhibitions of their paintings in San Francisco, where he lived and worked. By 1949, however, he had tired of what he viewed as the egocentrism of New York School abstraction and returned to figurative painting, while retaining the gestural handling of paint.

In *Standing Couple*, Park formed the figures' facial features with emphatic smears of black paint, and bluntly described the swimsuits that distinguish male and female bathers, who stand in an undefined, shallow space. Despite the abstract quality of the composition, the artist created the illusion of realistic elements, such as the effect of light, the atmosphere of the environment, and the expressive poses of the figures. Light appears to enter from the right to suggest a sunlit day, and the vibrant blue and green background establishes an oceanside setting. Heavy brushstrokes evoke the breaking of waves on the shore. Despite the everyday subject matter, the figures are heroic and monumental. Wolfskill

David Park
United States
1911–1960

Standing Couple
1958
Oil on canvas
75 × 56 3/4 inches
Educational Grants and Provost's Funds,
Festival of Arts Purchase Fund
1961-11-1

Modern critics often refer to Jess as an outsider or an eccentric. Though some associate his collages made from pieces of comic books and magazines with the pop art movement of the 1960s, his work is romantic and philosophical rather than deadpan. He was drawn to children's tales, folklore, the occult, Egyptian mythology, and advertisements in popular magazines such as *Life* and *Time*. Jess began his "paste-ups," as he called his "romantic fantasies" based on novels, in 1951.

The flayed figure in *Hang'd Man* hangs by his ankles from a rope formed of entwined bodies. The tarot card referred to in the subtitle is the Death card, but the number 13 typically associated with bad luck implies simply the passage of events and time. The Plexiglas over the collaged shade and screen door makes the work reflective; as a result, the viewer's image merges with that of the hanged man. Barnes

Jess (Burgess Collins)
United States
1923–2004

The Hang'd Man: Tarot XIII
1959
Mixed media
79 1/2 × 30 inches
John Needles Chester Fund
1983-27-1

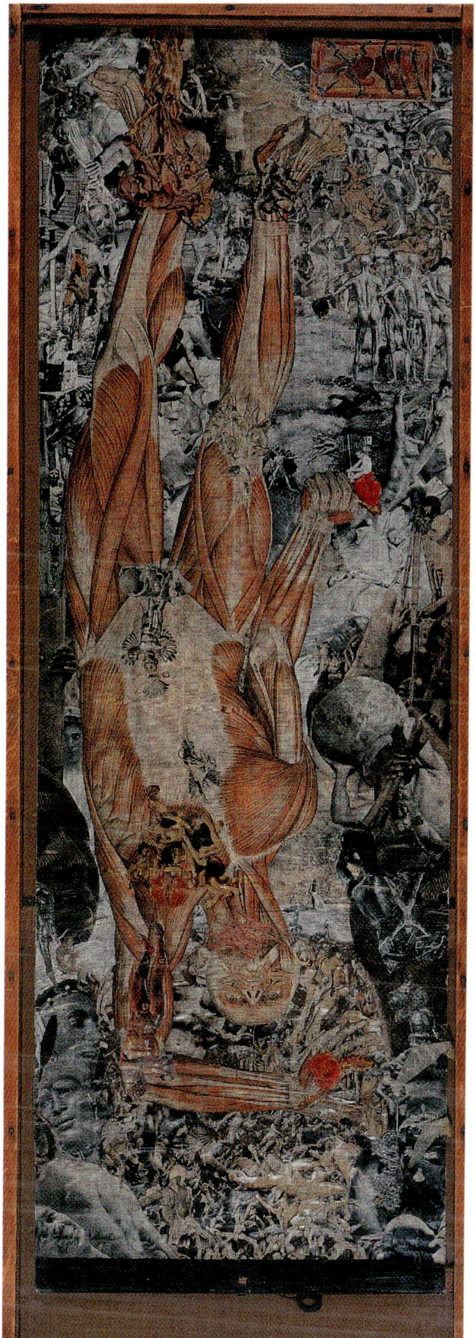

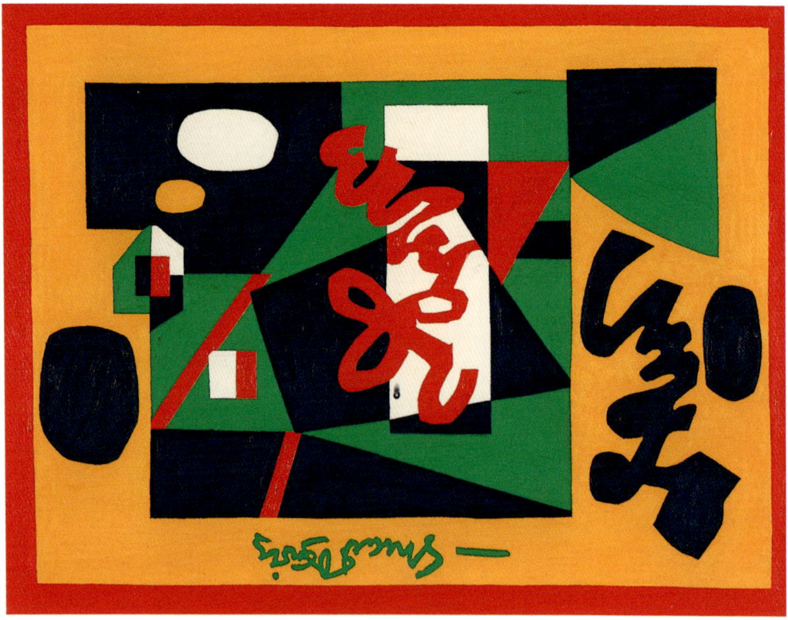

Stuart Davis moved to New York City at age seventeen to study with Robert Henri, the leader of the so-called Ashcan School, a group who looked to their daily environment for subject matter. Davis's commitment to the gritty realism of this group waned, however, when in 1913 he exhibited five watercolors at the *International Exhibition of Modern Art* in New York, later known as the Armory Show, and first encountered European modernist art. Enthralled with what he saw, Davis began experimenting with cubism and over the next decade adapted it to his distinctive vocabulary. He traveled to Paris in 1928 and returned even more committed to an abstract art that would be infused with the pattern, rhythm, and vitality of the American scene. During the tumultuous 1930s, Davis championed abstraction as a social and political vehicle. He believed that if form were grounded in the sensations of daily life, abstract art would be accessible to everyone.

General Studies is a late work in which Davis looks back to his previous paintings, specifically his 1932 *Composition with Red Polygon* (private collection). Davis transformed what was primarily a black-and-white armature of line into a structure of intensely colored planes. Since the 1950s, Davis had restricted himself to working with no more than five hues in a single work, but his paintings from the 1960s are limited to a palette of black, white, red, yellow, and green. Unlike many of Davis's works, Krannert Art Museum's painting shows a calligraphic script that does not form words but serves an exclusively visual function. Its title may refer to the basic, and in Davis's mind the most vital, aspect of making art: the creation of meaningful forms with shape, color, and line. Even his signature, which is often placed at unusual angles in his later paintings and in this case is upside down, is a creative exploration of form and meaning. Morgan

General Studies
1962
Oil on canvas
27 1/4 × 36 1/4 inches
Festival of Art Purchase Fund
1963-16-1

Stuart Davis
United States
1894–1964

Art Sinsabaugh worked in the tradition of the Institute of Design in Chicago (where he studied) and its predecessor in the same city, the New Bauhaus, founded by László Moholy-Nagy in 1937. Moholy-Nagy taught the value of arriving at self-expression through experimentation and encouraged students to challenge and stretch traditional forms. Sinsabaugh brought these values to his art, and taught them to his students.

Sinsabaugh's *Chicago Landscape* series was completed after his famous *Midwest Landscape* series, in which he used a radically unconventional format, printing his 12 × 20-inch negatives as small as 1 × 20 inches in order to emphasize the prairie's flatness and the visual activity on the horizon. He once said, "I began to think of Chicago again and I wanted to show it as a prairie city – I felt it to be a horizontal city."

Sinsabaugh made the photograph *Chicago #85*, like much of the work in the series, along one of the expressways that had recently been cut through city neighborhoods, opening up perspectives that had not previously been available. Here Sinsabaugh, typically, describes the space through a procession of narrowing strips – highway surfaces, fences, rail tracks and platform, secondary roads, lines of parked cars, and, finally, the strip of houses and commercial buildings that constitute the neighborhood. It is a space that denies the viewer entry. Sinsabaugh again and again used this approach to describe, in his words, "the neighborhoods ... laid bare and their very bowels exposed." Meanwhile, on the sunny expressways, the speeding cars are so blurred by movement as to resemble pure energy. Zagorski

Art Sinsabaugh
United States
1924–1983

Chicago #85
1964
Silver gelatin print
11 3/4 × 19 1/2 inches
Gift of Ed Zagorski
1985-38-1

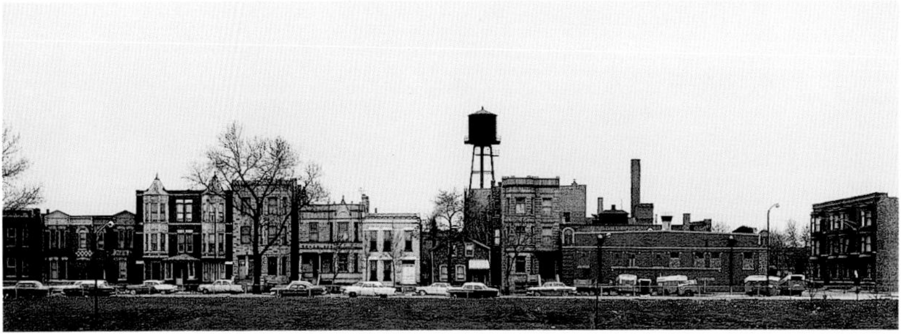

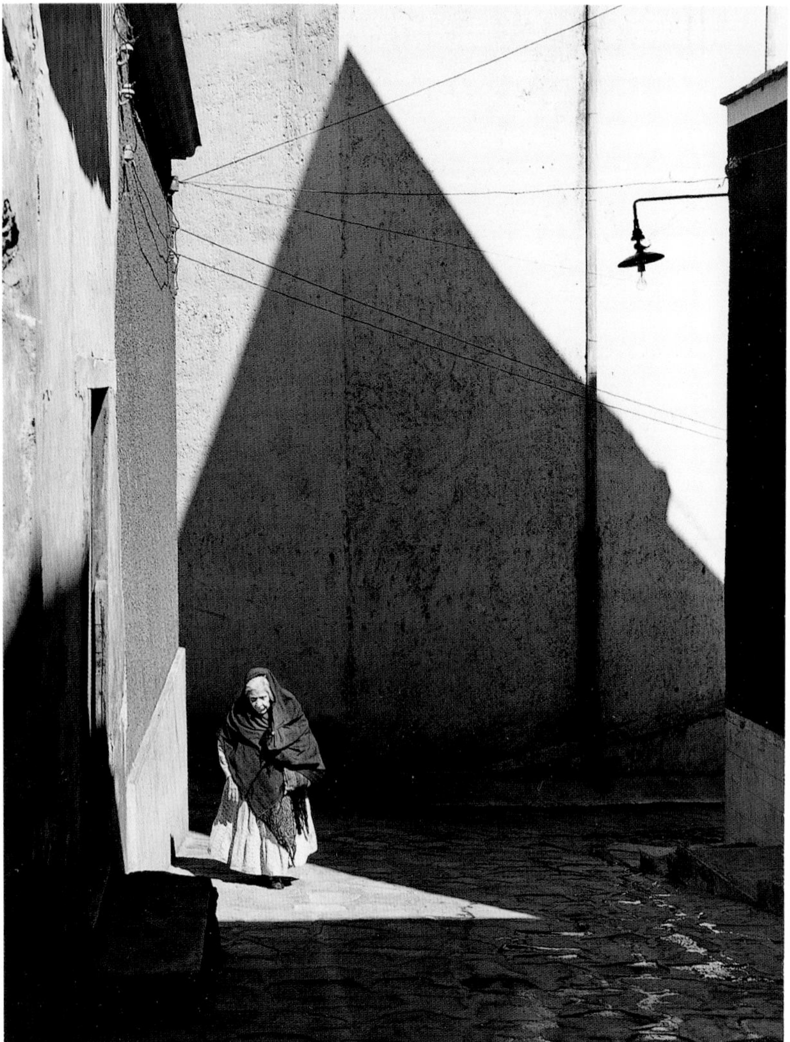

Manuel Carrillo grew up in Mexico during the decades of the Mexican Revolution and its aftermath. After spending his teenage years at a military academy in Mexico, he moved to New York where he lived for eight years. During that time, he often returned to Mexico to work for the Illinois Central Railroad. At age forty-nine he joined the Club Fotográfico de Méjico and the Photographic Society of America, and began a second career as a photographer. His first international solo exhibition, *Mi Pueblo* (*My People*), took place at the Chicago Public Library in 1960. Carrillo became known for his descriptions of daily life in rural Mexico and his exploration of personal, cultural, and national identity in Mexico's post-revolutionary era. He brought together documentary, cinematic, and modern formalist approaches in black-and-white prints that often portray the relationship between people and the natural landscape. In *Mexico City*, an old woman appears alone in an alley, dwarfed by a stark geometric shadow looming behind her. The dramatic contrast of light and dark recalls Hollywood *film noir* of the 1940s and '50s, as well as the geometric abstraction of American modernist photographers Paul Strand and Edward Weston. By the time of his death in Mexico City at age eighty-three, Manuel Carrillo had exhibited his work in hundreds of exhibitions and established an international reputation. His distinctive vision earned him the moniker "*el maestro mejicano.*" Mitchell

Manuel Carrillo
Mexico
1906–1988

Mexico City, D. F.
1966
Silver gelatin print
13 × 11 inches
Gift of Arnold M. Gilbert
1982-22-27

Associated with the New York pop art movement, which emerged in the late 1950s as a reaction to abstract expressionism, Robert Indiana (born Robert Clark) is perhaps best known for his *LOVE* print, which he designed in 1964 as a Christmas card for the Museum of Modern Art. Whereas other artists, such as Andy Warhol, represented objects of mass production in their works as a commentary on American consumerism, Indiana used commercial techniques such as stenciling to create an art resembling signs – road signs in particular – through the incorporation of text, simple geometric shapes, and numerals. The interplay of the verbal and visual is a striking aspect of Indiana's work, in which the words and numbers themselves become art. He chose words and expressions familiar to the general public but situated them within unfamiliar contexts to give them new layers of meaning.

Indiana, who called himself an "American painter of signs," was fascinated by American history, politics, and literature, and integrated related themes into the seemingly simple designs of his paintings. The two works at Krannert Art Museum vary greatly in size, but both show Indiana's interrogation of aspects of American culture. *Yield Brother John* (p. 305) is a variation on Indiana's earlier *Yield Brother* series. It was made specifically for the pianist John Wustman of the University of Illinois, who was invited to give a recital in celebration of Indiana's thirty-ninth birthday. The composition, with its stenciled text and central circular shape, is derived from a work the artist created in 1963 to warn against the dream of the perfect American family. The title contains both the cautionary warning implied by a yield traffic sign and a more intimate, biblical evocation through the use of the word "brother." The central circle is bisected by vertical blue stripes, which Indiana described as symbols of the North Star, Polaris.

According to Indiana, technically perfect works are meaningless unless they have more than one level of symbolic association. In *Louisiana: The Confederacy* (p. 304), Indiana's view of the civil rights struggles in the South is made explicit in his text. This work is one of four paintings dealing with the attacks on nonviolent civil rights demonstrators in Louisiana, Alabama, Florida, and Mississippi. The center circle contains the text "the fair city Bogalusa." This city, located on the border of Louisiana and Mississippi, was at one time the heart of Ku Klux Klan country and the site of civil rights disturbances. The three rings of text draw the viewer's eye to the center of the painting like the rings of a target, with a red star acting as the bull's-eye. Kuechler

(following pages)
Louisiana: The Confederacy
1966
Oil on canvas
70 × 60 inches
Contemporary American Painting
and Sculpture Exhibition
1967-7-1

Yield Brother John
1967
Oil on canvas
40 × 30 inches
Gift of John Wustman
2005-2-1

Robert Indiana
United States
b. 1928

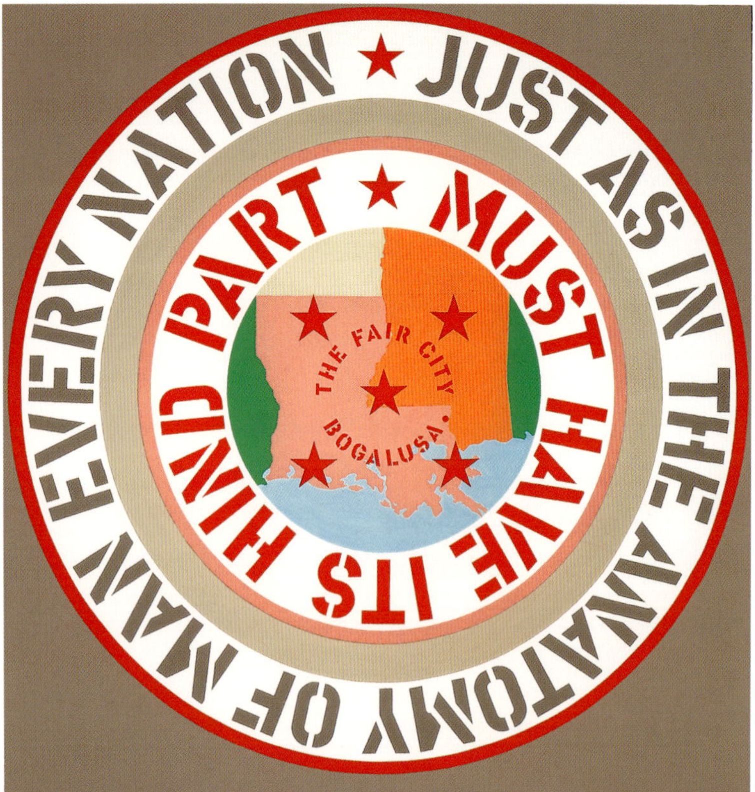
JUST AS IN THE ANATOMY OF MAN EVERY NATION
MUST HAVE ITS HIND PART
THE FAIR CITY
BOGALUSA.
LOUISIANA

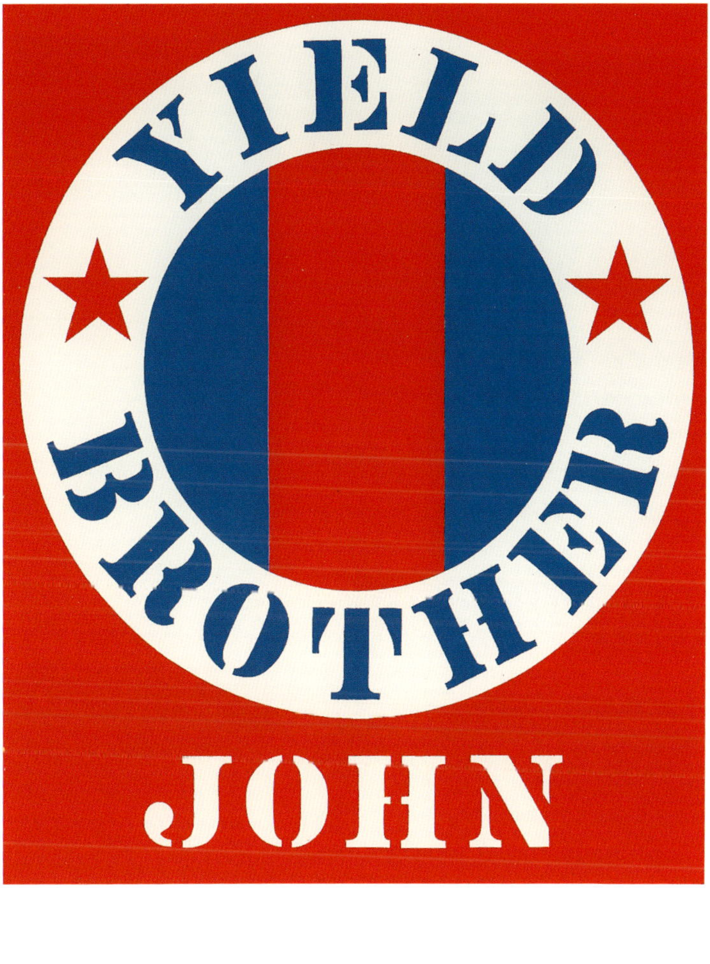

Louisiana: The Confederacy
Yield Brother John

The designer and artist Harry Bertoia came to the United States as a teenager to visit an uncle in Detroit, and decided to stay. He was trained at the Detroit Society of Arts and Crafts before receiving a scholarship to the Cranbrook Academy of Art, where he studied with architect Walter Gropius. The director of the school, architect Eliel Saarinen, asked Bertoia to stay on to reopen the department of metalworking. At Cranbrook, Bertoia was to collaborate with Florence Knoll, Charles Eames, and Eero Saarinen – all leading figures in American design. When Bertoia decided to try his hand at prints, and sent 100 to art patron Peggy Guggenheim, she added most to the holdings of her avant-garde museum and placed the others in important collections.

After Cranbrook, Bertoia joined Eames in California to experiment with molded plywood. This work stemmed from the Eames/Saarinen chair design that won the Museum of Modern Art furniture competition in 1940, but could not be successfully produced. In addition, Bertoia contributed to the war effort by making airplane parts manufactured by Evans Products, where Eames was director of research and development. Bertoia then spent two years in San Diego at the Point Loma Naval Electrical Lab, where he worked on a project involving human engineering and stroboscopic photography. After hours, he made sculptures there.

Bertoia moved to Pennsylvania in 1950 to collaborate with Hans and Florence Knoll on furniture that was produced under his name by Knoll. His now ubiquitous Diamond Chair went into production in 1952. In 1960 he began making tonal or sound sculptures, which he continued to create until his death in 1978. *Tonal Piece* is composed of a grid of tall rods forming a visual and harmonic grove. There is a wide range in the number, configuration, and height of rods in this sculptural type, creating a broad spectrum of sound, all gently haunting. The largest installation of tonal sculptures is in Chicago, designed for the reflecting pool in front of the Standard Oil Building and installed in 1975. Fox

Harry Bertoia
United States
(born Italy)
1915–1978

Tonal Piece
1967
Bronze plate and rods
59 × 10 inches
Gift of Robert D. Kleinschmidt
1998-21-23

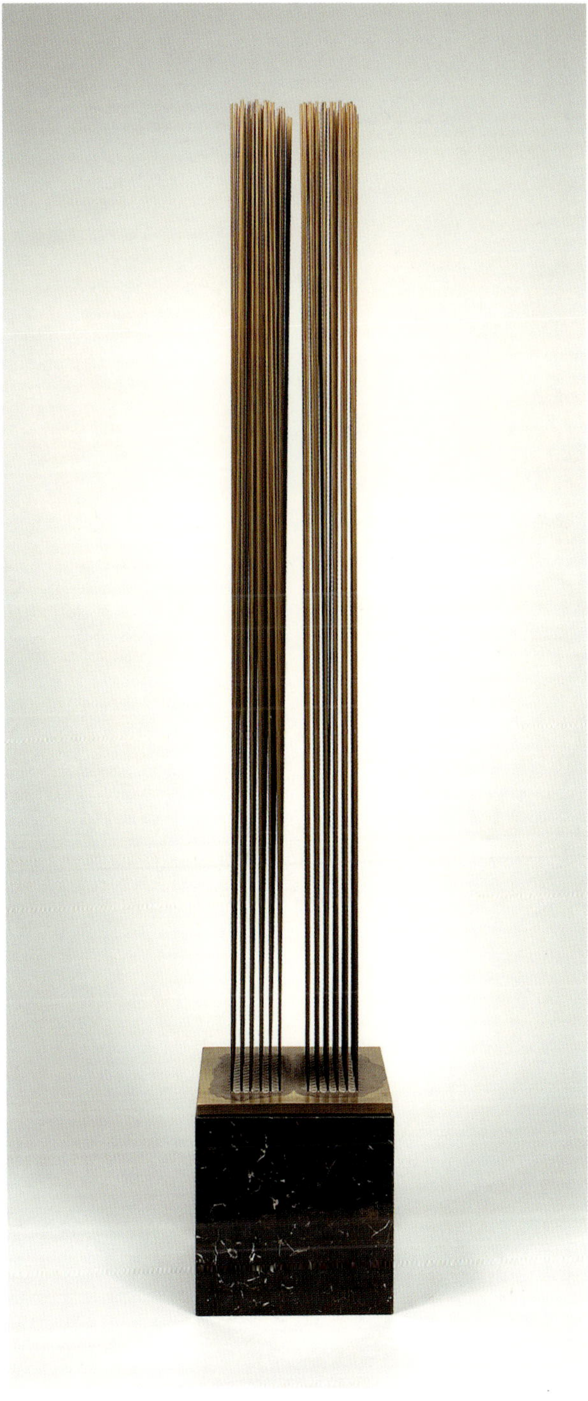

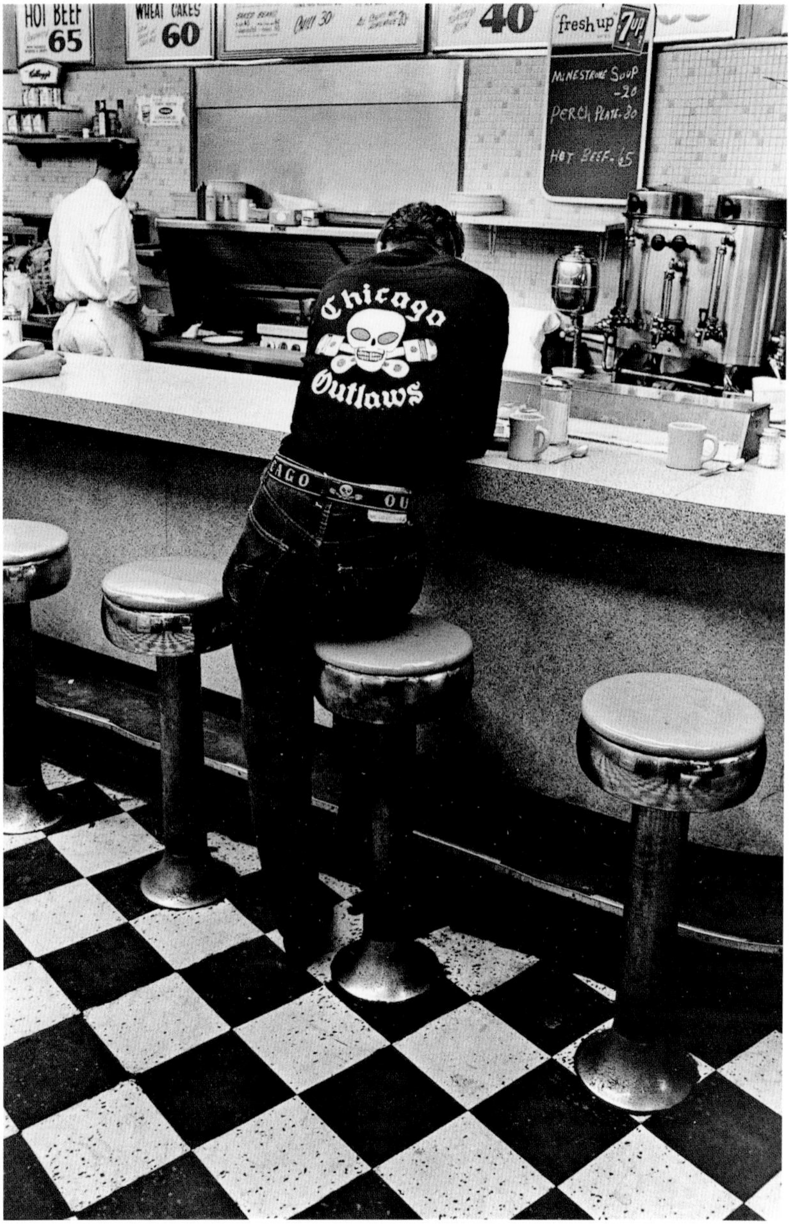

HOT BEEF
65
WHEAT CAKES
60
40
"fresh up"
7up
MINESTRONE SOUP -20
PERCH PLATE-80
HOT BEEF-65
Chicago
Outlaws

Influenced by the documentary work of Walker Evans, James Agee, and Robert Frank, Danny Lyon has spent his career photographing American subcultures. Originally from New York City, Lyon began experimenting with photography at age seventeen. He studied history at the University of Chicago and joined the civil rights movement in 1962, becoming staff photographer for the Student Nonviolent Coordinating Committee. From 1962 to 1966 he worked intensively on photographs and interviews for his book *The Bike Riders*, published in 1968. He rode, socialized, and made friends with members of the Chicago Outlaws, eventually joining the motorcycle club.

In *Jack, Chicago*, a biker drinks coffee at a small diner. Jack is shown from behind, his membership in the club signified by the insignia on the back of his jacket. Centered in the composition, he appears to be unaware of being photographed. The cook in the upper left-hand corner also has his back to the camera, lending a candid quality to the image. Many photographs in the series are directly related to bike riding, races, and drinking, while others, such as this one, show quieter, less dramatic moments. Ritsma

Jack, Chicago
1967
Silver gelatin print
12 3/4 × 8 3/4 inches
Gift of Arnold and Temmie Gilbert
1988-14-32

Danny Lyon
United States
b. 1942

Claes Oldenburg was one of the first artists associated with the American pop art movement in the mid-1960s, and has been at its forefront ever since. Like Roy Lichtenstein, Robert Rauschenberg, and Andy Warhol, Oldenburg used anti-aesthetic strategies to convey an ambivalent fascination with consumer culture. These artists rejected the dominant abstract expressionist mode in which art served as a vehicle for personal and mystical expression. Pop artists also kept their distance from the popular reform movements of the 1960s that sought social and political change through direct action. Pop artists questioned many of the same institutions and social patterns, but did so through parody, as in Oldenburg's *Proposed Chapel in the Form of a Swedish Extension Plug*.

In *Proposed Chapel*, a powerful perspectival effect and carefully weighted contour lines create an imposing architectural form, however loosely sketched. Oldenburg's nonchalant mastery of graphic technique complements the wit of his visual puns. *Proposed Chapel* also illustrates Oldenburg's variation on the surrealists' techniques of juxtaposition and their use of object-art. He synthesizes two unrelated everyday objects by noting their purely visual similarities, and expands the resulting hybrid to a disconcerting scale. The fusion of religious architecture and mass-produced household convenience undermines the customary separation of sacred and middle-class domestic spaces. This visual and conceptual sleight-of-hand raises questions about the function of religion in a modern leisure society. Over the years, Oldenburg has erected dozens of highly implausible monumental works. Still, the early date of *Proposed Chapel* and its architectural conception identify the concept as more rhetorical device than genuine aspiration. Wetzel

Claes Oldenburg
United States
(born Sweden)
b. 1929

Proposed Chapel in the Form of a Swedish Extension Plug
1967
Crayon, wash
22 × 30 inches
Art Acquisition Fund
1968-4-1

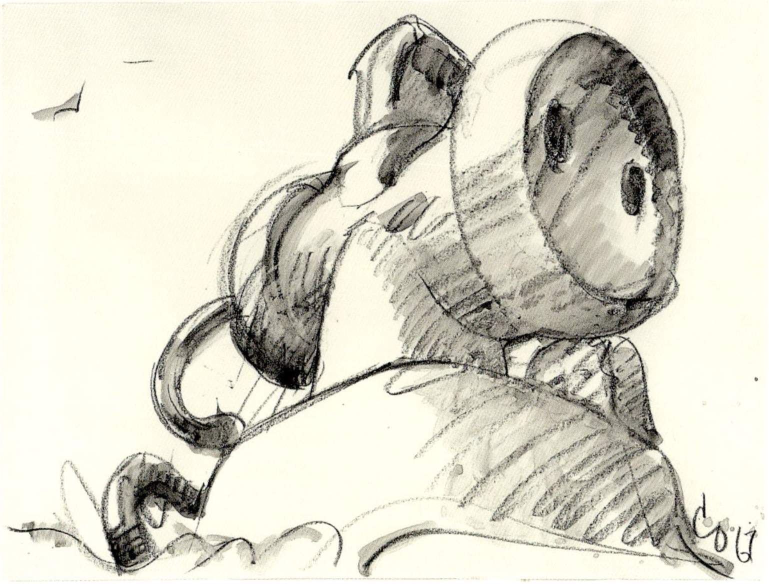

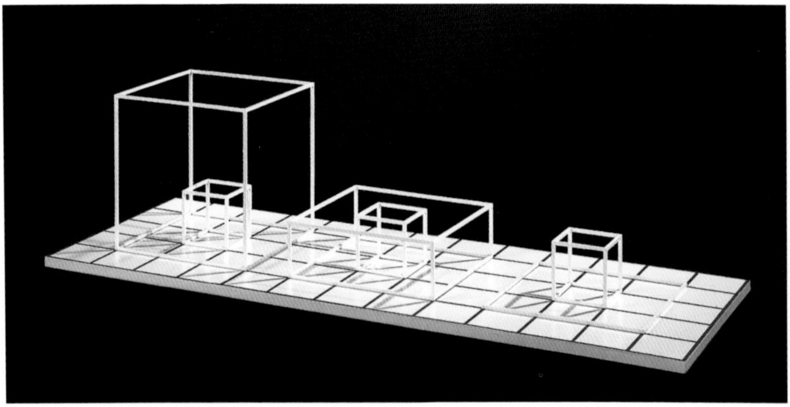

A seminal contributor to both the conceptual and minimal art movements of the 1960s, Sol LeWitt built his oeuvre – prints, drawings, paintings on canvas and walls, and sculpture – on the vocabulary of the grid. This vision may owe something to his early experiences in the office of the architect I. M. Pei. In an interview in 2001, LeWitt said:

I was part of the group that wanted to reinvent art as an opposition not only to Abstract Expressionism but to the whole history of Modern art. We felt that Modern art had come to some sort of conclusion with, on one hand Piet Mondrian, and on the other, Jackson Pollock. Some other kind of thinking, another kind of art was necessary because there was a vacuum there with no other ideas coming out of it. By going back to square one and trying to reinvent the whole idea of what art could be, a new kind of art could be made.

Sol LeWitt's work is based on his belief that ideas, even if irrational, should be logically pursued: "The idea becomes the machine that makes the art" and "conceptual art is made to engage the mind of the viewer rather than his eye or emotions."

A 2 5 8 dates from the time LeWitt started working with fabricators to make his sculptures. His close involvement with and oversight of such collaborators and assistants have become integral to his working method. It was important to LeWitt that his works be kept freshly painted and restored to their original pristine condition even in his absence. Fox

Sol LeWitt
United States
1928–2007

A 2 5 8
1968
Baked enamel on steel
19 1/4 × 81 inches
Festival of Arts Purchase Fund
1969-3-1

Critics first linked Peter Saul with pop art on account of his references to Mickey Mouse and imagery from popular culture. However, Saul departed from the neutrality and ambiguity of pop to express his opposition to war and racism. On his return from Europe in 1965, the artist's response to the tension produced by the Vietnam War was to intensify his already edgy, politically charged imagery. In *Typical Saigon* (pp. 316–17), grotesquely exaggerated images of soldiers and Vietnamese women rendered in glaring red, green, and orange are taken from such widely disparate sources as *Mad Magazine* and religious iconography. The message along the left side of the canvas, written in pseudo-Chinese characters, may have served as a cryptic warning to American soldiers concerning the exploitation of Vietnamese women. The women, tied to crosses, are given holy status by means of halos. But the seeming victims double as aggressors: they are aggressively hyper-sexualized and fire weapons like the men. They appear to be devoured by gruesomely distorted and wounded soldiers.

In addition to making pointed political commentary, Saul makes fun of the understated aesthetics of the minimalism then current in the art world with his outrageous themes and garish colors. Barnes

(following pages)

Typical Saigon
1968
Acrylic, oil, and enamel on canvas
93 × 144 inches
Festival of Arts Purchase Fund
1969-4-1

Peter Saul
United States
b. 1934

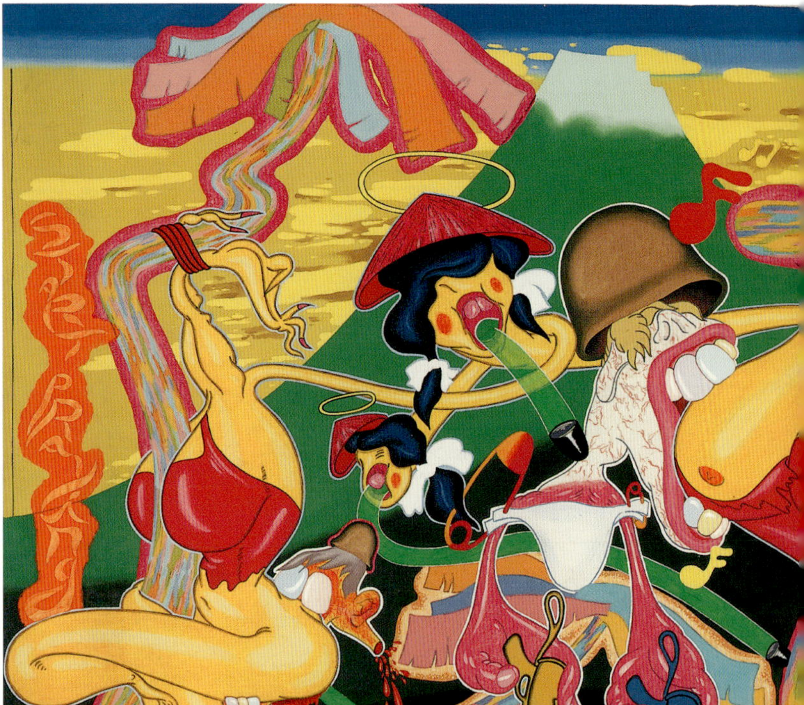

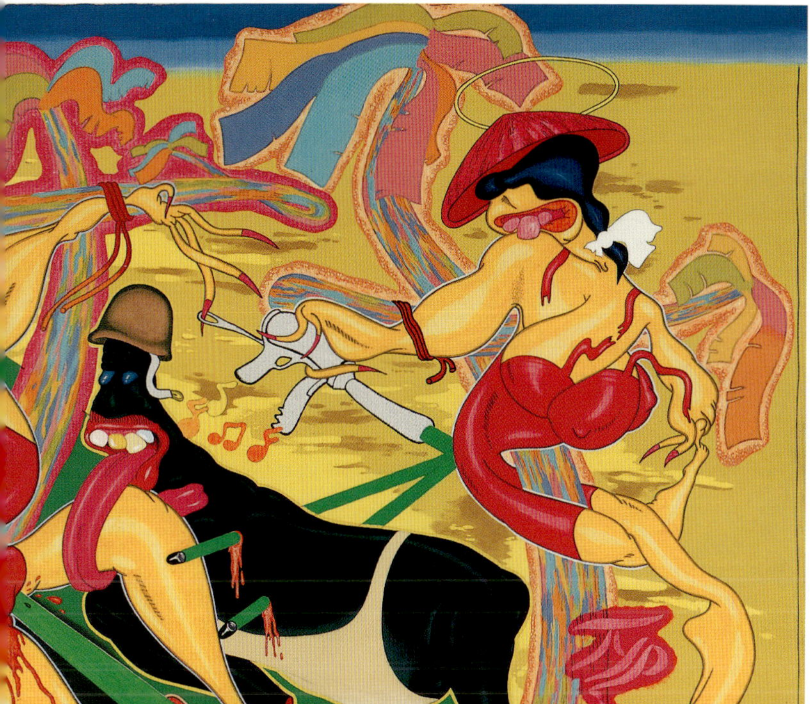

9/27
Barnett Newman 1969

The New York–based abstract expressionists dominated the American art scene from the late 1940s to the mid-1960s. Their individual development tended to evolve from early surrealist-related imagery to abstract mature works. Among them, Barnett Newman is known primarily for his paintings, but he also created a significant number of sculptures and prints during the final decade of his life. The untitled etching in the collection of Krannert Art Museum marks the culmination of his work as a printmaker. Though many of his colleagues enjoyed increasing critical acceptance, Newman faced severe criticism or indifference during most of his career. Detractors condemned his work as either inaccessible or altogether devoid of meaning. Late in his career and following his death, however, his work and theoretical writings on art influenced a generation of color-field and minimalist painters.

In this simple and contemplative work, a vertical black band is bordered by two off-white blocks of identical size. The aquatint technique has created subtle irregularities in tonal quality throughout the image, which is bordered by the white color of the paper support. The understated variation, as seen here, is typical of Newman's mature work. Wetzel

Barnett Newman
United States
1905–1970

Untitled
1969
Etching, aquatint
32 × 22 inches
John Needles Chester Fund
1985-7-1

Painter, sculptor, printmaker, photographer, and performance artist Robert Rauschenberg began working in the late 1940s. Throughout his career, he maintained a sophisticated interest in representational art and in novel combinations of media. His artistic development was shaped by his experiences at Black Mountain College in North Carolina with artist Josef Albers, composer John Cage, and dancer Merce Cunningham, and by his later residence in New York. In the mid-1950s, Rauschenberg began mixing techniques and incorporating found objects into his work, creating what he called "combines."

In 1969 Rauschenberg was invited by NASA to witness the launch of Apollo XI, the manned flight to the moon, at the Kennedy Space Center in Florida. Inspired by the experience, he created *Stoned Moon*, a series of 33 lithographs. The punning title refers to the lithographic stone as well as to the high induced by one of America's great technological achievements. In *Sky Garden* from the series, images provided by NASA of the blast-off and technicians at the control center are juxtaposed with pictures of the Floridian landscape and the official NASA seal. A large diagram of a rocket is superimposed over the images.

At the time, the production of *Sky Garden* and *Waves* – also from the series – represented a technological milestone in printmaking. They were the largest prints ever made on a hand-operated lithographic press. As printer Timothy Isham from Gemini G. E. L., which published the series, recalled: "Sky Garden was so long that there was no way a single person could roll it out. We had two printers and two spongers." Rauschenberg's printmaking and design skills as demonstrated in the *Stoned Moon* series made it a critical success. Critic Lawrence Alloway praised the artist for having "produced the first persuasive public art of the space age," and compared his depiction of the space program with Peter Paul Rubens's Medici cycle "in its pomp, wit, and fidelity." Stanulis

Robert Rauschenberg
United States
1925–2008

Sky Garden
1969
Lithograph, silkscreen
89 × 37 3/4 inches
Art Acquisition Fund and
NEA Matching Grant Fund
1978-7-1

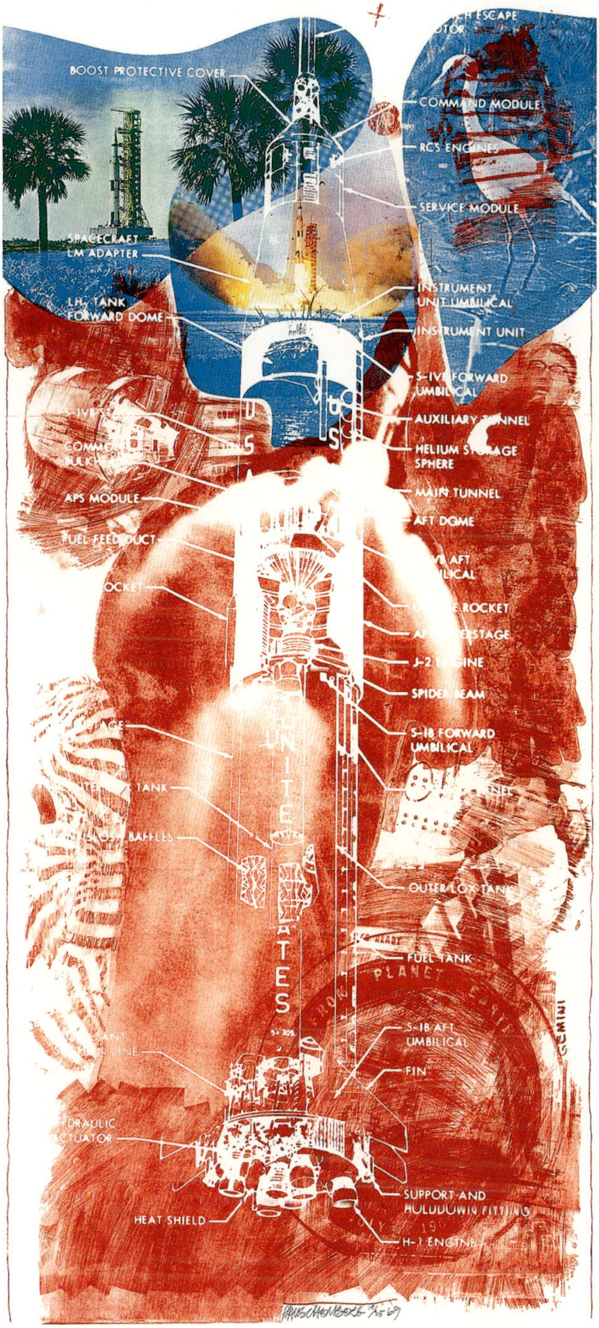

BOOST PROTECTIVE COVER
COMMAND MODULE
RCS ENGINES
SERVICE MODULE
SPACECRAFT
LM ADAPTER
INSTRUMENT
UNIT UMBILICAL
FORWARD DOME
INSTRUMENT UNIT
UMBILICAL
AUXILIARY TUNNEL
HELIUM STORAGE
SPHERE
APS MODULE
MAIN TUNNEL
AFT DOME
SPIDER BEAM
S-IB FORWARD
UMBILICAL
OUTER LOX TANK
FUEL TANK
UNITED STATES
PLANET
GEMINI
S-IB AFT
UMBILICAL
FIN
SUPPORT AND
HEAT SHIELD

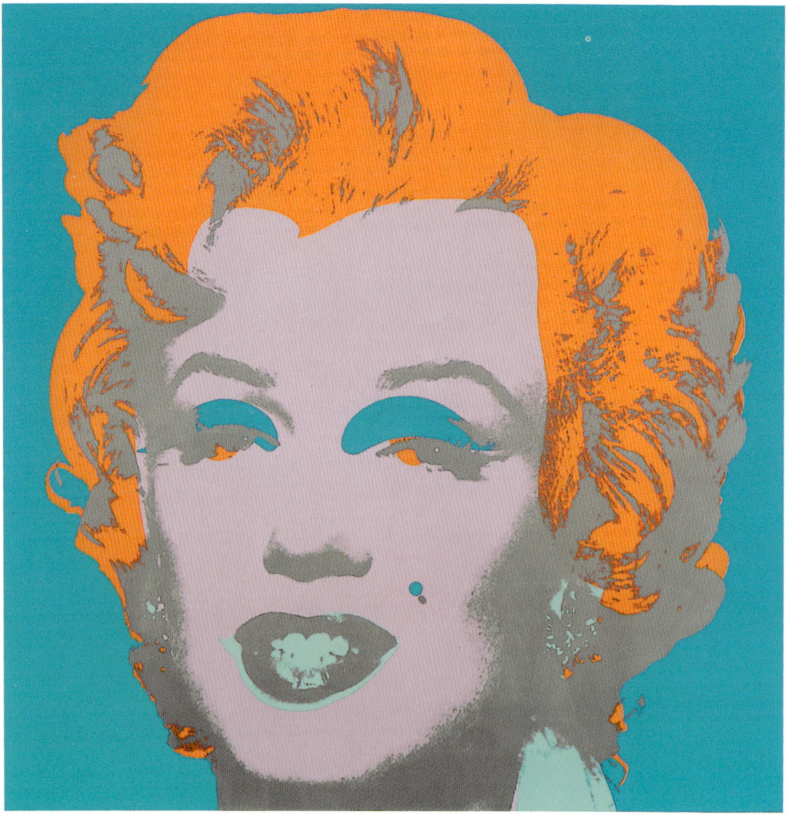

After graduating in graphic design from the Carnegie Institute of Technology in Pittsburgh in 1949, Andy Warhol soon became a successful commercial artist. In the early 1960s, he became one of the leading figures of the American pop art movement. Warhol used the silkscreen process borrowed from advertising to repeat single images of consumer goods, such as Brillo boxes and Campbell's soup cans, and Hollywood celebrities, including Elvis Presley and Marilyn Monroe. The *Marilyn Monroe* series, initiated soon after the movie star's death in 1962, exemplifies Warhol's practice of equating commercial goods and celebrities; all are transformed into icons to be painted and subsequently sold at galleries.

Marilyn at Krannert Art Museum illustrates Warhol's deliberately sloppy approach; its forms and contours are flawed by the intentional misalignment of screens, uneven inking, and occasional smears. The a betrays no trace of expressive gesture or artistic individuality. The image is not a representation of Monroe so much as a mechanical reproduction of her image as a popular icon. Warhol detaches the signifier (the image) from the signified (Marilyn Monroe) to demonstrate the power of representation in the commodity-centered culture of America. Tseng

Andy Warhol
United States
1931–1987

Marilyn
1971
Silkscreen
35 3/4 × 35 3/4 inches
John Needles Chester Fund
1983-8-1

In the 1960s, Frank Stella emphasized the flatness of paint and the two-dimensionality of the canvas as an alternative to the introspection of abstract expressionist painting. In his paintings from this period, Stella eliminated both depth of field and emotional content in order to explore the purely formal properties of painting. He started work on *Kozangrodek III* (pp. 326–27) in October of 1970 by making more than forty drawings from photographs of buildings burned in Poland by the Nazis. In the relief collage, the artist inserted lines and shapes taken from the two-dimensional photograph into the viewer's three-dimensional space. By layering planes of vibrant color and dynamic materials that tilt and interlock with one another, Stella moved beyond the flatness of painting to new concerns. Saggese

(following pages)
Kozangrodek III
1973
Canvas, corrugated cardboard, felt, plywood, Masonite, paint
114 × 98 inches
Art Acquisition Fund and NEA Matching Grant
1976-10-1

Frank Stella
United States
b. 1936

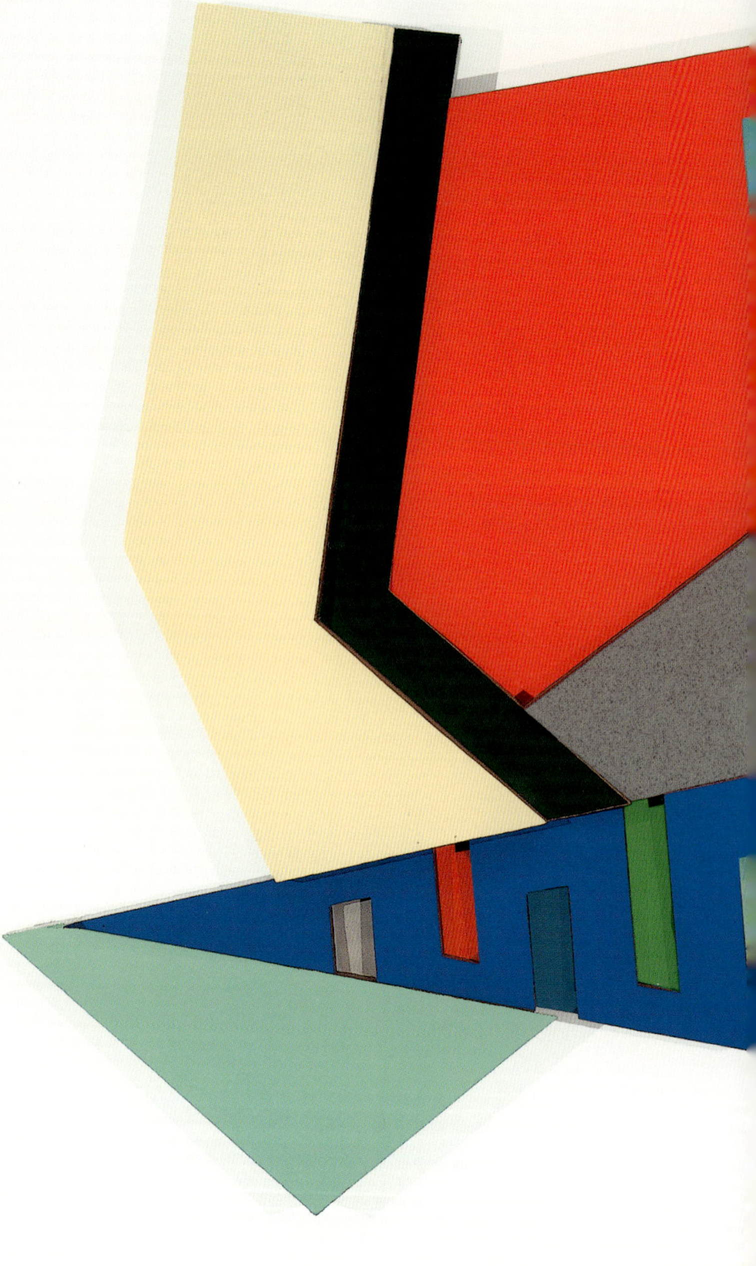

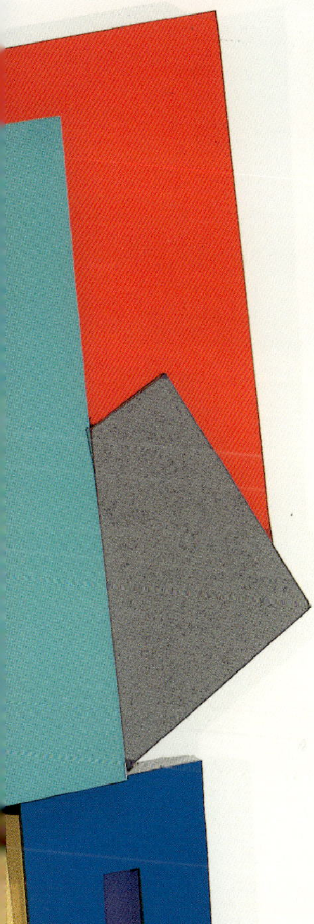

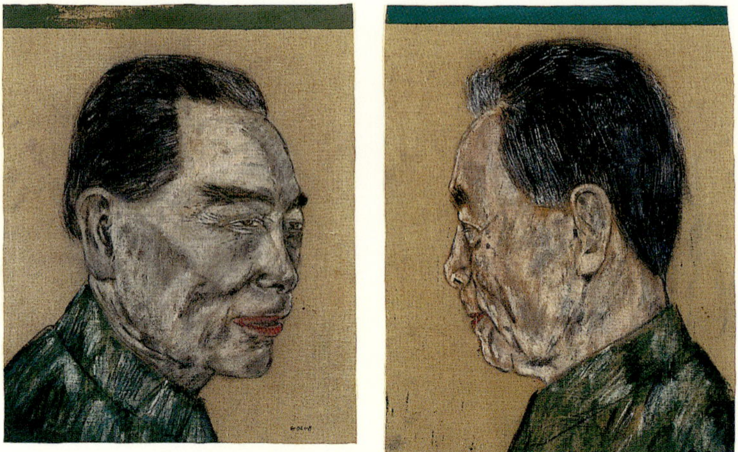

Between 1966 and 1973, Leon Golub's depictions of the atrocities of the Vietnam War were among the most conceptually adventurous and technically demanding paintings of the period. His Napalm and Vietnam series served as an antidote to the psychological and sociological isolation of art in previous decades. By the mid-1970s the war was over, national media attention had shifted to Watergate and the scandal of President Nixon's impeachment, and Golub's focus changed.

From 1976 to 1979, Golub completed more than one hundred portraits of political and cultural leaders – including Fidel Castro, John Foster Dulles, Francisco Franco, Ho Chi Minh, and Nelson Rockefeller. The artist claimed that he was interested in the figures "not as good guys, not as bad guys, but men who have political power in their hands." Drawing on news photographs, Golub was less concerned with specific political arguments than with the politics of representation in the media age. More specifically, these portraits illuminate the divide between public perception and political truth. Scholars, however, have argued that they are, above all, investigations into the performative and mediated aspects of identity.

In *Two Head Studies of Zhou Enlai*, the artist subtly critiques the representational value of painting by playing with the conventions of portraiture. First, he eliminates the intimacy of traditional portraiture by portraying Zhou Enlai in a military uniform, emphasizing his public role as the foreign minister of China under Mao. The deep scratches on the surface and the ambiguous space of the background diverge from the devices that enhance the subject in conventional formal portraits. The unfinished quality of the rough cloth and its irregular edges contrast with the self-consciousness of the poses. Saggese

Leon Golub
United States
1922–2004

Two Head Studies of Zhou Enlai
ca. 1976–79
Oil on woven cloth
33 × 43 inches
Estate of William S. Kinkead
1984-44-5

The artist Robert Motherwell described his source material as "familiar objects which make part of my daily life." Throughout the 1970s, he incorporated into his collages personal artifacts such as cigarette packages, wine labels, and symphony programs. *St. Michael III* is one in a series of lithographs that includes a *trompe l'oeil* rendition of a Belgian cigarette package and label. The use of a sweeping splash of black ink points to Motherwell's artistic interests, most notably abstract expressionism, Chinese calligraphy, and Zen painting. Like the abstract expressionists, Motherwell often capitalized on the unpredictability of his materials, and constantly varied his processes. As one scholar has asserted, Motherwell "found a way to paint that allowed the nature of the materials to collaborate with him in the processes of creating the artistic result."

The premises of Chinese calligraphy and Zen painting have some analogies with those of abstract expressionist painting, in that the American notion of character driving the artistic process can be compared with the East Asian idea of brushwork being formed by the artist's inner nature. Motherwell was immediately drawn to East Asian art when he first encountered it during a trip to San Francisco.

Though the ink in *St. Michael III* looks spontaneous, in fact the artist transferred the splatter shape onto the aluminum plate from a lithographic stone used to make an earlier print of 1975 titled *Monster*. *St. Michael III* embodies the Zen aspiration to a balance between transcendence and everyday life: the expressive black strokes complement the mundane cigarette package. Saggese

Robert Motherwell
United States
1915–1991

St. Michael III
1979
Lithograph
41 1/2 × 31 1/2 inches
John Needles Chester Fund
1982-24-1

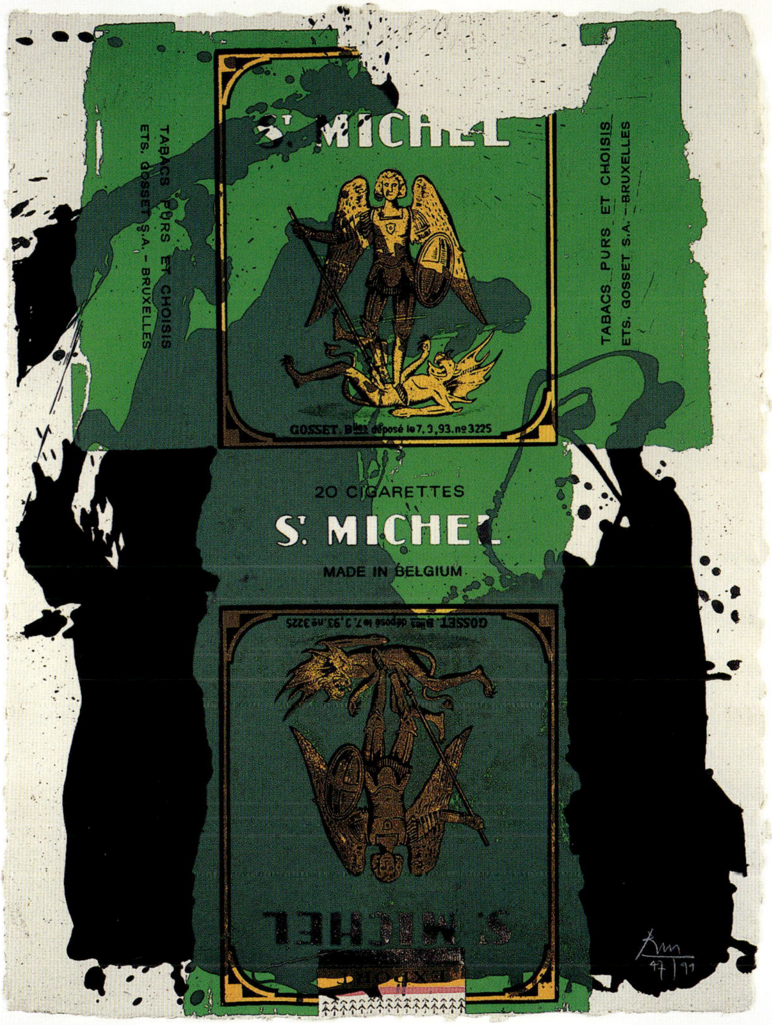
St MICHEL
TABACS PURS ET CHOISIS
ETS. GOSSET S.A. - BRUXELLES
20 CIGARETTES
St MICHEL
MADE IN BELGIUM

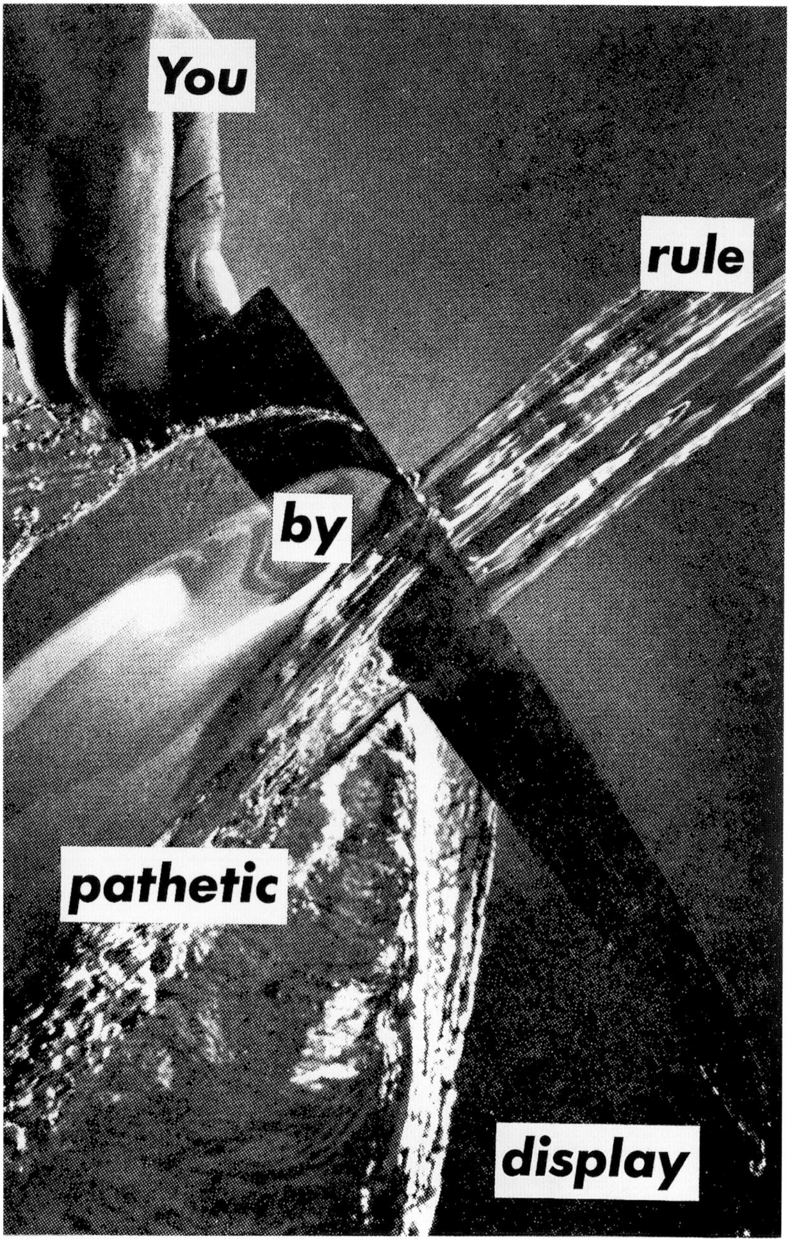
You
rule
by
pathetic
display

Born in Newark, New Jersey, Barbara Kruger attended Syracuse University and Parsons School of Design. Her early experience in advertising and design for publications such as *Mademoiselle* and *Aperture* is readily apparent in her later art. In this example, Kruger combines text and image to incite the viewer. In contrast to her contemporary Jenny Holzer, who uses text alone, Kruger juxtaposes well-known phrases and appropriated images in a style reminiscent of Dada photomontage, but with a seamless presentation and a feminist political agenda.

Like advertisements, Kruger's posters are easily produced and displayed; her work has appeared not only in private galleries and museums but also on billboards, where it is available to a wider audience. Kruger incriminates the viewer by addressing him or her directly ("You rule by pathetic display"). In this way she prompts the the questions "Who rules?" and "Who wields the knife?"

In other untitled works, such as those presenting the phrases "I am your immaculate conception," "Your gaze hits the side of my face," and "We will no longer be your favorite disappearing act," images and words suggest gender relations in which "I," "my," and "we" appear to be female, while "your" is male. The text allows her audience, both male and female, to try on the roles themselves. Kuhl Cox

Barbara Kruger
United States
b. 1945

Untitled (*You Rule by Pathetic Display*)
1982
Photo-offset lithograph, serigraph
73 × 49 inches
Art Acquisition Fund
1986-36-1

Educated at the California College of Arts and Crafts and Mills College, Robert Arneson was one of the best known of the twentieth-century ceramic sculptors who took ceramics from "craft" to fine art. His sculptures, often inflected with humor, usually portray art-world figures, from the collector Gilda Bookbinder (*In Pursuit of Asian Gilda*, 1981) to Vincent van Gogh (*Vince*, 1978). This bust represents Arneson's most frequently explored theme both in his drawings and ceramic work: himself.

Arneson's balding, bearded head, in patinated bronze, is monumental in scale. His thumbprints are visible in the modeling of the bust, which has the expressive qualities of his frenetic drawings. Placed on a column adorned with a narrative bas-relief of Arneson classically posed, it conveys the mock heroism of the figure of the artist. In conventional museum displays, detached busts often rest on classical pedestals. Here the support is an integral part of the work. As in *Klown* (1978), in which Arneson represented himself wearing clown make-up with his tongue sticking out, here he reveals his sense of humor: green-glazed foliage climbing up the pedestal unsuccessfully conceals his genitals. In other works, Arneson directs his humor to social criticism or personal reflection. Kuhl Cox

Robert Arneson
United States
1930–1992

Untitled
1984
Bronze, terracotta
74 × 24 inches
Harlan E. Moore Charitable Trust
1985-2-1.1/.2

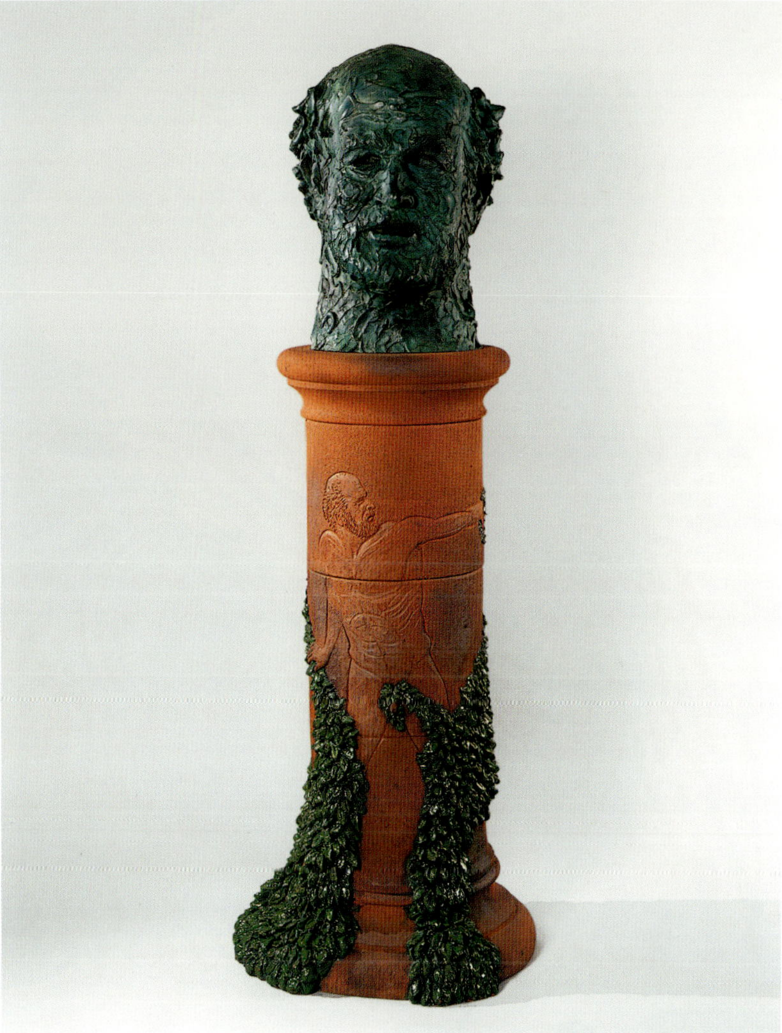

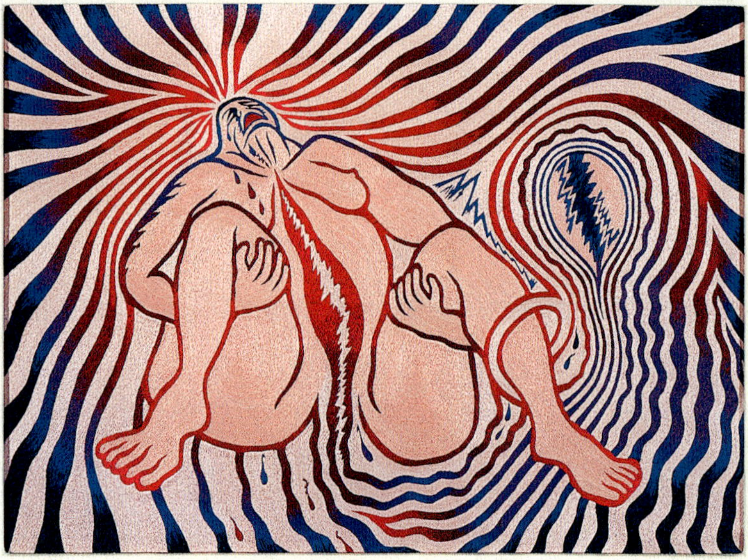

In 1971 Judy Chicago co-founded with artist Miriam Schapiro the Feminist Art Program at the California Institute of the Arts in Valencia, initiating her commitment to feminist activism and teaching. Throughout her career, Chicago has sought to revise male-dominated art and art history by elevating artistic crafts traditionally associated with women, such as embroidery, to the status of fine art. In *Birth Tear Embroidery*, she merges needlework with painting.

Chicago created the *Birth Project*, a series of approximately one hundred textiles executed between 1980 and 1985, to explore both the mythical and factual aspects of birth. The project was a group effort, as Chicago employed 150 needleworkers to transfer her painted or drawn images to fabric. The use of embroidery in the *Birth Project* is especially evocative, as the soft, undulating surface of the stitching resembles the texture of real skin. Chicago has used vaginal imagery throughout her career as a symbol of biological womanhood. In *Birth Tear Embroidery*, she exaggerates the female anatomy to accentuate the physical intensity of giving birth. The image illustrates the tearing of a woman's body as she cries out, colored ripples evoking her pain. The work honors the birth process as a powerful and remarkable event. Chicago avoids objectifying the female nude by creating not a sanitized and ideal figure with erotic content but one that expresses physical endurance. She views women as essential creators and links the generative powers of birth with artistic creativity. Wolfskill

Judy Chicago
United States
b. 1939

Birth Tear Embroidery
1984
Sharpie ink on pink silk with embroidery
19 1/4 × 24 1/2 inches
Gift of Through the Flower Corporation
1985-21-1.1

Vernon Fisher's title *Bikini* (pp. 340–41) refers to the test site where atomic bombs were exploded in 1946, on Bikini Atoll in the Pacific Ocean. The enormous size of the two abutting canvases and the clarity and drama of the photographic image tend to engage the emotional participation of viewers. However, a countervailing distance is achieved by the intrusion of a smaller image in red tones on the monumental image. This detachment is reinforced by the monochrome of the dominant image and the reproduction of stains from the photographic source, giving it the character of historical evidence. On examination, the smaller image proves to be a view of a miniature golf course, dominated by an obstacle the shape of which echoes that of the mushroom cloud above the atoll. This association is key to one interpretation of the painting: the implicit presence of global dangers in a local context.

Fisher graduated from the University of Illinois in 1969. His artistic methods, themes, and imagery reflect the preoccupations of his generation. His estrangement of image and reality, use of mass-media sources, and demand that the viewer participate in the creation of meaning, all forecast postmodernist concerns. Wetzel

Vernon Fisher
United States
b. 1943

(following pages)
Bikini
1987
Acrylic on canvas
11 1/2 feet × 18 1/2 feet
Acquired with funds from the
John Needles Chester Fund 1994,
Benefit Dinner Fund, and
John Patrick Mooney Jr. Memorial Fund
1994-7-1

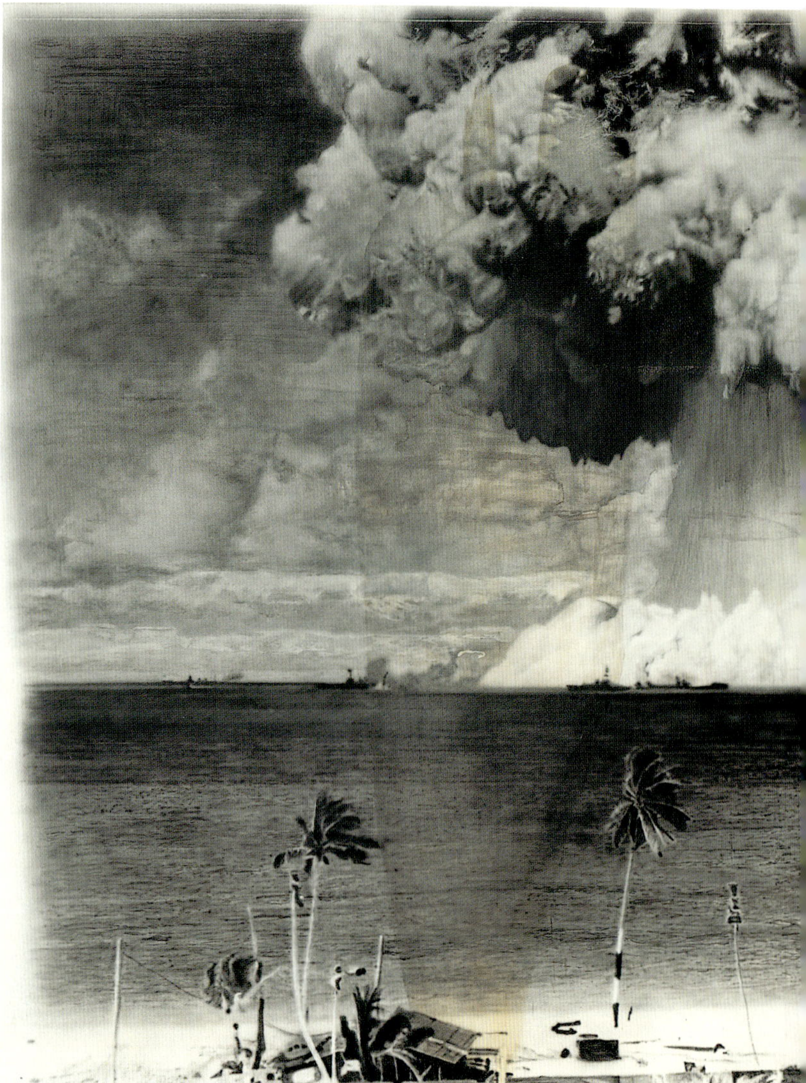

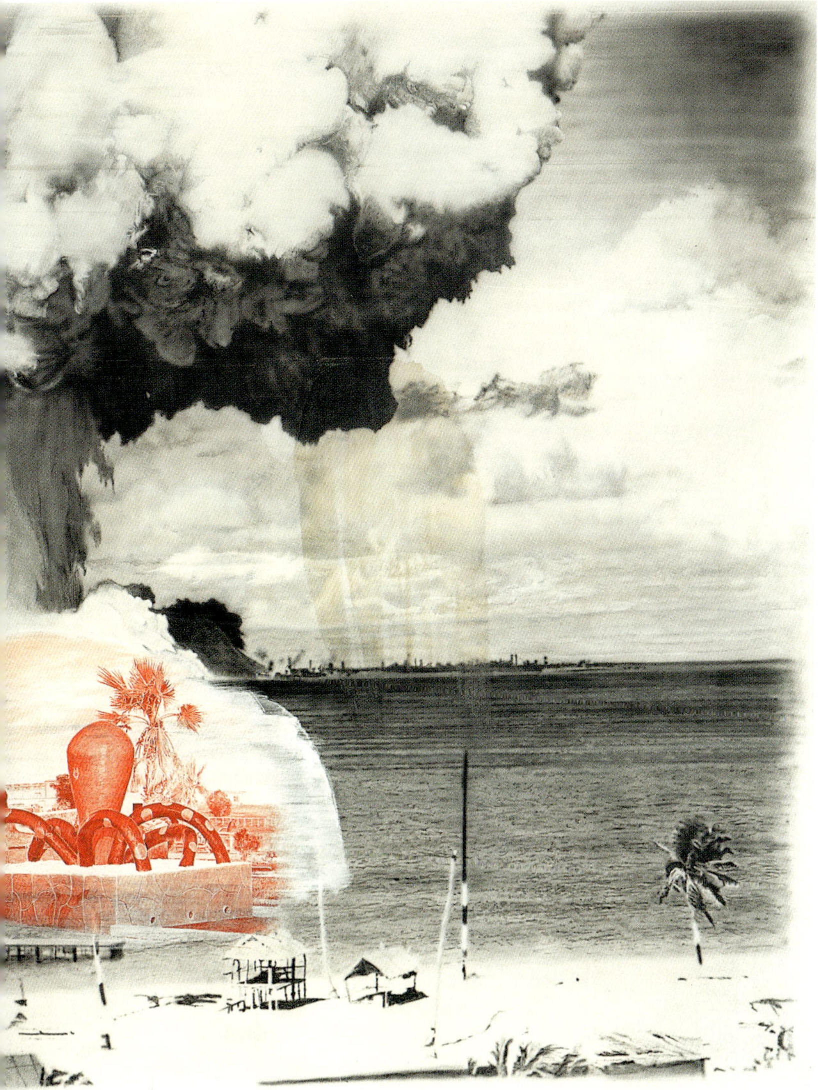

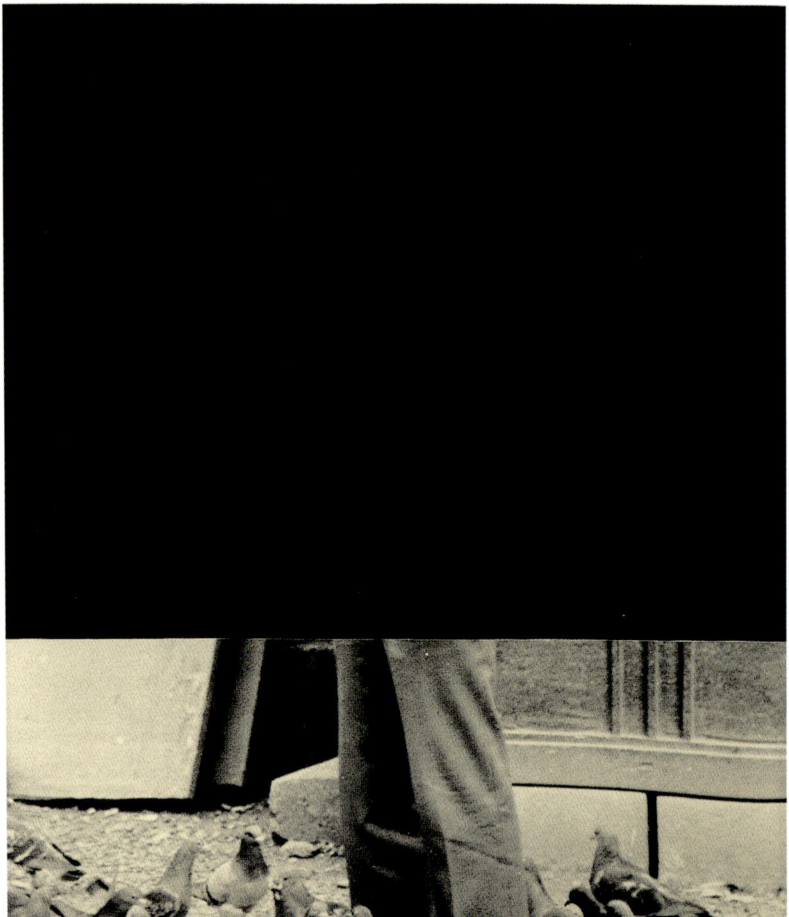

Annette Lemieux joins an intellectual analysis of social codes to a primary emphasis on psychological and emotional content. This enterprise leads her to devise processes and techniques incorporating a wide range of materials, from marble to scrim. Her approach has expanded from an early use of found materials laden with cultural meanings and evocative of personal memories to the more traditional processes of painting, printing, and carving. *Weight* is a powerful re-visioning of an earlier work – a small photograph of a man feeding pigeons that gather around his feet and perch on his shoulders with wings spread. It is typical of Lemieux to exploit her own prior work, which she appropriates virtually intact and significantly alters at the same time. Here the scale, medium, and device of blacking out over half of the canvas transform the original image, one of ascendance, into one of compression and oppression. Fox

Annette Lemieux
United States
b. 1957

Weight
1990
Water-based inks
and oil on canvas
102 × 79 inches
Gift of Peter Michael
2006-8-1

A former child prostitute, the openly homosexual David Wojnarowicz challenged political and social structures, cultural norms, and mainstream ethics throughout his career. With collagelike compositions he created his own mythology, deconstructing and reorganizing fragments of his experience in symbolic form. He often juxtaposed depictions of nature in vibrant and sensual colors with symbolic representations of cultures in dull, muted tones. In *Earth and Wind*, Wojnarowicz divided his composition in half vertically. To the right, a grid of five- and ten-dollar bills serves as background for two vividly colored vignettes. At the top, a bird eats a worm, and below, four tornadoes rise from a rural landscape to surround the Treasury Building printed on the currency. Nature would seem to represent life, innocence, and vitality, while culture might signify greed, corruption, and banality. It may be that the tornadoes allude to the power of the unpredictable and uncontrollable forces of nature to assault cultural constructions.

The left side of the composition shows a globe of the earth ripped open to expose an emerging brain. Wojnarowicz often tore apart maps – symbolically loaded representations of government and nation – to propose the elimination of the boundaries that separate peoples and cultures. Ritsma

David Wojnarowicz
United States
1954–1992

Earth and Wind
1990
Lithograph
23 × 30 inches
Art Acquisition Fund
1997-3-1.1

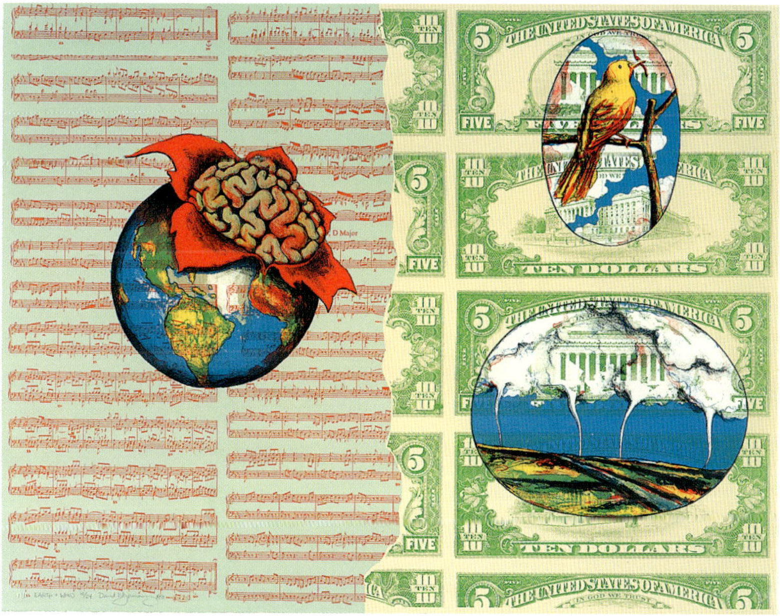
D Major
THE UNITED STATES OF AMERICA
FIVE
TEN DOLLARS
FIVE
THE UNITED STATES OF AMERICA
TEN DOLLARS
THE UNITED STATES OF AMERICA
IN GOD WE TRUST

In the early 1990s, Carrie Mae Weems explored the culture of the Gullah in her *Sea Islands* series. The Gullah are a people living on islands off the coast of Georgia and South Carolina whose ancestors were African captives brought to America during the antebellum period. The two photographs from the series in Krannert Art Museum's collection (pp. 348, 349) show the exterior and interior of a praise house, a modest building devoted to religious and other community purposes. Weems notes the mix of the spiritual and the banal in the structure. In one image, a mouthwash bottle serves as a container for blessing and healing oil. In the other, a hand-painted sign identifies the building and visually balances an electricity meter and climbing vine on the facade.

The straightforward images testify to the Gullahs' rich spiritual life, which has persevered through the ordeal of slavery and ensuing chronic poverty. Weems disrupts the spatial coherence of the interior view with mirrors that insert the disorienting reflections of the room to the left and a man casually waiting to the right. In the exterior shot, she places the motif slightly off-center and leaves a plain strip of road across the foreground, suggesting the modesty and grace of the community. O'Brien

(following pages)
Praise House
1992
Blessing and Healing Oil
1992

From the *Sea Island* series
Silver gelatin prints
Each 21 × 21 inches
Art Acquisition Fund
1997-5-2.1/2.2

Carrie Mae Weems
United States
b. 1953

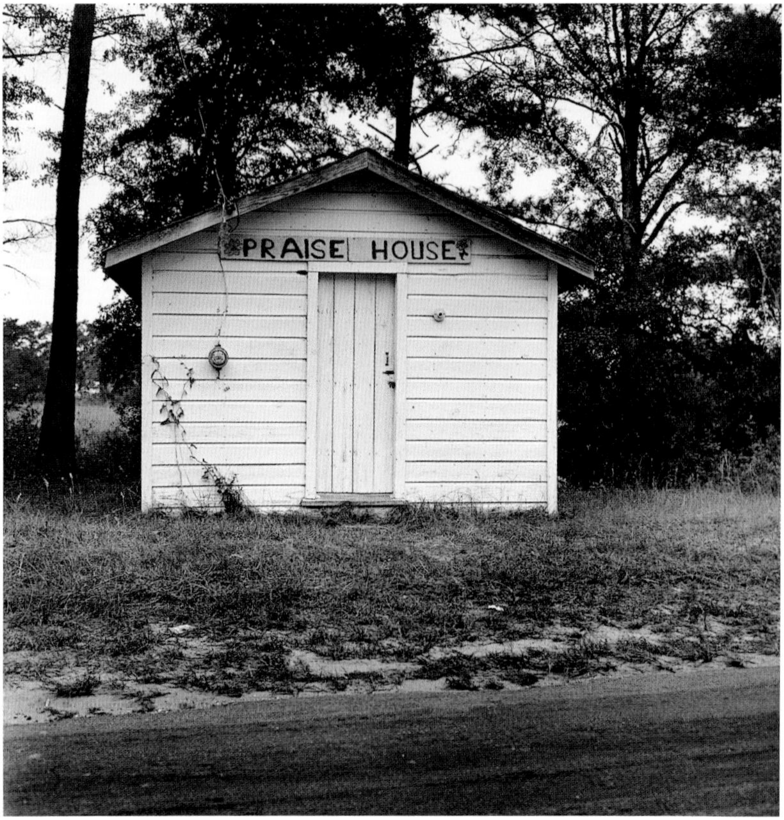
PRAISE HOUSE

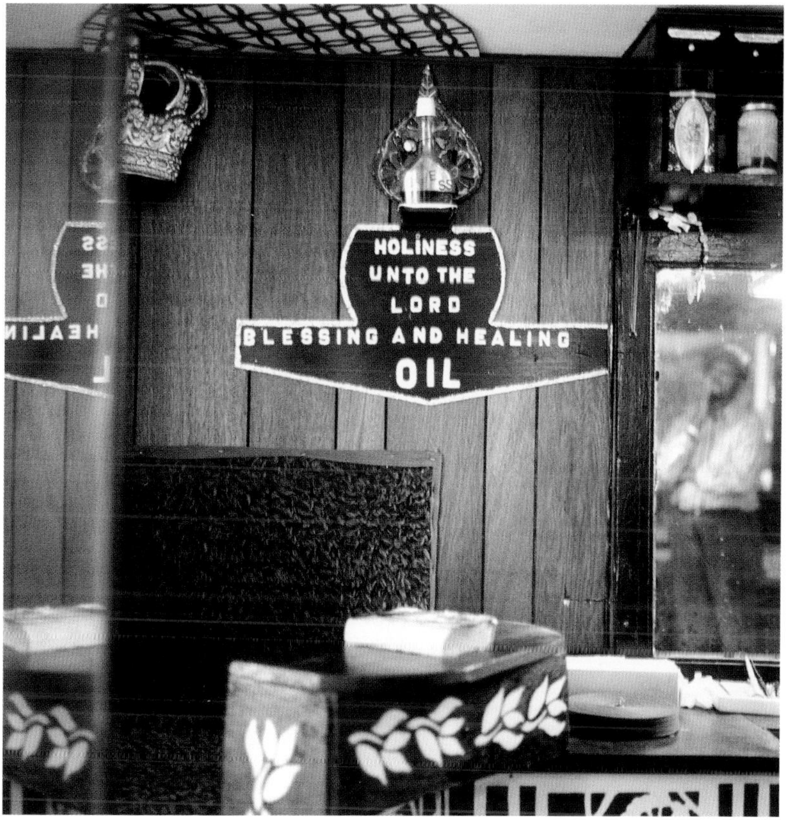

Praise House
Blessing and Healing Oil

Art donors and funding sources

Max Abramovitz
Albert L. Arenberg
Art Acquisition Fund
Walter Bareiss
William Becker
Benefit Dinner Fund
George P. Bickford
Mr. and Mrs. Willis Bruce
John Needles Chester Fund
City of Chicago
Class of 1908
Contemporary American Painting and Sculpture Exhibition
Mr. and Mrs. Herman Cooper
Arnold H. Crane
Department of Ceramic Engineering, University of Illinois
Alice and Donald Dodds
Educational Grants and Provost's Funds
Richard J. Faletti Family Collection
Festival of Arts Purchase Fund
Arnold M. Gilbert
Arnold and Temmie Gilbert
Professor Anita J. Glaze
J. Theodore Gleick
Mr. and Mrs. Philip C. Goldstick
Sheldon Good Family Charitable Foundation
Estate of Musa Guston
Joseph B. Harris
Estate of William S. Kinkead
William S. Kinkead
Robert D. Kleinschmidt
Knoedler & Company
Ellnora D. Krannert
Ellnora D. Krannert Fund
Mr. and Mrs. Herman C. Krannert
Sophie and Brian Leung Fund
Jacques and Yulla Lipchitz Foundation
Estate of Katherine Trees Livezey
Estate of Felicia Meyer Marsh
Peter Michael
Ruth Miller
John Patrick Mooney Jr. Memorial Fund
A. Doyle Moore
Harlan E. Moore
Harlan E. Moore Charitable Trust
Theresa E. and Harlan E. Moore
Rosann and Richard Noel
NEA Matching Grant
Mr. and Mrs. Roy R. Neuberger
Fred Olsen
Grant J. Pick
Gordon Ray
The Judith Rothschild Foundation
School of Art + Design, University of Illinois
Cecilia and Irwin Smiley
Herman Spertus
Through the Flower Corporation
George S. Trees
Mr. and Mrs. Merle J. Trees
University Foundation
University of Illinois Foundation Fund
University of Illinois Purchase
James Russell Vaky
Wang Dongling
Eva-Maria Worthington (in honor of Dr. Maglione)
John Wustman
Ed Zagorski

Insert 2

1 Board of Trustees of Illinois Industrial University, 7th Annual Report (Springfield, 1875), 91–92; *Champaign County Gazette*, Mar. 4, 1874; "Editorial," *Illini*, May 1876, 226–27.

2 *Chicago Tribune*, Jan. 2, 1875; "Editorial," *Illini*, May 1876, 227. Actually, the University of Michigan had the only comparable collection west of New York, and Gregory must have known of it from his years of educational work in the state. Professor Andrew D. White, a collaborator in assembling Michigan's group of plaster casts and engraved and photographed views of antiquity, visited Gregory in Urbana in 1871.

3 College of Literature and Arts, "Annual Report for 1906–07," Mar. 1, 1907.

4 President's Report 1927–1928 (Urbana, 1929), 31. The cornerstone for the Architecture Building was laid November 16, 1926. Classes were first held there in February 1928.

Insert 3

1 Frank Roos to Rexford Newcomb, "A Proposal for a Revised Use of Funds Requested by The College of Fine and Applied Arts, for the 1947–48 Budget," May 5, 1947.

2–3 Ibid.

4 Rexford Newcomb to Nelson Rice, May 18, 1950.

5 George D. Stoddard, foreword to *University of Illinois Competitive Exhibition of Contemporary American Painting* (Champaign: University of Illinois, 1948).

6–7 Ibid.

8 Peyton Boswell, "Progress in Illinois," *Art Digest*, March 1, 1948, 7; Copeland Berg, "Illini Art Show Opens on March 2," *Chicago Herald-American*, Feb. 23, 1952.

9 Fran Myers, "Broadway Tatler," *News-Gazette*, Feb. 26, 1948; "Times Critic Lauds U. I. Show," *News Gazette*, Feb. 29, 1948; Bob Wilbert, "Realism, Surrealism, Abstract, Non-Objective Art to be Seen at Exhibition of American Painting," *Daily Illini*, Feb. 28, 1948.

10 The usual biennial exhibition was cancelled in 1971. In its stead, all works purchased from earlier shows for the permanent collection were brought together for the first time.

11 Allen S. Weller, College of Fine and Applied Arts, "Annual Report 1970–71," 17.

Insert 4

1 Muriel Scheinman, "Celebrating Art: From Plaster Casts to Contemporary American Arts Festivals," in *No Boundaries: University of Illinois Vignettes*, ed. Lillian Hoddeson (Champaign: University of Illinois Press, 2004).

Copyright and photography credits

Robert Arneson, Untitled, 1984: Art © Estate of Robert Arneson/Licensed by VAGA, New York, NY; Milton Avery, *Bouquet with March*, 1948: © 2006 Milton Avery Trust / Artists Rights Society (ARS), New York; William Baziotes, *Moon Animal*, 1950: Courtesy of the Estate of William Baziotes, New York; Max Beckmann, *Beaulieu*, 1947: © 2005 Artists Rights Society (ARS), New York / VG Bild-Kunst, Bonn; Ruth Bernhard, *Two Forms*, 1963: © Ruth Bernhard / All Rights Reserved; Harry Bertoia, *Tonal Piece*, 1967: © 2008 Estate of Harry Bertoia / Artists Rights Society (ARS), New York; Albert Bloch, *Die Höhen,* 1914: Printed with the permission of the Albert Bloch Foundation; Pierre Bonnard, *France-Champagne*, 1891: © 2008 Artists Rights Society (ARS), New York / ADAGP, Paris; Louise Bourgeois, *Depression Woman*, 1949–50: Art © Louise Bourgeois/Licensed by VAGA, New York, NY; Wynn Bullock, *Child in Forest*, 1951: © 1951/2005, Bullock Family Photography LLC, all rights reserved, courtesy Archive Consulting and Management Services LLC, New York, NY; Charles Burchfield, *The Four Seasons*, 1949–60: Reproduced with permission from the Charles E. Burchfield Foundation; Manuel Carrillo, *Mexico City, D. F.*, 1966: University of Texas at El Paso Library, Special Collections Department, Manuel Carrillo Photograph Collection, MS288; Judy Chicago, *Birth Tear Embroidery*, 1984: © 2005 Judy Chicago/Artists Rights Society (ARS), New York; Stuart Davis, *General Studies*, 1962: Art © Estate of Stuart Davis/Licensed by VAGA, New York, NY; Otto Dix, *Leuchtkugel erhellt die Monacu-Ferme*, 1924: © 2005 Artists Rights Society (ARS), New York / VG Bild-Kunst, Bonn; Jacob Epstein, *Head of Wynne Godley*, 1956: © Tate, London 2006; Walker Evans, *Negroes, Tallahassee, Florida*, ca. 1941: © Walker Evans Archive, The Metropolitan Museum of Art; Vernon Fisher, *Bikini*, 1987: Courtesy of Vernon Fisher; Leon Golub, *Two Head Studies of Zhou Enlai*, ca. 1976–79: Art © Estate of Leon Golub/Licensed by VAGA, New York, NY; Adolph Gottlieb, *Romanesque Facade*, 1949: Art © Adolph and Esther Gottlieb Foundation/Licensed by VAGA, New York, New York; George Grosz, *Nach Ladenschluss* (*Rush Hour*), from *Ecce Homo* series, no. 45, 1919: Art © Estate of George Grosz/Licensed by VAGA, New York, NY; Philip Guston, *The Porch*, 1945, and *Combat II*, ca. 1978: © Estate of Philip Guston; Hans Hofmann, *Apparition*, 1947: © 2005 Estate of Hans Hofmann/Artists Rights Society (ARS), New York; Robert Indiana, *Louisiana: The Confederacy*, 1966, and *Yield Brother John*, 1967: © 2006 Morgan Art Foundation Ltd. / Artists Rights Society (ARS), New York; Jess (Burgess Collins), *The Hang'd Man: Tarot XIII*, 1959: Courtesy the Jess Collins Trust; Ilya Iosifovich Kabakov, *Woman as Fountain: Courtyard Sculpture Project*, 1998: © 2005 Artists Rights Society (ARS), New York / VG Bild-Kunst, Bonn; André Kertész, *Dunaharaszti*, 1920: © 2006 Estate of André Kertész / Courtesy Stephen Daiter Gallery / Chicago; Chris Killip, *XMAS, Castleford, N. E. England, 1976*, 1976: Image courtesy of Chris Killip; Paul Klee, *Bärtiger Mann*, 1925: © 2005 Artists Rights Society (ARS), New York / VG Bild-Kunst, Bonn; Käthe Kollwitz, *Self-Portrait*, 1938: © 2005 Artists Rights Society (ARS), New York / VG Bild-Kunst, Bonn; Barbara Kruger, Untitled (*You Rule by Pathetic Display*), 1982: Courtesy of the Mary Boone Gallery, New York; Annette Lemieux, *Weight*, 1990: Courtesy of Annette Lemieux; Sol LeWitt, *A 2 5 8*, 1968: © 2006 Sol LeWitt / Artists Rights Society (ARS), New York; Jacques Lipchitz, *Portrait of Mademoiselle Coco Chanel*, 1921, and Untitled, ca. 1927–29: © Estate of Jacques Lipchitz; Danny Lyon, *Jack, Chicago*, 1967: Danny Lyon, courtesy Edwynn Houk Gallery; Reginald Marsh, *Coney Island Beach*, 1947: © 2005 Estate of Reginald Marsh/Art Students League, New York/Artists Rights Society (ARS), New York; Matta, *L'horreur du mal, l'ultime, l'ennemi intérieur, la memoria cósmica*, 1951: © 2006 Artists Rights Society (ARS), New York / ADAGP, Paris; Robert Motherwell, *St. Michael III*, 1979: Art © Dedalus Foundation, Inc./Licensed by VAGA, New York, NY; Gabriele Münter, *The Blue Gable*, 1911: © 2005 Artists Rights Society (ARS), New York / VG Bild-Kunst, Bonn; Barnett Newman, Untitled, 1969: © 2005 Barnett Newman Foundation/Artists Rights Society (ARS), New York; Claes Oldenburg, *Proposed Chapel in the Form of a Swedish Extension Plug*, 1967: © Claes Oldenburg; Pablo Picasso, *Salome*, 1905: © 2005 Estate of Pablo Picasso / Artists Rights Society (ARS), New York; Robert Rauschenberg, *Sky Garden*, 1969: Art © Robert Rauschenberg/ Licensed by VAGA New York, NY; Mark Rothko, *No. 13*, 1949: © 2006 Kate Rothko Prizel & Christopher Rothko / Artists Rights Society (ARS), New York; Peter Saul, *Typical Saigon*, 1968: Courtesy of Peter Saul; Kurt Seligmann, *High Priest*, 1950: © 2005 Orange County Citizens Foundation/Artists Rights Society (ARS), New York; Ben Shahn, *Second Allegory*, 1953: Art © Estate of Ben Shahn/Licensed by VAGA, New York, NY; Art Sinsabaugh, *Chicago #85*, 1964: © Katherine Anne Sinsabaugh and Elisabeth Sinsabaugh de la Cova; Frank Stella, *Kozangrodek III*, 1973: © 2005 Frank Stella/Artists Rights Society (ARS), New York; Hedda Sterne, *Machine 5*, 1950: © 2005 Artists Rights Society, New York; Alfred Stieglitz, *The Terminal*, 1893: © 2005 The Georgia O'Keeffe Foundation/Artists Rights Society (ARS), New York; Yves Tanguy, *Le malheur adoucit les pierres*, 1948: © 2005 Estate of Yves Tanguy / Artists Rights Society (ARS), New York; Andy Warhol, *Marilyn*, 1971: © 2005 Andy Warhol Foundation for the Visual Arts/ Artists Rights Society (ARS), New York, TM 2006 Marilyn Monroe, LLC by CMG Worldwide, Inc. www.MarilynMonroe.com; Carrie Mae Weems, *Praise House*, 1992, and *Blessing and Healing Oil*, 1992, from the *Sea Island* series: © Carrie Mae Weems; Edward Weston, Untitled (*Nude*), 1925: Collection Center for Creative Photography, University of Arizona © 1981 Arizona Board of Regents; Guy C. Wiggins, *Wall Street, New York (Winter, New York)*, ca. 1930: © Guy A. Wiggins; David Wojnarowicz, *Earth and Wind*, 1990: Courtesy of Tom Rauffenbart; Wang Dongling, *Ling Shan*, 1989: Courtesy of Wang Dongling

Krannert Art Museum staff

Damon Baker
Art, Design, and Technology Associate Curator

Erin K. Donovan
Curatorial Assistant

Mona Dye
Accounting Technician

Virginia Erickson
Resource Center Coordinator

Chris Grant
Associate Director

Kathleen Harleman
Director

Mark Hix
Security Guard

Kathleen Jones
Registrar

Sarah Kent
Manager of Systems Services

Kathryn Koca
Curatorial Assistant

Robert G. La France
Associate Curator for Pre-Modern Art

Eric Lemme
Design & Installation Specialist

Donald Matejowsky
Supervisor/Security Guard

Joseph Miller
Security Guard

Brenda Nardi
Associate Director of Development

Walter Rohr
Security Guard

Christine Saniat
Associate Registrar

Anne Sautman
Director of Education

Chris Schaede
Office Administrator

Diane Schumacher
Director of Marketing

James Stuart
Security Guard

Casey Swink
Security Guard

Phyllis Williams
Building Maintenance Worker

Walter Wilson
Design & Installation Specialist

Editors Maria Bailey, Anne Burkus-Chasson, Erin K. Donovan, Lucy Flint, Marcel Franciscono, Anne D. Hedeman, David O'Brien, Diane Pelrine, Dana Rush, Diane Schumacher, Judy Stubbs, Oscar Vázquez

Designer Studio Blue

Production Assistance Maria Bailey, Michael W. Conner, Jenifer K. Dapper, Erin K. Donovan, María del Mar González-González, Karen Hewitt, Alexander Hovan, Kathleen Jones, Kathryn Koca, Joyce M. Kuechler, Robert G. LaFrance, Kerry Morgan, Diane Schumacher, Roxanne Stanulis, Heidi Strobel

Photography Chris Brown, Thomas Nowak, Wilmer Zehr

Krannert Art Museum Handbook Committee Gisele Atterberry, Michael W. Conner, Kathleen Harleman, Josef Helfenstein, Karen Hewitt, Kathleen Jones, Kerry Morgan, James B. Sinclair (chair), Robert B. Smith, Roxanne Stanulis, Heidi Strobel

Library of Congress No. 2008936269

ISBN 978-1-883015-41-1

Published by Krannert Art Museum and Kinkead Pavilion

Krannert Art Museum and Kinkead Pavilion
College of Fine and Applied Arts
University of Illinois at Urbana-Champaign
500 East Peabody Drive
Champaign, IL 61820

t: 217.333.1861
www.kam.illinois.edu